DEADBEATS, DEAD BALLS, AND

THE 1914 BOSTON BRAVES

DEADBEATS, DEAD BALLS, AND THE 1914 BOSTON BRAVES

MARTIN H. BUSH

◆ ◆ ◆ ◆ ◆ ◆ ◆ ◆ ◆ ◆ ◆ ◆ ◆ ◆

The Kent State University Press   *Kent, Ohio*

© 2025 by The Kent State University Press, Kent, Ohio 44242
All rights reserved
ISBN 978-1-60635-494-0
Published in the United States of America

No part of this book may be used or reproduced, in any manner whatsoever, without written permission from the Publisher, except in the case of short quotations in critical reviews or articles.

Cataloging information for this title is available at the Library of Congress.

29 28 27 26 25   5 4 3 2 1

For

MARTIN J. BUSH

my father

a ball player, an umpire,

and a good man

CONTENTS

Preface ix

PART I

1. The Best Manager in Baseball 3
2. They'd Delivered Disappointments for Years 14
3. Rogers's Rules 19
4. The Newly Named American League 27
5. Something's Wrong Here 33
6. A Memorable Era in Baseball History 39
7. His Focus Was Sound 48
8. Self-Serving Pronouncements 52
9. Rowdies Run Riot 57
10. A Deep Freeze Developed 63
11. Everyone's Dirty Little Secret 71
12. Tried to Show That He Belonged 78
13. Surprising Success 82
14. The Price the Yankee Manager Paid 87
15. Always a Truth-Bender in the Crowd 93
16. A Stand-Up Guy 101
17. Full of Insincere Sincerity 104

PART II

18. The First Real Gem 115
19. He Talked Himself Out of More Ball Games 122
20. Damn That Man 127
21. A Symbol of Greed and Selfishness 131
22. A Whiff of Score-Settling 138
23. A Self-Styled Hand Grenade 141
24. Misery and Suffering 144
25. Confidence Grew Stronger Day by Day 151

26 You Call Yourselves Big Leaguers?   162
27 The Crab and Rab   171
28 Without Charge   177
29 The Bad Boy   179
30 I Seen It Done   182
31 A Change in Strategy Was Unthinkable   186
32 He Did Not Cross the Line   190
33 A Man Who Can Do Anything He Sets Out to Do   198
34 Mathewson Was Brilliant   204
35 Braves Watchers Were Everywhere   213
36 It Was the Spirit of the Team   219
37 Just an Old-Fashioned Nose-Thumbing   225
38 An Unappeasable Hunger   233
39 Kid's Gonna Blow Sky High   236
40 Solid Ivory   242
41 The Most Spirited Team I Ever Saw   244

PART III

42 Rejoicing in Boston   249
43 It Was a Bad Scene   252
44 The Boys Rocketed Out of Their Seats   255
45 Not Your Run-of-the-Mill Mascots   257
46 Just Keep Quiet and Listen   264
47 The Dr. Jekyll and Mr. Hyde of Baseball   267
48 Royal Rooters   272
49 A Boom-Boom Voice   277
50 Rooftop Seats   281
51 Puzzled by What He Sees   284
52 It Was Like Looking Down Murderer's Row   295
53 The Braves' Best Pitcher Was in Trouble   301
54 In the Spirit of Good Sportsmanship   307
55 He Was Looking at His Worst Nightmare   311
56 The Voices Told the Story   322
57 It Was High Drama Time   328
58 Lightning-Bolt Talent   336

Acknowledgments   342
Chapter Sources   345
Bibliography   357
Index   365

PREFACE

My father was a semipro ball player and a minor league umpire, and baseball played an important role in my early years. He'd often take me and my sister, Kay, and my pals to ball games. And while he was at work behind the plate, we wandered around the grandstand entertaining ourselves and, once in a while, even watched the game. It was great fun.

My daughter Lisa was well aware of my love of baseball and, in September 1996, she called my attention to an auction about to take place at Christie's East in New York: the photo archive of *Baseball* magazine, a popular monthly published from 1908 until 1963.

I was looking for an investment at the time, and attended the auction and purchased 834 vintage baseball photographs, most of them dated before 1920. As I was leaving, a nicely dressed man approached me and asked if I'd consider selling the 40 pre-1920 Boston Braves photographs I'd just purchased. I politely brushed him off.

"What are you going to do with them?" he asked.

"Oh, I don't know. Maybe I'll write an article or something."

"You ought to write something about the 1914 Boston Braves."

I nodded and smiled and said, "Maybe I will."

His remark got me thinking: What was so special about the 1914 Boston Braves? A few days later I decided to find out.

Reading loads of Boston papers of the era in the microfilm room of the New York Public Library, for hours on end, led me to the conclusion that the man knew what he was talking about. The Braves were strangely likable. Ordinary and wonderful. They demanded attention.

But in most people's minds in 1996, they were little more than dry statistics in history-skimming books based on inch-deep scholarship.

The story was the stuff of a good book, a once-upon-a-time tale set against a backdrop of early baseball lore. I'd always wanted to write a book about baseball, and here it was staring me in the face. So I decided to take up the challenge.

A historian by training, I broadened my knowledge of baseball's early days by studying thousands of inches of newspaper reports, magazine articles, interviews, court records, and the clipping files (articles cut from newspapers and magazines) at the Baseball Hall of Fame library in Cooperstown.

Ten years of research unearthed an enormous trove of information, and more than once laid bare a memory-branding revelation. I even visited the cities and ballparks they played in, and the hotels they stayed in.

I've told the story exactly as it happened, stressing the human element, allowing the participants themselves—on all sides—to voice their feelings and beliefs. These guys were not always batting and throwing.

First-person players' accounts enabled me to write scenes with an immediacy seldom seen, and to use dialogue that would otherwise have been impossible.

And I didn't shirk from controversy or pull my punches in describing the crafty actions and schemes of the lords of baseball. The readers see them as they were, sometimes aiming for excellence and superiority, sometimes displaying a willingness to act dishonestly when it came to gaining the upper hand.

PART I

♦ ♦ ♦ ♦ ♦ ♦ ♦ ♦ ♦ ♦

CHAPTER 1

THE BEST MANAGER IN BASEBALL

They were awful. They were bad news. They were what you'd expect to see if you peered up the anus of baseball. The Giants pounced on them like a lion on a lame antelope and swept both ends of a doubleheader. All the bruised and confused Braves could do was hold their own in batting practice; it was all downhill after that.

George Stallings, a highly successful manager, shared the games with Jim Gaffney, the Braves' owner, who was under intense scrutiny in the press. The two friends spent most of the afternoon scanning the action on the field, discussing the team's strengths and limitations, and analyzing and evaluating the failed club's prospects and possibilities. What jumped out at Stallings was the indifference of the players, the whiff of futility about them.

Twisting uneasily in his seat, Stallings mopped his brow, squeezed his chin with his thumb and forefinger, and studied the faces on the Braves' dugout bench, silently asking himself, "Do I want to manage this ball club?" The answer was "no," a resounding "no."

But he liked Jim Gaffney, liked him a lot. Jim was a good guy, a man's man, and "George from Georgia" wasn't about to hurt Jim's feelings. Common courtesy would not allow it. And for the sake of agreeableness, the "Big Fellow " began rehearsing in his own mind the words he'd use in turning down Jim's proposal.

The two men sat quietly after the second game drew to a close, the cool shadow of the stands at the Polo Grounds surrounding them, their eyes following the thousands of fans moving toward exit ramps and streaming onto the field, an adoring crowd of ordinary folk, childlike in their joy in having seen the Giants clinch the pennant, feeling pride in the home team on a pleasing afternoon.

Gaffney struck a match, fired up a fine Cuban cigar, blew out a fog of smoke, and cast a glance in Stallings's direction: "Well, George," he said, "what do you think of my ball club?"

The sentence hung in the air.

A gregarious sort, with playful blue eyes and a big laugh, Jim Gaffney was prominent in New York's construction industry and a big wheel at Tammany Hall. He'd always been a rabid baseball fan, and fancied himself owning one of the local teams, an idea that puffed up his ego and fed a little-boy infatuation that had tugged at his mind for years. It also made good business sense. He'd been so eager to buy a big-league outfit that he'd once attempted to seize control of the Brooklyn club, miscalculated badly, was outmaneuvered, and got nowhere.

"You don't go in cold turkey and buy a team," Giants manager John McGraw told him. "You need to know what you don't know before you jump into the business. You have to rub elbows, develop relationships, learn the politics of the industry, the back-room nature of the game."

Gaffney heeded McGraw's advice, took a deep breath, sat back and waited for the right set of circumstances to develop. And develop they did. In 1911 an opportunity of immense potential turned up in Boston: the city's long-suffering National League franchise was available.

Earlier in the year, a predatory investment group, led by New York attorney William Hepburn Russell, added the ball club to its array of holdings for the bargain price of $100,000 (the equivalent of $2.5 million in today's dollars), with the intention of getting into and out of the baseball business as rapidly as possible.

Instead of plowing cash into the Rustlers and putting the team on a solid financial footing, as many new owners do, Russell focused on running a lean operation as a means of raking in a larger return on a quick sale. It was all about rich men getting richer; it had nothing to do with baseball. To manage the enterprise, the cost-conscious Russell hired Fred Tenney, one of the biggest stars of Boston's championship seasons, and sweetened his contract by including a built-in bonus clause. Not a bonus based on the number of games the team won, as you might imagine, but an incentive for dashing into the grandstand and retrieving foul balls.

Yes, things were that bad.

In the face of these management blunders, anguished fans stayed away in droves, the Rustlers lost money, and the franchise found itself in a dangerous downward spiral. The obvious distress of the organization raised questions among insiders about how long the rudderless ball club could survive in view of the relentless competition it faced from its far more popular municipal rival, the Boston Red Sox, the glamour team in town.

Besieged by ankle-biters and emotionally and physically worn down, Russell collapsed and died unexpectedly of a heart attack and the ball club went up for sale.

A fellow attorney, John Montgomery Ward, sensing a chance at making a killing, secured an option on the franchise and emerged as the power broker of any future deal. Aware of Jim Gaffney's interest, and knowing that the Tammany stalwart's checkbook was wide open, Ward contacted the genial Irishman and gave him the news he'd been waiting for: the Boston club was available.

Was Gaffney interested?

Of course he was. It was a noteworthy opportunity, and the price did not give him pause. As the lead investor of a Tammany group, Gaffney struck a deal with the Russell estate, paid the staggering sum of $177,000 (approximately $4.4 million in today's dollars) for 945 shares of capital stock, and took control of the club.

The well-funded Tammany boys also assumed a $350,000 albatross, the mortgage on moldering South End Grounds, the team's decaying home field, which, everyone agreed, was badly in need of a makeover. The task of rebuilding the organization—more of a teardown than a fixer-upper—was placed in the capable hands of the same John Montgomery Ward, a former big-league star, widely respected in early baseball circles as a player, a lawyer, and an executive. He was named president and general manager.

Significant hurdles remained, but Gaffney and his cronies had the cash cushion necessary to breathe new life into the business and make the ball club a formidable presence in the National League. They rebranded the team the Braves, had the profile of a Native American Indian stitched on the left sleeve of the team's jerseys, and a swastika—an ancient sign of the sun and a symbol of good luck—on the button top of the caps.

But the clueless gang of misfits continued to struggle and fail miserably; they lost more than a hundred games in 1912 and cemented a spot for themselves at the bottom of the standings for the fourth season in a row. Gaffney had expected a few rocky patches going through the gut-wrenching transition of rebuilding an ailing franchise, but nothing like this chronicle of ineptness. After weeks of turmoil in which Ward failed to improve the ball club, the Tammany bigwig bought out most of the minority stockholders, assumed the presidency himself, fired Ward, and made known his intention to clean house and breathe new life into the ball club.

Behind the scenes, the Braves' boss met with his friend and confidant John McGraw over drinks at the Lamb's Club to get John's take on the man he (Gaffney) had selected as his new manager. McGraw chided him about the choice. "He's not your man, Jim," McGraw said, speaking earnestly in the manner of someone who meant to be convincing. "It's George Stallings. He's the man you want. He's managing Buffalo of the International League right now. You can get him, too, if you want him."

"You think so?"

"There's no doubt in my mind . . . George is a leader of men, intelligent and professional. He has a passion for excellence and knows how to develop young talent and bring out the best in veterans . . . You saw what he did with the Yankees. Go after him, Jim. You sign him and you'll have the best manager in baseball."

Stallings shook his head and said nothing. Unfailingly cordial, "Gentleman George" frowned, looked down, examined his hands, and made a vague gesture. "I have to tell you, Jim," he said, in a firm pleasant voice. "I've seen some pretty bad ball clubs in my day . . . but these guys . . . these guys . . . " He kept shaking his head. "These guys beat them all."

Though his guest's response was about as pleasing as heat stroke, the Braves' owner managed a half smile. He was determined, actually more than determined, to sign the highly regarded Stallings to a contract. "Here's the deal, George," he said. "If you accept my proposition, you will be the boss in every sense of the word."

Stallings raised his eyebrows as high as they would go and looked fixedly at Gaffney. "Big George" had always been at the mercy of restraints imposed on him by owners in the past, several of whom were pretty bad owners. He threw Gaffney a quick questioning look.

"How's that, Jim? . . . You mean that?"

"I sure do. You can buy or sell whoever you please. I want you to run the club just as if it were your own."

Never before had anyone offered him autonomy in assembling a team. "Will I have the authority of the general manager too?"

"You sure will."

This was almost unheard of. Stallings offered a rhetorical shrug and went into deep thought. After a while, he looked up, tilted his head to one side, squinted at Gaffney, and asked, "Will you put that in writing, Jim? I mean, in my contract? That I have absolute control of the ball club on and off the field? That I have the power to purchase and trade players as I choose? That my authority is absolute? That under no circumstances will I be interfered with?"

Gaffney chuckled, cut him off, and offered assurances about his role. "You have my word, George," he said, and offered his hand. "You will be the boss."

The two men shook on it; for the fourth time in his storied major-league career, George Stallings would play the role of savior for an organization trying to get back what seemed lost. He would be the primary architect of the Boston Braves reclamation project. How long that might take was hardly clear.

"There's no quick fix in baseball," he explained. "It's gonna take a lot of work . . . luck too. You'll have to bear with me through at least the 1915 season."

"You have my promise, George. You do what you have to do. My lawyer will draw up the papers."

Who was this George Stallings? What was his story? Where did he come from? Though not as well known today as many of his contemporaries, George Tweedy Stallings was a master builder of championship teams, one of the most extraordinary managers in baseball history.

Born on November 17, 1867, in Augusta, Georgia, young George was as well ancestored socially as anyone, and he inherited a military pedigree. Everyone in the family fought in the Civil War, and the names of Shiloh, Sharpsburg, Gettysburg, Chickamauga, and Appomattox were in his blood. Is it any wonder, then, that he enrolled at the Virginia Military Institute, a small college committed to leadership training in bucolic Lexington, Virginia, a place unspoiled by industry, idyllic, green, and altogether country.

Impressively tall, whip smart, and endowed with the fetching good looks of a heartthrob, young Stallings was an inch, perhaps two, over six feet, and as lean as a greyhound. A star at football, track, and baseball, he was a cerebral tough guy, a mixture of will, fight, and an unyielding desire to win, always charging, exhorting, ordering, a leader of men.

Off the field, his charm was enormous. Fellow cadets thought of him as an intelligent, friendly, self-effacing classmate with a cheerful word for everyone, invariably bustling across lawns with an armful of books, flashing a smile, the soul of politeness, a decent, principled southern gentleman who, without exception, seemed like the smartest one in the room.

"It was my speed in college," he said, "that brought me whatever bid I had for athletic prominence. There were perhaps a handful of men in the whole country in those days who could really run a hundred yards in ten seconds . . . I was one of them."

The likable young plebe didn't always apply himself in the classroom. Being a bit of a cut-up as well, he was more than once given sharp verbal dressing-downs for transgressions. Things eventually fell apart. His academic status collapsed, and he was expelled from VMI and told in no uncertain terms not to come back. There was no handwringing. No worrying. No regrets. The former cadet confronted the situation head on. This was one of the potholes of life, that's all. The world awaited him.

When he found himself wondering what he might do, his thoughts naturally turned toward medicine, a boyhood reverie: he was enthralled by the idea of becoming a surgeon, a profession that held the promise of a bright future. This pleased his father, William Henry Stallings, a well-to-do contractor, in as much as it would keep George in school where he belonged.

Admission to medical school was little more than a moot question for an upper-middle-class young man with a quick intellect and some college, and things fell into place quickly. George enrolled full time at the Washington University School of Medicine, the College of Physicians in Baltimore, and was soon on his way to becoming a practicing surgeon.

The Stallingses, who traced their roots back to 1086 England and William the Conqueror, were a tightly knit household, and spring breaks and vacations invariably brought George back home, wherever home might be at the moment. In the winter months of 1886–87, the peripatetic family was living in Jacksonville, Florida, where William Henry's firm was constructing a custom house on the Jacksonville waterfront.

Everyone in the Stallings clan was crazy about baseball. And George, like his four brothers, was in the habit of spending most of his free time on the diamond while visiting the folks in Florida. This is where Philadelphia Phillies outfielder Ed Andrews discovered him. Andrews wasn't scouting for talent. It was just that a local semipro ballgame seemed like a lot more fun on a hot humid day in the off-season than tending his orange grove; the oranges could wait. The big leaguer was immediately captivated by the bold, hard-driving, outspoken catcher working behind the plate. The kid was really engaged: he had above-average tools and a passion for the game that poured out of every cell in his body.

"He wasn't the greatest talent," Andrews recalled in later years, "but the kid showed enormous potential. He could run like a deer. And he was brainy and quick behind the plate; and his arm was surprisingly strong and accurate." What influenced the big leaguer more than anything else was the strength of the big fellow's personality: he was bossy and didn't try to hide it.

George's demeanor off the field was striking as well. Andrews was especially captivated by the young man's innate intelligence, his infectious likeability, and the ease and polish and fine manners he displayed in social situations. Simply put, George Stallings was a cut or two above most young men his age.

When Andrews got back to Philadelphia, he brought the tall, trim collegian to the attention of his boss, Phillies manager Harry Wright, one of the most influential pioneers of early baseball. Andrews urged Wright to take an interest in the kid. And Wright did.

On an open day in the Phillies schedule, the Philadelphia manager hopped a train to Baltimore for a quick look at Andrews's prodigy, and somehow he got the dates mixed up. No game was scheduled. Wright did learn, however, that young Stallings was competing in a track meet nearby, and he hurried over just in time to see the fleet Georgia boy run away with the 100-yard dash. He did it with such ease that Wright, taking the long view, invited the young man to sign a Phillies contract right then and there. "You're too good an athlete to be wasting your time in medical school," the Philadelphia skipper told him. "I want you to join my club next season."

It was an honor.

"I was young and full of ambition to excel in sports, like most young men of my time," Stallings said in later recountings, his faced wreathed in smiles. "And, unlike most, I had a chance right away to go with a major-league ball club."

Brash, aggressive, and confident, he reported with high expectations in the spring of 1887, the year the Phillies dedicated a new state-of-the-art wooden ballpark in North Philadelphia (later known as Baker Bowl) that attracted 253,671 fans, a lot of eyeballs in those days.

The magic of big-league ball was intoxicating at first, but it wasn't long before young Stallings's initial exhilaration gave way to reality. He was shunted aside and left to rot on the bench—at least that's the way he looked at things—while two pretty good receivers did the catching. The young man felt thwarted. His iffy reasoning gave rise to a good deal of silly muttering and sulkiness, and an undertone of impudence.

"Look," Wright told him. "We're in a tight pennant race. Every game is important. I can't take a chance on playing an amateur . . . Watch and learn. You'll get your chance."

The combative rookie issued a withering objection: "You think it's fun watching?" he shouted. "You're holding me back." Wright didn't hold him back long. He cut him loose the following day.

"I got to the majors in a hurry," Stallings recalled, "but didn't stay long . . . I guess I must have wanted to start at the top and work my way down." It was a staggering blow. At the same time it taught the big fellow not to regard the profession too lightly. "I struck a stronger pace than I could follow," he later said of his embarrassing mistake, "although I didn't realize it at the time."

After three years of hopscotching around the bush leagues, the likable young catcher rapidly ascended the food chain of minor league ball and was taken under the wing of manager Bill McGunnigle, the highly successful mastermind of the Brooklyn Bridegrooms, a first-rate big-league outfit. (The team was tagged with the name because six players had gotten married in the off-season.) Stallings didn't last long. More experienced catchers did most of the work behind the plate, and George was excess baggage.

But Bill McGunnigle was refreshingly human, a surprisingly good soul, and he made certain that "George from Georgia" got a cameo appearance in the big show before the front office sent him packing. It was a nice gesture. (Stallings handled four games behind the plate and went hitless in 11 at bats.)

The young man had a good head for business, and thanks to a loan from his father, he bought a small noncontrolling interest in the Augusta Electricians of the 12-team Southern League, and was given the job of steering the ball club. Though only 23 at the time, his career took off. He focused on helping players make the most of their skills and quickly earned a reputation for being a smart, straight-shooting, strong-willed disciplinarian, a courageous warrior who motivated his troops with a rough, tough, theatrical manner.

"Stallings' teams were always out there hustling and fighting," Grantland Rice wrote, "working for everything. They either played ball for him or went elsewhere to loaf."

The following season he acquired an interest in the Nashville Vols, a Southern League outfit entrenched in last place, and assumed the managerial reins of the ball club. More than a few hard-boiled local geezerati wondered out loud about the new stranger in town. The tall, dark, mustachioed dude, impeccably appareled in stylish custom-tailored suits, displayed a sartorial sense seldom seen in Nashville. He looked like an actor, a bank president, or a lawyer; he didn't look like a ballplayer.

He was, though. And a good one.

The downtrodden Vols had finished far behind the pack the previous year, a split season (20–44 and 13–16), but the novice manager was not shy about taking on the knotty task of molding the rough-hewn bunch of losers he inherited into a winning outfit. Starting from scratch, he dug in and, acting much like a crusading evangelist, made the most of his opportunities, preaching, teaching, exhorting. He lifted the Vols in the standings through the sheer force of his personality, telling them what to do, how to do it, and when to do it. He was relentlessly positive, and his natural exuberance made everyone believe they could win. And they did win.

A melodramatic incident that took place early in the season is worth repeating here for posterity. When Stallings and Ollie Beard, Stallings's predecessor at Nashville, met for a series in Evansville, hundreds of Nashville fans accompanied the team on a 132-mile rail excursion to witness the clash between the two rivals. The first game, a bitterly contested pitcher's duel—no runner crossed home plate in the first seven innings—was well worth the trip.

Stallings, a right-handed hitter, came to bat in the visitor's half of the eighth of a scoreless tie, and was fooled by an elevated fastball. Swinging late, he sliced a high drive down the right field line that disappeared over the fence. "Foul!" the pool-room bum umpiring behind the plate called out.

Disdainful shouts erupted from the stands. "You big ham!" "You robber, you!" "Get him outta there!" Stallings raised a hand. The voices quieted.

The big fellow met the next pitch squarely and pulled a screamer down the left field line that just did clear the fence. With meanness of mind, the hometown umpire trumpeted, "Foul ball!"

Stallings's head jerked around, his eyes bulging: "Jesus, Mary, Joseph," he bellowed. "That was a fair ball." A barrage of expletives followed.

Gripping the heavy bat low on the neck, he stepped back into the batter's box and readied himself for the seventh pitch of the at bat. This time, a fastball drifted over the heart of the plate, shoulder high.

Thwok! A pure, clear sound.

The ball went flying high and deep into straightaway center field and disappeared over the fence. The go-ahead run. As Stallings trotted across home plate, he turned and looked at the loutish umpire: "Well," he said, "what do you call that one?"

Whenever someone mentioned the incident in later years, the "Big Chief" would silently reminisce, smile broadly, and say, "I certainly looked like a player that day."

A myth? Perhaps. But a nice myth.

That same season, he split his playing time behind the plate and in the outfield while guiding Nashville to a fourth-place finish in the first half of an abbreviated season and to a first-place finish in the shortened second half of the season, a far cry from the team's 33–60 record in 1893.

The following year he led Nashville (now named the Seraphs) to a second-place finish, one game behind the pennant-winning Atlanta Crackers, in a neck-and-neck race. Though the Seraphs didn't capture the flag, it was a banner year for Stallings nonetheless. He batted .341, stole 29 bases, thrived at first base and in the outfield, and kept the team in championship contention throughout the season.

By this time, word of his expertise in taking over losing minor-league clubs and turning them into something better had propelled his résumé into the national spotlight. A proven winner (his track record was indisputable), he was being hailed as something of a genius in baseball circles. If managing had a rising wunderkind, someone who was brilliantly creative, it had to be George Stallings.

In 1896 he took on the formidable task of installing new life, on a shoestring budget, into the forlorn Detroit Tigers of the Western League, replacing the incumbent manager in midseason. Not surprisingly, the ingenious Stallings seeded the players' enthusiasm with his own infectious optimism, kick-started the ball club, and engineered a turnaround in a remarkably short period of time. The youthful Tigers gained traction, climbed back into the top half of the league in the second half of the season, and, though pretenders more than contenders in the pennant race, finished third, 10 games behind the first-place Minneapolis Millers.

Here is a twist. After batting a respectable .302 and leading the team to a first-division finish, Stallings, unlike so many others before and after him, recognized his limitations, determined that he was not talented enough to keep playing, and cheerfully decided at the age of 28 that it was time to put aside his dream of making it to the Bigs as a player and focus instead on getting there as a manager. It was a carefully thought-out decision.

His reputation for having improved every team he'd ever managed caught the notice of Al Reach and John Rogers, co-owners of the Philadelphia Phillies, and Reach and Rogers decided that the brilliant young southerner was exactly the kind of leader they were looking for: a manager who left no doubt about who was in charge, a tough guy who could light a fire under the tempestuous gang of underperforming stars who wore Philadelphia uniforms.

In 1896 the Phillies had stumbled into eighth place and ended up 28½ games off the pace set by the pennant-winning Baltimore Orioles. It was Philadelphia's worst finish since becoming members of the National League in 1883. A change was in order.

On Sunday, December 26, Reach and Rogers gave George Stallings a belated Christmas present: a two-year contract as manager of the trophy-hungry Philadelphia Phillies. Close friends advised George not to take the job, told him it was hopeless, said he wouldn't last long. Colonel Rogers was a difficult man to work for. Eager to manage at the highest level, perhaps too eager, Stallings embraced the faint promise of success, genuinely believing that he could prove his well-meaning friends wrong.

CHAPTER 2

THEY'D DELIVERED DISAPPOINTMENTS FOR YEARS

Stallings took charge of the biggest bats in baseball, an explosive ball club that included three future Hall of Famers ("Big Ed" Delahanty, Napoleon Lajoie, and Sam Thompson), all intent on building mountains of personal statistics for themselves.

When these guys were on a tear, balls jumped off their bats, hits rattled off walls, runs scored in bunches; when they went into a slump, the results were corrosive. They swung at everything, hacked away in frustration, seldom thought of manufacturing a run, even to win a game. That's one of the reasons why they'd delivered disappointments for years. It was loosey-goosey baseball played by tough-talking, beer-guzzling, fist-flinging malcontents out for personal glory, not victories.

This was the morass George Stallings stepped into. "They may have been stars," he said, "but the spirit that wins games was lacking."

Reasonably clear-eyed, the rookie manager set out to break the cycle of low expectations: change the ball club's chemistry, breathe new life into the organization, put everyone on the same page, and shape the boys into a clever, aggressive, well-conditioned machine. No small feat for a team populated by social misfits.

His guiding principles: play together, fight together, win together. His message: Win. Win. Win. Winning is what mattered. All that mattered. "You're a big-league ball club," he told them. "You've got to play like big leaguers. Devotion to the team must override personal ambitions."

Most of the booze-addled, ill-tempered, semiliterates who reported for spring training in 1897 viewed their new manager's every move with suspicion and wondered how a 29-year-old with practically no major-league experience could handle a bunch of big-league stars. They regarded him as humorless, hot-tempered, and arrogant, a bigmouthed disciplinarian who ruffled a good many feathers and bruised more than a few egos.

Necessarily a tough guy in a world of tough guys, Stallings was enormous physically, solidly muscular, and terrifyingly strong. His hulking, breathing, no-nonsense persona flooded the field, and his body language said it all: Don't mess with me.

He spat out instructions like an army drill sergeant: "Work as a team . . ." "Play the percentages . . ." "Anticipate . . ." "Keep the pressure on . . ." "Wait the pitcher out . . ." "Work the count . . ." "Get a good pitch to hit . . ." "Run hard . . ." "Take the extra base . . ." "Keep mistakes to a minimum . . ." "Don't beat yourselves . . ." "Execute, execute, execute." And he insisted that the players match his own will to win.

Every now and then his bullying provoked caustic contempt, sometimes to the point of spilling blood. "What the hell does he know?" a disgruntled player would say. "Goddamn parade-ground martinet . . ." "Treating us like white trash . . ." "Ordering us around . . ." "We're not in the goddamn army . . ."

A few mocked him behind his back: "Win, win, win . . . I want victories, not heroes . . ." "Fuck him . . ." "Who cares whether we win or lose?" "What difference does it make?" "He's takin' all the fun out of it."

The cards were stacked against the young manager, and the names on those cards were Nap Lajoie, the first baseman and a rising star; Big Ed Delahanty, the left fielder and an honest-to-goodness superstar; and Colonel John Rogers, the greedy majority owner of the team.

The 22-year-old Napoleon Lajoie (pronounced la-zha-way), a top talent better known as "Larry," was easily led astray, particularly after falling under the influence of unruly Phillies veterans who were invariably bickering with and sniping at Stallings.

Larry debuted as a first baseman after Big Ed Delahanty, the team's regular at that position (Delahanty disliked playing there), convinced him that he'd have a better chance of sticking in the Bigs as a first baseman than he would as an outfielder. "I had no experience at first base," Lajoie later recalled, "and decided to give it a try."

The "Big Frenchman," a 200-pound six-footer, was an instant success and rapidly won the hearts of Philadelphia fans with his superb fielding and splendid hitting. Larry seemed to glide around the bag with the smooth swiftness of a panther on the prowl. He may well have been one of the most graceful athletes ever to play the game. And how he could hit. A right-handed batter, powerfully built, the thick-legged Lajoie had a sharp eye for pitch location, a smooth swing, and tremendous power. Over the course of a 21-year career, he compiled a .345 lifetime average and won the then-mythical Triple Crown in 1901 with a league-leading .422 average.

When Larry was hot, he was such a good hitter that pitchers preferred to walk him rather than risk pitching to him. One day Russ Ford, one of the New York Yankees' best pitchers, decided on an intentional pass. Just put him on. The fourth pitch was wide, but not too wide. The beautifully coordinated Lajoie reached out, bat in one hand, and punched the ball into right field for a double. Ford was more careful the second time around, but the result was the same. The Big Frenchman got a third one-handed double to right on Ford's third attempt at an intentional pass.

Not taking any chances the next time Lajoie came to bat, Ford delivered four balls behind Larry's back and walked him. Even the great Lajoie couldn't hit them there.

Big Ed Delahanty was a lethal hitter, tough, crude, efficient, a big headache, never really tethered to reality. Blessed with extraordinary skills, he set all kinds of records for excellence for batters of his day. Three times he averaged over .400 (Delahanty, Luis Arraez, and D. J. LeMahieu are the only hitters ever to win batting titles in both the American and National Leagues), and once he hit safely in 10 consecutive at bats. What he had you couldn't teach.

A fixture in the Phillies lineup, Big Ed was everybody's hero, an exciting player, fun to watch, adored by fans. They say pitchers never discovered his weakness. "When the ball seems to me to be coming in to my liking," he once remarked, "I'm going to belt it. I don't care where it comes in."

One afternoon Delahanty stepped up to the plate against the great Cy Young. Two men were out and the catcher ordered an intentional pass: "Put him on." Young's first offering was wide, almost a wild pitch. That didn't slow Del one bit. He reached out and slammed the pitch out of the ballpark.

The catcher looked at Young questioningly: "I thought I told you to put him on?"

"You did," Young replied. "That's what I was trying to do . . . I thought I'd thrown a wild pitch until I saw the damn thing going over the fence."

Though an immense talent, Del was anything but a manager's dream. A dark, temperamental side of his personality frequently intruded on his game. Dangerously unstable, bipolar, and prone to rage, he spent much of his time and money satisfying infantile impulses and making himself less capable. He was overly fond of drinking, gambling, and loose women, and he devoted a lot of energy to getting soused.

Most evenings were spent stumbling from gin mill to gin mill, his favorite haunts, in downwardly sloping nights of partying and barhopping. He'd grown up brawling with bullies, and his idea of guilt-free fun was a noisy fistfight outside a saloon. After hours, drowning in the tide of his own thirst, he found it impossible to cork the bottle and would sometimes wander around aimlessly throughout the night in the seedier parts of town, looking for one last drink.

Baseball wasn't Colonel John Rogers's main interest in life. His bank account was. The team represented power, prestige, and money. The almighty dollar was his religion, and maximizing corporate profits was uppermost in his mind. Seeking to improve discipline (at least that's the excuse he gave), the cantankerous old coot tossed a hot potato in George Stallings's lap even before he signed a contract: a "code of conduct," a foolishly impractical set of rules that could not help but undercut Stallings's authority and cause friction between the players and the manager, and between the manager and the front office.

The code would have a devastating effect on the environment Stallings expected to put in place. Rule 4, for instance, the temperance rule, held the manager responsible "for a player's abstinence from the use of both spiritual and malt liquors in the ballpark and the player's rooms at home or while on road trips or in public conveyances." Political and religious discussions, card playing, quarrelling, profanity, obscenity, and rowdy or ungentlemanly conduct at home, away, or traveling were also prohibited.

According to rule 7, "Only the captain or other player designated by the manager could address an umpire, and then only in strict accordance with the Playing Rules, in respectful language. Profane, indecent, vulgar or ungentlemanly language, gestures or conduct directed against an umpire would subject the offender to punishment."

Clauses inserted in each player's contract allowed management to defer $300 of the player's salary, $7,500 in today's dollars, until the end of the season, and stated that "the money would be returned to him if, and this was a big if, the player lived up to the rules [there were 11 of them] and played ball to the owner's satisfaction." So there you have it.

◆◆◆

Stallings did what he was hired to do throughout the 1897 season: he ended the rowdy bad behavior of the self-indulgent players who had dragged down the ball club for years, weeded out the worst of the wrong-headed actors, imposed restrictions, ratcheted up the concept of team play, and scheduled skull sessions at nine o'clock sharp each morning, followed by a stiff workout, except on Sundays when the team was at home.

Most of the alcohol-soaked whiskey swiggers didn't buy into all of the rah-rah-rah-let's-crush-'em-like-a-bug stuff, and the ball club languished and finished 10th in the 12-team league. So far as the boys were concerned, their manager was a madman. "Stallings harps too much on system," one of them said. "What we need is less system and more runs."

But Stallings believed a player should be familiar with every conceivable game situation, be prepared for every exigency, even things not encountered very often. The players would sit around him in a half circle and talk over, discuss, and analyze good and bad plays, mental errors, and plans for new modes of attack.

The way Stallings looked at things, major-league baseball was not a social game; it was men at work. A business. If players did not willingly climb the ladder of success, Stallings was determined to drag them up right along with him. Most of the time he was about as subtle as a jackhammer.

Drawing on his manager's reports of fines and verbal reprimands as indicators of bad conduct, Colonel Rogers nattered on endlessly about the team's 10th-place finish in 1897 and the failure of its players to live up to the code. Their performances did not add up to what he thought appropriate, and he announced a series of salary reductions at the end of the season: final paychecks would be withheld.

The to-do was considerable.

Expressing disbelief at being denied their rightful earnings, the players refused to admit any wrongdoing and demanded their money. This opened a contentious debate. Nap Lajoie, for one, called it a gimmick. He would not sign a new contract in which he was to receive $2,100 and an additional $300 at the end of the season, provided he lived up to the abstinence clauses of the contract.

"The $2,400 salary is fine," Lajoie said. "But I don't intend to dissipate, so why should I sign a contract with an abstinence clause in it?"

When asked to comment, Stallings sidestepped the issue. What could he say? Any criticism of the colonel might cost him his job. Silently, though, he felt a touch of foreboding in his bones and deplored the implications of Rogers's actions.

CHAPTER 3

ROGERS'S RULES

"The standard of rum, riot and rebellion has been hauled down," an approving Philadelphia writer declared in February 1898.

The worst troublemakers had been jettisoned, sent packing, at least those considered expendable, the serial brawlers, the drinkers, and the womanizers. Well, not all of them. Dumping some of the other drink-infected rabble-rousers was unthinkable. Who in their right mind would entertain the thought of trading the likes of Big Ed Delahanty, a .377 hitter? Or Nap Lajoie, .363? Or, for that matter, Duff Cooley, .329? Sluggers of that caliber weren't discovered every day of the week.

Expectations were high at the opening of the season. The revamped lineup was strong from top to bottom. But whipping the team into shape would not happen overnight. A lot of hard work lay ahead of them before they turned into a smoothly running, efficient machine. It would be a long, difficult slog.

Of the five new pitchers, two, rookie left-hander Wiley Piatt and veteran right-hander "Red" Donahue (acquired in a trade with St. Louis), would become big winners. Piatt would throw six shutouts in winning 24 games (he would win 23 the following season), and Donahue would win 16, and go on to become a 20-game winner in three of the following four years.

The all-new infield of "Klondike" Douglas at first, Nap Lajoie at second, Monte Cross at short, and "Kid" Elberfeld at third was excitingly brilliant. Stallings's decision to shift Lajoie from first to second could not have been more successful. When complimented on the shrewdness of the move, the Phillies manager replied, "Oh, well, Larry would have been great wherever I played him."

Slick-fielding Monte Cross and feisty Kid Elberfeld would be disappointments. Cross, who typically covered a lot of ground (he'd led National League shortstops at one time or another in putouts four times and in assists twice), made an astonishing 93 errors in 149 games. And an early-season knee injury wrecked Kid Elberfeld's major-league debut, limiting the Kid to just 38 at bats in 14 games.

The refusal of the Philadelphia front office to re-sign third baseman Billy Nash as a backup for the Kid also hurt the team. Rookie Ed Abbaticchio, a utility infielder, was thrown into the gap at third to shore up the infield when Elberfeld went down and simply could not get the job done. Abbaticchio was wobbly and unsure of himself and kicked a lot of easy ground balls. The unexpected weaknesses at shortstop and third base cost the Phillies a number of early-season games.

An opening-day 7–6 loss to Brooklyn did nothing to dampen Stallings's spirit. Always superstitious, he viewed the setback as a good omen. Things looked good after the first week of play. Philadelphia was 4–1, tied for first in the standings. Giddy smiles abounded in the City of Brotherly Love. It looked like it was going to be a good year for the Phillies. A very good year.

But the offense stalled and things began to unravel. The inconsistent attack was proficient one day, ragged the day after, and quiet the next. When wins proved elusive, smiles turned to frowns. Bats went limp. Wheels jammed. The team went into a six-week slumber and was a bust of major proportions, lethargic, inept, and as dull and flat as yesterday's party balloon.

For all the talk about their vaunted power, the hitting wasn't worth a lick and showed no signs of improving. On the 12th of May, 14 games into the season, bad luck further enfeebled the team. "Big Sam" Thompson injured his back. It was a terrific blow. The 6'2", 200-pound future Hall of Famer was leading the team in hitting when an injury cut him down. Sam knew every inch of the wall in right field, every angle, every eccentricity. No one took balls off the wall better.

"There was as much difference between Thompson's hitting and fielding," the Philadelphia Inquirer remarked, "and that of the two players who tramped around right-field after him, as there was between a thoroughbred race horse and a plow horse."

Sam was not only a great hitter and fielder, he was a decent, straightforward, honorable person, the kind of individual the troubled ball club could ill afford to lose. When asked when he'd return to the lineup, Big Sam smiled apologetically and said, "I'm afraid I'm through." And he was. Two weeks later the front office announced his retirement.

Whatever expectations Stallings might have had about succeeding were dashed by injuries and the backward-tugging force of Rogers's rules—the code. Getting fined for doing their job was a big worry for the players. They were uptight, shaky, and in a constant fret.

Most fans were unaware of Rogers's interference, and the wholesale salary reductions generated by the code, until news of the sordid mess broke into public view in St. Louis on June 24. A former Phillies player sued Colonel Rogers for back pay, claiming it was due him. A St. Louis judge apparently saw some merit in the charges and attached the gate receipts from the Phillies-Cardinals series at Sportsmans Park until the salary squabble was resolved.

Five Cardinal teammates, all Phillies outcasts traded to St. Louis, also threatened lawsuits.

Growing frantic over a sharp drop in home attendance and what he perceived as the failure of the ball club, Colonel Rogers conjured up another pseudo-motivator: "Win now, or else." Though aware of the implications of the ultimatum, Stallings pretended to give it no importance. He realized when he took the job that things might turn out this way. It was beyond concern.

Unable to accompany the team on its swing through Boston and New York, or personally cover the games in those cities, several Philadelphia writers, disregarding anything so tedious as "the truth," managed to get into the act nonetheless, using unfounded gossip about the possibility of discontent in the ranks to put into play a lot of foolish rubbish, doing more or less what they liked with rumors.

The Big Chief scoffed at the stories and denied that there was any friction on the ball club. There was not a word of truth in the gossip.

The players themselves went on record as saying "that nobody blamed Manager Stallings. They didn't have any grievances against their skipper. They knew of no one else they'd rather play for than George Stallings." They were quite fond of him.

On the way to Boston, Cooley and Lajoie were fined for excessive drinking in public, and the same pair were again fined for carelessly breaking the rules before the team left the Hub City, something Stallings seldom did. He was attempting to jolt the boys into playing better ball. And what did Colonel Rogers do? He interfered. Playing the part of the good guy, he overruled his manager and made the Big Chief look like the bad guy. Stallings was furious. He wasn't interested in being used as a pawn against his players.

The Phillies lost two of three in Boston, largely because of an inability to hit with runners in scoring position. The offense veered between feeble and nonexistent.

It was on to New York where Wiley Piatt, the Phillies starting pitcher, and his teammates virtually gift-wrapped the first game of the series for the home team, an 11–3 Giants victory. Piatt gave up 10 walks, and his teammates, playing ragged ball behind him, committed an astonishing nine errors. "They performed like men in a trance," the *New York Times* reported, "like men afflicted with nervous prostration."

New York humiliated Philadelphia again the following day, 16–4, a game in which the visitors mystifyingly committed six more costly errors, bringing the total to 15 errors in two games. It was awful.

A sports-page headline in the *Philadelphia Record* pretty much summed up the reason for the Phillies' protracted slump:

WHAT THE PHILLIES NEED
MORE COMMON SENSE MANAGEMENT
AND FEWER CLUB RULES

The folly of attempting to control a team of ball players by a written set of rules which impose a fine or punishment for so many different things is a joke.... Manager Stallings has not been free to handle the ball players as he thought best, but was expected to control them in the way the club owners thought wise. This has been a severe handicap on Stallings and the result has been a dismal failure....

It is hoped that Rogers' rules will be thrown into the sewer.... The long list of failures indicates that Rogers' way of doing business is wrong. A change should be made at once.

Home for a day after the wretched trip to Boston and New York, two or three members of the ball club called on President Reach, the Phillies' minority owner, in an effort to address the team's shortcomings and at the same time offer some advice as well as do some not-so-subtle prodding during the air-clearing meeting.

They reminded President Reach that players should not be treated as enemies, and they vigorously assailed the hated code. Rogers's rules were the reason the team was languishing in tenth place. The men confessed to being uptight and unable to focus on the game because of the corrosive power of the rules, and they admitted that the code had sapped their incentive to give their all for the team. They urged President Reach to give them a chance. Suspend the rules and ease the stress. Eliminate front-office control of the club on the field. "If you do that," they promised, "you'll see results. The team will perform closer to what you and Colonel Rogers expected in the first place."

Reach was well enough aware of the situation to understand that some owners are not always wise owners. Colonel Rogers had gone too far. It was clearly a failure of upper management. Mr. Reach promised the boys that he'd talk to the majority owner and urge him to suspend the 11-rule code. He'd do it immediately.

News of the meeting leaked to the press, and a money-grubbing hack from the *Evening Bulletin,* not knowing what happened, grasping at straws, cooked up a twisted scenario of his own making, imagining a player rebellion against the manager, embellishing and ignoring and manipulating the facts. "There has been too much management," he wrote. "Some of the players rebelled and forced the issue on the owners of the club."

Later that same morning, President A. J. Reach relieved Stallings of his managerial duties for a limited time, or at least that's what was said publicly (Stallings was under contract for six more months). The majority owner of the franchise, Colonel John Rogers, not always a straightforward individual, had laid out the plan of action before the team returned from New York, and he remained at his summer home on Cape May when President Reach relieved the Phillies manager of his duties.

Unfailingly courteous, Stallings skillfully deflected questions about the announcement and issued a carefully worded reply: "The owners looked for results in the form of victories. They didn't get the results they expected, and action was taken."

With the possible exception of Duff Cooley, who, as team captain, would handle things that afternoon, the players were unaware of what had happened. Shortly before game time, Ed Delahanty approached Stallings fully expecting a scolding. Del requested permission to wear his gray road knickers. The usual excuse. He'd overslept and didn't have time to retrieve the home whites from the cleaners.

"Wear anything you like," Stallings replied snappishly, turning his face away.

The response struck Del as odd. He looked at his manager uncomprehendingly. "Is something wrong, George?" he asked, showing sincere concern.

Stallings ran his thumb over his lip and mumbled, "I've been let go."

Del stared at him, hardly believing his ears. Somehow it seemed inconceivable. He looked at the ground, shaking his head, and muttered, "I'm sorry, George. I'm sorry. I'm really sorry."

Minutes later, the club's secretary, Billy Shettsline, appeared on the field and in a solemn voice announced the change. "Manager Stallings will not accompany the team on the road trip which opens in St. Louis on Monday. It's been decided to keep him home on this journey."

Questions about Stallings's status went unanswered. Asked whether he had resigned or been released, Shettsline was noncommittal. "Neither one nor the other," he said. "Mr. Rogers is on Cape May at the moment, and matters will . . . remain just as they are for a time. I will go away with the team myself and manage until we return, or something else is done."

A likeable sort, big and portly, good-humored, the 34-year-old Shettsline, a former ticket taker, bookkeeper, and front-office factotum, had no baseball credentials to speak of, but people enjoyed having him around, particularly Colonel Rogers.

Late Saturday afternoon, there was a mixed bag of feelings in the clubhouse after a 6–5 Philadelphia victory over the New York Giants. Most of the boys were terribly upset. Not so much about the managerial change—those things happen. What bothered them was the *Bulletin*'s inappropriate and unjust coverage.

The tough-talking extroverts on the team decided to publicly rebut the *Bulletin*'s story. It had to be done, and done quickly. There wasn't much time. There was a train to catch for St. Louis. A statement was hurriedly prepared.

> We, the undersigned players of the Philadelphia Ball Club, having noticed in a Philadelphia paper that we requested the release of Manager Stallings, wish it distinctly understood that there is positively no truth in the statement. We have the greatest respect for Manager Stallings and wish it known that he has always acted in a straightforward and manly manner toward us all. W. B. Douglass, W. H. Piatt, N. Lajoie, D. G. Cooley, Ed J. Abbaticchio, N. Elberfeld, A. T. Orth, E. W. McFarland, George L. Wheeler, Ed Dunkle, E. J. Delahanty, Newt. Fisher, Monte Cross, F. L. Donohue.

When told of the players' public gesture on his behalf, Stallings was not surprised. "Every member of the team is my friend," he said, "as they should be. I've been a friend to every one of them."

"How is it possible for anyone to blame George Stallings?" the *Evening Item* asked. "He's a splendid judge of young players and was good at breaking them in. . . . For the players he picked up by purchase and otherwise, he deserves a great deal of thanks."

The writer then posed a question. "If a team isn't hitting, if there's a letdown in the pitching, if the pitchers are walking eight or nine batters a game, and hit one or two others, and if there are a lot of errors, ghastly errors, can you blame the manager?"

> "From the beginning to the present time," Francis Richter wrote, in *The Sporting Life,* taking a careful look at the season, "George Stallings has experienced nothing but misfortune. The team did not get proper spring training; it was handicapped in the choice of a competent captain (Duff Cooley) to work with the manager; and the team struck a prolonged batting slump, during which games upon games—totaling at least a score—were lost for lack of a hit by anyone of the 'big four' of the team—Cooley, Douglas, Delahanty and Lajoie—who fell down together. Enough games were lost in this aggravating way, to have put the team in the first division, right up with the leaders. The loss of Elberfeld was also a hard blow; it unbalanced the infield."

Rogers rejected the arguments, saying he made the change because of the ball club's unfulfilled promise. They had now been less than a .500 team for more than a year. They were much better than that on paper.

An even more flagrant misrepresentation of the facts took place 50 years later. Sportswriters Fred Lieb and Stan Baumgartner, perhaps in a quest for a juicy story for their history of the Philadelphia Phillies, repeated the unfounded rumors and chronic false statements as facts, interpreting the incident as "the first big league team to go on strike against their manager."

Doing more or less what they pleased, Lieb and Baumgartner fabricated, distorted, and invented things, and they attributed "a cute little" sign-stealing trick to Stallings, something that occurred more than two years after the Big Chief had been relieved as manager.

Once these stories appeared in print, others repeated the rubbish so many times that people got so they believed them. The canard was too good to retire, and others insisted on retelling the hoary tale. Since nobody heard Stallings's side of the narrative, what really happened got lost in the stew.

When Stallings faced Reach and Rogers in the Phillies' offices Monday morning, the points at issue played out in an atmosphere of tenseness.

Stallings admitted he was a tough taskmaster (wasn't that why they hired him?) and bristled at suggestions that he might have been unfair. In a furious exchange, he stood up to the touchy, vainglorious, and devious Rogers and refused to accept responsibility for the fines levied in Boston. He was carrying out orders, enforcing Rogers's rules. He reminded Reach and Rogers that they as owners had acted improperly in rescinding the fines. That they undermined team discipline. That they made relationships fail.

"Sometimes," Stallings said, acknowledging his own mistakes, "things go the right way, sometimes they don't." He insisted that the ball club's 19–27 record didn't reflect the true character of the team. But it didn't matter. Gentleman George was swimming with sharks. So far as Reach and Rogers were concerned, Stallings had bungled the job. Talking like lawyers and speaking legalese, they reached a decision. It was time to part ways. They paid off Stallings. It was over.*

---

*Whatever Stallings's shortcomings might have been, he left Reach and Rogers and Quaker City fans with a solid team. The Phillies, after Rogers's rules were abandoned, blossomed under manager Billy Shettsline and played winning ball for the remainder of the season, eventually climbing into sixth place in the standings.

CHAPTER 4

THE NEWLY NAMED AMERICAN LEAGUE

Within days of the upheaval in Philadelphia, George Vanderbeck, Stallings's former boss and principal owner of the Western League's Detroit Tigers, jumped at the possibility of bringing the Big Chief back into the fold. When reporters asked why, Vanderbeck explained, "It's simple, George is the best there is. He's a baseball architect who knows how to build and maintain competitive teams." What Vanderbeck might have added, and did not, was that George Stallings functioned perfectly well at a low level of spending.

An unreasonable boss, the mercurial Detroit owner was intensely belligerent. He alienated players, angered fans, and churned through managers at a breakneck pace. He'd already sent two of his skippers spinning through exit doors that season.

But Stallings, cocky and self-assured, willingly undertook the task of rebuilding the Tigers, a disheartened, disoriented, and defeated band of losers who lacked any sense of self-esteem or seriousness about winning.

Working tirelessly, George from Georgia juggled players and positions and lineups, sorted out the effective from the ineffective, and sent the regular second baseman and third baseman packing. He himself took over the duties in left field and personally captained the team, as well as managing it.

When not actively engaged on the field of play, the young manager spent hours burning up the wires, looking for dribs and drabs of talent, any player who might strengthen the ball club. The Tigers pulled themselves together, came up from the bottom, and finished sixth. The following year, they became a grassroots success story of sorts, making a bid for second place and staying competitive all season before falling back and finishing fourth, a game and a half behind the third-place Indianapolis Hoosiers.

◆◆◆

President Byron Bancroft Johnson of the Western League (friends called him "Ban") was the executive responsible for running the circuit. (Johnson also served the league as its secretary and treasurer.) A tough, cold, ruthless character, Johnson's unwonted administrative acumen in commercial matters earned the respect of the cigar-chomping owners who tended to rely on his decisions. They were making money, some of them for the first time, and willingly followed the lead of this new breed of hands-on executive.

Reared in Avondale, Ohio, a sleepy town on the outskirts of Cincinnati, Johnson didn't have the faintest idea of what he wanted out of life. An underachiever in college, he cut classes and shunned homework, fell behind in his studies, quit school, and took a fling at professional baseball, only to learn that he did not have enough natural talent to make a career of it.

His first taste of life in the real world came as a $25-a-week reporter for the *Cincinnati Commercial Gazette* (a good salary in those days), where he encountered the manageable chaos and the pressure-packed last-minute heart palpitations of a newsroom before a deadline. It was a galvanizing experience. The brash young man showed a gift for communicating and loved the brutal competition for stories. His restless, active mind embraced the possibilities of the profession, and he showed no compunction in proffering a few white lies in putting together any vaguely newsworthy story. The not-always-savory reporter impressed those around him as being one of those individuals who was going somewhere.

Within a year, the ambitious Johnson caught the attention of Hurat Halstead, the *Gazette*'s editor. Halstead made young Ban the paper's sports editor, an appointment that put the big fellow on a career path in professional baseball. The daily grind in the press box at Cincinnati Park, pounding out reports about games, opened the young sports editor's eyes to the vagaries of the business and gave him a purpose in life.

The full significance of the experience registered six years later when, at the urging of his friend, Cincinnati manager Charlie Comiskey, Johnson accepted an offer to fill a vacancy as president of the Western League, a high minor league. Without delay, Johnson laid out a clear agenda for what he wanted to do: strengthen the organization financially, reduce rowdyism, and make the game more respectable. The frequently repeated slogan "clean baseball" became his mantra.

Johnson's ideas encountered serious challenges from hard-nosed players and managers, most of whom had been schooled in the anything-goes, ask-no-quarter, give-none years of professional baseball. Rough-and-ready veterans of the diamond resented talk of rescuing the game from rowdyism and tended to ignore Johnson's edicts. Winning alone counted. Nothing was too vicious.

This was the mindset of Detroit manager George Stallings, he of the take-no-prisoners school of baseball. An independent contrarian, Stallings believed a team going into battle was better off with a little meanness in its game—an "edge." That's the way the big fellow was wired. He was well known for restlessly prowling the bench, shouting and screaming and making disparaging gestures. Bad calls touched off barrages of splendid vulgarities. Four-letter words. The Fuck Patois. The heathenish talk of manliness. His furious tongue heaped insults on anyone and everyone in sight, a mindset that established a cocky atmosphere.

The *Cleveland Plain Dealer* chronicled the rowdyism of the era with a fictitious diary entry told through the eyes of a mythical umpire. A few paragraphs are worth quoting here:

Monday—Got along pretty well today. Captain Soaker called me a liar twice, but I pretended not to hear him. I'll fix him later on. Larry Gahan shook his fist under my nose on a close decision in the third, and he'll get the benefit of no close calls from me.

Tuesday—For half the game, I had both teams around me four deep. The balance of the time I was dodging souvenirs from the crowd. In the sixth there was a rush for me from the right field bleachers, but the police stopped 'em in time. I have only words of praise for the police. They saw that the home team still had an even chance of winning, and they didn't want the game interrupted. In the seventh, Pete Husky swung at me, but I dodged his fist and the blow struck catcher Feeney square in the ear. He told me I dodged on purpose, and we had quite an argument. Finally, I sent him to the bench.

Wednesday—I told the police this afternoon that if they didn't stop the fans from throwing beer bottles, and cigar boxes, and shoe shine brushes at me, I would forfeit the game to the visiting team. They said they'd try.... Toward the end of the ninth, I stood as far back of the catcher as I could, and, when the last man was out, I ran for my life—and the streetcar. As I started through the door, I heard beer bottles crashing against the ground behind me.

Thursday—Fergy Maguire complained too much in the second, and I sent him to the bench. He tried to hit me with an uppercut and I punched him in the jaw. He didn't go to the bench. They brought the bench to him.

> Saturday—It took seventeen policemen and a patrol wagon to save me this afternoon. The trouble began when I called Finigan out on a close play in the fourth. The crowd called me a "robber" sixteen minutes without cessation. In the sixth, when I called "Mugsy" Swipes safe at second on another close play, the crowd finally broke loose. Men swore, women fainted and dogs barked. The crowd swarmed onto the field and I backed away, surrounded by police officers. They ran in a patrol wagon, chucked me into it, and then the whole outfit raced around the field—three times—with the crowd in pursuit.

The diary underscored the enormous challenge Johnson faced. But he did not hesitate. Defying conventional wisdom, he took command, laid out his expectations, tightened his grip, intensified the clampdown, and steered the league into the center of public attention. The press coverage was incredible; attendance exceeded expectations, and the quality of play was higher than expected. His leadership skills made all the difference between teams making money and losing money.

A contentious figure of fascinating contradictions, Johnson single-handedly, or so he made it appear, put the Western League on a sound financial footing and laid the groundwork for future assaults on new markets. Inherent in his approach were big picture aspirations, a vision of playing a larger and more important role in the business of baseball. Having forged an even tighter bond with Charlie Comiskey, the owner of the St. Paul Saints, Ban and Charlie conceived the seemingly improbable scheme of reorganizing the Western League into a second major league, what Johnson liked to call "a cleaner alternative to the rowdyism of the long-established National League."

The idea was not without risk. The strategy called for the invasion of big eastern cities where there was a large and enthusiastic audience for baseball. The first step of the plan took place at the Western League's annual meeting in Chicago (1899). With a press release, Johnson announced that "the Western League had gone out of existence, and the American League of Professional Baseball Clubs had taken its place."

Though the American League was still a minor league, the rechristening marked the beginning of a series of organizational moves that would make success a certainty. But it wasn't all white nights and around-the-clock sunshine, all happiness, all the time; it was part frustration, part crises, and part circus.

Crushing debts and lawsuits were overwhelming Detroit owner George Vanderbeck. His properties were being auctioned off, by order of the Wayne County court, and everything was soon gone, except for the ball club. Nobody wanted it. This really got Johnson's dander up. Fearing for the future of the nascent American League, he hurried to Detroit in search of a well-heeled buyer, someone under whom the club might prosper, and ran into a stone wall. The league had lost its luster in Detroit, and the public perception of its future was badly damaged.

James D. Burns, a local businessman and politician, and George Stallings, an entrepreneur and the club's manager, stepped forward. It was an opportunity thing. They agreed to purchase the franchise for $12,000 in cash ($450,430 in 2024 dollars) on the condition that Johnson and the American League guarantee Detroit a berth in the circuit when it became a second major league. Johnson agreed. The franchise was on its feet again, and that's what mattered.

Despite shallow pockets and a prolonged controversy with the National League, Johnson obtained permission, under the National Agreement then in effect (the document that helped guide all of organized baseball), to transfer two American League teams into major-league cities: Comiskey's St. Paul Saints into Chicago and the Grand Rapids Prodigals into Cleveland.

The move, as it turned out, came at a bargain price. Johnson and Jim Hart, the president of Chicago's major-league team (the Orphans and future Cubs), after much wrangling, struck a deal. Hart agreed to share the Chicago market if the name Chicago were not used in identifying the new team in town and if the American League played its games on Chicago's South Side, which were easily managed restrictions.

Johnson and Comiskey shrewdly got around the name problem by adopting the identity and the uniforms of Chicago's original National League team, the Chicago White Stockings. The boys from the press did the rest. Within a year, writers were calling the team the Chicago White Sox. The name fit headlines better. And it stuck. The condition calling for the team to play on Chicago's South Side was just fine with Johnson and Comiskey. So far as they were concerned, it opened up a whole new constituency. And the franchise prospered.

Cleveland was a different story. It was a city of promise, and it was a city of limitations; promise because it once supported a strong major-league team—the Cleveland Spiders, and limitations because the National League had abandoned the city after the Spiders' fortunes soured.

Frank DeHass Robison, the team's owner, panicked when attendance suffered a sharp and unexpected decline in 1897. In an effort to extricate himself from a messy financial situation, Robison came up with an exit strategy, a master plan that would enable him to get rid of the Spiders and remain in baseball. He purchased a second National League team at a bankruptcy auction: the St. Louis Browns (the future Cardinals).

Robison immediately traded, transferred really, the Spiders' most popular players to the Browns, including three future Hall of Famers—Jesse Burkett, Cy Young, and Bobby Wallace—for a troupe of misfits, no-names, and has-beens (none of whom were destined to make much of an impact) in one of the most lopsided trades in baseball history. The jarring announcement destroyed whatever fan loyalty remained in Cleveland, and the franchise was dismantled at the end of the season.

While all of this was going on, Ban Johnson was scurrying around Cleveland, wooing investors, lighting fires under potential backers, working to raise capital for a new minor-league team. When things looked bleakest, he hit the jackpot.

Charles Somers, a wealthy young coal millionaire, and John Kilfoyle, a local haberdasher, expressed interest. But they were reluctant to back a minor-league team in a city unable to support a major-league team. And rightly so. When Johnson assured them that the fledgling league would become a major league once Chicago and Cleveland established a local following, Somers and Kilfoyle came on board; Somers went on to become the linchpin on which the future success of the league rested.

With teams in Buffalo, Chicago, Cleveland, Detroit, Indianapolis, Kansas City, Milwaukee, and Minneapolis, the newly named American League took on a national identity. Chicago became the hub city when Johnson established league headquarters there, sharing the same suite of offices with his good friend, Charles Comiskey.

CHAPTER 5

SOMETHING'S WRONG HERE

There were so many stories about bad calls by umpires in the Western League that the tales seemed like part of an endless loop of the same narrative. An incident at South Side Park in Chicago served as an example of why the men in blue were the subjects of so much searing criticism.

With one out in the bottom half of the eighth, the White Sox were leading the visiting Tigers 7–1. Runners were on first and third. Dick Padden, behind on the count, rapped a nubber in front of the mound. "Dummy" Hoy, the runner on third, sprinted home. It was a gutsy move but not a wise one; he was out sliding across the plate.

Whether intentionally or not, Hoy bumped the catcher's arm as he was about to throw the batter out at first base and complete the double play. But umpire Joe Cantillon, widely condemned for being more skilled at starting fights than preventing them, made no call. He just stood there and said nothing. The Detroit players howled, "Interference!"

Arms flailing, yammering, "You dumb bastard . . . " manager George Stallings charged in from right field. "Didn't you see the play?" he hollered. "Padden's out . . . a clear case of interference."

Eyeball-tight, Stallings and Cantillon went at it up close, jabbering at each other. Cantillon mouthed something. Stallings's eyes widened. He tweaked Cantillon's nose; or did he shove him or smack him? Nobody was quite certain. Things happened so quickly. Cantillon shot a pointed finger at Stallings: "You're outta here."

Two days later, Joe Cantillon was in hot water again. It happened in the fourth inning of the final game of the series. The Tigers were leading 5–3. The White Sox were at bat. There was one out and a runner on first base.

Frank Isbell, the Chicago first baseman, rapped a bouncer to the left side of the mound. The pitcher pounced on it and snapped a throw to second base. Kid Elberfeld took the throw and fired the ball to first, completing the twin killing. Most fans thought the visiting Tigers had executed a perfect double play. Cantillon called both runners safe. And Elberfeld went berserk. He threw his cap on the ground, tore at his hair, danced on the cap, punted it, and cursed until he was purple in the face. Not surprisingly, he was put out of the game for the breach of decorum.

The Kid was a smart-talking, pugnacious little beast, one of the most volatile players in the game. He had the temper of a fiend and the mouth of a hyena, and Stallings was often uncomfortable with the young man's outbursts.

Three days later, Johnson sprung a jack-in-the-box sensation. He suspended manager George Stallings for 10 days. The reason? Bad language during the run-in with umpire Joe Cantillon. Not a word was said about Elberfeld.

Stallings looked slightly aghast when handed the notice. "I can't believe it," he said. "Ten days? For what?" Suppressed rage boiled inside him. "What the hell was I supposed to do?" he asked of no one in particular. "That son of a bitch called me a nigger. I'm a Georgia boy. I couldn't let him get away with that."

Jim Burns, president of the Detroit ball club, was even more upset. "Something's wrong here," he growled. "Johnson is picking on us . . . It's discrimination . . . That's what it is." Burns bristled at a reporter who said Johnson was "only doing his job."

In a burst of fury, Burns bellowed, "Only doing his job? Only doing his job? Well, let me tell you something, mister. Johnson gave us a crooked deal when we claimed Dick Padden and Jack O'Brien . . . Our check was in the mail . . . What did Johnson do? . . . He bollixed the deal. Cut our throats. Instead of completing the sale with Nick Young [the National League president], like he was supposed to do, he sold Padden to Chicago and O'Brien to Kansas City. He didn't send them to us. The dirty bastard."

The reporter raised his brows, a silent invitation for Burns to continue.

"Johnson was determined to strengthen the White Sox," Burns said. "Make them contenders. He didn't care if he weakened us or prevented us from getting stronger."

To this end, Johnson was dead set on proving that the American League's franchise in Chicago, though a minor-league team, could outdraw the resident major-league team in the same city in a head-to-head competition. On

July 3 a mere 11½ games separated first-place Chicago from eighth-place Buffalo. It was a fan's paradise. Burns and Stallings and several others who wisely chose to hide their irritation didn't like the idea of the league's president rigging the pennant race.

Burns's anger did not subside. The following morning he boarded a train for Chicago, and when he reached American League headquarters, he didn't feel obliged to muzzle his previously expressed opinions. With cold fury in his voice, he unloaded on the American League president, pointedly accusing him of ordering umpires to "roast" the Tigers and give them the short end of the stick, especially Stallings. "It's got to stop," Burns shouted. "And stop now." Johnson's face crimsoned.

Responding publicly, Johnson sneered in print: "Jim Burns is new to baseball. When his friends [he was clearly referring to Detroit manager George Stallings] tell him he is being robbed, he believes it. . . . As far as umpires go, mistakes may be made, but the charge that umpires have been instructed 'to roast' Detroit is puerile."

They traded blows in the press.

"Mr. Johnson should remember that he is the hired man in the league," Burns said in response. "He works for us. We are the only people who select men who shall be associated with us. . . . Mr. Johnson has no right to talk about the men who pay his salary."

One Saturday afternoon, there were two outs and runners on first and second in a game at Bennett Park in Detroit. Chicago manager Charlie Comiskey signaled for a double steal. Anticipating the play, Joe Cantillon kept his eyes glued on the lead runner. But Detroit catcher Al Shaw crossed him up. Shaw threw to second base instead, the ball clearly beating the runner. Elberfeld made the tag. Just about everybody in the ballpark thought the runner was out, except Joe Cantillon. He ruled both runners safe. The Kid slammed his glove on the ground, leaned over, and spat between Cantillon's feet, deliberately provoking the partisan crowd.[*] It was bedlam.

Fans hooted and jeered every decision after that, and the uproar continued. In the top of the fourth a Chicago runner reached first base on a scratch hit. Dick Padden, the next batter, dumped a twisting looper over the

---

[*] Kid Elberfeld was a tough competitor. He was always out to prove that he wasn't afraid of anybody. "A little guy just had to be tough to get by," he explained. "The only way I could prevent those big guys from picking on me was to be just a bit tougher than they were." He thought nothing of blocking second base and challenging a base runner to slash him out of the way. As a result, he was repeatedly "bunged up." His legs were badly scarred, and he'd sit in the clubhouse after games, pouring whiskey on spike wounds to cauterize them.

first baseman's head. The ball hugged the right-field foul line and dropped just foul. Cantillon, out of position, hesitated, then called it a fair ball. A torrent of boos cascaded out of the stands. The next two batters popped out, but Chicago first baseman Frank Isbell smacked a sharp ground ball up the middle, driving home both runners, the visitors' margin of victory.

Outraged fans swarmed onto the field and surrounded Cantillon. Seeing this, Jim Burns jumped into the middle of the melee and shouldered his way to the umpire's side. Burns, a former prizefighter, was there to protect Cantillon. A squad of policemen supported Burns and ended up escorting Cantillon to safety at the nearby Trumble Avenue police station.

The umpire did not register a complaint with the president of the American League. Charlie Comiskey did, an account of the donnybrook that was, to put it mildly, less than fully credible. The Chicago papers quoted Comiskey as saying: "It was the worst exhibition of rowdyism he'd ever seen on a ballfield." The Chicago manager blamed George Stallings for inciting Detroit fans to riot. It was a shocking comment. No one present so much as mentioned Stallings in connection with the episode.

Ban Johnson, influenced by Comiskey and the Chicago papers, suspended Elberfeld for 10 days, fined him, and publicly rebuked George Stallings: "He could not or would not maintain order," Johnson said. "He's no good. . . . We want good managers in this league, not men who are always talking to newspapers about imagined wrongs."

Fairly or unfairly, Stallings and Burns were being blamed for the misconduct of the Detroit players and the ham-handedness of Joe Cantillon. But that's not what bothered them. Elberfeld deserved to be suspended. What bothered them was the arbitrary and willful way the aggressive Johnson was handling things.

A mad nine weeks followed. Burns and Johnson hammered each other in a running dialogue. "Burns might as well do his roaring now," Johnson said. "He'll never have another chance. . . . The other owners are getting tired of the continued trouble, and it's almost certain that Burns and Stallings will not be owners of the Detroit team next season. . . . They will undoubtedly find themselves . . . without a franchise, which will mean either a new manager in Detroit or a new city in the American League when the league is reorganized."

The warfare was nonstop.

Burns brought up ownership's desire to sell the Detroit team and get out from under the control of Johnson and his inner circle. He spoke acidly. "We're ready to sell," he said. "We'll deliver the club, lock, stock and barrel, to the first comer for $20,000. Johnson has been notified that he can have the first chance to purchase at that price if he wants to."

"I have no fear of their carrying out the threat to sell the club," Johnson replied. "The Detroit magnates have apparently forgotten that they cannot sell without the consent of the other seven owners."

"That son of a bitch," Burns shot back, his voice needlessly loud. "He's sore because he didn't get a piece of the Detroit club, as he did with Comiskey's club."

"Humph!" snorted Johnson. "Is that a fact?"

"Notice," Burns told a beat reporter. "He didn't say I was wrong."

Though feelings were bitter, a move to the National League was not an option. National League officials had no intention of returning to the unwieldy and unprofitable 12-team format they'd so recently abandoned. To renew the money-losing arrangement less than two years later would have been absolute folly.

After returning from the 10-day suspension, Elberfeld played nothing short of brilliant baseball, behaved himself, and actually quieted down for about a month—that is, until a Saturday game in Cleveland, when his penchant for self-immolation once again got the better of him. Like steam from a kettle reaching its boiling point, he talked himself into a frenzy, kicked dirt on umpire Jack Sheridan, and jumped around like a lunatic. Spittle hit the umpire's cheek. Sheridan jerked a thumb in the direction of the Detroit bench: "You're through for the day."

A navy-blue-sweatered Stallings, seated at the end of the Detroit bench, lifted a hand, let it fall, and gave Elberfeld a dark look, a quiet rebuke, as the Kid took a seat. That was not the end of it. Elberfeld kept up an angry chatter on the bench as the game wore on. Smoky, quarrelsome language. Sheridan finally had had enough, and turned and chased him out of the ballpark.

Ban Johnson surprised everyone. Instead of suspending Elberfeld, as was generally expected, Johnson spoke of the Detroit management in only the kindest terms and dismissed the incident as two people caught up in the moment after a grueling season.

Johnson even wrote a gracious letter to Burns and told him the past would be forgotten if Elberfeld did the right thing for the balance of the season. He struck an even more conciliatory note, indicating that he realized

Detroit was the best baseball town in the league, virtually suggesting that the stories published in the Chicago papers about Burns being frozen out of Detroit the next year did not come from him.

Johnson's unexpected change in attitude went a long way toward closing the breach between the two parties. Burns couldn't contain a smug smile when he read the letter. He also took a modest step toward improved relations by quickly editing his own past comments, and acknowledging that several remarks about Johnson were ill advised. Johnson readily accepted the explanation.

It was a Kafkaesque situation. With the swirling controversy surrounding the league's systemic umpiring difficulties put on the back burner, and Burns working in harmony with the league's "inner circle," Johnson reasoned that he would have the votes needed to push ahead with plans to take the American League deep into National League territory as a second major league.

With this in mind, he invited Burns to accompany him and a few friends on a fishing and hunting trip up in the wilds of Wisconsin. Charlie Comiskey of Chicago, Matt Killilea of Milwaukee, Jim Manning of Kansas City, and Charles Somers of Cleveland—the "inner circle"—were the other invitees.

Meanwhile, the Tigers pulled themselves together, made a bid for second place, tired after a terrific struggle, and staggered to a fourth-place finish, 13 games behind Comiskey's pennant-winning Chicago White Sox.

What was perhaps more significant was the way Detroit fans backed the team, particularly when the Tigers were not winning. The Detroit franchise posted one of the best attendance records in the business, and the figures were not padded for public consumption. In a wonderful irony, Johnson, when pinned down, was forced to admit that Detroit's attendance led almost all other teams, the exception being Chicago. The drawing power of the Tigers was even more remarkable when you consider that Detroit, with a population of 330,000 in 1900, was the 12th largest city in the United States, while Chicago, with a population of 1,843,578, was the second largest city in the nation.

"We cleaned up a $10,000 [$371,000 in today's dollars] profit on the season," Detroit president Jim Burns said, "and we will be in the American League next season."

CHAPTER 6

A MEMORABLE ERA IN BASEBALL HISTORY

On Monday, January 28, 1901, delegates from American League teams pushed forward a significant first step in the story of baseball, a seminal moment, a period of adventurous expansion. With almost no discussion or opposition, President Ban Johnson, imperious, self-approving, and utterly self-confident, stood before the league's owners and executives in the ballroom of Chicago's Grand Pacific Hotel and laid out a far-reaching plan for a second major league.

"The baseball economy is booming," Johnson said, a smile tugging at the corner of his mouth. "The time has come to declare ourselves a major league. We can't wait." He paused and gazed at the faces around him, gauging reactions, then continued, "Reorganization won't be easy. We all know that. The structure of the league will fundamentally change."

Johnson pointed out that plans were afoot to establish new franchises in major population areas, cities whose names were familiar nationwide: Baltimore, Buffalo, New York, Philadelphia, St. Louis, and Washington. "The people seem to be with us," he said, and "we have every indication of goodwill in the cities which we propose to enter."

It was a gut-check moment. Johnson was outlining a bold new plan, a radical reshuffling of the league, a strategy favoring stronger teams in big cities, particularly those in large eastern cities, at the expense of the weaker teams in small cities. Baseball was a returns-driven business; empty seats didn't pay bills.

A stinging chorus of resentment arose from those who were afraid the shakeout would leave them behind. Beleaguered executives, suddenly at odds with Johnson, were increasingly resentful of the powerful role the man had assumed in managing their affairs.

All but deaf to the withering criticism, Johnson did not waver from his script. "The league and the 'Circuit Committee' have no interest in propping up underperforming franchises larded with debt. This will mean the elimination of a number of teams. That can't be helped. We can't stand still. Expansion is crucial for the survival of the American League."

The aggrieved owners of the Indianapolis, Kansas City, and Minneapolis franchises, fearing the loss of substantial investments, gave voice to real concerns. Several called Johnson's plan "draconian," Kansas City magnate Jim Manning, a member of Johnson's inner circle, among them.

Drawn into Johnson's orbit early, Manning was somewhat of a starstruck admirer of the big poohbah, loyal and obedient, an unwavering advocate for the benefits of expansion. Some months before, Johnson had given Manning his personal assurances that the Kansas City franchise would be part of the reorganized league. Manning was now taken aback by the realization that the Kansas City Blues would not survive the shakeout.

That didn't matter, nor did Manning's many contributions to the league's expansion committee, the so-called Circuit Committee. The American League's voice of authority approached the issue with a ruthless mindset: "Kansas City was too far west to be a viable member of a reorganized American League." And he wasn't the least bit fazed about doing something completely different from what he'd promised a friend just weeks before.

"The National League," Johnson said, "has reduced its roster of clubs from twelve to eight teams. That gives us a window of opportunity. We must seize it. There won't be another like it. The time to act is now." The appointed leader of the American League had not misfired yet, and the delegates, led by proponents of expansion, agreed to anything that would enable the American League to operate on a competitive level with the National League.*

Backed by the ample cash of the very supportive Charles Somers, the can-do Cleveland businessman, Johnson announced plans for franchises in Baltimore, Philadelphia, and Washington. Although the public declaration drew criticism from the National League, Johnson was unapologetic. He took to his bully pulpit and cited fundamental problems with the Na-

---

* The founding president of the American League, Ban Johnson, was cantankerous, greedy, and unprincipled. And those were his good qualities.

tional League's treatment of the American League, as well as the shortcomings of the National Agreement. "The American League," he said, "has decided to explore its options."

Big-shot National League moguls yawned and ignored Johnson. Why not? They had little incentive to cooperate. To them, Johnson was a nobody. Hard-liners, like Colonel John Rogers of the Phillies, dismissed him as a "joke," called his statements nonsense: "Mr. Johnson apparently considers himself outside the pale of the National Agreement," Rogers said. "So be it. We have a great deal of money invested in the National League and we intend to protect our interests."

Embracing the underdog role dealt him, Johnson cut ties with the National League and pursued alternatives that were more promising than the small-market franchises in the American League. New York and Philadelphia were the prime targets.

Displeased with the prospect of competition in New York, Andrew Freedman, the majority owner of the New York Giants, choked off Johnson's aspirations in New York before the American League could mount a serious challenge. Freedman and his friends intentionally set out to preserve the Giants' turf and destroy the new league, or at the very least cripple it and reduce it to its former "subject status."

Taking what he could get, Johnson focused on Philadelphia, Baltimore, and Washington, cities capable of maximizing the American League's presence in the East. He assigned Connie Mack, a trusted acolyte who possessed the expertise necessary for a start-up enterprise, the task of organizing a ball club in Philadelphia, a team capable of challenging the National League's supremacy in the Quaker City.

Mack moved quickly. Knowing how heavily baseball depended on free publicity in newspapers, he contacted two Philadelphia friends, Frank Hough, sports editor of the *Philadelphia Inquirer*, and "Butch" Jones, sports editor for the Associated Press, whose friendship he'd cultivated for years. Mack placed a secret side deal on the table. No one was to know. Not even their employers. Especially their employers.

The two sportswriters were offered a 25 percent ownership stake of nonvoting stock (Mack shrewdly retained the voting rights for himself) in the new franchise, divided equally between them, if they would provide favorable regular news coverage about the new ball club, bearing the historic name the Philadelphia Athletics, and pave the way for its entry into the City of Brotherly Love.

Speak out they did, often and loudly, with ringing headlines:

NATIONAL LEAGUE IS PROVED TO BE RESPONSIBLE FOR THE FAILURE TO AVERT CLASH WITH THE AMERICAN LEAGUE

AMERICAN LEAGUE WILL TREAT PLAYERS AS MEN, NOT SLAVES

NATIONAL LEAGUE MAY LOSE ALL ITS GREAT STARS

And so it went.

Meanwhile, Ban Johnson, looking to put financial firepower behind the new business, busily searched for a backer, a full-fledged investor, from among the many financially powerful businessmen in the Philadelphia area. The individual he set his sights on was Ben Shibe, a partner in the A. J. Reach Company, one of America's leading sporting goods manufacturers.

Shibe voiced reservations about the wisdom of investing so much capital in a far-reaching economic enterprise whose fate remained uncertain. The venture was too risky. Nor was that all. The most serious stumbling block, it seemed, was the cost of constructing a new ballpark. Although Johnson urged Shibe to think big, negotiations stalled.

Talk about frustration.

Not knowing what to do, Johnson wired Charles Somers, the financial engine whose money was purported to have made American League expansion possible, and asked his advice. Somers wired back: "We will cure Shibe of his shyness. Tell Connie Mack to find the grounds and I'll put up the money."

When Shibe continued to drag his feet, Johnson played his trump card. The A. J. Reach contract to supply baseballs for the American League games was scheduled to run out at the end of the season, and Johnson made an offer. If Shibe took a 50 percent stake in the Philadelphia Athletics franchise and served as its president, the American League's ball committee (of which Ban Johnson was the sole member) would extend indefinitely A. J. Reach's exclusive contract for the manufacture of official American League baseballs. That was the "icebreaker." It clinched the deal.

For his loyalty and outstanding work in helping bring American League baseball to Philadelphia, Ban Johnson awarded Connie Mack managerial and ownership positions in the ball club, including a gift of 25 percent of the remaining stock. (Mack now controlled 50 percent of the voting stock.)

By all accounts, Johnson also set in motion a move into Baltimore without having locked down any financing for the new franchise. Over a number of months he'd pursued a relationship with John McGraw and

Wilbert Robinson, particularly McGraw, two ballplayers who had once starred with Ned Hanlon's famous Baltimore Orioles. Johnson told them that he was about to put the American League on the national stage and wanted them to be part of it, McGraw as manager and part owner and member of the American League's board of directors, and Robinson as a coach and stockholder.

To secure McGraw's support, Johnson promised him the managerial reins of the new ball club in New York when the American League moved into the city, probably within a year or two. That's exactly what McGraw wanted to hear. He cast his lot with Johnson and promised to assist in gaining a foothold in New York City, where he had many contacts.

The American League announced the incorporation of the Baltimore Baseball and Athletic Company—the Baltimore Orioles—in November 1900. The stated capitalization was $40,000 ($1,000,000 in today's dollars). Sidney Frank, a 29-year-old local money player, acquired the largest stake in the franchise, and McGraw, Robinson, and a host of others became minority stockholders.

Ban Johnson took on an unusually personal role in putting together the Washington franchise. Seeking a well-qualified manager for the nation's capital, he coaxed the reluctant Jim Manning into bidding Kansas City goodbye and signing on as the principal owner, president, and manager of the Washington ball club.

When Manning said he wasn't certain that that was what he wanted to do, Johnson had some advice for him: "Forget Kansas City. Get over it." The appointed leader of the American League explained his thinking about expansion: "It's an ambitious endeavor." He was devising and executing strategies that were in the long-term best interest of the American League, not what was in the best interest of individual owners. He was trying to expand into populous cities where there were the most potential customers. The American League needed to maximize its chances of success and minimize its risks. It was just good business, that's all.

Once Manning signed a contract, his business affairs took an unforeseen twist. Before long, he learned that he had not been made the principal owner or the president of the ball club, as he was led to believe. Fred Postal, a Detroit hotel executive, was named president. Manning's reward for caving in to Johnson's entreaties turned out to be nothing more than the manager's job and a modest financial stake in the ball club. Not bad, really. Yet Manning felt used. It was a gut punch. But a one-year contract tied him to the deal.

The principal owner held the purse strings, 51 percent of the outstanding stock, and exercised control over every aspect of the operation. He made all of the big decisions. Who was the principal owner of the Washington ball club? It was none other than the president of the American League, Ban Johnson, an often-overlooked fact; he used his position to reap huge financial gains.

This exposed thorny ethical territory. Critics harrumphing about ethical standards viewed Johnson's personal ownership as a conflict of interest, claiming that his contradictory priorities endangered objectivity. He would not be impartial in behind-the-scenes decisions. They considered it incestuous of Johnson, as president of the league, to hold a majority interest in the Washington club, and stock in other clubs as well.

Did Ban Johnson do anything wrong by enriching himself and his cronies while hiding his own financial ties to ball clubs? Legally? No. Ethically? Well, readers can decide that for themselves.†

Overnight, or so it seemed, the American League was progressing—at least on paper—from being a minor league of regional importance to being a major league of national importance, independent and equal to the National League.

President Johnson made the radical reshaping of the league official in an announcement during a press conference at the Great Northern Hotel in Chicago. "After a vote of the delegates," Johnson said, "the American League has been reorganized into an eight-team major-league circuit for the 1901 season.... We have in the West, Chicago, Cleveland, Detroit and Milwaukee, and in the East, Baltimore, Philadelphia, Washington and ... " He paused, before continuing. "The eighth team in our stable will be Boston."

"How's that?" ... "Boston?" ... "In place of who?" Reporters turned and exchanged glances.

"The hostile attitude of the National League is responsible for our adding Boston," Johnson said. "Boston is just the logical extension of the American League's growth strategy. The timetable is being quickened, that's all." Pause. "We are firmly of the opinion that in communities like Boston, Philadelphia and Chicago there is room for two clubs and continuous baseball during the season. We are here to stay."

---

† Johnson owned the Washington Senators and was co-owner, with Charles Comiskey, of the Chicago White Sox (he and Comiskey shared the same office), and Johnson also had financial stakes in other American League teams.

Continuing, he said, "Charles Somers will sponsor the club in Boston. He is the agent in this transaction. In time, the franchise, now held by the American League, will be transferred to Boston parties. The ball club is capitalized at $100,000 [$2,500,000 in today's dollars]."

Joseph D. O'Brien, who represented the rival American Association, knew something of the economics of baseball and questioned Somers's financial worth: "According to Dun [now Dun & Bradstreet, a financial credibility firm that provides data on credit history], and other authorities," O'Brien said, "Somers is worth $100,000. Where's the money coming from? How can they keep the league solvent?"

Did Ben Shibe's 50-percent purchase of stock in the Philadelphia Athletics provide the funds for the move into Boston? It appears that way. The numbers are hard to pin down. And Ban Johnson and Charles Somers would not discuss any aspect of the financing of either franchise.

This was news to Jim Franklin, the principal owner of the Buffalo Bisons. Six weeks earlier, when the decision about the eighth franchise in the league appeared to be in limbo, Johnson assured Franklin that Buffalo would be the fourth member in the Eastern Division.

Insulted, cheeks flushed, Franklin got up from his chair and stormed out of the meeting. Sensing the turbulence of his emotions as he moved through the lobby, several reporters chased after him, peppering him with questions. Franklin stopped abruptly, turned on them, scowled, and blasted the delegates in session upstairs as mere pawns under Ban Johnson's stewardship, men who'd given him too much power in the decision-making.

"I have stands that cost me $100,000," Franklin said, shaking his head, his face expressive of controlled distaste. "Now I'm left out in the cold. They're baseball pirates. A lot of cold-blooded cutthroats. That's what they are. Men of no moral principles."

Johnson spoke contemptuously of Franklin when informed of the Buffalo owner's aspersions, calling them "the thoughtless prattle of a disappointed man."

The conclave at the Great Northern dragged on and on and on, the afternoon of the official announcement, continuing, except for a short recess, until a little after midnight. Talk centered on the new constitution under which the American League would operate for the next 10 years.

Part genius, part con man, Ban Johnson set the stage for his proposals. His preferred tactic was to stand up and glare at people seated around the conference table, raise a bit of a ruckus, then slam his fist down and bellow,

"That's the way I think it is, and that's the way it is." The owners understood that they were not to provoke their leader. If they did, Tyrannosaurus Rex would come after them, and retaliation would be swift and certain.

On this occasion, Johnson favored a more subtle approach. He smiled the smile of misdirection, more cordial and polite than usual. The 13 delegates shifted in their chairs and faced him, listening with a commercial mindset.

Speaking loudly and proudly with an entrepreneurial bent, Johnson reminded them of the staggering profits the league had made in the past, and he told them there was a lot more money to be made in the future. The way he saw it, no money would be lost in the process. Rewards would flow in abundance. The American League would be the biggest success story in sports history—but only if they followed his advice. There was no middle ground.

After a brief, mostly positive discussion, the delegates reached a consensus: give Johnson tighter control over league affairs—unilaterally. A hawkish member of the Johnson clique seized the moment and slapped the table with the flat of his hand: "Sounds good to me," he said. "Let's do it." The others nodded. Agreed. Why not? They'd all be rich. Motion approved. Unanimously.

That Johnson had orchestrated the overhauling of the league's constitution to his advantage was hardly noticed; that he had extended the range of his influence in restructuring the league didn't seem to matter; that central governance over the disparate franchises had been handed over to the president's office hardly crossed their minds; that they had entrusted practical control of their ball clubs in one individual's hands didn't bother them; that they had granted him dictatorial powers over their organizations didn't raise concerns. His arguments prevailed, possibly because of a conviction by those present that his leadership skills were crucial to the continued financial prosperity of the league.

The 13 men present pledged to "stand together, burn their bridges behind them, and sink or swim together."

His status cemented, Johnson's power was well-nigh absolute. He was overlord of the American League, its president, its secretary, its treasurer. He would remain the league's leader for almost 20 years.

Contractually bound by an ironclad agreement, a 10-year membership pact, each owner relinquished 51 percent of the team's stock to be "held in trust" by the president of the league. Options on the franchises themselves, on the ballparks, and on the grounds on which the games were played were also placed in Johnson's hands.‡

And that wasn't all. The league's by-laws set the championship schedule at 140 games for the first full season, equalized travel expenses among the teams, limited the number of players on each team to 14 (after the completion of the first two weeks of the season), retained the attractive 25-cent base admission rate for all American League games, and last and most important, required the eight franchises to share receipts equally.

The American League was a corporate trust.

---

‡ The American League was created as a trust in 1902, much like John D. Rockefeller's Standard Oil Company; teams shared expenses and profits equally, though attendance reports had a complicated relationship with the truth.

CHAPTER 7

HIS FOCUS WAS SOUND

With Machiavellian cunning, Ban Johnson patterned his stratagems in shaping the American League after the most successful business of the "Gilded Age," John D. Rockefeller's Standard Oil Company, the richest corporation in the world. Johnson looked upon the power-mongering Rockefeller with great admiration, and he embraced Rockefeller's immoral philosophy of selfishness and trampling on the rights of others as virtues in the greedy pursuit of profits.

"The way the American League is organized and controlled," a writer for the *Kansas City Journal* observed,

> It cannot help being a "syndicate league" [in other words, a trust]. Not only is there evidence that certain American League magnates will be financially interested in more than one American League team, but the proof of "syndicatism," as "Muggsy" McGraw chose to call it, is found in the further fact that the club owners . . . have turned over to President Johnson the major portion of their capital stock, club options and ground leases. Never were club owners so bound as the American League owners. The actions of the league magnates amount to a pooling of the interests of each to draw out an equal amount.

Several owners felt Johnson was moving too fast. They wondered where the quality players would come from and doubted the new league's ability to attract National League stars. What about the reserve clause, the backbone of baseball, the rule that bound a player to a team for life? How would the American League get around that?

A lesser man might have run for cover. Not Ban Johnson. His focus was sound. He had analyzed the situation correctly and pushed ahead. The National League's downsizing from a 12-team to an 8-team circuit left a large pool of big-league talent available for the taking. And discontent over the National League's $2,400 salary limit and certain restrictive clauses in the league's standard player's contract were also causing a good deal of unhappiness.

Seizing the opening the National League had unwittingly presented them, Ban Johnson encouraged swift approval of a contract aspired to by the players, with a few minor changes. It was a brilliant stroke—a setback for the National League.

Player grabbing had been going on for months. Everyone got involved, even Johnson and the American League's recently elected vice president, Charles Somers. League representatives were told to ignore the National Agreement and the reserve clause, since they were no longer in effect, but to respect signed contracts.

A secretive air pervaded the signings, particularly when it came to inviting a well-known athlete to put his name on the line. American League agents pushed hard, successfully luring a small group of major leaguers into the fold, as well as a larger number of former players, mainly minor-league journeymen, individuals whose names would attract fan interest and help put the American League on the national stage.

Thanks to the $2,400 ceiling on National League salaries, several big stars were swayed by seductive offers: Jimmy Collins, Hugh Duffy, Clark Griffith, Fielder Jones, Nap Lajoie, Joe McGinnity, and Cy Young, future Hall of Famers all. They would play key roles in the American League's coming-out party.

Strong overtures were made to "Shoeless Joe" Jackson, who would become the most famous of the eight Chicago White Sox players banned for fixing the 1919 World Series. Jackson refused a Federal League offer of $41,000 a year for three years—$1,226,567 in today's currency—because of his loyalty to owner Charles Somers and his Cleveland teammates. Jackson's annual salary at the time was $8,000. His trueheartedness kept him from becoming a millionaire. (Would a man like that throw a World Series?)

The incomparable Hans Wagner[*] was another who received bids far above anything the National Leaguers were offering. But Wagner, an

---

[*] His name was Johannes Peter Wagner. Teammates, fans, and contemporaries called him Hans, not Honus, as most people do today.

intensely loyal person, liked working for Barney Dreyfuss, the Pirates' genial president. Dreyfuss had always treated him well. And Hans liked his teammates. Playing before hometown friends was a privilege for Hans, an honor not easily surrendered. Pittsburgh was in his blood. When he and Dreyfuss sat down to talk things over, Dreyfuss laid it all on the line. He did not equivocate. "Hans," he said, "you worked hard for me last year. How much do you want?"

Wagner rubbed his cheek, rocked backward and forward, opened his hands, his shoulders suggesting a shrug, and looked at Dreyfuss thoughtfully: "Well," he said, "I'll take a thousand dollars less than the American League is offering." Somewhat taken aback by Wagner's modest proposal, Dreyfuss nodded and, without a qualm or a doubt, said, "That's fine with me." They shook hands on it.

Within days, Dreyfuss also signed most of the other Pirate regulars. The team's only significant loss was Jimmy Williams, a .264 hitter, snared by John McGraw for the Baltimore Orioles.

There was no mass exodus from National League ranks as some writers maintain. National League executives didn't lose any sleep over the possibility of losing players or filling rosters. It may have been hubris, but they were largely unconcerned; predictably, most National Leaguers gravitated toward the security of the older league rather than risk the insecurities inherent in the new start-up league.

Of the 182 players who inked American League contracts for its inaugural big-league season, 111 had played in the National League at one time or another, most of them for only a few games. The remaining signees were minor leaguers with no previous major-league experience.

Baseball in the dead-ball era, as it is today, was an image-conscious business. Everything was manipulated. The acknowledged stars were assigned to the big-market teams: Chicago, Philadelphia, and Boston, franchises that dominated the league until 1920.[†]

Johnson's thumbprint was on everything. He even choreographed pennant races. A level playing field was of secondary importance, an issue to be dealt with later.

A somewhat heroic renegade faction, led by John McGraw and George Stallings, was quite vocal in its criticism of the disparity Ban Johnson was

---

[†] Only the 1907, 1908, and 1909 Detroit Tigers, led by Ty Cobb and Sam Crawford, the most feared one-two punch in baseball, were able to break through the three-team domination during the dead-ball era, although, now and then, other teams did make a close race of it.

purposefully creating. They worked hard, spent their own money, and vied for the same big-name players who were being signed by the league and assigned to big-city teams, individuals capable of making one ball club more competitive than another. McGraw and Stallings, though rebellious, accepted Johnson's high-handed methods with a dissatisfaction that rumbled, for the most part, under the surface. Their principal yardstick for success was winning games. That's what counted most for them: where the team finished in the standings. Financial gain was secondary. And, with unapologetic directness, McGraw sought to deep-six Johnson. He urged fellow owners to oust the president of the league. Get rid of him.

CHAPTER 8

SELF-SERVING PRONOUNCEMENTS

Enormous crowds greeted festivities at American League ballparks on the opening days of the inaugural season (April 1901), even in Boston, Chicago, and Philadelphia, where the new league faced head-to-head competition from established National League teams.

Turnstiles were still spinning two weeks into the season, and the moguls, as owners liked to call themselves, were prospering. Full of brio and spin and aglow with justifiable pride, President Ban Johnson, answering a smattering of questions, told a crowd of journalists: "I can say without fear that our expanded organization is an assured success."

Opening Day at Bennett Park in Detroit started as a big disappointment. The visiting Milwaukee Brewers were giving the home team an emphatic 13–4 drubbing, putting a damper on an otherwise celebratory mood. Disappointed faces filled the park. Oom Paul, the Tigers' canine mascot, lay half asleep at his handler's feet as the game drew to a close.

Manager George Stallings didn't like what he was seeing any better than Oom Paul, particularly the ears-pinned-back looks on the players' faces. Stallings's arteries pulsed. His face darkened. Pent-up rage finally erupted. Hollering at the top of his lungs, he tore off his brown fedora and angrily slammed it on the ground. "Goddamn it to hell," he bellowed, in an ear-battering barrage. "What kind of birds are you anyway? Letting a bunch of bozos make monkeys out of you. Do something about it. Fight. Look alive. Show me something."

An audible communal gasp rose from the Detroit bench. The young Tigers were a smart, scrappy, close-knit lot, drunk on camaraderie, and highly susceptible to the all-consuming primal appeal of their leader, a genuine plea meant to spur the flow of an athlete's blood. The outburst was contagious. Something switched on. Faces came alive.

Guns blazing, they attacked the Brewers in the bottom of the ninth, their assault relentless, their onslaught unforgiving. Hit followed hit, run followed run: two singles, four doubles, five runs batted in, all before the Brewers could get a man out. There was no mistaking the Tigers' channeled fury. They were playing like warriors in the grip of a force outside themselves.

Three batters later, there was still only one out as the ninth inning progressed. Seven runners had crossed the plate; the Tigers now trailed by only two runs, and there were runners on first and second.

Eyes shined with excitement. Hands exploded in applause. Cheers mounted. Boys pleaded. Women shouted. Men jumped up and down. Everybody was hoping for a miracle. One keyed-up bleacherite flung up his arms and tossed his coat into the throng. When he got the coat back it was in two pieces. He didn't seem to care.

Just beyond the right field and left field foul lines, the standing-room-only crowd pressed closer, momentarily holding up the game. Stallings ordered his players to push them back so the Milwaukee outfielders could field their positions.

The delay was a godsend for Brewers hurler Bert "Pete" Husting. It enabled the hard-pressed pitcher to regroup before facing Jimmy Barrett with runners on first and second.

An air of expectancy swept over the ballpark. "Come on, Jimmy me boy, lean on one," fans shouted. "Bang one out there."

Husting fell behind on the count, two balls and no strikes. Barrett swung through a curve for a strike. He took another curve. Strike two. The umpire raised his hands showing the count: two fingers extended on the right hand and two on the left hand.

Husting broke off still another curve, vicious and inside. Barrett started his swing, then held up, but the umpire brayed "Stee-rike three," leaving Barrett shaking his head amid a smattering of boos.

Tiger luck was fading.

"Kid" Gleason moved into the batter's box, the weight of the world resting on his shoulders. Cheers, whistles, and foot stomps greeted him. Swinging at the first pitch, Gleason rapped a high bouncer toward third. You could hear the crowd utter a lot of "Uh-ohs," and "No, nos," and not a few "Son of a bitches."

Jim Burke, the Brewers' third baseman, moved quickly to his left, knocked down the ball, scrambled to pick it up, and hurried a throw over to first baseman Johnny Anderson. The throw pulled Anderson off the bag. Gleason's speed did the rest. And Detroit fans let out a collective sigh of relief. Pete Husting's body language shouted disgust.

Detroit's cleanup hitter, "Ducky" Holmes, toting a black bat and adjusting his cap, walked toward the plate. Before stepping into the batter's box, Ducky bent down, rubbed his hands in the gravelly dirt, and wiped them on his uniform.

There were two outs and the bases were loaded in the last of the ninth. Milwaukee held a two-run lead.

Husting's first pitch was high. Ball one. Eyes squinting with displeasure, Pete glared at the umpire and walked slowly around the mound, cursing, buying time. He was tired. Very tired. He'd thrown a whopping 56 pitches— in this inning alone. Exhaustion was taking over. His pitches were flying all over the place. He just couldn't keep them down, much less get his curve over the plate.

With the count 3–1, Holmes tapped a slow roller down the third-base line. Once again Burke came rushing in, barehanded the ball, and made the only play he had, an off-balance throw across the diamond to first base. The umpire bellowed, "Safe!" The runner on third scored. It was 13–12, Milwaukee. Now Detroit had a real chance of stealing the game.

Tumultuous applause greeted "Pop" Dillon, the Tigers' fourteenth batter of the inning. Pop was swinging the bat well. He'd already had a three-hit afternoon, all of the hits doubles, including one earlier in the same inning.

Hoping they could make something happen, Tiger fans stood, cheered, clapped, and sang. The noise was fantastic. You could feel the energy.

Dillon was the sixth consecutive left-handed batter to face Husting's right-handed slants.

George Stallings, a student of the game, was known for playing the percentages. He had purposefully stacked the Detroit lineup with left-handed hitters to face the Brewers' right-handed starting pitcher that afternoon, "Pink" Hawley, who had lasted six innings.

Dillon tapped his bat against each shoe, knocked off clumps of dirt, then tapped the plate, set himself, rocked back and forth, and waited. Adrenaline iced his veins. He reminded himself to stay back and wait for the pitch he wanted.

Sweat darkened the bill of Husting's cap, trickled down his nose. He no longer felt good about himself; his arm was as limp as a dick after a night of frolicking with a slutty blond. And there was no relief was in sight. Milwaukee manager Hugh Duffy had already used three pitchers that afternoon, the first of the four-game series. He would not call on another.

Husting again fell behind in the count, 3–1, a hitter's count. This time he made the mistake of leaving a hanging curve high in the strike zone.

Thwok! The fat part of Dillon's bat sent the ball slicing down the left field foul line. Thousands of eyes followed its flight. The Detroit players burst off the bench for a better look. Fans stood, wondering whether the ball would go fair or foul. It landed deep in the overflow crowd.

Fair ball. A ground-rule double. One healthy swing of the bat had lifted the Tigers to an exhilarating 14–13 victory.

A wave of electric emotion broke over the stands. Men surged onto the field. All the elements of chance had come together to produce one of the most astonishing finishes in big-league history.

Oom Paul, the lucky mascot, stood at his handler's side, wagging his tail, watching the milling crowd. Oom Paul had done his job. He had done it well.

The following day, a Friday, there were two outs in the last of the ninth, no one was on base, and the Tigers were trailing by a run, 5–4. The count on the batter, Ducky Holmes, was three balls and two strikes. Chances of a comeback were slim. One more strike and the game was over.

Sensing the inevitability of defeat, Oom Paul's handler started for the exit gate.

Stallings stopped him. "We're still alive," he growled.

Oom Paul stayed.

Holmes walked.

The next batter, that man Pop Dillon, nestled in at the plate.

The crowd howled, whistled, and called for Pop to do it again. "Come on, Pop." "Make him put it over." "Get a hold of one." "Give that mother a ride."

Dillon didn't disappoint. He got hold of the first pitch and ripped a too-hot-to-handle screamer off the first baseman's glove. Holmes advanced to third on the play. Runners were now on first and third. A moment later, with Kid Elberfeld at bat, Dillon picked the right pitch to steal on, a breaking ball, and scampered down to second base unchallenged. Runners were now on second and third. Tension filled the park. Seconds took hours. Minutes took days.

Elberfeld, looking for his second hit of the game, swung at a 2–2 pitch and lined a shot deep into left center. The center fielder turned to his right, took one step, stopped, and watched the ball disappear into the roped-off area of the crowd—a ground-rule double, scoring Holmes and Dillon. The

Tigers had pulled off another win by the narrowest of margins, 6–5, an outcome nobody expected.

Milwaukee rolled out to commanding leads on several occasions Saturday, the third game of the series, before 9,000 exceptionally noisy ticket holders. Each time the Tigers came clawing back. Before long, the Brewers found themselves desperately hanging on to a 9–8 lead. It was the last of the eighth. Stallings's relentless Tigers rallied once again, scored five runs, and broke the game wide open for a stunning 13–9 victory.

Feeling snake-bitten, the Brewers vowed things would be different on Sunday, the fourth and final game of the series. They scored early and often, jumping out to a seemingly insurmountable 11–5 lead after seven innings, only to see it disintegrate as Stallings's boys came roaring back. The unstoppable Tigers scored three times in the eighth and four times in the ninth for another memorable come-from-behind victory, a 12–11 win that compelled admiration from the record-breaking throng of 10,858.

What a way to start a season.

CHAPTER 9

ROWDIES RUN RIOT

Umpiring was a flaw in the league, as we have seen, a flaw everyone recognized—everyone, that is, except Ban Johnson. His confidence was such that he never doubted the absurd idea that a single umpire could handle the nuances of the game. But the men in blue simply could not position themselves to make difficult decisions on close plays taking place simultaneously 90 or 180 feet apart. It was simply impossible.

Mistakes made umpires targets of a storm of criticism. So far as players, managers, and fans were concerned, an umpire seldom called a good game. And umpires were constantly forced to deal with underhanded behavior taking place behind their backs.

The Baltimore Orioles were known to sneak a ball into an umpire's ribs and hurl a bat at him when he wasn't looking. John McGraw, Wilbert Robinson, Mike Donlin, Billy Keister, and one or two others displayed a deep-seated arrogance toward the men in blue. They bulldozed. They argued. They claimed every close decision. And they constantly tried to intimidate them. When they didn't get their way, they'd ignite trouble. Acting like a knuckle-dragging thug, McGraw would wag a forefinger beneath an umpire's nose and say, "Do you remember what I told you? Remember what I said I'd do to you? Well, this is your last chance. See?"

Should anyone have been surprised by an umpire's anger and frustration in the face of such aggressiveness? Who could blame an arbiter who chose to stand tall in a confrontation over a tough judgment call? A real bruiser of a fight was inevitable.

And trouble did burst upon the league like a strike of lightning out of a clear blue sky:

ROWDIES RUN RIOT

DISGRACEFUL SCENES AT TWO AMERICAN LEAGUE PARKS

UMPIRE CONNOLLY ASSAULTED BY BALTIMORE PLAYERS AND FANS

UMPIRE HASKELL GETS THE SAME TREATMENT IN WASHINGTON

Blatant mistakes by umpire Tom Connolly during a string of six games in Baltimore so angered Orioles fans that many of them expressed nagging suspicions about Connolly's motives. Could he be intentionally giving the home team the worst of close decisions? The question was on the lips of hordes of Baltimore fans, ardent supporters known throughout the sports world as the loudest, rudest, and most insolent in all of baseball—and they worked hard at living up to their reputation.

After a questionable decision in the first inning of the seventh game of an August homestand, ill will toward Connolly exploded, provoking an unfortunate chain of events. Shouts and cries of "You rotten bastard" rang out from a nasty din, and a helpless here-we-go-again feeling swept through the stands. Enmity was palpable.

Two innings later, with one out and the bases loaded, and Baltimore nursing a 3–2 lead, Detroit's "Doc" Casey, batting right-handed, lifted a harmless fly into shallow right field, down the line. The right fielder came crashing in, realized he couldn't make the catch, eased up and watched the ball drop in front of him, foul by more than a foot. It rolled to the wall.

"Fair ball!" Connolly called out from his position behind the pitcher's mound.

A howling cacophony of catcalls and boos rolled down from the stands. Inarticulate voices hurled vulgar epithets at him: "Wassat? Wassat?" fans screamed. "Fair ball?" "You gotta be kidding." "You big rummy! You got nerve!" "Open your eyes!" "You oughta be umpiring for a blind school." "Rotten . . . Rotten . . . Rotten . . ."

Four runs scored in the inning and Baltimore fans attributed all of the runs to the missed call by Connolly.

The Tigers were ahead by a score of 7–4 after three and a half innings, not an insurmountable lead, and the hometown fans felt there was plenty of time for a Baltimore comeback. They were certain of it.

Orioles third baseman Jack Dunn was the first batter up for Baltimore in the last of the fourth. Batting from the right side, Dunn took two fastballs for called strikes; the noise in the stands increased in volume with each pitch. Dunn fought off a third fastball with a short, choppy swing, slicing the ball on one hop directly at the Tiger first baseman.

Busting down the first-base line with the momentum of a sprinter, Dunn hit the dirt head first, his outstretched hand reaching the base just as the first-sacker stepped on the bag. Umpire Tom Connolly, on top of the action all the way, bellowed, "You're out!" It was the correct call. Didn't matter.

Fists clenched, eyes ablaze with indignation, Baltimore's "Iron Man" Joe McGinnity rushed at Connolly like an attack dog, sputtering, "You no-good fuck," and with his spikes deliberately stomped on both of Connolly's feet. Then, still breathing curses, the muscle-bound goon shot a long squirt of brown tobacco juice in Connolly's face. McGinnity spat not once but twice. Brazen, blatant acts.

Connolly, eyes hot, mouth tight as a seam, teeth grinding in rage, pulled a folded handkerchief out of his pocket and slowly wiped his face. He would not tolerate this kind of treatment. With anger on his side, he reacted: "Game forfeited to Detroit, 9–0." (The actual score at the time was 7–4 in favor of Detroit.)

Decorum disintegrated.

Feeding off McGinnity's ire, the wild, crazy, howling mob clambered over seatbacks, tumbled over walls, broke through gates, and stormed onto the field. They came in rushes and jumps like animals taking over the zoo. The chaos was pure Hieronymus Bosch, a breathtaking sight unlike anything seen before.

Forty policemen, trying to restore order, formed a protective shield around Connolly. But one overzealous fan, focusing his wrath on the umpire, managed to break through the police line and get in a punch or two.

Joe McGinnity, the Oriole who did the spitting; Billy Keister, an Oriole pitcher who claimed he was just standing around looking on; and the rabid fan who punched Connolly in the face were arrested for breach of the peace.

Some 40 miles away, the second-division Washington Senators were manhandling the league-leading Chicago White Sox, who were desperately clinging to a slim lead in the tight pennant race. Washington was leading 1–0 in the fourth inning when trouble broke out. Runners were on first and second, two men were out, and the count was 3–2 on the batter, the Senators' third baseman. Sox pitcher Jack Katoll, being extra careful not to give the guy anything too good to hit, whistled a fastball just off the outside corner of the plate, a pitch not spotted well.

Catcher Joe Sugden, trying to entice a strike call from umpire Jack Haskell, moved his glove ever so slightly toward the plate.

Haskell wasn't buying it. "Ball four," he growled. The bases were loaded.

Katoll was livid. He felt the pitch had caught the corner of the plate. Hands on hips, pawing the earth, and shaking his head in disgust, he verbally cursed the call.

Umpire Haskell burst into rude, jeering laughter and told Katoll he couldn't put the ball over a barn door if he had to. And he was pretty officious about it too.

The very next batter, the Washington shortstop, hammered a one-one pitch off the left field fence, a three-base hit, driving in all three runners.

Red-faced mad and struggling to keep from losing it, Katoll toed the rubber, read the sign, took a deep breath, exhaled, and delivered a spitter. The pitch broke down into the dirt, bounced off the catcher's chest protector, and rolled away. A wild pitch. The runner scored easily from third with the fourth run of the inning. Washington led 5–0.

Losing did not come easily for Jack Katoll. His temper reached fever pitch. He glowered at the umpire and started after him, thought better of it before he reached home plate, stopped, lifted his glove, received the ball from the catcher, turned, and took a few steps back toward the mound. Suddenly he stopped, wheeled, and hurled the ball—point-blank—with tremendous force, right at Haskell. The ball caught the astonished umpire on the instep.

He grimaced and bent over double in pain, the color draining from his face. Seconds later, he rose, limped toward the pitching mound, and, furious, ordered Katoll out of the game. The two men squared off for a brawl.

As the emotional and verbal abuse between them gathered steam, White Sox shortstop Frank Shugart rushed over to put in his two cents' worth; he shoved his jaw in Haskell's beefsteak face and screamed terrible things at him. Catcher Joe Sugden and Shugart and Haskell went at it, piling insult upon insult. Attempting to quiet Sugden and Shugart and put an end to the shouting and shoving, the husky umpire finally said, "All right . . . All right . . . That's enough jawing . . . Let's get out there and play ball."

Haskell then unthinkingly put a hand on Shugart's shoulder, pushed the Sox shortstop aside, and started another combative exchange with Sugden.

An instant later, Shugart's fist smacked into Haskell's mouth, blindsiding him. Down he went.

Seeing the fracas erupt, a horde of Washington fans itching for a fight swarmed onto the field, adding to the confusion. Minor skirmishes broke out here and there, and Shugart was not treated well. Men shouted at him, pushed him, and shoved him in the melee. Other Chicago players were harassed as well.

The sprawling free-for-all was an unpleasant sight. Fortunately for Shugart and his pals, enough police were on hand to keep the mob at bay. The incident was defused, and order restored. Shugart and Katoll were arrested, but the police took no further action. After a short delay the game was completed. Washington defeated Chicago, 8–0.

Umpire Haskell was in a pitiable condition after the game: bloodied and angry, his face badly swollen (a cut on his lip required 13 stitches), and his leg twice its normal size. (A bone in his instep had been broken.)

Ban Johnson was outraged by the violence. These were not the kinds of goings-on he wanted to hear about at American League headquarters. Things had to be brought under control, and quickly, before the embarrassing behavior tarnished the league's carefully cultivated claim of "clean baseball."

Sanctimonious as ever, Johnson was quick to act on newspaper reports alone. He did not wait for evidence from the combatants. When questioned by reporters, Johnson didn't hold back. "I've expelled Shugart for life," he said, "for assaulting Umpire Haskell... And that's final."

"It's the former National Leaguers," he said, naming names (Duffy, Griffith, McGraw, Stallings), "who have caused all the trouble... We don't intend to stand for it." He paused for breath. "McGinnity will have to walk the plank, too. He's been suspended and should be blacklisted."

The outspoken McGinnity was not shy about responding to the blathering president of the league. "So, it's back to the iron mines for me, is it? Well, what a pity it would be if Ban Johnson should drive me over to the National League and compel me to accept some of the big offers that have been made me. [The Iron Man had been offered a $2,000 bonus to sign with St. Louis and turned it down.] I think I can still get a job if it comes to that."

Owners, worried about their investments and players, and about their future in the league, thought Johnson was shirking his responsibilities, denying, minimizing, and disregarding the season-long disagreements over appearance and reality. So far as they were concerned, the president showed too little consideration for players adversely affected when it came to evaluating umpiring standards. Johnson viewed them as disposable instruments, rather than people, and did not make reasoned decisions.

John McGraw, of all people, was a catalyst peacemaker. He ceased talk of a rebellion, abandoned his defiant air, and stopped urging fellow owners to oust Johnson. With his recently injured leg in a plaster cast, McGraw hauled his junkyard body out to Chicago and called on the big poohbah.

The meeting was hardly routine. Johnson tended to be cool and formal at first. The two hadn't spoken for months; they had difficulty communicating. But McGraw eventually broke through; the conversation lasted long into the evening. McGraw found Johnson much more inclined to listen to his side of the argument than he thought possible, and Johnson was impressed by McGraw's grasp of the situation. What emerged from the talk was a tentative deal, an understanding about McGraw's future behavior, as well as that of the suspended McGinnity.

The agreement represented a 180-degree reversal from Johnson's earlier stance: "I have reinstated McGinnity," Johnson declared, "fined him and told him to apologize to Connolly. . . . The circumstances, I find, were not all against the pitcher, and, as McGinnity shows a disposition to rectify his wrong, I'm glad to put him back in the game." Johnson also promised to implement a two-umpire system. But he didn't say when he'd do it.

The ruling was effectively a slap on the wrist.

On Saturday, the fourteenth of September, President Johnson granted Shugart a hearing. Shugart was contrite. He apologized for his tawdry behavior in Washington and made a plea for clemency, promising good conduct in the future. A number of American League stockholders, worried about their investments, supported Shugart. They urged Johnson to reinstate the Chicago shortstop and put an end to the aggravating on-field controversies. Johnson reinstated Shugart.

The show of public reconciliation and mutual friendship was good politics, little more. Like a cobra incapable of being charmed, Ban Johnson was a vindictive person. He held grudges and had a powerful memory for slights. If you got in his way, he was going to lash out at you. He would not soon forget his bitter history with McGraw. The president of the American League resolved to rid himself of the Baltimore manager in some future shakeup, and other pollutants like him as well.

CHAPTER 10

A DEEP FREEZE DEVELOPED

The metamorphosis of the American League from a high minor league into a thriving major league was an enormous success. A total of 1,683,584 fans wheeled through the turnstiles that first season, and attendance showed no signs of dropping off. The strong support compared favorably with the 1,920,031 people who attended games in the more established National League. Clearly, the ever-expanding upstart circuit had a promising future.

The budding enterprise generated most interest in Chicago, Boston, and Detroit. Chicago attracted 354,350 fans, an average of 5,288 per game; Boston 300,000, an average of 4,900 per game; and Detroit 259,430, an average of 3,815 per game. Philadelphia and Washington were also moneymakers.[*]

Boston was the most striking success. In a head-to-head battle for fan support with the Boston Nationals, the Boston Americans attracted more admirers by a surprisingly wide margin. Attendance in Cleveland was about adequate, in Baltimore disappointing (enough to clear expenses and then some), and in Milwaukee discouraging. The Brewers lost money.

"Milwaukee cannot support a high-priced team on one good day a week," Ban Johnson remarked. Everyone knew what that meant. Milwaukee would be dropped from the league. Johnson didn't believe in trying to turn lemons into lemonade.

At the close of what was a very successful season for the Detroit franchise, both on the field and at the gate, George Stallings returned home

---

[*] Johnson rigged pennant races and transferred players (by executive fiat) from small-market teams to large-market teams—think Boston, Chicago, and Philadelphia—so they would dominate the league. And they did.

and eventually got around to examining the company books. What he found was a mixture of surprise and anguish: the books were in disarray. Bank accounts were empty or overdrawn. Records were incomplete. Receipts were missing. And the organization was hemorrhaging money.

Caught off guard by the disclosures, Stallings kept asking himself, How could Jim Burns do this to me? It seemed impossible. There was no paper trail to document the extravagant spending; there was little accurate information; and absurdly falsified books concealed a thicket of machinations. It seemed that Burns had loosely handled cash—much of it for inappropriate personal expenses. He pocketed money, acted irresponsibly, and made no meaningful attempt to keep finances sound.

Where the ball club should have shown a $20,000 profit, about $742,000 in today's dollars, it showed a $6,000 loss. Overcome by disbelief, Stallings demanded an explanation.

Burns not only swept aside Stallings's concerns, he denied any wrongdoing, asserted his innocence, and dismissively answered questions in a manner best described as flippant. "The money went for legitimate expenses," he said with a faint smile. "The expenditures were appropriate."

"All told," Stallings said, "I drew $2,081 out of the club for expenses . . . Burns' personal account shows that he took $9,000. Where the rest of the money went is yet to be determined."

The Big Chief's outrage mounted as details emerged about Burns's dodgy practices and fraudulent behavior. He'd posted 501 shares of stock owned by Stallings as collateral for a personal loan of $2,500 from the Central Savings Bank of Detroit, a transaction unknown to Stallings.

Stallings had given Burns the stock to be deposited in escrow with the president of the American League. Burns never surrendered the stock. The only documents he turned over to Ban Johnson were those related to the franchise agreement and the leases on Detroit's two ballparks.

Because of Burns's deception, the president of the American League was led to believe that Burns was the majority owner of the Detroit ball club, its president, its secretary, and its treasurer, an impression Burns encouraged. Johnson had no idea that George Stallings was the real owner of the ball club, that Burns was nothing more than a minority stockholder, the appointed president, secretary, and treasurer.

Stallings initially heard news of the shocking subterfuge when Burns defaulted on the loan from the Central Savings Bank. To protect himself from losing control of the ball club and avoid getting involved in months of endless litigation, Stallings paid off Burns's personal loan, recaptured the stock, retained control of the business, and accepted Burns's personal note for the debt.

At an emergency meeting of stockholders (to which Burns was not invited), Stallings, alleging unlawful accounting, described the precarious condition of the franchise, the extent of the greed involved, and the monetary damage the ball club had suffered at the hands of Burns, and he told those present that Burns had no respect for the rules of accounting.

"To be precise," Stallings said, "we are all victims of a financial fraud. Instead of the thirty percent dividend we've been expecting, we are facing a probable default." His recommendation for solving their financial woes? Bankruptcy. Put the company in the hands of a receiver.

Two stockholders, attorneys Frank C. Cook and James McNamara, opposed bankruptcy as a solution. "It's a short-term liquidity issue," they argued. "Why not treat it as an internal problem? Deal with Burns as an in-house matter, refinance our obligations, and avoid a criminal inquiry. Otherwise we might find it difficult to raise money or sell the team. After all, the economics of baseball are outstanding, and it's crucial that we keep the club functioning."

Burns was called in for an explanation. A lot of blustery talk and blunt questioning followed. Burns insisted that he was blameless, expressed disdain for details, and maintained there was a huge misunderstanding. An indignant back-and-forth followed: rudeness, sarcasm, and sometimes vulgarity. Boardroom tensions boiled over. Demands were made. Stallings, a Vesuvius of emotion, snarled, "Either you buy the club or sell your share in it."

"No," Burns responded icily.

Eventually, Burns admitted that he was in a bit of a financial bind, and he agreed, somewhat reluctantly, to sell his holdings for $3,000, about $111,000 in today's dollars. Stallings accepted without hesitation.

The following morning Burns was back demanding more money, twice the original amount, $3,000 more to be exact. Stallings refused. He would not budge. He'd had enough of the double-dealing bastard and immediately wired President Ban Johnson at American League headquarters, advising him of the ball club's financial instability. He suggested that Johnson hurry to Detroit and intervene, and extricate his friend from the convoluted mess.

Burns also contacted American League headquarters and urged Johnson to dispatch a letter in which he (Johnson) endorsed Burns. Johnson acted swiftly, initiating an aggressive public relations offensive designed to protect the reputation of his friend, Jim Burns: "The American League franchise," Johnson wrote, "was granted to James Burns alone. He is the only person who has been recognized by the league as the representative of Detroit's franchise rights."

But financial turbulence was engulfing Burns. He was sinking fast. The issue flared into the open when the Peninsula Savings Bank of Detroit laid bare information about Burns being in default on still another personal loan, a loan for which he'd pledged most of his own baseball stock as collateral.

The stock had been taken over by a local financier, Sam Angus, President of the Detroit, Ypsilanti, Ann Arbor, and Jackson Railway, a 76-mile intercity electric trolley line. According to insiders, Burns's ownership stake in the ball club had been reduced to 300 shares of unhypothecated stock.

On the seventh of November, a Thursday morning, President Ban Johnson, much overweight but tireless, arrived in Detroit on an all-night sleeper, and immediately sought out Burns for a briefing at the Griswold House.

Always a pitchman with a folksy appeal, Burns served up an impressive slander-laden stew, flattered and fooled the president of the American League, touched on the difficulties confronting the franchise, told some false stories, explained what went wrong—concealing his own shortcomings—and laid the blame at the feet of George Stallings, saying Stallings was trying to wrest control of the ball club away from him in a grab for money and power. Burns even brought along an incomplete set of the books, showed them to Johnson, and explained: "Stallings kept them. Stallings routinely fudged the books. It's Stallings who is responsible for the disordered finances."

Burns's treachery was breathtaking. A lot of harrumphing ensued.

Hearing of Johnson's arrival in town, Stallings rushed over to the Griswold House to see him. There was much to discuss. But Johnson and Burns were already cloistered somewhere in the hotel. Johnson would not see Stallings. All Stallings could do was scratch his head and grumble, never dreaming of what was taking place upstairs.

Stallings hung around the lobby until 11 in the morning, then left for a previously scheduled appointment at the Majestic Building. When asked about Johnson, Stallings made no comment.

Later in the afternoon, the media-savvy Johnson, completely bamboozled by the slick-talking Burns, ruthlessly, and with almost missionary zeal, rushed into print, issuing a statement in which he steadfastly defended Burns. "The franchise," he said, "belongs to Burns personally. No one else will be recognized by the American League." Johnson then held an impromptu news conference in a room swarming with journalists. Once again George Stallings was in his sights.

Speaking in characteristically blunt terms, the president of the American League, a supremely confident and striking individual, told reporters about Stallings's involvement with the books, publicly accusing him of egregious mismanagement of funds, spotty paperwork, and a stunning lack of accountability, stopping just short of using the word "embezzlement." Everyone was shocked.

Johnson didn't stop there. Battering Stallings like a boxer's speed bag, he kept up a blistering attack, slamming Stallings unmercifully, offering comments considered at best inaccurate, at worst lies. It was the way Johnson operated. He also lashed out at what he claimed was Stallings's betrayal of the American League and accused him of negotiating with the enemy, of trying to sell the Detroit ball club to the National League.

Knowledgeable people were appalled. This wasn't the George Stallings they knew. The charges were totally unfair. They were not, as they say, reality based. The president of the American League was using Stallings as a piñata in a bookkeeping scandal.

Johnson left the Griswold House shortly after lunch, carefully keeping his distance from Stallings, and spent the remainder of the day hopscotching around town, touting the ball club's strength, sounding out wealthy businessmen, anyone who was supposed to have money, coaxing, cajoling, prodding, seeing if he could scare up enough capital to staunch the bleeding and rescue the franchise from its financial malaise, and save Burns's interest in the ball club. But support for Burns was shallow. Few people in Detroit had a high opinion of the man. Not a penny was forthcoming.

The level of Johnson's rancor mortified Stallings. He'd been the target of Johnson's attacks before. They'd both taken shots at each other. But this was different. This was emotional, down and dirty, with deep-seated overtones. On questionable grounds, Johnson had succeeded in tarnishing Stallings's reputation in a relentless push to drive him out of the league.

A deep freeze developed between the two men.

Infuriated by the malevolent way his activities were being portrayed in the press and intent on protecting his reputation, Stallings took off the kid gloves and launched a blistering bare-knuckle attack of his own.

Almost choking with rage, Stallings vented righteous anger and offered the press his side of the story. "Johnson stated last night that I had charge of the books. I tell you now, I had nothing to do with the bookkeeping during the past year. I can prove it. And, if they can show me where I made one single entry, I will make Johnson and Burns a present of my stock in the club."

Passing a handkerchief over his moist brow, he explained, "The money was counted every night, by myself, Clarence Loomis and Jimmy Casey, and turned over to Burns who deposited it in the bank. Burns was the treasurer of the club. Not a cent could be drawn out of the bank without his signature on the check."

In a bitter voice, Stallings spoke about the charge that he had tried to sell the club to the National League. "That's the most asinine thing I've ever heard of," he said. "How the hell could I sell the club? Even if I wanted to. I'd given Burns my stock. He'd placed it in Johnson's hands, in escrow. Or at least I thought he had. I believed at the time that Johnson had my stock in his safe. I couldn't get at it if I wanted to." Stallings frowned, stared down at his hands, and shook his head. "I hope Johnson will be man enough to give me a chance to appear before him and be heard, and not dodge me, as he has been doing."

Confident of his position, Stallings went looking for Johnson Friday morning at the Griswold House, a tempest of thoughts flashing through his mind. Johnson wasn't there; he'd spent the night at the Oriental Hotel. Stallings tried contacting him at the Oriental. Three times Stallings sent word to Johnson. The replies: "He's not up yet." "He's indisposed." "He's left."

Responding to the barrage of questions from reporters, Stallings expressed moral outrage and implied a not-so-veiled threat to sue. "I did not create the problem," he said, with an acute sense of injustice. "My interests are fully protected by all the money necessary, and I will spend whatever it takes."

Friday morning, Johnson met with the club's attorney, James McNamara, and devoted hours to examining, interpreting, and trying to piece together a nearly complete set of books. It was pretty damning evidence. The truth hit him with a thud: James Burns was a liar, a manipulator, and a thief, the true culprit behind the mess.

The books cleared up a lot of things. It was Burns who kept them. It was Burns who had entire charge of business affairs. All moneys were paid to Burns. Grandstand receipts were counted in the presence of three witnesses. Burns banked the money. All expenditures were made by check through Burns. Johnson learned for the first time that George Stallings was the real owner of the Detroit club, that Stallings controlled a majority of the stock, that Stallings owned more stock than Burns and all of the other stockholders put together.

With dramatic tension rising, Stallings and Johnson finally met behind closed doors at three o'clock Friday afternoon for a one-on-one conversation about their options. The two strong-willed individuals had been at loggerheads for years. Amazing animosity and long-simmering resentments motivated them. Their blunt exchanges were like hand-to-hand combat: they clawed at each other like jungle beasts.

Driven by long-standing grudges and unsettled scores, Stallings went after Johnson with a vengeance, using language laced with four-letter words. He cornered Johnson and forced the president of the American League to admit that his only source for the statement about Stallings's purported betrayal—selling out to the National League—was James Burns himself. No one else.

Unleashing pent-up anger and loudly proclaiming his innocence, Stallings conveyed his unhappiness over Johnson's devastating putdowns and ill-considered public remarks. He berated Johnson and argued that his own conduct had been impeccable, and Johnson and the American League lacked the authority to expel him.

It was a remarkable comedown for the increasingly costive president of the American League. He'd taken a beating. But his legal training served him well; a cool, crass operator, he endured the verbal thrashing, took it in stride, all the while silently plotting in his own mind what he'd do to Stallings.

As the clock neared four, they were joined by James McNamara, a key Stallings ally, the ball club's attorney, one of the people in whom Stallings confided. McNamara was a diplomat. He knew which buttons to push. And he was well aware of Stallings's willingness to sell the ball club, cut his ties with the American League, and liberate himself from the kinds of chains Ban Johnson had imposed on him.

Even as they verbally jousted and engaged in tough talk, the two adversaries indicated a willingness to explore alternatives and figure out how they might make targeted moves to address their concerns and arrive at a peaceful settlement. McNamara convinced them to cut a deal. Oral agreements were made. Plans for the sale of the ball club were mapped out. The talk centered on a private investor capable of providing the franchise with a revitalizing lift. Sam Angus was anointed as the most desirable potential owner. It was agreed: Angus would be approached.

Stallings was explicit about what he wanted to complete the deal: $22,500, about $835,000 in today's dollars, in cash for his holdings (par value). He was prepared to let his interest go and insisted that he was in a position to do the dictating in the matter of terms. He would not budge.

Johnson did not say much, other than issue a terse statement. "The books," he said, "as closely as I can figure them out, show receipts of $65,000 for the year, and expenditures of $71,000. The club should have been run last year, including every possible expense, for $36,000, on which there would have been a $29,000 profit" (about $1,076,000 in today's dollars). The announcement was an act of cleverness, a way of sending a message to potential investors and making an indirect financial pitch to Sam Angus.

A tumultuous seven days followed.

Thinking major-league baseball a glamorous business and believing there was a big payoff on the horizon, a syndicate, led by Sam Angus, acquired Burns's holdings and assumed his indebtedness. This, "it was supposed, amounted to quite a figure. Burns walked away from the mess adequately compensated with a check for $6,500." In a parallel backroom deal, Sam Angus, perhaps for past or future political favors from Burns, pulled out his checkbook and paid whatever Burns owed the ball club, including the disputed grandstand receipts.

On Saturday morning, November 16, 1901, the syndicate acquired George Stallings's majority stake in the ball club, picking up an attractive asset at a fire-sale price, and took control of the franchise, a move encouraged and approved by the president of the American League.

Johnson lost no time in going after Stallings. Using strong-arm methods, he set afloat a good deal of misinformation about the Big Chief, perpetuating lasting misconceptions and unfortunate notions about the man, notions that persist today.

Asked if he'd been railroaded out of the league, Stallings replied, "No," he'd simply gotten tired of being systematically beaten up and taking abuse, most of it coming from the president of the American League. He refused to place his manhood in Ban Johnson's hands.

Paraphrasing the words of journalist Bill Granger, who wrote about the management style of a modern-day executive of the same ilk: "You get the feeling that if you were marooned on a desert island with Ban Johnson, you would want to make sure he had enough to eat."

CHAPTER 11

EVERYONE'S DIRTY LITTLE SECRET

Late in the autumn of 1908, George Stallings emerged from baseball's minor-league wilderness to take over the managerial reins of the New York Yankees, a ball club called the "Highlanders," the "Kilties," the "Invaders," the "Hilltoppers," and a lot of other names, a pathetic last-place outfit in total disarray.*

The Yankees hadn't started the season that way. They'd played winning ball in April, climbed into first place in May, stumbled badly in June, touched bottom in July, did a belly-flop in August, and almost self-destructed in September.

In one way or another the preening egomaniacs who wore New York Yankee uniforms routinely managed to lose games in the most uninspiring ways. Chicago's "Big Ed" Walsh beat them on nine different occasions; Boston's Cy Young, at 41, the oldest pitcher in the game, hurled a no-hitter against them, an 8–0 gem; and Washington's 20-year-old Walter Johnson, on the way to his first winning season in the big leagues, shut them out three times in four days.

Tiring of the team's unhappy dynamics and the owner's ham-handedness, manager Clark Griffith resigned halfway through the season, during an angry telephone call with owner Frank Farrell.

---

* The *New York American* first called the New York American League ball club the Yankees on Monday, February 23, 1904, page 8, column 3. The team has been known, for the most part, as the Yankees ever since. The name appeared in syndicated articles on sports pages across the nation and soon became popular everywhere. This is the headline for the story in the *New York American:* "M'Guire to Catch for the American Nine Here: Privileged by Detroit to Go Where He Pleased, the Great Backstop Has Signed with Griffith's New York Yankees."

Managerial candidates were plentiful. Among those seeking the top job were three Yankee hopefuls, left fielder Jake Stahl, shortstop Kid Elberfeld, and first baseman Hal Chase.

Owner Frank Farrell's appointment of Elberfeld gave rise to a lot of head-scratching. "Elberfeld?" a roomful of reporters asked in a chorus of skepticism. "You've got to be kidding!"

The unlikely choice of Kid Elberfeld displeased both Jake Stahl, a former big-league manager, and Hal Chase, the team captain, who naturally thought they would be next in line. The two men made known their displeasure, so much so that Stahl was shipped off to Boston, while Chase quietly, and sometimes not so quietly, worked behind the scenes to undermine the hot-headed Elberfeld. And it was not difficult to do.

The Kid made a hash of things. Under his inept leadership, New York played 27–71 ball, a .276 percentage. Players accused one another of not hustling; Elberfeld himself, shouting expletives, treated the boys like something on the sole of his shoe. The resulting toxicity destroyed whatever morale remained on the rudderless ball club.

Premier players like "Wee Willie" Keeler, whose skills were rapidly diminishing, became exceedingly unhappy with what was going on. When exasperation flooded over into anger, Wee Willie quit the team and baseball.

The phenomenally gifted Hal Chase, a folk hero of sorts, was the best first baseman in the business. A handsome rooster, the celebrity of "Prince Hal" was almost impossible to exaggerate. His name alone sold tickets. In the eyes of Ed Barrow, a longtime Yankee executive and career baseball man, "'Hal' Chase was unmatched and without a doubt whatsoever the greatest fielding first baseman who ever lived."

Although no more than above average at the plate, Chase's speed and extraordinary glove work put him on a pedestal alongside the biggest stars of the day. Smoother and quicker on his feet than any first baseman in baseball history, Chase had the sure hands of a pickpocket and the unbelievable ability to swoop across the diamond and field bunts on both sides of the mound—with either hand—then rifle an accurate throw to any base. And he made it look easy.

"If he tries that stuff on me," Cleveland's Nap Lajoie once remarked before a series in New York, "I'll fix it so he won't try it again on me or anybody else." The first time Lajoie came to bat in the series, runners were on first and second with no outs. The Big Frenchman shortened up as if to bunt, then took the pitch for a called strike. Sure enough, Chase was almost on top of the plate when the ball pounded into the catcher's mitt.

That was exactly what Lajoie wanted to see. He'd teach the bastard a lesson he'd never forget.

The Yankee pitcher prepared to deliver again. Chase edged forward. Lajoie shortened up as if to bunt. Chase came charging in. Lajoie drew back his bat and swung away. A savage swing. He caught the ball squarely, a shot right at Chase. You'd think Prince Hal would duck. Not in the slightest. He stuck up his glove, speared the ball, and made a snap throw to second base to double up the disbelieving runner hung up between second and third. The crowd went wild.

Elberfeld and Chase hated each other. They were always at cross-purposes, constantly bickering and waging war. The unending animosity was a deep cut in the Yankee clubhouse, and the bad blood and ill will disoriented the team. Elberfeld constantly challenged Chase's integrity. He felt Prince Hal was a bad guy, an idol with clay feet, getting away with all kinds of stuff, quitting on the team, performing erratically, manipulating and throwing games. Ironically, there was nothing illegal about throwing a baseball game in 1908: throwing games was not illegal until after the Black Sox scandal more than a decade later.

Growing more and more exasperated with Chase's insubordination and distorted sense of self, Elberfeld shifted Prince Hal to left field, a move the great first baseman took as an atrocious insult. "Infuriated, he made a sorry spectacle of himself."

As the bad blood between them became more pronounced, the tabloid press began asking uncomfortable questions about Chase's gambling connections. But it was Yankee owner Frank Farrell, an unsavory character himself, who introduced Hal Chase to the world of big-time gambling, a milieu in which Prince Hal was most comfortable.

Yankee teammate "Gabby" Street provided history with a glimpse of Chase's personal conduct, in which you can see that the Prince was an aberrant cheat. Yet, for all his flaws, and they were legion, he was not totally blackhearted. One afternoon, the Yankees were playing host to the Boston Red Sox in a double bill at American League Park. Chase turned to utility catcher Gabby Street, waiting his turn in the cage at batting practice, and said, "Poker game down at McGraw's tonight, Gabby. Eight o'clock."

"Pass on me, Prince. The stakes are too high."

"Come anyway, Gabby. You don't have to play. There's plenty of good food, and a lot of good-looking dolls. They've got that good beer you like, too."

McGraw's was a popular pool hall in the Marbridge Building on Herald Square. (Giants manager John McGraw originally owned the business.) It was the place to see and be seen, a gathering spot for the beautiful, the well-heeled, and the decadent, a lively bar and restaurant and gambling scene where an ever-evolving roster of newsmakers were part of the in-house entertainment. Mobs of visiting tourists and locals would go out of their minds when they spotted a celebrity.

"Say, isn't that George M. Cohan over there? That guy looks enough like George M. Cohan to be George M. Cohan."

It sure was. "Yankee Doodle Dandy" himself.

When Gabby arrived, the Prince was in a poker game, seated across from his Yankee teammate, Guy Zinn, and Harry Hooper, the Red Sox star. One or two big-time gamblers were also in the game. It was the most popular table at McGraw's. The stakes were high. And it attracted the bulk of attention. Chase, handsome, smiling, and smoking an expensive Havana cigar, the bellybands still on it, was thoroughly enjoying himself.

"He was always smiling," Gabby recalled. "He sure as hell loved life."

Street stood a few feet behind Chase, kibitzing; Hal didn't seem to mind. Not at all. And Gabby could easily see the cards Prince held in his hand.

Chase played conservatively, for the most part, waiting for an opening. As the evening wore on, beer flowed, folding money slapped the table, a new deck of cards was introduced. The cards were cut. Each man at the table drew for the deal. The high card belonged to the Prince.

He rocked the deck on the polished wood and dealt the cards. The players studied their hands.

"How many, Zinny?" Chase asked.

"I'm good, Prince," Zinn replied. "I'll play these." Zinn had drawn a pat hand.

Silence fell over the table. Hooper and the others folded.

Gabby watched the action with keen interest. "I'm looking over Prince's shoulder," Gabby says. "He has a pair of Kings going in, and draws three cards. I see the cards. No help there. Prince is dead in the water. All he has is two Kings."

Zinn bets $100 and Prince takes a drag on his cigar and says, "And $100." This goes on a couple of more times. Gabby thinks: "Prince is nuts."

Zinn doesn't fold and drop out. A carload of money finds its way onto the table, a lucrative pot, about $2,500 ($81,000 in today's dollars), most of it coming from Zinn and Chase.

"Finally," Street says, "Guy calls Prince. Hal fans out his cards in front of Zinn and says, 'Four Kings, Zinny, can you beat 'em?' Zinn's full house is second best."

Gabby is speechless. "Four Kings? Where the hell did the other two Kings come from? I'm standing right behind Hal, and he turns a pair of Kings into four-of-a-kind. Right in front of my eyes. It's the damnedest thing I'd ever seen."

Smiling broadly, Prince turned to Gabby and said, "Ain't life beautiful, Gabby, me boy?"

Gabby continued. "Later that night, I see Zinn talking to a pretty young thing at the bar. He's happy, smiling, and I'm thinking to myself, 'What an actor.' He calls me over and buys me a drink and tells me what a swell guy Chase is. He says Prince calls him over and says, 'What's the matter, Zinny? Have you lost your best friend?'

"It was worse. Zinn had lost six months' pay. And with that, Chase dropped $1,000 in Zinn's pocket and said, 'Hell, Zinny, it's only money.'

"I never thought of it as cheating," Gabby recalled. "It was more like beating the system. Hal was showing off for me. He wanted to show me he could palm a pair of Kings out of his sleeve in that tough company and not get caught. It was like he wanted somebody to know."

That was Hal Chase, charming and maddening, a mystery wrapped in an enigma.

Gambling flourished in New York City, a town full of high rollers and old-style gambling houses; it was part of sports culture. Betting was heavy, particularly at racetracks and gambling dens. When state officials shut down the local tracks, gamblers reestablished themselves at ballparks and wandered around the grandstands taking bets from fans who wanted a piece of the action before and during games. The availability and ease of betting in the big leagues was systemic, escalating, and becoming ubiquitous, too prevalent to ignore.

More than a few barflies, talking baseball over half-full glasses of warm beer, felt that some of the games were rigged, and their suspicions may have been correct. Players and gamblers mingled freely. In fact, quite a few players admitted that they'd been asked to throw games and had heard of others as well who'd been approached by gamblers.

Between 1903 and 1912, an era of peace in baseball, the propaganda blitz of selling the public on our national pastime shunted aside gambling problems, according to sportswriter/author Leonard Koppett:

> Organized Baseball's response during the increasing prosperity of the two-league system was a deliberate policy of sweeping the dirt under the rug. It whitewashed cases it couldn't ignore and ignored as much as it could. Praising

itself as publicly as possible for presenting a "clean sport," it chose concealment over cleaning up the instances that arose. At the same time, the gambling proclivities of managers and club owners were well known, especially at racetracks and gambling clubs, and condoned by their fellow authorities.

How did American League potentate Ban Johnson react to the possibility of Chase being engaged in dubious conduct? Did he investigate? Did he take aggressive action? Did he implement much-needed reforms? He did not. The self-righteous Johnson ignored the whole range of evidence that Chase might have been doing something improper or illegal and willfully turned a blind eye to it; the thought of a ballplayer throwing a game did not play well in the nation's newspapers. Any acknowledgment of deviousness, that is to say, a game being fixed, would have a chilling effect on the prosperity of big-league baseball. That wouldn't do at all.

For Ban Johnson, a cold-hearted opportunist, one idea was paramount: the American League must continue to thrive. It was a huge profit machine. And after so many pious pronouncements about "clean baseball" and the high standard of sportsmanship and discipline in the junior circuit, the league's president could not suddenly admit to imperfection, even when it was staring him in the face.

Viewing the past with pride, the present with satisfaction, and the future with confidence, Johnson huffed and puffed and covered up scandals or ignored wrongdoing, and merely dispatched a bulletin alerting league executives to the problem, as if they weren't already aware of it.

Chase lived life recklessly; he had an inflated sense of entitlement that trumped any moral considerations. As slippery as a fish out of water, he was not rattled by assaults on his integrity, and he disavowed any wrongdoing, explaining to reporters how he'd been out there competing when he was too ill to play.

"Of course I made errors," he said, in imperturbable good humor. "Who wouldn't the way I felt ... I should have been home in bed." Then he paused and sneered with a cocky half smile that bordered on the verge of a sulk. "And this is the thanks I get for it." Continuing, he said, "Don't you guys know about the petty jealousies going on in the clubhouse?"

Rumors began circulating about Chase leaving the Yankees and managing an outlaw team in the California State League.

A worried Frank Farrell confronted Chase about the rumors after the Yankees split a doubleheader with the Athletics on the first day of September (Chase got four hits). Chase denied any knowledge of the gossip and assured the boss that he "was more than satisfied," and he gave the Yankee owner "his word of honor as a man that he wasn't leaving." Three days later, the shocker of shockers hit the streets in the form of bold black type on the sports pages of the morning papers: "HAL CHASE, YANKEE FIRST BASEMAN, PICKS UP WITHOUT GIVING NOTICE AND THREATENS TO MAKE SOME STARTLING REVELATIONS."

Chase, in his hubris, promised he'd spring a sensation if he wasn't left alone. Shaking his index finger at a reporter, he issued the following threat: "If any attempt is made by the management of the club to 'roast' me, I'll tell a story that will rip the baseball world wide open." Chase wrapped things up by saying, "I'm not satisfied to play under a management that sees fit to give out a story detrimental to my character, and questions my integrity and honesty . . . and I've decided to quit."

Farrell defended himself. "In order to overshadow his unmanly action, Hal Chase tries to blame a published article. . . . But he has repeatedly defied organized baseball and . . . has caused more trouble than any other ballplayer in the league." As an afterthought, Farrell added, "Regarding Chase's threat to disrupt baseball in New York City, I would welcome any statement he might see fit to make."

One can only wonder what Farrell was thinking. Was he wary of a verbal broadside from Chase? Did he think that, if enough rocks were overturned, something that smelled bad might be exposed? And what message did baseball's high tolerance for rule-bending send to other players? Not a good one. Little by little the years would do their work.

CHAPTER 12

TRIED TO SHOW THAT HE BELONGED

Fans wondered who would replace Kid Elberfeld as Yankee manager. One name stood out on a very short list: George Tweedy Stallings. Farrell and Stallings were friends, good friends, but Stallings wasn't interested in the job. He was thriving as the owner-manager of the Newark Sailors, a highly profitable Double-A Eastern League franchise, and thought it best that he stay there.

But Stallings was the kind of leader the Yankees needed, a take-charge manager, respected for turning around hopeless ball clubs, and Farrell aggressively recruited him.

"It won't work," Stallings said. "Ban Johnson will raise a rumpus." He reminded Farrell of the bad blood between them.

"Oh, that was years ago," Farrell replied. "He's mellowed. We get along well. He's very supportive."

Stallings wasn't so certain. He kept shaking his head.

"Look," Farrell said, "I'll tell you what . . . If there's trouble, the New York club will back you . . . I promise you that."

Farrell's word was good enough for Stallings. He signed a two-year contract and was given complete control of retooling the team even before the formal announcement was made.

Sporting Life first broke the news in August: "George Stallings will be manager of the Yankees next year. A report from the West has it that the club will have a bench manager next year, and if such is the case, there is little doubt that George Stallings will be that man."

Ban Johnson did a slow burn as he read the article. The president of the American League worked himself into a lather, summoned Farrell to

Chicago, and upbraided the Yankee owner for hiring Stallings without the league's permission.

"What do you mean by signing that man to a contract?" Johnson growled, his neck reddening. "You know he isn't wanted in this league . . . Get rid of him."

"He's already signed a contract," Farrell said, his voice subdued.

"I hope you didn't sign him for more than a year."

"He's signed for two years."

Johnson drummed his fingers on the desk. "That contract is not to be renewed . . . You understand . . . Not under any circumstances." Continuing after a pause, Johnson dredged up conveniently embellished tales about Stallings's supposed missteps in the past, tales in which the truth was a trivial inconvenience.

Trying to show that he belonged, Farrell nodded assent. "That stuff happened before I was in the league," he said. "I thought it was long since forgotten."

"Forgotten . . . Forgotten," Johnson brayed, his chest heaving, his nostrils swelling with air. He stared at Farrell angrily for a moment, then launched into an incoherent harangue about Stallings, portraying the Big Chief as a baseball loony.

The harsh reaction took Farrell by surprise. This obsession about keeping Stallings out of the league was bizarre. Johnson was not only intent on keeping Stallings out of the league; he wanted Stallings's head on the wall as well.

A thought suddenly crossed Johnson's mind. Maybe there was a way out of this mess: just pay Stallings his salary and get rid of him. He looked the question at Farrell as clearly as if he'd asked it. The two understood each other at a glance. Like coconspirators in a Gilbert and Sullivan operetta, they began exploring managerial possibilities. Frank Chance, manager of the world-champion Chicago Cubs, topped the list. Chance was at odds with Cubs owner Charlie Murphy, and Charlie Murphy was at odds with everyone else in baseball.

The word got around that Farrell's appointment of George Stallings had been sidetracked because of opposition from Ban Johnson. Details began emerging. According to an article based mostly on anonymous sources, Farrell had gone to great lengths in trying to sign the number-one candidate:

> While Farrell signed Stallings three months ago, it is known that last month he offered the manager of a National League team a five-year contract,

agreeing to pay him $50,000 for five years. Farrell offered to deposit the money in any bank the manager might name, to be drawn according to the stipulations of the contract. The man to whom the offer was made has a good team and refused Farrell's offer for the reason that he would have to build up an entirely new team in order to land . . . in a good position in next year's championship race.

The controversy offered a telling glimpse of Johnson's iron-fisted, in-your-face management style. A lot of behind-the-scenes squabbling went on, but when he called the tune, the owners danced. It was an unusual mix of free enterprise and authoritarianism, all part of the business.

The unflattering tabloid coverage that was developing bothered Johnson, particularly the belittling way he was being portrayed in the press. Trying to keep the lid on the situation, he backed off.

Ten days later the Yankees made the long-awaited announcement: "After considering numerous possible candidates for the job," Farrell said, "I have today closed with George T. Stallings to manage the New York American League team. . . . The engagement of Stallings meets with the approval of President Ban Johnson and the team owners of the American League."

It was a bold-faced lie, all hugs and hopeful rhetoric. Johnson and Stallings would coexist uneasily. Nothing more.

Stallings's upbeat mood was a breath of fresh air in Yankeeland. Little by little he cobbled together a promising team. Wee Willie Keeler agreed to return for one more season because Stallings felt Wee Willie still had something to give, but not in right field, the sun field at American League Park. "I have been playing the sun field for some years," Willie said, "and after I came out of the field on a real sunny day, it was some time before I could see things clearly. It hurt my hitting."

Kid Elberfeld was another surprise. He too was retained, and so too was that other fellow with rebellious tendencies, Hal Chase, the player thought to be the linchpin of the Yankees' lineup. And why not? Stallings described Chase as "the greatest player he had ever seen."

Chase made his peace with the National Commission, paid a modest $200 fine, and was reinstated by the American League. Big-league baseball was a business in the guise of a sport, and without a star attraction like Hal Chase in the lineup, baseball executives believed they could not satisfactorily entertain fans in New York City. The franchise would not be an economic success.

The decision left the willful Chase more confident than ever and exposed the hypocrisy that helped sustain American League baseball.

CHAPTER 13

SURPRISING SUCCESS

The unenviable task of putting a humpty-dumpty ball club back together again didn't faze Stallings. Not one bit. It was just a matter of revamping the system, of getting a tough bunch of guys in the right frame of mind, of creating a make-no-excuses environment in which everyone worked together and played together as a team. The boys learned quickly that the Big Chief was comfortable being in charge.

Nothing was done randomly. Practices were planned to the minute. He was always the first one on the field in the morning and the last to leave in the afternoon. "Rain or shine," he said, "there will be a two-hour skull practice every day." At the first session he questioned Willie Keeler, one of the few players with whom he was acquainted, about the team's hit-and-run sign. Willie cocked an eye, smiled sheepishly, shrugged, and "practically admitted there wasn't any."

It wasn't long before the meetings were awash with chatter about tactics and strategy, about aggressiveness as an asset, about the importance of the running game, about deciding where each player should position himself for a cut-off throw, about the value of physical conditioning and other things, things that helped good teams win more games.

At first, most of the gang looked upon the sessions as a joke: "Stallings's Baseball School." But before long attitudes began to change. Some of the less hostile players acknowledged the value of emphasizing the little things, things that most of them seldom thought about, things like which outfielders among their opponents charged the ball the quickest and threw the hardest and most accurately. Like who was the best shortstop? Or which shortstop could reach hard-hit balls up the middle? Like who was the fleetest center fielder? Or which outfielders had the most arm strength?

The training honed skills other teams lacked. It gave the Yankees an edge. The Big Chief steered the ship calmly and correctly. He raised expectations and reinforced the importance of loyalty within the team. It was never about anyone other than the team. He convinced the boys to believe in themselves, to feel valued. And he pushed guys who got too comfortable, and put others at ease when they needed a boost. The approach quickened competitive impulses and inspired best efforts.

As a result, the Yankees' 1909 season was a comparative success. Not the kind of success where newspaper clippings are worth keeping, but a success in the way synergy developed among the players, the way they worked together, the way they pulled together. They finished an unexpected fifth, missing out on a first-division finish by only three and a half games.

The change of philosophy, the infusion of fast young talent, and the rapid development of several splendid young pitchers gave rise to high expectations for the future. Attendance soared, and the franchise realized a profit for the first time in its seven-year history.

Stallings's surprising success and increasing popularity in New York grated on Ban Johnson, but the American League president kept his disdain under wraps and waited for an opening. The time will come, he kept reminding himself, and when it does . . . He chuckled inwardly—like a big fat unpleasant cat, its tail twitching, ready to pounce—as he followed Stallings's every move. And then something did attract his attention.

Manager Joe Cantillon of the Washington Senators—yes, the same Joe Cantillon players once condemned for being an incompetent umpire—was shamelessly spreading nasty rumors about Stallings, saying he was systematically stealing opponents' signs at American League Park.

According to Cantillon, the Yankees were positioning a sign-stealer on a platform behind the Young's Hats sign in right center field, where the outfield fence stood 16 feet high. Peering through field glasses, the culprit got the visiting team's signals as they were being flashed by the catcher, then, moving the crossbar in the letter H in the word "Hats," he relayed the information to the batter. When the crossbar was turned a certain way, the batter knew a fastball was coming; another way, a curve; another way, an off-speed pitch.

In September the Detroit Tigers, locked in a struggle for a third consecutive pennant in a tight race, made their final appearance at American

League Park in New York. On the alert for chicanery, Tigers manager Hughie Jennings came up with an entirely new set of signals for the series.

And to be certain that it was Joe Cantillon's paranoia and intense dislike of Stallings and nothing more, Jennings asked the team's trainer, Harry Tuthill (who happened to believe Cantillon's accusation), if he'd slip outside the ballpark during the Saturday afternoon doubleheader for a "looksee." Tuthill unobtrusively left the dugout in the middle innings of the first game and walked along the outside of the outfield fence. And what do you think he discovered? Nothing. Not a single piece of physical evidence. Nothing, that is, except a hole in the outfield fence and some kind of iron lever on a post.

Detroit played like champions that day, taking both ends of the Saturday doubleheader from New York, 2–1 and 10–4, before an excited crowd of 20,000 fans. All the Yankees could manage were four hits in the first contest and 10 in the second.

Because of blue laws the teams did not play on Sunday. On Monday the Yankees rebounded and defeated the Tigers, 4–1, "bunching four scratch hits, none of which left the infield."

Tuesday, in the final contest of the four-game set, Detroit right hander "Wild Bill" Donovan shut out New York, 5–0. The Yankees managed only five hits. All told, they hit safely just 23 times in 35 innings, the only extra-base hits being a double and a home run. The Yankees weren't exactly knocking the cover off the ball.

But Ban Johnson was determined to believe the worst, seemingly by rote. He demanded George Stallings's scalp, wanted him drummed out of the American League and barred from organized baseball for life. "Stallings is not too well liked by other club executives," Johnson said, regurgitating an outright lie, "and in order to prevent trouble among them, the man . . . must be made to give up his ideas of continuing to serve Frank Farrell as manager."

Stallings offered no comment when told of Johnson's statement, though an appropriate response might have been: What a crock of . . .

On December 15, 1909, American League executives got together at the Hotel Wolcott on 4 West 31st Street in New York for their annual meeting. The gathering was untroubled by any differences of opinion. Everyone was prospering. Major-league attendance had reached a new high. A total of 7,978,108 fans passed through turnstiles in 1909. American League attendance was 3,740,570 (an increase of 129,204), while the National League totaled 3,637,580. In other words, the comparatively new American League had attracted a larger following than the senior circuit by 102,990 paid admissions.

Magnificent new concrete and steel ballparks in Philadelphia, Chicago, and Cleveland almost assured record-breaking profits in the future. The potential for lavish growth was tremendous.

Ban Johnson, the majordomo of the American League, reported the gratifying "increase in business," and the board of directors (formerly the league's governing body; now little more than a rubber-stamp committee under Ban Johnson) transacted all of the league's yearly business in two hours, then adjourned until the following year. There was no debate, no discussion, no differences of opinion. The meeting ran smoothly because Ban Johnson, a godlike figure and leader of his own parade, made the bulk of the decisions beforehand, and crossing Johnson would have been like crossing Attila the Hun.

The board of directors did, however, review the signal-tipping evidence, and, on President Johnson's recommendation, "promptly disposed of the scandal and cleared the New York Yankees of all complicity in the matter."

When Johnson emerged from the meeting, a reporter covering the story for the *Tribune* asked, "What about the lever Harry Tuthill discovered on a post behind the right field fence?"

His patience worn thin, Johnson minimized the significance of the charge of wrongdoing. "The investigation," he said, "determined it was nothing more than abandoned equipment used earlier in the year to operate acetylene gas lamps that were strung around the outfield fence for a 15-mile match race—held at night—between two of the world's premier long-distance runners, Henri St. Ives of France and Alfred Shrub of England."

But the sign-stealing controversy did not go away. The rumors seemed to take on an almost mystical presence. They persisted and seemed to have the clinging power of a blood-sucking leech, and the taint on Stallings's reputation did not go away.

Thirty-five years later Frank Graham Jr., in a book titled *The New York Yankees: An Informal History,* further embellished the sign-stealing tale that demonized Stallings. Graham described Tuthill's "raid" on a sign near the scoreboard on the center field fence (there was no scoreboard on the center field fence) and told how the sign-stealer signaled Yankee batters, using the letter O instead of the crossbar in the Young's Hats advertisement. "When the center of the O was open," Graham wrote, "it meant that a fastball was about to be delivered; when it was closed, a curveball; when it was half open, an off-speed pitch."

Yet, when you unpack the statement, there is nothing inside. The letter O was at least two feet high. How could visiting teams and crowds who attended Yankee games fail to see the obvious changes in the letter O, or the movement of the crossbar on the Young's Hats sign, when talk of the subterfuge was all over the papers?

One fan summed up the view from the bleachers: "I ain't much smart," he said, "but even I can figure out that nothin's goin' on." And Detroit trainer Harry Tuthill himself admitted to a reporter from the *World* that he "found no evidence to substantiate the warning Joe Cantillon had given the Tigers in Washington."

Besides that, there was no rule prohibiting the practice of sign-stealing in 1909. The tactic had always been part of the game, so much so that Brooklyn Dodgers manager "Chuck" Dressen, a noted sign-stealer himself, once famously told the 1953 National League All-Stars: "Don't worry about a new set of signs for the game, boys. I'll just use the same signs your teams have been using all season."

CHAPTER 14

THE PRICE THE YANKEE MANAGER PAID

A string of disabling injuries struck Yankees regulars at almost every position in 1910, but Stallings, master juggler that he was, mixed and matched combinations, maneuvered 20 part-timers in and out of the lineup and, in some unfathomable way, managed to get the team to play first-division baseball, an achievement worthy of high praise.

Utility man Jack Knight proved a godsend. A virtual jack-of-all-trades, Knight performed yeoman duty at almost every position (he did not pitch or catch) before becoming a fixture at shortstop. Rookie Bert Daniels brought the outfield together and became a fan favorite, and Ed Sweeney, one of six catchers Stallings used behind the plate, though weakened by health problems, showed the potential of a first-rate backstop.

The splendid work of a corps of young pitchers, led by rookie right hander Russ Ford, made the Yankees a pennant contender. Ford posted Cy Young–like numbers, 26–6, a record that included eight shutouts and a sparkling 1.65 earned run average. Rookie left-hander Jim Vaughn, though bothered by a sore arm, was 13–11, with five shutouts and a 1.83 ERA, and, when Vaughn experienced soreness in his shoulder, Jack Quinn, a right-hander, known for doctoring the ball, took up the slack and fashioned an 18–12 record in a workhorse role.

Hal Chase, the last remaining regular from Clark Griffith's regime, was an invaluable cog in the lineup. When Prince Hal was in the game, there was something of an aura about the team, an electric feeling. You might call it compelling theater. And people in the "Big Town" appreciated a good show.

That anything was amiss was inconceivable. Yet, as early as spring training, idle gossip hinted of friction in the club. There were noisy internal squabbles, most notably differences between team manager Stallings and captain Chase.

Things appeared to be running smoothly, though, two months into the season. The Yankees were in first place, sporting a superb 27–11 record, when Chase decided to feed several friends in the press tidbits of gossip about the team's surprising success. Fans didn't know what he was up to until mid-June when the Yankees visited Detroit for a series with the Tigers. It was then that a story on the sports page of the *Detroit Evening News* brought the issue into focus: "CHASE TO SUCCEED GEORGE T. STALLINGS AS HIGHLAND BOSS." The subhead added: "Hal Practically in Charge of Yankees This Season; Former Detroit Manager Ending Two-Year Contract."

Written by H. G. Salsinger, the story seemed maliciously inspired. According to Salsinger, Hal Chase was made captain last winter and "given a rather firm hold on the managerial reins. . . . Chase is the real manager," Salsinger explained. "On the field the Yankees are under his sole direction. They follow his orders. And the selection of pitchers lies mostly with Chase."

Stallings was spitting mad when he read the article and quickly made clear how troubled he was. "How," he asked reporters, incredulously, "can a member of the press entertain such an idea, much less write about it? Anyone who knows me will tell you that I would not manage a club unless I had absolute charge. No second fiddle for me."

Eyes bulging, face a deep reddish color, chest heaving with emotion, he reminded the boys from the press that a St. Louis paper had printed a similar story, and that Yankee players "made an awful kick about it." He paused abruptly. "Maybe the story in St. Louis inspired the article in Detroit." (He didn't believe that for a second but was wise enough not to get into a public confrontation with Chase.)

Chase remained tight-lipped. A smart, manipulative man, he was aware that he had undermined the no-nonsense Stallings and realized that his own actions were inappropriate. Meetings between Stallings and Chase— the few there were—usually turned into shouting matches. But Stallings did not hesitate to confront Chase and articulate his thoughts. "The stories," Stallings said, "are a distraction aimed at undermining the ball club." He asked Chase to refute them.

Though averse to interviews, Chase debated the advisability of talking to reporters. Stallings insisted, pointing out that, if left unchallenged, the stories were a serious rebuke to his (Stallings's) authority and a detriment to the ball club. Chase finally agreed to talk to the press and promised to disclaim and deny the stories. Reporters were summoned.

Wearing surface smiles, the two men greeted the press, and Chase freely expressed himself when asked if there was any clash in judgment between manager and captain. "It's absurd," Chase said, dispassionately. "Mr. Stallings is a warm friend of mine and my superior on the team. Our relations are most amiable. He is the manager of the team and I have no desire to pose as one trying to usurp his power. As captain, I know my duties and try to carry them out on the field. The players will bear me out when I say that Mr. Stallings runs the club."

The Yankee players were well aware of what the Big Chief expected: teamwork, industry, and selflessness. He demanded that they go all out all the time and perform even when hurt. He wanted them to live and die with every pitch, just as he did. "There is no 'I' in the word team," he reminded them.

But that's not the way he handled Prince Hal. When Chase loafed or claimed an injury or said he was too beat up or too sore to play, putting his own interests ahead of the team's, Stallings held back criticism of the talented first baseman.

Instead of hustling, mentoring, and setting a good example as the ball club's captain, Chase sat out several important series early in the season, one at home against Detroit, another in Boston, as the boys struggled to compete with a crippled lineup. On one occasion only 14 men were suited up to play. It was at this juncture in the schedule that Chase, complaining about some sort of mysterious illness, unexpectedly left the team and returned to New York.

Chase did not rejoin the ball club until just before game time on August 1, after he and his pal, Jim Vaughn, the supposedly sore-armed pitcher, had narrowly escaped serious injury as passengers on a New York Central express that rammed a stalled engine 45 miles west of Amsterdam, New York. Chase, though shaken up, was unhurt after being thrown into the aisle among other passengers, one of them a woman who was taken off the train in critical condition.

Two days later Chase was back at first base for the second game of a four-game series in Cleveland, a 5–2 Yankee victory.

After Cleveland it was on to Bennett Park in Detroit, where admiring sportswriters praised his play around first base. "Chase is back, playing the great ball for which he is famous," Howard Pearson wrote in the *Detroit*

Journal: "His fancy fielding was the one bright light in a 4–1 Yankee loss. Shortstop Jack Knight made a bad throw on a double play ball, low and wide, but Chase clawed it with his bare hand in one of the classiest bits of first sacking seen here all year."

But it was the fleet and controversial Ty Cobb who provided most of the excitement at Bennett Park throughout the series. Always intensely wrapped up in the game, Cobb said he would not play if Tigers left fielder Davy Jones was in the lineup. The Georgian was furious with Jones for having missed a hit-and-run sign earlier in the week.

"If I missed Ty's sign, it certainly wasn't intentional," Jones said, excusing himself. "He's doing me an injustice. . . . That's not right. When Ty had trouble on the field and a mix-up threatened to engulf him, I stood by him, and he knows it." It didn't matter. Cobb had a mean toughness about him. And he wanted Jones thrown off the team.

Cobb and teammate Sam Crawford were also out of sorts. They hadn't spoken since the second week in May, after Crawford objected to a remark Cobb made about Tigers shortstop Donie Bush. Donie had also missed a sign. Crawford got in the middle of things and ended up threatening Cobb. This wasn't anything new. At one time, Cobb and outfielder Matty McIntyre did not speak for three years after—what else—McIntyre had missed a hit-and-run sign, and they had only recently patched things up.

The Detroit team was in an uproar. Cobb grudgingly agreed to dress for the first contest of the Yankee series, but then he was furious when Tigers manager Hughie Jennings kept him out of the game.

"Discipline must be maintained at any cost," Jennings explained.

After things quieted down, Cobb returned to action, and his hitting and fielding were instrumental in two Tigers victories over the Yankees.

Everyone seemed happy. Fans applauded Ty's every move, that is, except for some obnoxious heckling by a couple of crumbums in the left field bleachers. They showered unrelenting abuse on the Georgian. Smart-alecky remarks. Insensitive, lacerating, malicious insults. One of the motormouths really unloaded on him, shouting vulgar words, stupid things, personal things, making a lot of noise with meaty fingers cupped around his big mouth.

Cobb's ears caught snatches of phrases of the abuse above the drone of the crowd; his eyes swept across the bleachers, trying to pick them out. "Who are those guys anyway?" he kept asking himself. His eyes moved. Paused. Shifted. Paused again.

Suddenly, he caught sight of one of the loudmouthed ruffians. Then another. And another. It was the eighth inning. His mouth went tight. His eyes flashed. He stared. Hatred welled up in him. Tore at his insides. His expression maniacal, his face purple with rage, he climbed the low bleacher fence, nimbly shoved past a startled cop, and knifed his way through the crowd.

"Uh-oh," someone said.

Almost before the three uncouth characters realized what was happening, Cobb was on top of them. The faces of the motormouths registered disbelief. Cobb never hesitated. With dizzying suddenness, he unloaded a wild punch that just grazed the top of a Black man's head. Cobb spluttered, snorted, and blurted out obscenities, called the man a "black bastard" and a lot of other names he didn't learn in Sunday school.

A special officer hurriedly jumped between them and hustled the terrified Negro away while other arms held Cobb back. Much shouting followed. Threats and counterthreats. Cobb turned on the Black man's two white friends: "Hang around another inning," he snarled, as special officers pulled him away. "We'll finish this then."

Immediately after the game, a 5–0 Tiger victory in which Cobb starred, he was back in the stands, eager to deliver the promised beatings, but the two white guys had disappeared.

Two hours after the getaway game, and 30 minutes before the team boarded a train for St. Louis, the Yankees experienced another you've-got-to-be-kidding moment. Hal Chase once again did his walk-off-the-team routine. He was leaving indefinitely. No explanation. Nothing. He only said he was "too sick to play." It was the third time he had pulled the stunt that season.

Though irked, Stallings said nothing and made the most of it. It was a trust/confidence issue. "I always let him use his own judgment," Stallings explained, "and made a point of never questioning his actions."

This was the price the Yankee manager paid for trying to get along with the franchise superstar. Chase's leaving didn't really matter. He hadn't been playing with conviction since the first game of his return. The Yankees were 1–6 with Hal in the lineup and 6–5 without him.

Prince Hal immediately made a beeline for the Reed & Barton Building at 320 Fifth Avenue in New York City, the offices of Yankees owner Frank Farrell, where he complained about Stallings and a lot of other things.

Then it was off to Far Rockaway, a popular seaside resort on Long Island, where he vacationed at "Big Bill" Devery's estate. Big Bill was well known around town as New York's recently retired police chief who had run the department like one enormous racket, using police payoffs extorted from clip joints, dance halls, gambling dens, nightclubs, saloons, and whorehouses in the city's Tenderloin district (the red-light district) to purchase a few shares in the Greater New York Baseball Association, better known as the New York Yankees.

Even today smiles cross the faces of those who are acquainted with Big Bill's reputation, perhaps because of a remark he made while accepting the appointment as New York's chief of police: "They tell me you fellows are the fiercest ever on graftin'," Big Bill told his officers. "Well now, that's going to stop . . . If there's any graftin' to be done around here, I'll do it . . . Leave it to me."

Big Bill's motto: "Hear nothin', see nothin', and say nothin', eat, drink, and pay nothin'."

"The man was no more fit to be chief of police," muckraking journalist Lincoln Steffens wrote in his autobiography, "than a fish seller is to be director of the Aquarium." Yet Steffens liked Big Bill—liked him a lot. "As a character, as a work of art, he was a masterpiece," Steffens wrote. "Not only I myself but every reporter I ever assigned to roast the man came back smiling and put that smile in his report."

While visiting Devery, Chase talked baseball and spent afternoons at Far Rockaway beach relaxing in the summer sun and enjoying an occasional dip in the ocean. It was the good life. After dinner Chase would invariably deposit himself in an easy chair opposite Big Bill, and buoyantly articulate his thoughts about the Yankee team, indulging in a gruff show of badinage, soapboxing for his own promotion, as Bill, rolling a cigar between his fingers, radiated clear-eyed affection. Prince Hal had Big Bill's complete support.

Drinking until they were both numb and dumb, they talked and laughed and bellowed and boasted as Big Bill wistfully told stories about the good old days, stories that lost nothing in the retelling.

On Sunday Hal left early in the day to play baseball (under an assumed name) with Andy Coakley's semipro team, something he did regularly when the Yankees were in town.

CHAPTER 15

ALWAYS A TRUTH-BENDER IN THE CROWD

By the time Hal Chase rejoined his teammates, their feelings toward him had cooled. How, they asked, could he, their captain, walk out on them when they were fighting for second place in the standings? Hadn't other crippled teammates played through injuries, sometimes leaving a sickbed to fill in in an emergency? Sure they had. Why didn't Hal make more of an effort to play through his aches and pains, particularly after having been generously, perhaps too generously, given sick leaves in the past?

A shadow was looming over the Yankees' roller-coaster season. The ever-confident Chase, toting an increasingly bloated ego, was not playing by the rules. He was quitting on the boys, and his insufferable arrogance was an unwarranted distraction and destabilizing influence. It made everyone's job a lot more demanding.

The ball club's day-to-day level of play suffered, and Stallings grew more and more exasperated. The simmering tensions between the two men soon became a big story, steady fodder for the papers, a drama that transfixed readers of sports pages across the nation. George from Georgia no longer refrained from smoothing over differences between himself and Prince Hal, and the two crossed swords more than once. Special privileges for the Yankees captain were withdrawn. Stallings no longer cut Chase slack and came on strong whenever Chase did not play up to expectations.

Prince Hal did not like it, not one bit. He was always raising a fuss about one thing or another, and was singularly incensed by Stallings's tongue-lashings. "One day I dropped a ball," he whined, the tone of his voice reptilian, "a thing which any player might do, and I drew severe criticism and ridicule from Mr. Stallings. If the 'roast' had been brought on by a bone-headed play, I could have understood that and I would have felt that I deserved it."

An essentially duplicitous character with an edge on amorality, Chase's play set off alarms. He'd switch signs on the field so the bench (manager Stallings) couldn't interfere with him. Though teammates did not confront Chase directly or speak about his questionable play publicly, more than a few suspected him of being a "dumper," quietly accusing him, among themselves, of throwing games.

With the score tied and nobody out in the eighth inning of a game in Detroit, and the heavy artillery of the New York batting order coming up, Chase, who had doubled to lead off the inning, disregarded Stallings's orders and attempted a steal of third. He was an easy out, committing one of the cardinal sins of baseball, being the first out of an inning at third base. The out made a huge difference. New York dropped the game, a squeaker, by one run.

Stallings was upset. Something fishy was going on. But he was wary of denigrating the cunning athlete's contributions to the ball club, and to baseball in general. The formidably talented Chase was New York's biggest draw. His box-office appeal was deemed crucial to the team's financial success. To charge a star of his magnitude with throwing games was dangerous, if not foolhardy, particularly when the individual's speed, innate grace, and spectacular daring made him one of the darlings of the game. Chase's macho flamboyance kept the picture murky, and concealed misconduct in saggy performances.

September 17, Sportsman's Park, St. Louis. During the first leg of the Yankees' final swing of the season through the league's western cities, one of the St. Louis Browns players, a friend of the Yankees' clean-up hitter Jack Knight, presented Knight with a beautiful black bat. "Jack," he said, "this stick has been a jinx for me lately. Maybe it will be all right for you . . . Why don't you take it? . . . Give it a try."

Knight graciously accepted the offer and, as sometimes happens, drove out a single and two doubles in four trips to the plate the very first time he used the bat, leading the Yankees to a 5–1 victory. The black beauty became an object of instant reverential respect.

The following afternoon, the Yankees' number-three hitter, Hal Chase, who preceded Knight in the batting order, picked up the precious piece of lumber, took a couple of practice swings, liked the balance and feel of the thing, and started for the plate.

"Hey! Wait a minute," Knight called out. "You can't use that bat. That's the only stick I have. . . . If you break it I'm a goner."

The rebuke gave Chase pause. Though he said nothing, he adopted the stance of a gangster, glowered at Knight, and spat in his direction. You could smell the tension rising. Before throwing the bat down, Chase turned and with one mighty swing slammed it against the wall of the dugout. The Yankee bench was speechless. From then on a strong sense of grudge marred the relationship between the two men.

Chase's best friend on the team, "Hippo" Vaughn (he weighed a few pounds less than a hippopotamus), started for New York that afternoon and didn't have a thing. Leading off for St. Louis, Frankie Truesdale, a submissive .213 hitter, walked on four straight pitches and then stole second. Vaughn also gave a free pass to "Red" Corriden, another big basher (Red, a utility player, was carrying a sickly .105 average into the game, and it was only a few days before the end of the season). George Stone then drove Truesdale home with a single through the left side of the infield, Corriden stopping at third. After Hub Northen flied out, Roy Hartzell ripped a liner into left field, driving in Corriden with the Browns' second run of the inning.

Vaughn was just lobbing pitches in there with nothing on them.

Stallings's body language shouted disgust. "Good gawd," he said to himself. "These are the lowly Browns, the lowest of the low, the most impotent team in the majors [the St. Louis Browns lost 107 games in 1910], and here they are pushing Vaughn around. And making it look easy."

Vaughn's performance was so far below standard that it triggered Stallings's suspicions. The Big Chief signaled for the "Vermont Schoolmaster," Ray Fisher, who taught Latin in the off-season. Unfortunately, Fisher unleashed a sharp curve into the dirt on his first pitch, and it got by catcher Lou Criger. George Stone scored from third. After that Fisher escaped without allowing another run in the inning. St. Louis led, 3–0.

The surprising Browns weren't finished. They came right back at Fisher in the second inning. Weak-hitting Bill Killefer got things started with a high chopper up the middle. Fisher leaped for the ball, knocked it down, made a quick recovery behind the mound, and flipped an off-balance toss to first base right at the sure-handed Hal Chase.

Prince Hal was in position to catch the ball, yet, as good as he was, he allowed it to glance off the heel of his glove and bounce to the fence. Killefer took second on the play. Fisher couldn't believe his eyes. Nonplussed, he stared at Chase for a long few seconds, thinking how easily the great first baseman should have handled the play. He always did. But young Fisher reasoned, logically: Who am I, a rookie, to criticize the finest-fielding first baseman in all of baseball?

Stallings almost choked with rage from his perch on the bench. The Yankee skipper pondered questions uppermost in his mind. Should he denounce the team's golden boy? Or should he conveniently forget the incident? And what about Chase's pal, Jim Vaughn? Was he in on the fix too?

St. Louis, thanks largely to Hal Chase's sloppy play, scored two more runs, and the Browns' lead swelled to a commanding 5–0. The Yankees were a resilient bunch, though, a team whose character had grown during the season, and they managed to claw their way back into the game, closing the gap to 6–3 in the fifth.

With one out in the top of the eighth and runners on first and third, the momentum of the game was beginning to tip in New York's favor. "Red" Nelson, the Browns' pitcher, was visibly weakening. He was not keeping the ball down. And no one was up in the St. Louis bull pen. Jack O'Connor, the Browns' manager, was sticking with Nelson. Dripping sweat, Nelson's reddened face filled with a frown as he watched Hal Chase, the Yankees' captain, pull down the bill of his cap and take a couple of practice swings before stepping into the batter's box. Stallings ordered Chase to work the count. Wait out Nelson.

Nelson realized he was in trouble. Buying time, he took off his cap, glanced at the sky, ran the back of his hand across his forehead to keep the sweat from his eyes, put his cap back on, took a deep breath, and went to work, nibbling at the inside and outside corners of the plate with curveballs. The count leveled off at two and two.

And what do you know? Chase did the unthinkable. He canceled Stallings's orders and signaled for a "suicide squeeze": the riskiest play in baseball. Risky because there was little to gain and so much that could go wrong, particularly with two strikes on the batter. A foul ball was an automatic out; a pickoff play or a pitchout meant certain disaster. That's why they called it the suicide squeeze. With just five outs left in the game, the decision was amateurish. It was bad baseball. All the suicide squeeze could accomplish was give the Yankees a chance to score one run. They needed three to tie and four to win. It was a no-brainer. One run was meaningless.

Red Nelson bent forward to face his foe. He took a peek at Daniels on third, began his motion, his right hand cocking the ball, his arm whipping forward.

At that instant, Daniels sprinted for home. Chase squared to bunt. Shouts of "Squeeze!" "Squeeze!" "Squeeze!" rose from the St. Louis dugout. The ball smashed into the catcher's mitt as Chase's half-hearted attempt to get wood on the ball failed. Strike three. (Chase seldom failed to hit the ball on the hit-and-run play—when he tried.)

Daniels was an easy out sliding into home plate. The threat-shattering double play ended the eighth inning. Nelson and the Browns escaped unscathed in the ninth, and the Browns went on to win, 6–3.

It was a hey-wait-a-minute moment, writ large. The Yankee bench was furious. Flushed, sweaty faces, led by Daniels, screamed obscenities at Chase. He had deliberately changed the play to a suicide squeeze when he knew it was the wrong play.

Chase, defiant in the face of criticism, retorted furiously, asserted his innocence, claimed the signal was accidental. "I was forced to go through with it," he screamed.

His teammates weren't buying it.

Judging by Stallings's face, he wasn't buying it either. What Chase was up to was now apparent. Unable to bridle his infamous temper any longer, Stallings rendered a harsh judgment: Chase's intent was to throw the game.

Demonstrating extraordinary courage, integrity, and competitive fire, the Yankees' manager told his captain exactly what he thought of him. The air shivered. Chase's shoulders stiffened. The two eyed each other belligerently, Stallings a glaring, snarling badger, Chase a venomous, hissing viper. Stallings felt like strangling Prince Hal, and Chase felt like lashing out at Stallings's face. They jostled one another. Almost came to blows. But it didn't happen. The players separated them and prevented an angry scrap.

Reports of the confrontation preceded the arrival of the Yankees in Chicago. It was a tabloid-ready scandal. When the players stepped off the train at Union Station, the hellish hounds of the press swooped down on the entourage. "Is there trouble on the team?" a reporter asked. "I hear Chase and Stallings got into a fight?" "Is it true Stallings is going to resign?" another asked.

"Now listen, you guys," Stallings said, speaking for the team. "You folks oughtn't to write things like that. Those stories have been printed wherever we're at. They're attempts to create dissension on the ball club . . . That's all."

To expect that Stallings and Chase could get along peacefully on the same team in the future was now out of the question. Left without any choice,

Stallings wired Yankees owner Frank Farrell and asked him to come to Chicago and take charge of the deteriorating situation, "to look after your interests."

Farrell delayed his response. This bought him time. It seemed that three courses of action were open to the Yankees' owner: trade Chase for Ty Cobb or some other franchise player; suspend Stallings and appoint an interim manager; or name Chase manager of the Yankees. Prince Hal was money in the bank. An irreplaceable star. He was the player who attracted paying customers, a strong drawing card. He made the turnstiles spin and the cash registers ring, and he was already the darling of the Yankee roster.

The situation grew uglier Monday afternoon during the first of a three-game set against the White Sox. Bert Daniels singled and Harry Wolter walked to open things in the Yankees' first, and Stallings ordered Chase to move the runners over with a sacrifice bunt.

Chase, perhaps taken with a sense of his own prowess, once again ignored Stallings's orders and signaled for the hit-and-run. Then, according to the *New York American,* Chase "swung indolently, a foot under the pitch and Daniels . . . was nailed by a city block trying for third." After that neither Chase nor Knight could bring Wolter home, both dying on easy outs.

Though Chase's attitude exuded disdain, the frazzled Yankee dugout said little and went about its business. It was obvious, however, that hard feelings existed between Chase and his teammates. With one out and the bases loaded in the Chicago half of the third, the Yankees' starting pitcher, Jack Quinn, and Chase disputed the right of the other to field an easy roller to the right side of the mound (it was Quinn's play). Both grabbed for the ball, wrestled for possession, and allowed the runner on third to score the only run of the game. Had Chase not invaded the pitcher's turf, the game, an almost flawless pitcher's duel, would have remained a scoreless tie. As it turned out, the Yankees lost, 1–0.

It was not a feel-good moment. The crisis that had threatened the ball club for months was now at hand.

That night the Yankees' players spent an angst-filled evening lounging around the lobby of the Lexington Hotel in Chicago,* where the team was staying, clustered in small groups, speaking privately in low tones about the rancor between Chase and Stallings and what it meant for the team

---

* The Lexington Hotel at 2135 South Michigan Boulevard in Chicago later became infamous as the business headquarters of Al Capone, also known as "Scarface," the notorious gangster whose henchmen routinely patrolled the lobby with machine guns.

and for them personally. Every now and then a couple of the boys would glance over their shoulders and look around, making certain that no one was listening. Others were not so careful.

Hard-to-recognize local reporters from the Chicago papers, standing around nearby, unobtrusively scribbled notes on scratch pads, taking in bare-boned sentences from the gossip-laden talk. Bits of this. A little of that. Inside dirt. Things to pique the public's interest. The more outlandish the better.

"The prick . . . " "He's not helping us any . . . " "Didn't swing at a hit-and-run pitch and queered Daniels . . . " "The son of a bitch is wrecking our chances of finishing second . . . " "Let Farrell trade him for Cobb . . . " "Mr. Stallings blames him for many of our losses . . . " "Sunday he calls a squeeze play in the eighth when we're three runs behind . . . " "What an asshole . . . " "If he and his pal Vaughn put forth their best efforts, we'd be hustling Mack for the pennant right now."

The press was a carnivorous animal. Newsies were out in the street early the next morning, shouting bizarre news for all to hear.

"Extra. Extra. Read all about it. White Sox win and Yankees dissension rumors appear."

The story went on to say, "Fellow players accuse Chase of laying down [throwing games] . . . and seeking to disrupt the club for his own reasons." The writer concluded the article by saying, "The stories about Hal Chase throwing games are such common conversation . . . they need no official confirmation."

In a show of much-recycled sports non-wisdom, "Nie," a sad-sack journalist from New York City, in the business of myth-making, filed a totally fictive story in the *Globe and Commercial Advertiser,* a canard, laying bare the hypocrisy of the press, in which he did not let mere facts stand in the way. The story, picked up by other papers throughout the country, added momentum to the controversy: "There is no doubt in my mind that the Yankees are in open rebellion," Nie wrote. "On the way back to the hotel after yesterday's game, Chase and Stallings had a serious wrangle on the bus and came almost to the point of blows. Chase was the storm center, the other players blaming him for the opening 1–0 loss to the White Sox. . . . Stallings claims that men in Farrell's employ, but not traveling with the club, have been undermining him, and that he is glad now that things have come to a showdown."

Stallings shrugged off the article when asked about it. He was hardened to abuse in the public prints. It came with the job. "The story has no basis at all," he said. "Chase did not accompany the team back to the hotel.... He wasn't on the bus. So how could there have been a quarrel?" He laughed and shook his head. "You guys know how it is. There's always a truth-bender in the crowd. Somebody desperate for a story. It's harmless talk. That's all."

Chase too was polite enough to express surprise when questioned about the story. "Nothing to it," he said with his boyish habitual half smile. "Nothing at all.... Nothing was said by Mr. Stallings then [after the 1–0 loss to the White Sox] or later.... I went to the theatre after the game." Pause.

"To my knowledge, Mr. Stallings and I have no differences. Outside of baseball, I believe he is a perfect gentleman." A significant pause. "I hardly think he's a wonderful manager, though ... " Pause. "How he could get it into his head that I was a disturbing element on the team or even dream it, I cannot tell."

On returning to the Lexington Hotel, Stallings expected to find a telegram from Yankee owner Frank Farrell. Instead, he found a summons from President Ban Johnson, a man he abhorred, ordering him to report at once to American League headquarters right there in Chicago.

It would be an epic showdown.

CHAPTER 16

A STAND-UP GUY

Ban Johnson and George Stallings had not spoken for nine years, ever since the 1901 season when Johnson wrested control of the Detroit ball club away from Stallings and drove him out of the American League.

Though there was no evidence of the Yankee manager having leaked the story about Hal Chase, and indeed he had not, knowing it was on the not-to-do list, Stallings did nevertheless win the enmity of Johnson and the league's clay-footed owners, the inner sanctum of leadership, who recognized the seriousness of the allegations.

When the Big Chief arrived at American League headquarters, Johnson, whose ambition did not leave time for morals, brandished a willingness to offend and spoke acidly through his teeth, his tone curt, his voice poisonous, his thoughts full of malice. He denounced his visitor with venomous words, as if the very thought of what he had done was almost too painful to bear.

The self-infatuated president of the American League felt superior to Stallings and made no effort to hide it. Focusing on the longer term of league affairs, "the larger mission," as he put it, Johnson, with the deep chest croak of a bullfrog, expressed shame and embarrassment, saying that no evidence supported the allegations. Professional baseball, he noted, was in the business of public entertainment. Baseball was a commodity. An enterprise. An industry. Commerce came first.

With operatic gusto, the Lord-High-Everything ranted and raved about the destructive impact of the allegations and the risk a disgraceful scandal posed to the league, not to mention the legal and ethical harm it might unleash. Making Stallings feel the weight of his power, Johnson chastised him and, masking the stink of corruption, called Stallings's conduct perverse, apparently losing sight of the implications of a player throwing games.

Claiming to speak on behalf of the majority, the president of the American League brushed aside any thought of "doing the right thing" and placed the blame for endangering the league's future squarely on Stallings's shoulders, making him the whipping boy in the whole affair. No surprise there.

Power was at the heart of the confrontation. It was a clash of strong-willed men, a clash of egos, a clash of money. Vociferous and highly personal words were exchanged. Verbal roundhouse blows. It was a knock-down-drag-out fight. Nose to nose. Veins bulging.

Grounded on the concrete facts of life, Stallings had nothing but contempt for Johnson. He regarded the big poohbah as an arrogant, morally bankrupt phony and maintained that he (Stallings) did what he believed was best for the New York ball club, even though the scandal violated the omertà of professional baseball.

Johnson did little to hide his disdain, saying that what happened in St. Louis was no worse than what had been happening for years. Presenting his opinions as uncontroversial facts, he raised doubts about the veracity of the charges, defended Chase, and, with willful blindness to what was going on, called the accusations lies and unfounded allegations, an unsavory distortion of the truth, and took aim at Stallings for unfairly tarring the carefully cultivated image of the American League.

Stallings was obstinate. Trying to cope in the role of a combative crusader, he soon learned that the deck was stacked against him.

With typical abusive bluster, the autocratic Johnson skillfully played his hand, termed the charges against Chase "a high crime against the American League," and, with a dented moral sense, scornfully characterized Stallings as irresponsible, a disgrace to baseball, and demanded that Stallings step aside as manager of the New York Yankees.

It was a stark reversal of fortune. The accuser had become the accused. And for what? For exposing a crook.

Though the controversy cast a shadow over New York's hopes for a second-place finish in the American League, and a postseason City Series against John McGraw's New York Giants, the players were almost unanimous in support of their manager. They expressed every confidence in his ability and believed they would win the pennant in another year with the big fellow at the helm.

Not one but a half dozen Yankee players told the *New York American* that Stallings was a stand-up guy: "If he had been given a free rein this year, we would have won the pennant, or come close to it."

If Stallings had hoped to avoid public controversy by keeping the squabble in the Yankee family, he'd clearly miscalculated. He now faced a crisis of credibility and wondered if Yankees owner Frank Farrell would stand by him as promised. The answer was not long in coming. A telegram from Farrell awaited him at the front desk: "Impossible for me to come to Chicago," it read. "Kindly come to New York and talk things over. Turning the club over to Tom Davis [the team's traveling secretary, and Frank Farrell's brother-in-law] until you return." Uneasy doubts invaded Stallings's mind. The unspoken message did not bode well for him.

He spoke briefly with reporters but made no harsh criticisms. "I simply want to find out from Mr. Farrell who is running the New York ball club," he said, "Chase or myself. . . . If Mr. Farrell decides in favor of the first baseman, I will quit at once. If he upholds my regime, Chase will have to step down and out. There cannot be two bosses, especially when one is double-crossing the other."

Tuesday morning Ban Johnson capped a tumultuous few days by putting in a surprise appearance at the Lexington Hotel. The president of the American League had a long talk with Hal Chase, whose many indiscretions were ignored. Chase was not reprimanded. He was given support instead. Johnson's visit was a ringing endorsement, a testimonial on Prince Hal's behalf.

That same evening Davis spent so much time in Hal Chase's company that reporters were certain Chase would replace Stallings as manager.

The next day, before Stallings left for New York on the 20th Century Limited, a swarm of reporters caught up to him at Chicago's LaSalle Street station. Though tired and worn, he readily answered their questions.

"I wish Mr. Farrell had been able to come out here and talk to the men and learn their sentiments," he said, his voice filled with frustration. "I don't think he has any idea of how things have been going." He shook his head and said half to himself, "I'm relying on Mr. Farrell . . . I don't think he's capable of doing anything unfair . . . "

He paused, and toying with his watch fob, said, perhaps making a Freudian slip: "I would have liked to have led them to a pennant next season . . . At least I will have the satisfaction of knowing that I did the right thing."

He tried to smile but tears suddenly coursed down his cheeks, and he admitted, as he boarded the train, that the handwriting was on the wall. He doubted he'd be back as manager of the Yankees.

CHAPTER 17

FULL OF INSINCERE SINCERITY

Hal Chase remained silent until the 20th Century Limited, with George Stallings on it, was well on its way to New York. Late that evening, while chatting agreeably amid an admiring horde of newsmen in the lobby of the Colonial Hotel in Cleveland, the Yankees' next stop on the road trip, the irreverent Chase gave reporters what they'd been looking for, and at the same time largely settled the score with manager Stallings. He proudly pulled out a copy of a contract from an inner pocket of his suit jacket and showed it around. "My contract as leader of the team next season," he said, a merry look on his face, "has already been signed."

Eager eyes devoured it. A buzz resonated throughout the lobby. The contract called for a salary of $10,000 a year as player-manager ($263,000 in today's dollars). A few minutes later, Tom Davis added substance to the news by immediately placing Hal Chase in charge of the team, on and off the field. The astonishing disclosures came as close as anyone had publicly come to acknowledging what had appeared obvious for days: George Stallings was no longer manager of the New York Yankees.

Meanwhile in New York, Frank Farrell was on a long-distance telephone call with Ban Johnson, getting an earful, being told what to do, whether he liked it or not.

A little later in the day, Farrell faced members of the press at his business offices and fielded a barrage of questions. Never once did the Yankees' owner blame Chase for anything. On the contrary, whenever Prince Hal's name was brought up, Farrell defended the talented first baseman at every turn.

"Friction on the club?" he asked rhetorically, spreading his hands in a gesture of futility as he dodged uncomfortable questions. "I've had no real inkling of it other than what I've read in the papers . . . Stallings has only wired me and I've not heard from Chase . . . George and I will have a long conference tomorrow, but I won't decide anything until I've considered all the angles."

When the 20th Century Limited from Chicago pulled into Grand Central Depot at 9:30 A.M., a host of reporters from the city's 17 dailies were on hand, all eager for an interview. "Have you heard the news, George?" someone yelled out from the rear of the crowd as the Big Chief stepped onto the platform. "A dispatch out of Cleveland last night said Davis has turned the ball club over to Chase . . . It said he'd finish the season in charge of the team."

Anger flickered over Stallings's face for an instant, but he'd learned to mask powerlessness. After an uneasy pause, he played down the importance of the dispatch. "That's nothing more than customary," he said, in a sober and rational way. "It's only right that management should go to the captain in the absence of the manager."

"How are the players holding up under the strain?" another asked.

Stallings moistened his lips with his tongue. "The men," he said, a little hoarsely, "did the best they could in the games out west. Only two players on the team were not with me heart and soul . . . It's a good team and it's not for me or anybody else to say anything against it."

"What are you going to tell Farrell?" a man from the *Evening Sun* asked. Stallings gave the man a friendly nod and looked over the crowded platform, assembling his thoughts.

"I represent Mr. Farrell's main business interests," he said. "When I saw something was wrong on the team, I deemed it only right to acquaint Mr. Farrell with the situation. I'm here to explain things as they are . . . I'll present the plain facts."

A short time later, after a slight hesitation on both their parts, Farrell greeted Stallings with an extended hand and a friendly nod. "Sit," he said, indicating the move to be made with his hand. "Make yourself comfortable."

Stallings realized he was in a delicate position. His head was perilously close to the chopping block.

Trying to put his visitor at ease, Farrell said in a friendly and concerned way: "That Chicago trip is a long one." (It was 18 hours on the 20th Century Limited, 23 hours on other fast trains.) Stallings waved a hand as if to say, What are you going to do?

Small talk eased the way. Farrell gave Stallings credit for his contributions to the organization—the way he'd brought the team from last to second place in two years—and complimented him on being a keen judge of raw talent and getting the most out of the players available to him.

Stallings was uneasy. Behind closed lips his tongue passed over his teeth. He started to speak, stopped, and shook his head.

"Go ahead," Farrell said. "Whatever you say stays in this room."

Stallings had much to say. But where to start? Speaking in a soft, mollifying tone, he slowly shaped the account of Chase's alienation and the causes of the trouble, emphasizing the breakdown of communication between them. He sensed little support from Farrell, who remained deeply skeptical and strangely unaffected.

After a while, Farrell moved his head from side to side, scoffed softly, forced a half smile, and said: "You had ample opportunity to voice these concerns . . . which you did not do . . . You never said a word." Farrell's vague smile did not reflect approval or disapproval.

The blood rose in Stallings's cheeks. He replied laconically.

Farrell peered over the fatty bags beneath his eyes, lifted an eyebrow, and said he was astounded and exasperated by the charges. He hastened to add: "They were flawed from the beginning and probably should not have been brought out publicly." He paused, took out a handkerchief and blew his nose loudly, then continued. "Don't you realize that when you disparage one of my star players, on whom the franchise rests, through this person you disparage me? And you disparage the American League?"

Stallings was disappointed. This—this was too much. It was obvious now. Farrell had made a choice. He was pretty tightly behind Hal Chase. In all likelihood, Farrell had established an understanding with Ban Johnson.

All told, Stallings spent an hour and a half in Farrell's office. They broke for lunch at noon—Stallings went out to lunch alone—and resumed the conference at two o'clock. At three, Farrell ended the meeting, saying he had to catch the Lake Shore Limited, leaving at 5:30 for Cleveland, where he would assist the league president in conducting an investigation.

Learning this, Stallings asked Farrell's permission to accompany him, insisting it was only just that he, as the accuser, should be present when Chase was questioned. Farrell refused.

When reporters asked the Yankees owner if he'd arrived at any conclusion after conferring with his manager, Farrell waved off the question: "The matter is in abeyance," he said. "I have no statement to make at this time."

Shortly after arriving at the Colonial Hotel in Cleveland, Farrell, his oyster-pouchy eyes betraying an air of weariness, called the players together (except for Hal Chase) for an open meeting. His greeting was polite, even affable, although his look was grim and a little oily.

"Men," he said, "I've come to you in an attempt to untangle the threads of the controversy we've all been involved in. To this end, I'd like to hear from each of you about the charges and counter charges made by Manager Stallings and Captain Chase, particularly about Mr. Chase's so-called questionable performances on the field."

Farrell had raised uncomfortable questions, and the glum-looking bunch facing him behaved like wallpaper, staring in taut silence, not knowing what to think, glancing from one to the other, looking up at the ceiling, each waiting for someone else to say something.

All appeared embarrassed. Confused emotions surged up in them. One man stared down at the Stetson between his fingers and turned it around and around and around. A long interval passed. Nothing. No expressions for or against either man. Everything remained beneath the surface. They weren't going to talk.

One burly man, untroubled by the ownership of much of a brain, heaved himself to his feet, cleared his throat loudly and, a bit hesitantly, surprised everyone: "Mr. Farrell ... Maybe ... " He paused ... "Sir," a slight discomfort in his voice, "if," he hesitated, "you take each man aside and speak to him separately, you'll get the individual opinions you're looking for."

Private conversations did indeed loosen tongues and offer new details. As one might expect, the players took sides, but they found themselves in an awkward position. If they sided with Stallings, whom most had grown to appreciate, and Chase heard about it, they could expect hostility from Chase, whom they now understood would be named manager, if not immediately, certainly at the end of the season.

At first Farrell did not believe there was a substantial basis for Stallings's allegations, but the remarks of the players during the individual interviews threw him into confusion. Most supported Stallings's claims. A good number of them believed Chase had deliberately thrown games and done his best to discredit Stallings as manager. A very few sided with Chase.

At 10 that evening Ban Johnson arrived in Cleveland, hauling a considerable paunch, and immediately went into session with Frank Farrell and Charles Somers (owner of the Cleveland ball club and the league's vice president). Somers and Farrell briefed Johnson on the status of the investigation. Much turned on what the powerful American League president had to say.

Malice remained Johnson's animating impulse. Though the evidence backed the Yankees manager, the small-minded Johnson, a megalomaniac, judgmental and dismissive, rejected the players' testimony as ungrounded. Frowning with impatience, he played down their statements, his voice rising to a roar. "The assertions are unprovable. There is no irrefutable proof, only an array of indirect evidence. . . . New York must make a change of managers." This was his position, and he refused to budge.

Displaying a remarkable lack of character, Frank Farrell caved in to Johnson's demands and accepted orders without disagreement.

There were a number of reasons for Farrell's reluctance to tangle with the president of the American League. The Yankees owner badly needed Johnson's backing in a pending lawsuit filed against him by his former friend and business partner, Joseph Gordon. Gordon asserted in court documents that he owned 20 percent of the stock in the New York franchise and was entitled to 20 percent of the profits.

The charges were serious, the stakes high. Of that there was no doubt. Other than the legal issues involved, Ban Johnson's testimony would weigh heavily in the case. So Farrell, though skilled in circumventing the law, badly needed President Johnson's support. He did not dare oppose the big poohbah. If he did, he might pay dearly.

Joseph Gordon was not just some artful opportunist. An old-time baseball man, once associated with John B. Day of the American Association's New York Metropolitans, Gordon had been prominent in the game for 25 years. Court documents demonstrated how he conceived the strategy to bring an American League franchise into New York, and how he approached a number of possible investors about the plan, Frank Farrell being one of them.

A man of means, Farrell was said to be the operator of 200 illegal gambling establishments in the city. Though he had no experience in baseball affairs, he expressed an interest in the venture and agreed to furnish the financial backing for the enterprise ($140,000 in cash), if Gordon, known for his political clout, could meet four conditions: (1) secure membership in the American League, (2) locate a site for the ballpark, (3) hire the players, and (4) assume the executive responsibilities of running the ball club. For his contributions in bringing life to the fledgling enterprise, Gordon was promised 20 percent of the stock and 20 percent of the profit once Farrell had been repaid the money he'd invested.

Gordon, the first president and chief executive of the Greater New York Baseball Association (the New York Yankees), worked without pay while Farrell, mindful of protecting his financial interests, assumed the role of treasurer. "I didn't propose to let anyone carve me if I went into this thing," he remarked while testifying in court. "I controlled the financial end of it."

Seizing the opportunity in a world of lies, Ban Johnson welcomed the arrangement, using Joseph Gordon as a front man for the sleazy Farrell. It was all about money and deceit. New York would be a titanic struggle, and Johnson was afraid the American League might not succeed in the "Big Town" without the financial staying power of a wealthy supporter like Frank Farrell. His participation assured success.

Gordon took the position in documents filed in court that Farrell had gotten back all the money he'd invested in the enterprise by 1906. "The business is of great value," the complaint stated, "with large profits; the approximate receipts for the 1907 season were about $240,000. There have already been five seasons with the annual cost of operations about $80,000, and the net receipts over and above such costs have been large, and far exceed the money put in by the defendant Farrell."

After Farrell had been repaid from the ball club's hefty profits, his attorneys advised him to rid himself of Gordon, make Gordon the club's vice president, and assume the role of president himself. Unknown to Gordon, Farrell had capitalized the franchise at $200,000 ($7,166,000 in today's dollars) in 1903, and secretly issued himself most of the stock.

Four years later, following a plan laid out by his lawyer, Abram Elkus, Farrell raised questions about Gordon's judgment and performance and essentially pushed him out of the business, removing Gordon's name as president of the ball club from American League Park and from the team's stationery, setting the stage for a complicated lawsuit.

The legal dispute bounced around the courts for over four years before it reached the New York State Supreme Court in November 1911.

Farrell sat poker-faced on the witness stand and chose his words carefully in dismissing his former chief executive's claims as baseless, and worked hard at discrediting and destroying Gordon's credibility. "Gordon had nothing to do with organizing the association [franchise]," Farrell said, "and was not entitled to any profits. . . . He was simply a friend and was permitted to assist the owner in small details in which I in return permitted

Gordon to style himself as president, and gave him the run of the grounds until he made himself a nuisance and was ordered away."

Ban Johnson defended Farrell's actions, admitting that Gordon had negotiated with him for placing an American League club in New York, but he (Johnson) insisted on "seeing the man with the money." Gordon brought Farrell to Johnson's rooms at the Criterion Hotel, where, according to Johnson, Farrell asked if it would be necessary to divide the profit with anyone else if he were to finance the New York ball club. Johnson told Farrell, in Gordon's presence, that he (Farrell) would be the sole owner if he put up the money.

Judge Henry Bischoff struggled to decide whether there was enough circumstantial evidence to sort out the confusion during the following six weeks. He pressed both sides for more solid evidence. Then he waited. And waited. And waited. When none was forthcoming, Judge Bischoff issued his ruling:

> I am asked to find the fact of the contract, in the conflicting testimony of both parties, the plaintiff asserting that it was orally entered into and the defendant being equally emphatic in his denial. . . . Not a scrap of writing is introduced in evidence for or against the contract, and so far, therefore, the matter is evenly balanced. . . .
>
> That plaintiff aided the defendant in launching the enterprise is not disputed. Indeed the defendant concedes that he owes the plaintiff for the latter's services. . . .
>
> I am not persuaded by the evidence that any contract or partnership or joint venture existed between the parties as alleged in the complaint and therefore direct the dismissal of the complaint.

Information about Hal Chase's brazen and unseemly behavior was suppressed as being absurd; the facts given the press were controlled; and answers to questions were put together beforehand to produce the desired results. Ban Johnson was willing to go to great lengths to keep up appearances and preserve the myth of purity in big-league baseball, rather than expose anything wormy in the seamy underbelly of the game.

The twisted drama reached its climax at half past midnight on September 25 in Cleveland, when the weary figure of Ban Johnson emerged alone from behind closed doors and addressed reporters. "We have reached an understanding," he said, "but it's up to Mr. Farrell to make an official announcement of his plans."

Treating the Yankee manager the way a dog treats a fire hydrant, Johnson denounced the charges as unfounded and seized the opportunity to paint Stallings as a rogue manager. "He has utterly failed in his accusations against Chase," Johnson told reporters gathered around him. "Anyone who knows Hal Chase knows he is not guilty of the charges brought by Stallings, and I'm happy to say that the evidence of the New York players . . . showed Stallings up."

Frank Farrell's decision had been made for him by Ban Johnson. Stallings must step down at once. Hal Chase would replace him as manager.

A wall of skepticism greeted Johnson's statement. One reporter, who could not contain a smug smile, pointedly asked if the investigators had arrived at an objective decision. Another, his voice heavy with sarcasm, railed against the role played in the investigation by "the old boy network." A third wondered if the decision hadn't been arranged beforehand.

Johnson's pink-and-white jowly face swung quickly in the direction of each of the questioners, suppressed rage boiling inside him. Undeterred by the disposition of the press to doubt his words, he brushed off the unfavorable remarks, refused to divulge any details, and termed the hearing private. His neck reddening, he abruptly rejected the reporter's insinuations and branded the inkslinger's remarks as "utterly absurd," saying, "There will be no other announcements tonight."

Stallings's defenders in the press, and there were many, offered a good deal of support. "There was a prearranged plan to 'get' Stallings," the *St. Louis Post-Dispatch* editorialized, "although what the reason may have been has not yet slipped from the Sphinx-like lips of Ban Johnson."

"It is known positively," the *Evening Sun* stated, "that Stallings' removal was determined weeks ago."

A statement in the *Sporting News* was perhaps the most telling of all. It called the firing "a lasting disgrace to American League politics."

Readers can draw their own conclusions.

Frank Farrell waited until noon the following day before telephoning George Stallings at the Hotel Wolcott and asking if he'd come over.[*]

---

[*] On the night of April 18, 1912, the Hotel Wolcott took in many of the affluent survivors from the *Titanic*, three days after the sinking.

That Stallings's ties with the Yankees would be formally severed was understood. He refused to feel sorry for himself; like it or not, he simply had to accept the inevitability of it. The big fellow arrived a half hour later and entered through a side door unobserved by the crush of reporters waiting in the outer offices.

The meeting was brief (30 minutes) and not unfriendly. Stallings offered his resignation and it was accepted. Farrell handed him a check for the remainder of his salary through the end of the season; Stallings was then whisked out through the same door by which he'd entered.

Minutes later, Farrell strode into the adjoining room where the press corps had gathered and made the formal announcement: "Hal Chase has been signed to manage the Greater New York Baseball Club," he said. "He will succeed George T. Stallings." Farrell paused and glanced around the room before continuing. "After a thorough investigation I have found the charges against Hal Chase to be absolutely unfounded. I presented the evidence to Byron B. Johnson, the President of the American League, and he decided the matter. Beyond this I have nothing to say." He turned and left the room.

A few minutes later a band of reporters caught up with Stallings in the lobby of the Hotel Wolcott. "I don't care to say anything," he said, a poignant half smile breaking out across his face. "I'm out of a job and Chase is the new manager. That's all the fans want to know . . . So what's the use of talking?"

The reporters kept after him, firing question after question, all focused on the shabby treatment he'd received. After a while Stallings loosened up a bit and made a few brief comments. He was especially bitter about the way Johnson had blurred perceptions of guilt and innocence, and he confirmed that Johnson had indeed wielded the shiv that forced him out as manager of the Yankees.

He looked around at the boys, many of whom were friends, sighed deeply and said with dry-eyed dignity, "I'll tell you one thing here and now. I firmly believe that every charge I made against Hal Chase will be substantiated. You guys will see . . . Right now Mr. Farrell chooses not to believe my accusations. He's not convinced. But mark my words." He paused for dramatic emphasis. "In time he will find out the charges are absolutely true."

PART II

CHAPTER 18

THE FIRST REAL GEM

George Stallings brought the Boston Braves instant gravitas.

His first move?

Hiring Fred Mitchell.

Fred Mitchell? you say. A backup catcher? A part-time coach? Why Fred Mitchell? That doesn't make sense.

"I wanted brains," Stallings said. "You won't find a better teacher or communicator than Fred Mitchell." "Mitch" shared Stallings's vision. The Big Chief credited him with having turned the Yankees' pitching staff into the best in the league in 1910 when the two worked together in New York.

Smooth-featured, square-jawed, with an ever-impending five-o'clock shadow, the kind that needs a shave twice a day, Fred Mitchell was dedicated and dependable while playing the role of the devoted mentee, one of those stolid self-effacing individuals who stand on the sidelines, content to watch others bask in the glory of their accomplishments.

"Mitch was tireless," Stallings said. "Kind and approachable; he had a world of patience. Young pitchers loved him. He would slip on a big glove and take the young man off to a corner of the lot where they could be alone and no one could overhear his comments. Then he'd quietly talk to the man about his faults, never once getting after him roughly." The Braves manager cracked a smile and added, "He left the rough stuff to me."

When the Big Chief accepted the Braves' offer, he insisted on taking Mitchell, the Bisons' first-string catcher, with him as his second-in-command, leaving Buffalo without an experienced receiver. Desperate for catching, the Bisons' front office asked that Stallings lend them Hank Gowdy, a two-year major-league veteran with some experience behind the plate. This was fine with the Chief, so long as the Buffalo manager, Bill Clymer, a former catcher himself, agreed to play Gowdy regularly and smooth out some of his rough edges, enough of them, at least, to make Gowdy more valuable as trade bait.

Gowdy performed with passion and conviction, and the everyday discipline of handling different styles of pitching became second nature to him. He matured as a catcher, caught 87 games and batted a sparkling .317. Not bad for a player thought of as trade bait.

Hank was much improved as a late-season call-up in 1913, light-years ahead of where he'd been in previous appearances in the majors. Yet he was still viewed as a player useful only in attracting offers from other teams, that is, until the phone on George Stallings's desk jangled on a gray winter morning during the off-season. "What?" the Big Chief bellowed at the top of his lungs, his face reddening. He listened, slammed down the receiver, and snarled, "That no good son of a bitch. Bankbooks were always his favorite reading. The money-mad bastard."

The Braves' regular catcher, Bill Rariden, had defected, signing a three-year contract with the Indianapolis Hoosiers of the upstart Federal League for $6,000 a year. Who could blame him? The Hoosiers doubled what the Braves were offering.*

It was back to the blackboard. The Braves needed a catcher. But who? There weren't many around. Not good ones, anyway. Gowdy would have to do until a replacement could be found. And Stallings was not pleased.

Gowdy gangled. He made "gangling" a verb. His head appeared to have no more than a nodding familiarity with his neck, and his hands always looked as if they were about to fall off his wrists. It's no wonder that Stallings was on the lookout for another catcher.

Early in the autumn of 1913, the Big Chief went after several talented youngsters from the Northwestern League, Bill James, Bert "Moose" Whaling, and Les Mann of the Seattle Giants, each highly recommended

---

* The Federal League, a third major league, presented a formidable threat to the future of organized baseball. The Feds had some "big hitters" behind them, wealthy men like Harry Sinclair, said to have a net worth of more than $50 million ($1.6 billion in today's dollars). "I'll stand on the Battery" (the tip of Manhattan Island), Sinclair once boasted, "and take on any of the major-league owners in pitching dollars into the sea. We'll see who quits first." At the 1936 Kentucky Derby, during the height of the Great Depression, Harry Sinclair wagered $500,000 on the race ($11.5 million in today's dollars), and the horse—named Brevity—lost by a nose.

by umpire Amos Rusie, a former big-league pitching star and future Hall of Famer.

James seemed to have the most potential. Lean and lanky and all muscle at 6'3", 200 pounds, Bill looked like the real thing. His battery mate, Moose Whaling, was also a steal. Though only average with the bat and slow on the bases, Moose was almost flawless behind the plate during the 1912 season (seven errors in 138 games) and threw out 188 would-be base stealers.

Buffalo, aware of Stallings's high regard for Les Mann, grabbed the speedy outfielder in the September minor-league draft, before Stallings could complete a deal for him. Stallings chalked up the loss as an unfortunate missed opportunity. James and Whaling turned out to be an ideal fit for the Braves and were soon hounding their boss about Les Mann. "Get him at any cost," they would say. "He'll add lightning speed to the lineup and solve our outfield problems."

A juggernaut of energy, Les Mann began his diamond career at the age of 14, when he won a spot on the Girard Cycle Indians, a fast local semipro outfit in Lincoln, Nebraska. Two years later, while still in high school, he turned pro, played third base, and batted .292 for the Nebraska City Foresters of the Missouri-Iowa-Nebraska-Kansas League, a Class D circuit popularly known as the Mink League. His second season in professional ball was even more successful: he averaged .328 in 95 games for the Foresters and looked like a real comer.

The Northwestern League was a different story.

Home to a quarter of a million inhabitants in 1912, Seattle was a cosmopolitan port city whose claims to fame were bay views, forested hills, rain—lots of rain—damp, drizzly, overcast days, an environment totally alien to a 19-year-old brought up on the barren, sun-swept, rolling hills of the Nebraska prairie. Les Mann's start was hardly promising. He couldn't find his stroke and failed to fulfill expectations; his average hovered around .250 over the first half of the season.

"Quit worrying," teammates told him. "Settle down. Forget the weather. You'll get used to it. You don't tan in Seattle, you rust."

When the skies widened into pools of blue in late summer, the sparkling days of August ignited Mann's bat: he hit safely in 45 of 52 games, 81 hits in 200 at bats, a screaming .405 pace. By the season's end, his improbable heroics raised his average to a respectable .300. And he blasted a record-tying 23 home runs as well. With Mann's hot bat leading the way, Seattle swept its way to the Northwestern League title.

Buffalo wanted two players and cash for Mann, a huge demand, considering that a few months earlier they'd paid only $750 for him in the minor-league draft. Stallings vacillated and vacillated before finally agreeing to a two-for-one swap and cash.

Trying to live up to expectations, Les put too much pressure on himself, grew increasingly desperate, went cold, and floundered badly. With the Braves desperately struggling to score runs, "Cy" Seymour replaced Mann in the lineup, and writers thought the kid would drift back to the minors and disappear. That wasn't what Stallings had in mind. Les Mann was the best outfielder on the team. He had tremendous range, and the Big Chief felt that, given time, Les would relax, gain confidence, and show what he was capable of doing.

To this end, the Braves' manager platooned his outfielders and used Les exclusively against left-handed pitching. This did the trick. Les overcame his uncertainty, settled down, and learned that you shouldn't try to put certain pitches into play, that swinging at them was like giving away an at bat. His confidence soared. So did his average. It peaked at .291 in mid-August.

The Braves got their first big break in signing an exceptional talent when Fred Mitchell ran into Dick Rudolph on a train bound for spring training. It had been four years since the former teammates had seen each other, and Mitch was astonished by the unending flow of diatribes that poured from Rudolph's mouth.

"I won't go back to Toronto at my old salary," he told Mitchell, "or submit to a cut in pay after the way I pitched last season." (He won 25 games.) "My record entitles me to something more. If I don't get a chance now, I'm quitting."

Mitchell tried talking some sense into him. "Don't be too hasty," he advised. "Report for spring training. Get in shape. Maybe the Braves will be interested. I'll talk to George when I get to Macon."

Stallings was aware of Rudolph's work in the International League. In 1910 the Chief had attempted to acquire the Toronto hurler for the Yankees but didn't complete the deal. The asking price was too high. It was the New York Giants who met the Maple Leafs' demands. Rudolph was thrilled. Playing for John McGraw was a dream come true for a Bronx boy. The deal brought him to the promised land, the Polo Grounds. But he was a washout and was sent back to the minors. No one would touch the kid after that. Now and then a scout on the trail of a young prospect would appear in Toronto and Rudolph would point out that he, Dick Rudolph, had won 20 games in each of the previous five seasons. The scout would shrug and say, "What can I do? If McGraw canned you, the powers that be think there must be something wrong with you." Rudolph was trapped in the system.

Standing in front of his locker in the Toronto clubhouse before his first start of 1913, Rudolph turned to his manager, Joe Kelly, and said, "Joe, this is it. I won't be back. If I can't get any higher than the minor leagues, I'm going to try some other profession."

Rudolph was impressive that afternoon: he pitched a three-hitter and lost 1–0, the run coming on an infield hit, two ground outs, and a second infield hit. Immediately after the game he bid his teammates goodbye, turned in his uniform, and left the Maple Leafs for good. That same evening Mitchell called, and Rudolph learned that Toronto was demanding a fortune for him. They were trying to hold up the Braves. "Sit tight," Mitchell told him. "I'll get back to you. Whatever you do, don't go back. We'll force their hand."

When it became evident that "Rudy" was indeed gone, and that he was adamant about not rejoining the Maple Leafs, the secrecy surrounding the reasons for his long stay in Toronto came to light. The Giants, as it turned out, owned Rudy's contract. Jim McCaffey, the Maple Leafs' owner, wired Stallings and suggested a trade: a starting pitcher and $5,000 in cash. Stallings pointed out that McCaffey was going to lose Rudolph, one way or the other; Toronto might just as well sell him to Boston and get something for him. McCaffey placed a hurried call to John McGraw. McGraw agreed to the deal.

And, of all things, Rudolph refused to report. "No way," he said. "Not without a guarantee in writing that I won't be sent back to the minors."

Days passed.

Three weeks into the season, the Braves arrived in New York for a weekend series with the Dodgers. On Sunday, an off-day, Stallings telephoned Rudolph up in the Bronx: "Can we meet at the Hotel Somerset at 150 West 47th Street," he asked, "and talk things over?"

They met late that afternoon and Rudolph insisted on the guarantee that he would not be sent to the minors. Nothing less. "The kid had moxie," Stallings said. "He was not the type to back off from anything." A risk-taker himself, George shook his head, laughed, showed all of his teeth in an enormous grin, and held out his hand. Rudy got the guarantee.

◆◆◆

A week before the 1913 season opened, Joe Connolly's name appeared on the waiver list (the right to purchase the contract of another team's player at a stipulated price). Joey was being shipped back to the minors by the Washington Senators. "He's a fair player," manager Clark Griffith remarked, "but he'd be too old by the time I taught him anything."

Did Griffith know that Connolly had changed his baptismal name? That for years he'd misled people about his age? . . . Probably.

The son of Irish immigrants, Joey was born on a farm on the outskirts of North Smithfield, Rhode Island, on Friday, February 1, 1884. Eight days later, according to official records of the Rhode Island State Archives, he was christened Joseph Francis Connolly at St. James Catholic Church in nearby Manville.

Years later, in an attempt to escape the grim, harsh, exhausting routine of farm life and fulfill his boyhood dream of playing big-league baseball, Joey lied about his age, changed his middle name to Aloysius, and broke into professional ball, splitting the 1904 season between the New Bedford Whalers and the pennant-winning Haverhill Hustlers of the Class B New England League. He was 20 years old at the time.

George from Georgia had seen Connolly's bat at work for the Montreal Royals of the International League. The kid could hit. The kid could really hit. And Stallings quickly snapped up Connolly for the waiver price. Joey joined the Braves on their way north from spring training, took over in left field, won the job, and was hitting a solid .281 in late September, when he broke an ankle sliding into second base.

The Braves' roster was a work in progress in 1913, a shifting cast of characters, 45 in all. Of the 23 players on the ball club, only six were carryovers from the previous season: Otto Hess, "Rabbit" Maranville, "Hub" Perdue, Bill Rariden, Bill Sweeney, and George Tyler.

To think that a team with so many new faces was going to jell right away would have been overly optimistic. Not even Stallings's system could reverse years of mediocrity that easily. Dogged by the fates, the Braves started the 1913 season much like a car spinning its wheels in the mud of April showers. They couldn't get much traction and got off to a slow 2–9 start.

But they righted themselves, made modest progress, and took a doubleheader from the New York Giants at South End Grounds in Boston, something they'd not done in four years. "Boston caught me off guard," a shocked

John McGraw said. "It wouldn't surprise me to see them . . . on top of the second division before the season is over."

Stallings filled a pressing need at first base when he acquired "Butch" Schmidt in a six-player deal with the Rochester Hustlers of the International League. Rochester, worried about losing its best players for pennies in the September minor-league draft, offered the Braves an attractive package: pitcher Jack Quinn, center fielder Guy Zinn, and first baseman Butch Schmidt, in exchange for Art Devlin, cash, and two players to be named later. (Quinn, Zinn, and Schmidt had played for Stallings in 1910.) The key figure in the transaction was Schmidt. The handsome giant was the kind of defensive first baseman Stallings had been looking for.

Stallings's search for an answer at third base ended with the 1913 draft, when he acquired Charlie Deal, a former major leaguer at Detroit who had blossomed into a star in the International League. The former Tiger batted a solid .312 for the Providence Grays, and he put on a good show at third base when he was brought up by the Braves at the tail end of the season, averaging an impressive .316 at the plate.

Now the table was set for 1914.

CHAPTER 19

HE TALKED HIMSELF OUT OF MORE BALL GAMES

Easily recognizable, Braves manager George Stallings's bearlike walk and Cubs manager Johnny Evers's chiseled profile turned heads in February 1914 as they walked under the glittering porte cochere of the Waldorf Hotel in New York, one of the grandest hostelries in the world.

A pack of reporters intercepted the two baseball celebrities just inside the entrance. The local scribes liked the Big Chief. They liked his aura of baseball savvy. Liked the way he treated them. Stallings had done an outstanding job as Yankee manager, having turned a last-place club into a contender in two seasons, and the press's high regard for him had not diminished in the three years he'd been gone.

"Where do you think you'll finish this season, George? Will your boys contend?"

Stallings stopped, unbuttoned his overcoat, plunged both hands into the pockets of his tweed jacket, and turned on his good-fellow smile.

"Oh, I don't know about the pennant, boys," he said, a twinkle in his eye. "I'll tell you what, though . . . we'll finish higher than we did last year. Which means the first division."

"What's the word with you, Johnny?" another asked. "How do you feel looking back at your rookie managerial season?"

"Well," Evers said, "I came here with the idea in my mind that I had a pretty successful summer. A successful winter, too." Johnny was proud of what he'd accomplished. The Chicago Cubs came on fast in 1913—chalked up 88 wins and finished one game out of second place. Not bad for a team chosen by most experts to finish in the second division.

"What do you mean, John, when you say, 'successful winter, too'?"

"Oh . . . well . . . Back in December and early January, there was some danger of several of our guys signing with the Feds. My former partner at shortstop, Joe Tinker, was working for them, trying to sign some of our old teammates. I traveled around the country, from Florida to Tennessee, signing them up. Eleven days on the road. Ten nights on a sleeper. No fun. But it was worth it. Murphy even complimented me."

Stallings glanced up and down Peacock Alley, took in faces, smiled, and approached a happy gathering of baseball notables. Some were there to see, others to be seen. He shambled toward a group gathered around the popular Wilbert Robinson, the Dodgers' new manager, a former star of the famed Baltimore Orioles. Along the way, he stopped for a laugh here, a handshake there, slapping backs, putting friendly hands on shoulders, smiling and waving at everyone until he spotted Miller "Hug" Huggins, the Cardinals' manager. He gave Hug a big smile and an airy wave, and Hug smiled back. A few days earlier Stallings had proposed a trade. The deal fell through. No harm keeping the door open. Stallings headed toward Hug for a confab.

Upstairs, in Sun Parlor F, the assembled National League owners had just begun their annual meeting. They were listening to a report from Governor John Tener, the league's newly elected president. The governor was telling them what lay ahead.

A range of strong emotions filled the room. Happiness over past profits was muted by deep concern about baseball's future, particularly among the owners from Chicago, Pittsburgh, and St. Louis, cities that had been invaded by the outlaw Federal League. The possibility of the Feds succeeding as a third major league threatened the very existence of organized baseball as they knew it.

Seeking a cooperative effort in the face of the impending conflict, the governor laid out a proposal for the appointment of the three-member "war committee." The motion passed unanimously.

Veteran umpire Hank O'Day provided the big surprise of the afternoon when he requested a release from his umpiring contract so he could manage the Chicago Cubs. Somewhat taken aback, members of the board turned to Cubs owner Charlie Murphy for an explanation.

Murphy explained. He'd had serious differences with Johnny Evers and Evers resigned.

❖❖❖

While chatting with Miller Huggins, Stallings spotted Jim Gaffney coming down the main staircase. The clock in the corridor struck half past five. That's strange, Stallings thought to himself. The meeting isn't over yet. What's Jim doing down here? For a fleeting second his eyes met Gaffney's, and with a slight lift of the eyebrows, the Braves owner, almost imperceptibly, nodded toward Evers. Stallings's eyes followed the boss as he approached Johnny. Something peculiar was happening.

"Murphy says you resigned, John. Says O'Day is replacing you."

Evers's face colored. Incredulous surprise filled his eyes. He stared at Gaffney. Glanced around the room at the faces watching them. Then looked at Gaffney. "I didn't resign, Jim," he said, his voice choked. "If it's true that O'Day has been appointed in my place . . . " He hesitated, bit his lower lip, and shook his head. "I've been fired."

"So that's what's been going on up there," Gaffney said. "He let you go."

"Looks like it."

Gaffney looked directly at Evers. "John," he said.

"What?"

"Will you play for O'Day?"

Evers eyed Gaffney, his mouth a tight line, looking like he wanted to punch out somebody. "No," he said. "No. I'll never play for Murphy. I'll never play for that bastard again. Never."

Reporters, pads and pencils in hand, crowded around.

Gaffney and Stallings exchanged meaningful glances. Gaffney excused himself and worked his way through the crowded room toward Stallings. The two men leaned close, heads together, and covered their mouths. "Get Evers at any cost," Stallings whispered. "Make a deal."

Gaffney stepped back, his eyes flashing a grin. Back upstairs he went. As the afternoon session neared its close, Gaffney put an arm around Charlie Murphy's shoulder and offered the Cubs owner $25,000 in cash for Evers. Murphy was agreeable. Cash would not do it though. The Cubs needed players.

"That's fine," Gaffney said. "I'll talk to George. We'll work something out. I'll get back to you." They shook on it.

Johnny Evers was a star, not because he was a gold-glove fielder and a terror with the bat; he was a star because he was jaggedly smart, a player who knew how to win, and he did win. An incendiary presence, the querulous

Evers was the kind of competitor opponents loved to hate: abrasive, abusive, belligerent, an athlete who "took nothing from nobody—never." Something of a cross between a mob enforcer and a demented megaphone man, he feuded with everyone, talked all the time, and had an opinion about everything, especially about each and every ball pitched to him. His anger was all-consuming, and he never hesitated to toss his glove in the air or slam his cap on the ground, although these antics normally meant a quick shower.

Johnny talked himself out of more games than any player in major-league history. He even got himself thrown out of a game after an umpire awarded him a base on balls, on a called ball four. "See," he said. "That last one was a strike. That's what I've been telling you . . . you fathead . . . You've been missing them all afternoon."

While Miller Huggins of the Cardinals was batting in the third inning of a game one afternoon, Evers, playing on the infield grass near second base, expressed displeasure at the way umpire Cy Rigler was calling balls and strikes. They got into an argument. Shouting across the infield, Evers called Rigler a "fathead" and a lot of other things, and suggested that Rigler put on a Cardinals uniform so the fans wouldn't confuse him with a real umpire. Out of the game he went.

"The Cubs were always fighting and wrangling among themselves," Ty Cobb recalled, a trace of awe in his voice. (Keep in mind that Cobb could be among the meanest of them all.) "Twice I played against the Cubs in the World Series. Their tactics were the most aggressive of any team I'd ever seen. They were always crabbing. I thought there would be several fistfights among them, because of the vicious names they called each other. But how they did play ball together."

The Cubs' infield of Harry Steinfeldt, Joe Tinker, Johnny Evers, and Frank Chance was one of the best in major-league history, and the iron-willed Evers was its heartbeat, in spite of his sandpaper personality.

Reporters hanging around the Cubs' front office in the Corn Exchange Building in Chicago jumped to their feet when a telegram arrived. "What's up?" "Is it from Murphy?" "Something happen in New York?"

Charlie Thomas, the Cubs' secretary, nodded affirmatively. "See for yourselves," he said, holding out the telegram. It read: "The announcement made today that Henry O'Day is to manage the Chicago Cubs came as a great surprise, but it was well received in baseball circles."

"Holy smoke!" someone said. "What a story!" Johnny Evers, the idol of West Side fans, the best second baseman in the National League—bounced. The reporters rushed for the door.

"Wait a minute. Wait a minute," Thomas shouted after them. "I've got more for you." He opened a desk drawer and pulled out a stack of typed statements, dated the following day. Eager hands grabbed them. It wasn't a press release. The document took the form of an interview, a familiar gimmick Murphy employed, an interview with himself, written by himself.

Murphy had been rattling on for weeks about the Cubs' loss to the White Sox in the 1913 intracity series. In Murphy's mind, the Chicago City Series was just as important as the World Series. After all, the Cubs and White Sox drew 153,920 fans in the City Championship Series, slightly more than the Athletics and Giants drew in the World Series. "The Cubs should have swept the White Sox," Murphy said. "Instead, they blew the series to a second-division team." It was the third time in three years that the White Sox had beaten the Cubs for the City Championship.

CHAPTER 20

DAMN THAT MAN

Facing reporters early that evening, Evers's chin shot out, as was his habit when angry. A torrent of animosity poured from his lips, leaving no doubt about what he thought of Charlie Murphy's boorish behavior. "There is nothing I hate more," Evers said, "than having to kowtow to a blowhard." He laughed, a harsh derisive snort.

"I don't feel so bad about losing my job . . . but it's awfully hard holding in all the dirt I know about that brass-balled motherfucker." So far as Evers was concerned, Murphy was no better than public enemy number one on the FBI's most-wanted list.

Then, interrupting himself, he launched into the details of Murphy's front-office machinations as if enumerating them from a list: How Murphy routinely mutilated the truth. How Murphy refused to allow any significant move without prior approval. How Murphy overrode managerial decisions, putting him (Evers) at odds with players who suspected, correctly, that he did not have control of the team.

Talking a blue streak, Evers explained. "My first real battle with Murphy came right after the City Championship Series with the White Sox. Murphy tore into me for allowing the pitcher to bat instead of sending up a pinch hitter. He called it 'bad baseball,' said getting beat by the Sox cost him at least $50,000 in cash. 'That wasn't bad baseball,' I told him. 'Connie Mack made the same decision against the Giants in the World Series.'"

Evers scoffed belligerently. "Murphy kept harping on the loss of the City Series, and the amount of money it cost him. I asked him how much money he figured my play in 1908 was worth? When I got Merkle out for not touching second base, and the Cubs beat out the Giants and won the pennant. He said he failed to reckon it. He asked how much I thought it was worth. I said a quarter of a million dollars. He replied, 'Well, yes, I guess that's about right.'"

Much like a dysfunctional couple in a troubled marriage, Murphy and Evers were always at each other's throats, quarreling, finding fault with each other, trading insults. No quarrel was too petty for them.

Heated exchanges, disagreements, and altercations with players and key personnel also marred Evers's tenure as manager. From the day spring training in Tampa began until the season ended with the Cubs' loss in the Chicago City Series, the club's veteran players ridiculed Evers's every move.

Yet it might have been a near riot at West Side Grounds, provoked in large part by Evers himself, that undermined his tenure as manager and led to his departure. Mounted police had to be called in to quell the disturbance, and it was only a matter of luck that someone wasn't crushed in the melee. With six weeks remaining in the season, Murphy decided to seize the opportunity and dismiss Evers as manager.

But an odd coincidence saved Johnny's job. Journalistic bulldog Irving Vaughn of the *Chicago Tribune* got wind of Murphy's intention to fire Evers and leaked the story in an exclusive article.

Murphy detested Vaughn and reacted accordingly. "No damn numbskull writer can tell me when to fire my manager," he roared, and Johnny finished the season.

Evers found the prospect of managing the Cubs under the threat of instant dismissal humiliating, and he became increasingly troubled by Murphy's mood swings. So he asked him if he'd amend the managerial contract and agree not to override his (Evers's) orders any longer and make it more equitable for both himself and the club. Murphy appeared agreeable and set a date. On the appointed day, Murphy telephoned and told Mrs. Evers he couldn't make it. No new date was set.

Gossips claimed Evers was hanging onto the job by the tips of his fingers and predicted that he'd be dropped when convenient. Evers ignored the talk. After all, he felt that he and Murphy had resolved their differences—the boss had tacitly agreed not to override Johnny's orders any longer. To make certain of this, Evers sent Murphy a letter in which he reminded the boss of the items he wanted stricken from the contract. Murphy did not reply.

❖❖❖

Minutes after the afternoon meeting of the National League owners adjourned, Johnny cornered Governor John Tener, the league president, and asked if he might see him in private for a few minutes.

"Certainly, John. For an hour if you like." An Irish giant, born in the old country (County Tyrone), the well-dressed governor of Pennsylvania was a charismatic, fiftyish man, 6'4" and 270 pounds. He stood a head above everyone else in the room. The elephantine Tener put an arm around Evers and conspiratorially lowered his head in an effort at giving them some privacy.

"What I've got on my mind," Evers said, "is frankly confidential."

Together they made their way through the chattering, laughing crowd until they reached a quiet place where they could talk. Evers's mind tracked back and forth as he explained, his words burning with a sense of unfair treatment.

The man's resoluteness surprised the governor. He sensed an explosion brewing while Evers spelled out the relevant facts. The governor listened and raised an eyebrow. After a pause for reflection, he took a deep breath and let it out. He called Murphy's actions "an outrage." Evers was an icon in Chicago. Public sympathy would certainly be on his side. The nasty episode would give the outlaw Federal League an unwanted boost. Worst of all, Evers might join the outlaw league.

Evers claimed he was working under two five-year contracts, one as manager of the Cubs, the other as a player. "Murphy can't fire me from one without releasing me from the other," Evers said. "My lawyer in Troy has read them. 'If I'm dismissed as manager,' he told me, 'I'm dismissed as a player as well.'" He paused. "In other words, I'm a free agent. I'm going to fight for my release."

"I'll tell you what, John," the governor said, "leave the case with me. I haven't seen your contract, but if it is as strong a document as you say it is, I believe the League and the National Commission will see that your rights are honored." The governor promised to put the case before the National Commission that very evening.

After dropping the bomb, Murphy disappeared and was a block away in Herald Square, holed up in one of the three towers of the Hotel McAlpine, having given the front desk strict instructions that he was not to be disturbed.

Late that evening, a gaggle of reporters, having learned of his whereabouts, pounded on the door of Murphy's room.

"I did not get rid of Evers as manager," Murphy said, in an angry response to their questions. "He resigned in a letter I received on the second of February. I simply accepted his resignation. Here," he said, taking the letter from an inside pocket of his suit coat and shoving it in the reporters' faces. "See for yourselves."

The reporters read the letter: "I will not play under any contract," it read, "that gives you the right to do as you said you would do a short time ago," the pertinent sentence read, "and, if necessary, I will not play at all."

"Sounds like you were threatening to bounce him," a reporter said.

"No, no," Murphy said, irritably, in response to the comment, "not at all. The guy's a hothead. Can't you see? He resigned. It's plain as day."

CHAPTER 21

A SYMBOL OF GREED AND SELFISHNESS

Chicago was in an uproar. Twenty thousand Cubs fans took to the streets and signed "Never Again" petitions (hastily printed overnight), pledging they'd never again attend a Cubs game.

At the Waldorf in New York, Murphy, affecting the utmost nonchalance, was busy testing the tolerance of the majordomos of baseball. With a glued-on smile, the Cubs owner unwittingly pushed them to the limits of their patience by flat-out denying Evers's allegations, claiming that he (Murphy) was the one who was being unfairly defamed. Charlie portrayed himself as the victim of a mudslinging campaign. This was his mantra.

As documentary evidence, Murphy submitted Evers's contracts, read aloud from Evers's letter, then leaned back in his chair, put his hands behind his head, intertwined his fingers, and, with a look of self-satisfaction, laughed: "Gentlemen," he said, "that is a letter of resignation if I ever saw one."

Governor Tener bridled at the suggestion. "A man's imagination has to stretch pretty far to construe that as a resignation," he said. "Why, it's nothing more than a note from a man who's upset. A lot of managers write those things."

Murphy was completely unaware of how far from grace he'd fallen among his fellow owners, or what a pariah he'd become, or how much his latest blunder had stirred up old allergies.

The board recognized Murphy's right to fire Evers. In principle, they agreed with him. What bothered them was the timing, the way he'd gone about it. Barney Dreyfuss quizzed Murphy about the flashpoint of the episode: "Did you give him ten days' notice?"

Murphy passed a hand across his chin, gave a sort of suppressed laugh, and confessed that he'd not taken the routine step. He promised he'd do so at once and jotted a note on a pad.

"It seems to me you're in a bit of a fix," Dreyfuss said, not hiding his irritation. The others voiced similar concerns. Murphy acknowledged that he'd probably mishandled it.

Additional questioning brought out fundamental disagreements between Murphy and the other owners. His explanations were often ridiculed, and his honesty came under sharp attack. Banging his fist on the table, Garry Herrmann, president of the Reds, blistered Murphy so loudly that people out in the corridor could hear him. "You've been a monkey wrench in baseball's machinery for years," Herrmann roared, his face carved in pugnacious lines. "You talk too much for your own good, and for the good of baseball. You're always going off half-cocked and stirring up trouble among club owners. You've spoiled the face of America's pastime. You are a sneak and a rat."

Murphy made no comment.

From the day the *Cincinnati Times-Star* hired him as a sportswriter, Charles Webb Murphy, a compulsive self-promoter of the first order, irritated almost everyone he came in contact with, especially his peers. Charles P. Taft, the owner of the *Times-Star*, the brother of William Howard Taft, the future president of the United States, was one of the few individuals who took a liking to Murphy, and Murphy cultivated the relationship.

A small, plump man with a waxlike mustache and slicked-back hair, clever at sparring with words, Charlie Murphy was one of those exasperating characters most people can do without, jokey, annoying, and untroubled by a conscience. Other writers barely tolerated him. They viewed him as a press box pest, loud and unprofessional, and ridiculed the way he rooted for and against players and teams.

They called him "Chubby Charlie," not exactly an endearing name. This didn't faze Murphy one bit. He was happy in Cincinnati. It was the big time. For a young fellow barely out of pharmacy college and a two-dollar-a-week job at Keeshan's drugstore on Vine Street, writing about baseball for a major newspaper and hobnobbing with celebrities was the good life. He wanted more of it and hustled to make things happen.

His big opportunity came at the National League's annual meeting in New York. In those days, the owners seldom made public the nature of their business. If they made any statement at all, it was usually a bare-bones comment, nothing more. But sportswriters needed gossip and human-interest stories for their readers, and they weren't getting any.

While waiting down in the bar of the Fifth Avenue Hotel one afternoon, Murphy decided to liven things up a bit. He stood on a barstool and with a grand sweep of his arm introduced himself as the president of the National League.

"Gentlemen," he said. "I have here the information you desire." Pause for dramatic effect. "The clubs in session were represented by the delegates. The minutes of the last meeting were read and adopted. The pennant was awarded, and there was a unanimous vote in adopting the amendments of the constitution. That's all, gentlemen. Have a good day." It was a remarkably accurate parody.

Chubby Charlie's audience howled and cheered and laughed and raised many a glass in his honor. A few more drinks and a little prodding prepared Murphy for a boozy encore—this time a performance for the owners themselves. In an act of surprising hubris, Murphy, feeling no pain, went upstairs where the league meeting was under way, banged on the door and shouted, "Tell the magnates we have held a meeting in the bar at our own expense and we are going home. Staying here is a waste of our employer's money. We have the news."

The door opened warily. Nervous conversations filled the room with uneasy ill humor as nearsighted eyes peered at Murphy through wire spectacles. Unexpectedly, they invited him in.

Turning on his raffish charm, Murphy embraced the opportunity. Baseball writers, he explained, were sent to the annual meeting by their newspapers for gossip, something juicy for the home folks. The owners' stance of not releasing anything newsworthy put them at a disadvantage. "You're not giving us any news," Murphy said. "Don't you realize how much it would help baseball if you'd give us something worthwhile we could write about?"

Eyebrows went up. Heads nodded. Maybe there was something to what the man was saying. Profits might get a healthy boost. The lines of communication opened.

Sometime later John T. Brush, owner of the New York Giants, a devious, dried-up little man of 60, who admired Murphy's initiative (Charlie had known Mr. Brush from the days when Brush owned the Cincinnati Reds), offered him a job as the Giants' press agent and director of publicity. It was a good fit. The same likable humor and natural wit that earned Murphy the friendship of Charles Taft, won the approval of the Giants' owner. Murphy was one of the few men alive who could put a smile on Mr. Brush's dour, frostbitten face.

Murphy kept the sports pages of New York's daily and Sunday papers filled with news about the Giants. When nothing of interest was available, he'd make something up. It wasn't long before a reporter caught on and exposed him in a scathing article. You'd think the attack would set Murphy back a notch or two. Not at all. Instead of a show of indignation when he next encountered the author of the article, Murphy gave the man an expansive greeting, removed a pink carnation from his own lapel, and put it in the buttonhole of the man's jacket. "Keep up the good work, old boy," he said. "I don't care how much you roast me, as long as you keep the Giants in the paper. If you leave me out, Mr. Brush will think I'm not earning my coin."

One day Mr. Brush dropped a hint about the Cubs: the franchise was for sale. It might be acquired cheaply. Murphy acted quickly. He generally preceded the team as an advance man on road trips, drumming up interest before the ball club's arrival. When he got to Chicago, he cornered Cubs president Jim Hart about the rumor, and Hart admitted it was true. John R. Walsh, a tired old Chicago banker, was selling his controlling interest in the Cubs organization for $105,000. Hart would earn a bonus as the architect of the sale.

A born opportunist, Murphy made known his intentions: he would buy the team. After securing an option, he boarded a train for Cincinnati and told his former employer, the millionaire publisher Charles Taft, a compelling story. "If properly handled, the ball club is a gold mine." The freewheeling Murphy pledged all of his assets to the project, about $15,000. Would Mr. Taft be interested?

Convinced of Murphy's sincerity, Taft asked his lawyer, Charles Schmalstig, to evaluate the situation and analyze the confidential financial data. Schmalstig confirmed Murphy's judgment. The price of the ball club was a rare bargain. The company had substantial value. It was highly profitable, and the outlook for the future was rosy, provided Frank Chance was retained as manager.

Taft not only agreed to participate in the purchase, he offered to acquire all of the stock himself and pay cash for it. Unapologetic about his own aspirations, Murphy reminded Taft that the deal hinged on one stipulation, that he, Murphy, be allowed at any time to buy enough stock from Taft to assume a controlling interest in the ball club. Taft had no problem with the proviso. He wasn't all that interested in baseball.

Taft bought 40 percent of the stock for himself, 40 percent for Murphy, 10 percent for Schmalstig, and 10 percent for Frank Chance, the Cubs' manager. Now Murphy controlled a major-league club that was on the verge of becoming a dynasty. The 1906 Cubs won and won and won. They were a sensational 61–26 on July 29 and then picked up the pace after that, going 55–10 for the remainder of the season, finishing with a stunning 116–36 record, a .763 winning percentage, the best mark ever in major-league baseball. Over the next five years, the Cubs won four pennants, two world championships, and 530 games.

Earnings soared. The company paid hefty dividends. Within two years Murphy had repaid Mr. Taft from the returns on the investment and assumed a controlling interest in the organization, 53 percent of the stock, purchasing it from Mr. Taft.

Murphy's extraordinary success did not sit well with the other owners. Theirs was a rocky relationship punctuated by frequent fallouts. Hardly a week passed when one of the less attractive aspects of Murphy's personality did not rub one of the moguls the wrong way. An epithet-slinging fabulist, by turns affable and unsavory, he was always steamrolling somebody, or writing a letter demanding the firing of one reporter or another.

Murphy did not cooperate in 1906 when league officials ordered the installation of dressing rooms for the players in ballparks. He did, however, provide a dressing room and a shower for the umpires and cushions for the dugouts. It wasn't always about money, though. Murphy did up West Side Grounds (the Cubs' home field) in grand fashion. He enlarged the seating capacity of the ballpark; placed plush vermilion chairs in steel-topped enclosures for well-heeled fans; improved the cheap seating in center field for the bleacher faithful; created new spaces for concessions; and increased the team's cash flow.

Visiting players complained about the primitive conditions of the clubhouse. There were only four washbowls and two showers for 26 men. The plumbing was defective. Murphy did not take the complaints seriously until Garry Herrmann, president of the Cincinnati Reds, termed the visitors' dressing room "unfit for human habitation."

"You're crazy," Murphy responded in his typically undiplomatic way. "Your ballplayers are vandals. They tore off locker doors and threw them outside." It went back and forth this way for three years until the league cracked down on Murphy and ordered improvements.

❖❖❖

After the board questioned Murphy for about an hour, he was asked to step out of the room. William Baker of the Phillies, Schuyler Britton of the Cardinals, and Jim Gaffney of the Braves, owners not present during the hearing, joined the board so the league as a whole could address the issues. The panel conferred in low tones. Murphy's business practices, his character, and his motives were dissected and discussed. The owners ruled that Murphy was wrong in the Evers affair, that he had violated Evers's contract, that Evers had not been given his ten days' notice, and, since his contract as manager was tied in with his contract as a player, Evers was not discharged as manager. His release "was irregular and therefore invalid."

Murphy was mildly astonished when informed of the decision and quietly accepted it.

By unanimous vote, Murphy's vote included, the National League assumed both of Evers's contracts and guaranteed his salary for the next four years. And, for the good of the league, the panel demanded that Evers be traded to another National League team. Trading Evers suited Murphy just fine. He was finished with him and said he'd consider offers.

Evers would go high. Brooklyn and Cincinnati expressed interest. When they were slow to make an offer, Jim Gaffney, sensing their ambivalence, decided he'd knock them out of the bidding in one bold stroke. He offered Murphy two of the Braves' best players in exchange for Evers: pitcher Hub Perdue and second baseman Bill Sweeney. Murphy accepted immediately.

Gaffney hurried downstairs, a happy man as he stepped off the elevator. Grinning like a large friendly dog wagging its tail, Gaffney walked across the deep pile rug in Peacock Alley where Evers and Walter Hapgood of the *Boston Herald* were chatting. The two men turned expectantly.

"What's the proposition?" Evers asked.

"Well, John, I landed you," Gaffney said. "I'm going to assume your Chicago contract and give the Cubs Perdue and Sweeney. The agreement's already signed."

Johnny frowned heavily, stared into space, turned and looked at Gaffney. "I can't consider that for a moment, Jim," he said, a dry, blighting expression on his face. "I won't sign with you or anyone else if Murphy makes one penny out of it. I was faithful to him. I gave him my best for nine years, and he gave me a rotten deal. Tried to shame me . . . and what happens? The National League rewards him with a second baseman to take my place, and a good pitcher besides."

Clearly, the single-minded Evers would have no part in any deal where Murphy made a profit. Gaffney heaved a weary sigh, and he and Evers talked for some time. Johnny kept shaking his head. "No. No. No," he kept saying. "Absolutely not. No way." He was emphatic about wanting Murphy to take a dead loss.

Evers then dropped a bombshell. "I've been offered a big bunch of money by the Feds," he said, poker-faced. "More money than I could get managing the Cubs. And I'm sure of getting every penny of it. I'll tell you something else . . . if I follow my present leaning, I'll accept it."

Ogden Nash, the popular American poet, a lifelong baseball fan himself, was squarely on target in a witty four-liner about Evers's willingness to take risks:

E is for Evers
His jaw in advance;
Never afraid
To Tinker with Chance.

Reporters cornered Jim Gaffney a few minutes later. "Think he'll report to Boston?" they asked.

"Ohh . . ." Gaffney said, shaking his head. "He's awfully sore at Murphy. I guess I can't blame him. After he thinks it over for a while, I think he'll see that it's in his best interest to play for Boston . . . or at least I hope so."

"I hear the Feds are offering him a bundle of money," a reporter said.

"Yes. I've heard that too. Right here in Brooklyn. The Ward brothers, according to gossip. If what the Feds are saying is true, they won't do business with a player under contract. They can't sign Evers. He is signed up with the National League for four years. The league took over his contract."

Evers did not deny the rumors, saying only that he would not do anything until the next day, Friday the thirteenth.

A report began circulating in the press that a movement was afoot to oust Murphy: his tenure had reached long past its "sell-by date." Club owners, it seemed, had asked Governor Tener to get rid of the Chicago owner for good.

CHAPTER 22

A WHIFF OF SCORE-SETTLING

With Governor Tener away on business and the Feds poised on Evers's doorstep, Garry Herrmann took charge: he reconvened the board of directors in emergency session to deal with the situation. The three-member board, acting as judge and jury, quickly worked out a realistic strategy aimed at keeping Evers out of the outlaw's hands. The board canceled the Braves' option on Evers, nullified the Boston-Chicago trade, returned Perdue and Sweeney to the Braves, stripped Murphy of his star player (Evers), and fined the Chicago franchise $20,000.

The board also authorized an expenditure of another $20,000 as a means of augmenting any bonus a team might deem necessary to get Evers's signature on a contract, and "empowered President Tener to make an equitable settlement with the Chicago club for the loss of Perdue's and Sweeney's services."

There was a whiff of score-settling in these actions. The balance of power had shifted. Murphy had gotten his comeuppance, and Evers had gotten the best of Murphy.

Questions abounded. What would Johnny do? Sign with Boston? Join the Feds? What about Murphy? Would he drag the National League into court and air the dirty linen? Was there any truth in stories about his days in baseball being numbered?

Evers met with Federal League officials more than once at the Knickerbocker Hotel, 6 Times Square in New York City, where Maxfield Parrish's 30-foot-long mural *Old King Cole* hung and, it was said, the martini was invented. Each time they got together with Evers, the Feds opened a satchel full of thousand-dollar bills and dumped them on a table in the center of the room. This made quite an impression.

It seems the only thing that kept Johnny from signing with the Feds was the uncertain status of his contracts. He was wary of getting caught in a legal wrangle that might keep him out of baseball for the season. And it seemed that the Feds had similar doubts. Jim Gilmore, the president of the Federal League, was quoted in the press as saying, "Unless Evers can prove himself a free agent, the Federal League will make him no offer."

Gilmore's statement gave Gaffney the opening he'd been looking for. He placed a huge signing bonus on the table and publicly stated that he would outbid the Feds, no matter how high they went.

Evers was delighted. "I've agreed to meet Gaffney and Stallings tomorrow [Friday the thirteenth]," he said, "and I'm certainly going to be there with my lawyer from Troy, whether he tells me I'm a free agent, as I maintain, or whether he feels I'm not. I won't do business with anyone until after I've talked to Gaffney and Stallings."

Friday morning temperatures hovered around zero. The Northeast was bracing for a heavy snowfall and 70 mph winds. Jim Gaffney was out early, a little after six, and shivered and coughed in the darkness, the cold air punishing his lungs. He'd surprise Evers at his hotel, have breakfast with Johnny, and show him how eager the Braves were about signing him. Silent footfalls passed him on beaten paths in the snow. Somewhere on the street came the sound of the frosty scrape of a shovel on the sidewalk.

Gaffney rubbed his hands vigorously as he stepped into the lobby of the Hotel Somerset, trying to warm himself and shake the snow off his galoshes. The night clerk sat alone at the front desk paging through the newspaper, and Gaffney had to speak to get his attention.

"Mr. Evers's room, please."

The Braves' owner glanced at the newspaper headline: "Blizzard Tonight to Break Zero Cold."

The night clerk rang Evers's room.

No answer.

"Mr. Evers went out early," a helpful bellhop said, "a little before six."

Strange . . . Gaffney made some calls. He tried everywhere. No luck. Evers was not to be found. Gathering his scarf close around his neck, Gaffney buttoned his overcoat, pulled down the brim of his hat, and was about to leave when suddenly he lifted his hand and placed the open palm against his brow. An awful thought had struck him. The Feds had smuggled Evers into hiding. That's what happened. He was certain of it. They would announce the coup at a news conference later in the day. Gaffney shuddered at the thought. The whole affair seemed like some absurd Broadway farce. Everything was going wrong. And the laughs were on him.

CHAPTER 23

A SELF-STYLED HAND GRENADE

Hearst's morning papers, hot off the presses the night before, claimed the Federal League had signed Evers. It was space filling, vacuous babble. Nothing more. But Gaffney didn't know that. The source? Joe Tinker. Tinker denied that he'd said anything like that. "There's no truth to it," he said. "I just met Johnny for a few minutes and we shook hands. We haven't had a chance to talk yet. I expect I'll see him today."

To say that Evers was annoyed when he learned of Tinker's comments would be putting things mildly. The two hadn't spoken for years, much less shaken hands. Evers hated Tinker. And the thought of Tinker bossing him around flashed through Johnny's mind. His blood boiled in indignation. Tinker's big mouth had shattered the fabric, or whatever was left of it, of the Federal League's offer.

Much to Gaffney's relief, Evers and his lawyer arrived as scheduled at room 501 of the Metropolitan Life building, Jim Gaffney's office, carrying copies of Evers's Chicago contracts. Both sides examined the documents and saw nothing in them that would prevent Evers from signing with the Braves. Evers said he'd sign for four years at $10,000 a year ($320,000 a year in today's dollars), if Gaffney would give him a $30,000 signing bonus, $25,000 of the money in advance.

Hours of negotiations followed. At four in the afternoon, the two sides finally reached an agreement. Evers signed. He'd done well for himself: $40,000 for the season ($1 million in today's dollars), including the $30,000 signing bonus, of which he'd receive $15,000 in advance.

Glowing with a rush of schoolboy happiness, George Stallings was putting on his coat, hat, scarf, gloves, and galoshes when the boys from the press caught up with him.

"How do you see your chances after signing Evers?" they asked. "Will Johnny make you a contender?" "Or was the signing just a ploy to pull more fans through the turnstiles?"

"If everyone plays up to potential," Stallings said, "with Evers at second base, I feel we can win the pennant."

But pundits felt that the dial of expectations might be turned a little too high. There were questions: Would Evers be able to shine on the field when surrounded by a bunch of mediocre ballplayers? Would the fiery Evers follow the lead of the equally fiery Stallings? How much could a man like Evers, a self-styled hand grenade, help an inexperienced young team when he gets thrown out of games so often?

"Losing my temper is my one big fault," Evers admitted, "but I've reformed some in this respect. I was chased from the diamond only ten times last year, while in 1912, before I was manager, umpires found it necessary to tie a can on me twenty-five times."*

When Governor Tener returned from Harrisburg, he and the other owners ratified Evers's contract. "The Evers matter," Tener said, "so far as the Boston club is concerned, has been amicably adjusted." The governor continued with a slap at Murphy. "The day has passed when one man can say 'this is my club and I'll run it as I please.'" To deal with the Murphy situation, Tener scheduled a meeting of the board of directors at the Sinton Hotel in Cincinnati for the following Saturday, the twenty-first of February, where he hoped to force Murphy out of baseball, peacefully, if possible, and behind closed doors, rather than risk having the league smeared publicly.

Charles P. Taft, the wealthy Cincinnati newspaper mogul, was the key player in the affair. Governor Tener and Taft got together several days before the meeting, and the governor told Taft of the league's intention to rid itself of Murphy, even if it meant taking the extreme action of dissolving the league. He urged Taft to take over the Cubs franchise himself. It would be in the interest of all parties involved. Taft agreed.

"They called a meeting to have me quartered and boiled, or shot at sunrise," Murphy said, "I don't know which. I was confined to my bed with lum-

---

* In his 16 years as an active player, Johnny Evers was ejected from more games than any other big leaguer in baseball history. John McGraw may have been banished from games a greater number of times overall than Evers, because McGraw spent 41 years in the majors as both a player and a manager.

bago, unable even to talk, and couldn't possibly go to Cincinnati." After conferring with Mr. Taft, the battle-weary Murphy began thinking about how much money he might lose (most of his nest egg) if he took legal action, money he'd worked hard for. After some mental debating and a serious discussion with Mr. Taft, Murphy sold Taft the team, ending his stormy tenure as owner of the Chicago Cubs.

"The force used to drive me out of baseball was the checkbook," Murphy said, laughing. "Imagine? A man being forced to take $500,000 [$12,500,000 in today's dollars] for a baseball franchise. With a world on the brink of war and potential lawsuits in the offing, traitorous players, and the possibility of huge operating losses because of the presence of the Federal League, a rest looked good to me. I got out at the right psychological moment."

Murphy's comments raised more than a few eyebrows, among them those of Henry Berger, a Cubs fan, who planned on inviting Murphy to his office for an explanation of the discrepancy between the schedule Murphy filed with the tax collector, listing his personal property at a value of $6,650, and his being quoted in newspaper stories as saying, "I ran a shoestring into a million dollars . . . and sold my stock in the ball club for over $500,000."

Berger had a scrapbook full of Murphy clippings. And, as assistant state's attorney, he was in charge of investigating financial irregularities and financial fraud. He would assist the tax assessor in examining the discrepancy.

Murphy was expected to cooperate.

CHAPTER 24

MISERY AND SUFFERING

Most experts were anticipating a first-division finish for the Braves in 1914. "George Stallings is a fine manager and has some fair material," Ty Cobb remarked in his weekly syndicated column, "and he's likely to work his club into fourth place before it's over."

Stallings encouraged such thinking. He felt good about the team. "We'll play solid ball this year," he said. "The boys are fast, they can hit, they're well organized, and above all, they have confidence and a fighting spirit."

The season opener in Brooklyn turned into a sad affair. Football weather greeted "Lefty" George Tyler when the Braves took the field. It was bleak, dark, and disgusting. Tyler's frozen fingers couldn't get the feel of the ball, and Dodger hitters hammered everything he offered, scoring eight runs in six innings.

Worse yet, the Braves' offense failed to capitalize on most scoring opportunities. Loose play in the field further sabotaged Tyler's efforts to hold Brooklyn in check. The usually steady Johnny Evers bungled an attempt at stopping a double steal. Rabbit Maranville "went to sleep" chasing a fly ball. Tommy Griffith moved in slow motion in the outfield. And Butch Schmidt watched three balls trickle by him that should have been "eaten up." It looked like Butch was covering about three feet of ground around first base: he was playing like a fan pulled out of the grandstand.

Stallings was not upset by the loss. "This is one game I really don't mind losing each year," he said. "When Brooklyn beat us, I felt we would have some luck and were in for a good season."

But the calamities that followed shook even Stallings's faith in the superstition. The Braves lost seven of their first nine games, lost a few more—

heartbreaking losses—and after that went into a really bad skid. They were headed nowhere fast.

The daily menu of cold, rain, blustery winds, snow flurries, and frigid temperatures forced nine postponements in 22 days. (Sunday blue laws kept the team off the field on three other occasions.) The boys weren't getting in enough work on the field and their timing was off. They no longer looked to be in tip-top form.

"The same old mud puddles," Stallings lamented, "the same soggy landscape, the same dark skies. We've only had three morning practices since we left spring training in Macon."

The frigid weather sucked the life out of the boys. Ominous hacking noises came from every part of the dugout. At least a dozen players had severe colds. The raw, chilly days spawned other health problems as well. A persistent muscle-clenching charley horse slowed Charlie Deal; a strained back reduced the effectiveness of Johnny Evers; tonsillitis hindered Rabbit Maranville; an inflamed and swollen eye hampered Tommy Griffith; and a seriously sprained ankle and knee kept Larry Gilbert out of the lineup. "It's a sick-looking club," Stallings said, "because the men are sick, a good many of them."

Despite the losses, the dugout remained alive with talk. Fractious and cacophonous voices harangued umpires. Harsh, foul-mouthed obscenities abused opponents. The boys were incredibly antagonistic, and umpires admonished them for being too abrasive.

"We'll be up there," Stallings said. "It'll take us a month or so to get back in shape, then we'll be hard to beat." But luck ran badly. The slump deepened. The Braves won only two of 13 games. Attendance fell off. Most days there weren't enough backsides in seats to fill a trolley car. Fans stayed away in droves. Why go out to South End Grounds to watch the groan-inducing Braves dig a hole for themselves? It wasn't fun. One afternoon, a foghorn voice bellowed, "You guys are a double-A team. You'll be lucky if you finish in organized ball."

Holding an interview with George Stallings was no longer a pleasant experience. Every little thing upset him. All a writer had to do was call him a good "loser" and Stallings would bristle with indignation: "We won't win the pennant this year, but I still stick with my prediction. We'll finish better than we did last season."

Losing gnawed at the team. Some days they seemed hopeless. Mental mistakes were common. As brothers in frustration, they frequently beat themselves, finding different ways of doing it each day. Pitchers forgot to cover first base. Infielders bungled cut-off throws. A base runner was victimized by the hidden ball trick. Bert Whaling batted out of order. George Tyler walked 11 batters in one start. Hub Perdue failed to build velocity and his pitches seemed to have an affinity for connecting with rival bats. Butch Schmidt took awkward swings at the plate and looked like he was taking aim at a new strikeout record. The team as a whole stole only one base in the month of April. They were struggling and failing to right themselves.

A reporter asked Stallings about the head-scratching start. "What's wrong with the Braves?"

Stallings shook his head and sighed. "You know, I've been trying to figure that out for some time now, and I don't mind telling you, that's a 'humdinger' of a question." He paused, thought for a minute, and gave the scribe the best answer he could think of: "The pitching is fair," he said, "the fielding is first rate, but the hitting . . . that's where the catch is, the hitting."

Bats produced silence when punch was needed. Particularly the bats of outfielders. The offense hardly made the most of opportunities in clutch situations. At times they looked more like a bunch of schoolboys batting against the great Cy Young in his prime than experienced big-league hitters. The Braves needed some thump in the lineup. And they weren't getting it.

Striving to thread the needle of success, Stallings kept juggling players and playing time, hoping the changes would shake things up. It didn't happen. The team languished. The slump continued.

Umpires became villains in the eyes of the Braves. All hell broke out one afternoon at the Polo Grounds in a series against the Giants. After leading 6–3 in the eighth inning of the opener of the series, the Braves blew the lead and lost the game.

They suffered a second setback the following day. With runners on first and second and one out, Bert Whaling sliced a soft liner into shallow right field, near the foul line. Thinking a catch impossible, the runners took off. Fred Snodgrass, the Giants' right fielder, came tearing in, threw himself through the air, stuck out his glove, and snatched the ball an inch off the grass, between his glove and the ground, then somersaulted head over heels, jumped up, and thrust the ball over his head in his bare hand. Cy Rigler, the home plate umpire, called Whaling out. A quick flip doubled up the runner at first for the third out, ending the inning and a promising Boston rally.

The Braves felt wronged. The entire squad charged Rigler. They claimed Snodgrass had trapped the ball, that Whaling was entitled to a hit. "I can't believe it. I can't believe it," was on everybody's lips. There wasn't a man among them who didn't believe in his heart that the umpire had robbed them. They were certain of it.

Johnny Evers rushed heedlessly into the middle of things, gesticulating wildly with nostril-flaring anger, throwing off sarcastic sparks. He all but hit Rigler. "If you didn't see the play," Evers screamed nastily, "you should have left the decision up to Bob Emslie" (the umpire on the bases).

Legs splayed, hands on hips, Rigler held his ground. A mountain of a man, standing over six feet tall and weighing in at 240 pounds (he once played right tackle for the Massillon Tigers, an early professional football team), Rigler wasn't having any of it.

"Okay," he said. "I've heard it. That's enough. Another word out of you and you're out of the ball game." Afraid of losing his second baseman for the remainder of the day, Stallings motioned Evers over to the dugout and ordered him out to his position.

There were many differences of opinion about the controversial play. The 16,000 umpires in the stands and the press box believed what they wanted to believe. "Snodgrass without any doubt made a clean, legitimate catch," a New York writer from the *Sun* crooned. "It was perfectly apparent to those of us in a position to see the play."

A writer from the *Boston Globe* disagreed. "To those of us in the press box, it looked very much as though Snodgrass had scooped up the ball as he fell. He rolled on it, clutched it with his bare hand and then dazzled Rigler with his grandstand gesture."

Braves owner Jim Gaffney blamed Rigler personally for the loss. An outburst of furious indignation welled up in him. After the game, he made his way through the crowd on the field, confronted Rigler, called him every name in the book, and accused him of persecuting the Braves.

"What you don't know about umpiring would fill a book," Gaffney said, in his street-sounding voice.

Rigler fumed, every muscle in his body tensed. He pressed his lips together and did not answer.

Gaffney kept his blue eyes fixed on Rigler. "You're a fine one," Gaffney shouted, "handing it to us that way. I'll get you yet. I won't let up until I do."

"Don't tell me your troubles," Rigler snarled. "Take them to the office."

"You can count on it. Maybe if we bought some ballplayers off you, we'd get a square deal."

This was a nasty allegation. Struggling for control, Rigler continued walking toward the dressing room.

Fred Lieb watched the encounter from the press box: "We've heard of umps being chased by an irate mob," Lieb wrote, "also by frantic players, but to see an ump pursued by a wrathful club owner is a distinct novelty."

That evening at the Waldorf, Gaffney shared his feelings with reporters. "Now, don't misunderstand me, boys," he said, chewing a cigar back and forth in his mouth, "I'm not an umpire baiter. But it's a crying shame the way that that fellow Rigler always gives my club the worst of it. If he's not biased, he's not competent. I'm not going to stand for it anymore."

George Stallings filed an official protest, charging that Snodgrass's catch was not made legally. "If Snodgrass had caught the ball three feet from the ground and then fallen on it, as he did after he trapped it, Whaling would have been out. According to the rules of baseball, the sphere must be held momentarily. Snodgrass did not do that. *His glove was on the ground, palm down, when he righted himself.* Anybody who knows anything about baseball knows that an out is impossible under those circumstances."

Finding a way out of the situation was important. Comfortably uncomfortable, Governor John K. Tener, the National League's big, suave, dignified president, appeared unperturbed during a press conference at league headquarters. Skillfully handling the distasteful situation with great poise, the governor made light of the charges, and portrayed the budding scandal as nothing more than an unfortunate incident blown out of proportion. Tener called it an understandable disagreement among the parties involved.

"Jim is a good Irishman," Tener said, and laughed good-naturedly, ponderously shaking his head. "It's likely he is a little sore over losing. Jim is a new magnate and Rigler is an experienced umpire. I don't think anyone seriously believes any umpire is dishonest or has an apparent bias. Mr. Gaffney no doubt thought he got the worst of it and I admire the spirit that prompted the kick."

Governor Tener paused and made certain he had the attention of his audience. Then, drawing on the strategy of an ostrich, he continued in the same even voice. "I think it is a great tribute to the honesty of baseball, when a club owner will come out so pointedly and voice his sentiments of disapproval over an apparent grievance." Pause. "Of course I intend to investigate, but I know pretty well that friend James will not likely be so warm under the collar in a day or two, as he is just now. I am glad, however, that he asserted himself in the face of his fancied grievance."

Misery and suffering continued for the Braves. Losses piled up. Dick Rudolph pitched a near-perfect game for 10 innings against the Pirates (he gave up three hits) and all he got out of it was a 1–1 tie. A few days later the Reds beat him 1–0, another three-hit performance. Dick had allowed a total of two runs and six hits, pitched two complete games, 18 innings, and did not post a win.

Over a particularly bad five-game stretch, the Braves scored just three runs in 46 innings. Batters were not exactly wearing out the ball. The Braves were like a finely tuned machine rolling along with some of its main parts out of adjustment. Rabbit Maranville made four errors in a game for the second time in a week, a game in which the Braves committed five errors. (Maranville also made a couple of fancy belt-buckle catches.)

And when Hub Perdue took the mound, he was treated like a batting practice pitcher: he couldn't pitch hay. One hit followed another. Hub was so ineffective that he allowed 11 hits and three walks, and sandwiched in a wild pitch in six innings of a losing effort against the Giants.

On the sixteenth of May the Braves suffered a seventh consecutive defeat, a shutout, the sixth time they'd been shut down in 19 games. The season was spinning out of control. Not a single victory in 10 days. They'd gone 1–12–1 since the twenty-third of April.

Rock bottom came on the twentieth of May, five weeks into the season; their record stood at an inexcusable 4–18, a statistic no one could dismiss as bad luck.

When losses pile up, players lose confidence. They get lethargic. Hub Perdue was one of them. Johnny Evers directed volleys of insults at the hayseed and others like him, letting them know that he did not like their lack of spirit.

"I'm sick of this stinking losing," Evers snarled. "We've got to shake this losing mentality." To their credit, the boys did not tune Johnny out. They listened, interrogated themselves, and asked, What's going on here?

Though their spirits reached a low ebb, the players held firm. They looked a little better in the middle of May, better than they looked in late April. And their play gradually improved as Stallings drew every ounce of ability out of them.

The Big Chief's genius in handling players, especially pitchers, began to produce positive results. The pitchers who weren't throwing well began to exhibit a subtle excellence not seen earlier in the season. Boston hitters were working the count more effectively, connecting more often and driving the ball to all fields. On defense, the infield continued its nifty play, particularly around second base. Evers and Maranville, always fun to watch, pounced on balls like hungry dogs snapping at bones.

Playing every day helped the boys find their rhythm. They won more than they lost, and Maranville led the way. In a 3–1 victory over the Cubs, Rab tripled in the first, driving in Evers who had walked, then scored the winning run when Roger Bresnahan's pickoff throw got by Heine Zimmerman.

"Maranville covered about seven acres of ground around shortstop," a writer for the *Boston Journal* reported the next day. "He cut off several hits, and atoned for one slip by catching the runner at the plate after the error. In the same contest, he robbed 'Red' Corriden of a hit by digging into centerfield and grabbing Red's Texas Leaguer. Rabbit's back was to the plate when he made the catch, and it was so far out it didn't seem possible for him to handle the ball."

Rabbit put one over on umpire Cy Rigler in a hard-fought 3–2 victory over St. Louis after he missed Tyler's attempted pickoff of "Cozy" Dolan at second base. The ball went bounding into center field, and Dolan was about to take off for third when Rab fell on top of him, got a stranglehold on his leg, and didn't let go until the center fielder retrieved the ball. Cozy protested, but Rigler did not see things his way.

Johnny Evers's generalship also produced positive results. A natural fielder, resourceful, and an intuitive genius, Evers directed play on the field. He was everywhere, inspiring confidence in his teammates, making them fight, teaching them winning ways.

CHAPTER 25

CONFIDENCE GREW STRONGER DAY BY DAY

By the first of June, Stallings's "rah-rah-rah" no longer sounded like "blah-blah-blah." Things were changing. The signs were unmistakable. The boys were getting their swagger back. They were looking more like a team, like a really good team.

The strength of the club lay exactly where Stallings said it would, in the savvy hands of Johnny Evers, the team's iconic captain, a high-octane achiever whose genuine appetite for winning and field generalship, wisely delegated, led the charge. Evers was not only a gladiator, he was a first-rate hard-assed mentor, a baseball scholar who seemed to possess a preternatural instinct for smart play.

"The guy was psychic," Rabbit Maranville said. "He could sense where a player was going to hit the ball if the pitcher threw it where he was supposed to throw it. John, with his brains, taught me more baseball than I ever dreamed about." Rabbit followed Evers's example: listened when he spoke, asked questions, and watched the way John performed.

With runners on first and third, and one out, and the score tied in a game at Boston, a Cincinnati batter hit a screaming liner up the middle. Evers dived and knocked the ball down, recovered quickly, flipped a throw to Maranville, and got the first half of a certain double play that would end the inning.

"I was just about to throw to first," Rabbit said, "when Tommy Clarke came barreling at me. I tried to throw around him and my throw to first was late. The runner scored."

All hell broke loose. The very air shuddered. "What the hell?" Rab said to himself. He shot a glance at Evers, blinked and squinted, unable to believe his eyes. Gesticulating wildly, Johnny slammed his glove on the ground. Kicked it. Kicked up dust. Arms and legs flapping. Bellowing unprintable words at the top of his lungs.

"What's a matter?" Rabbit asked. "What'd I do?"

"What's the matter?" Evers shrieked, in a highly pitched nasal whine, mocking Rabbit. "You shoulda hit the cocksucker in the head. That's what you shoulda done. Make the motherfucker get out of the way."

"But—I—I didn't want to hurt him."

Evers grimaced, closed his eyes in disbelief and looked up at the sky, opened them, hunched his shoulders, worked himself into a frenzy, drew in his chin, then thrust it out like a raptor set to devour its prey.

"Now let me see," he said, slowly, with feigned calmness, drawing out each word. "Let me see if I can get this straight. You say you didn't want to hurt him."

Rabbit winced and shrunk back.

"That's nice. Real nice." Johnny's head nodded up and down in seeming agreement, a twisted smile on his face. Then came the explosion. "You goddamn idiot," he boomed, letting loose a torrent of abuse. "Haven't I learned you nothin'? The next time anyone comes at you like that, you hit the motherfucker in the head. Understand? Right between the eyes. You gotta want to bury 'em."

"Okay. Okay. Calm down. Gimme a break. I'll bust 'em the next time. I promise ya. I'll bust 'em good. You'll see. From now on."

Dismayed, Rabbit shook his head, turned, and droop-shouldered, walked back to his position at shortstop, mumbling to himself. "What a lunatic. The guy's outta his mind."

And there was Tommy Clarke, a shining example of dangerous stupidity, standing on second base, his chest puffed up, preening like a self-satisfied rooster, savoring the moment, exulting in the fun of it all.

Two months later, the Braves were locked into a scoreless tie with the Reds at Redland Field in Cincinnati when Tommy Clarke again reached first base with a runner on third and one out. The identical situation. It was brow-beating time. With animal vulgarity, the bull-necked Clarke, who had a mistrust of personal hygiene, looked out over the infield, cupped his hands around his mouth, and bellowed something unprintable at Maranville. The stands erupted in laughter.

Clarke called time, stepped off the bag, turned, faced his admirers, and bowed like Bluto in an animated Popeye cartoon, a broad smile filling his sweaty face. The fans loved it.

Clarke strutted and blustered and swaggered menacingly, directing his attention at Maranville. "Give me plenty of room, Midget," he said, "or I'll give you what I gave you in Boston."

The redness deepened on Rabbit's suntanned face, the only sign of fluster. He bit his lip, mopped the dampness from his brow with the back of his glove, traded glances with Evers, and set himself at the ready, like a bandy rooster.

A stir ran through the crowd. The fans smelled blood. Rabbit blood.

The word "Midget" echoed in Rabbit's ears. "Midget," he muttered. "I'll show that son of a bitch." He wet his parched lips, spat into the glove pocket, and smacked the leather with his fist a couple of times.

Evers looked over and barked encouragement.

Clarke moved off the bag with a menacing strut and went into an exaggerated crouch, his hands on his knees, rocking back and forth, eyes darting from the mound to Maranville.

"Pitch it, greenhorn," Clarke hollered at Dick Crutcher in a surly New York voice. "What are you waiting for?"

Crutcher, a rookie, scraped at the dirt and worked his foot into the hole in front of the rubber, peered in at the plate, got the sign. Shook it off. Got another. Nodded in agreement. Checked the runners, took a deep breath, and fired.

Swinging hard, the batter got on top of the ball and tapped a slow grounder to the right of second base. Evers pounced on it, scooped the ball out of the dirt, and fired it to Maranville, as Clarke charged like a maddened bull out to gore a picador who'd just shot a steel point into his shoulder.

"He was really coming at me," Rabbit said, "but I was determined. No backing down this time. No throwing around him."

Rabbit put everything he had into the throw.

Thonk!

The sickening sound of a baseball on bone. The ball skittered into right field.

"I hit him. Smack in the forehead," Rabbit said, "right between the eyes. The run scored. And Clarke dropped dead at my feet."

A hush fell over the crowd. The dugouts emptied. Evers dashed over to Rabbit's side, trying to pinch back a grin. "That's the way to do it, Rabbit. They won't come charging at you no more."

Rabbit didn't hear a word he was saying. The color drained from his face. He swallowed uneasily, kept shaking his head, staring at Clarke's crumpled body.

"I—I killed him," he stammered. "I killed him dead."

"Fuck him! Who cares?"

"But—"

"Look, kid. Forget him, will ya? The bastard got what he deserved. He ain't no fuckin' good anyway."

Players from both sides gathered around and peered down anxiously at Clarke's face. "Give him air. Give him some air . . . " "He don't look so good." "Somebody call a doctor."

Minutes passed.

Clarke's right leg twitched spasmodically. An inarticulate gurgle rose from deep within his throat.

"Don't let him swallow his tongue."

"Look. He's coming to." "Give him room."

Clarke blinked groggily, trying to focus on the blur of faces hovering above him. His eyes shifted slowly and glassily until he found the face he was looking for. He fixed a steady gaze on Rabbit Maranville. Clarke mumbled something. Tried to speak. His teammates pressed closer.

"What'd he say? . . . What'd he say?"

"Shut the fuck up, asshole. Don't you see? He's tryin' to tell us something. Come on, pal. What is it? We'll take care of you. You'll be okay. What is it?"

Clarke groaned, winced, tried to clear his raspy throat. "You . . . you . . . ," he whispered in a thick, throaty voice, directing the words at Maranville. "You . . . you got me, kid . . . You got me good . . . You're all right."

Everybody burst into relieved laughter. Clarke stayed in the game. The Reds won, 3–1.

The Braves' confidence began to grow stronger day by day. The boys were crawling back from the hopelessly lost. They were trying to regroup. But the outfield was holding them back. Stallings remained animated in spite of the discouraging circumstances. Every morning he had the boys out for batting practice. "Improved hitting," he said, "is all that stands between the team and the upper berths in the standings."

The Braves' inability to live up to expectations sank the franchise deep into red ink for the calendar year, a $70,000 deficit ($1,750,000 in today's dollars). With the business hemorrhaging cash, owner Jim Gaffney was "sorely tempted" to chuck the whole thing and get out of baseball. Over lunch in a quiet corner of Boston's venerable Union Oyster House in June, Stallings addressed the worries and the restless discontent of the boss.

"The team's luck is so bad it's bound to change," he said. "The odds are 100–1 that it will change. You've got to put your faith in the future."

"He spoke so enthusiastically about the club's potential," Gaffney said, "how solid it was. His unwavering commitment to it. I just had to believe him."

The Big Chief ordered two pieces of lemon meringue pie for dessert. "Maybe it will change our luck," he said, wistfully shaking his head.

Gaffney smiled and nodded.

The Braves won that afternoon, 3–2, behind left-hander Otto Hess. Thinking the win might be an omen, the start of something big, Stallings ordered the same meal the following day, including the two pieces of lemon meringue pie. The boys won again. After five consecutive days of lemon meringue pie, Stallings could hardly stand the stuff, but he kept ordering it until the Pirates snapped the Braves' winning streak.

Stallings kept improvising in an effort to get the most out of the material on hand. He managed to catch Pirates manager Fred Clarke off guard with a surprise move one afternoon, the result a 5–3 Braves triumph. Before the start of the game, Stallings wrote in the names of two rookies, a pitcher and a catcher, as the outfielders on the Braves' lineup card. When Clarke announced a right-hander as his starting pitcher, Stallings seized the upper hand before the first pitch of the game, replacing the names of the two rookies with those of Larry Gilbert and Joey Connolly, the Braves' most productive left-handed hitting outfielders. This injected more punch into the lineup.

The shift could not have been more successful. Gilbert and Connolly banged out six hits between them, including home runs onto Columbus Avenue by each of them in the seventh inning, the margin of victory.

Pundits viewed Stallings's maneuver as a stroke of genius. It was not. Ned Hanlon of the old Baltimore Orioles probably originated the idea, once he realized how much of an advantage a left-handed hitter had over a right-handed pitcher, and vice versa.

"Whenever a right-hander faces one left-handed batter after another, your strongest and most aggressive hitters," Stallings said, "it wears on his nerves. There are no soft spots in the lineup."

The strategy was an enlargement of a general practice drawn on by managers in selecting a pinch hitter. Stallings broadened the concept and shifted his entire outfield around, depending on whether the Braves were facing a right- or left-hander on a particular afternoon.

No big-league manager before him had shifted the entire outfield on a day-to-day basis. He was the first. The tactic gave rise to a bold new force in baseball, the platoon system. Besides improving the batter's chances of success, platooning kept outfielders in the dugout alert and eager when given an opportunity to play.

"The Braves batted .280 as a team and fielded .980 for the week," Melville West reported in the *Boston Globe*, "hardly figures of an habitual tailender."

Suddenly, or so it seemed, the Braves were busting right along. Stallings's men put 37 hits into play and scored 27 runs in taking three of four from the visiting Cubs.

There were concerns, though. The team lacked an effective right-handed hitting outfielder, and Charlie Deal was playing at less than full strength at third base. Then there was Hub Perdue, who was no longer applying himself.

Although Perdue had been a consistent performer in the past, the effort put forth by the big, shambling country boy had fallen off drastically; he wasn't of much use any longer as a top-of-the-line starter (2–5 in nine games). Hub's mind, not his arm, was his worst liability.

Stallings marked him as one of his failures, and the Big Chief hated to fail. Now it was almost a foregone conclusion that the Braves would trade Perdue. Get rid of him.

"I have a regular system of working pitchers," Stallings said. "I always follow it. I pick two pitchers for every game and call them number one and number two. As soon as the game starts, number two is supposed to hike out to the warm-up pen and take just enough pitches to be ready." The system allowed Stallings the luxury of keeping games from getting out of hand, if the starter opened badly. "I'm not caught without a warmed-up pitcher," he explained, "and many a ball game is saved that way."

While the Braves were on the road, Stallings announced his starting pitcher. "You're the number-one pitcher today, Bill [James] . . . and you, Hub, you're the number two." As the visiting team, the Braves were up first. They struck quickly, scored five runs in the opening inning, a good start, particularly for a club in an extended slump, but Bill threw poorly. He couldn't put the ball near enough to the plate for the batter to reach it with a pole, and they filled the bases on him.

This made the Big Chief anxious. Just then his eyes happened to sweep the dugout. There sat Hub Perdue slumped carelessly at the other end of the bench, lost in thought. "Why, you big, lumbering, lazy dub," Stallings shouted, his face purple, his eyes bulging, his veins popping. "Didn't you hear me tell you that you were the number-two pitcher today? . . . Goddamn it to hell," he snarled. "Get out there and warm up or get the hell out of the ballpark and never come back."

The lacing Stallings gave Hub was a strong one even for him, and the brutishness of it curled Hub up like salt on a snail. As it happened, Bill James settled down and there was no need of a relief pitcher.

Stallings didn't give the incident another thought until after the game, when he found Hub sitting in the clubhouse, terribly upset. "What's the matter with you, Hub?" Stallings asked, not having the slightest idea.

"Ah was just a tryin' to make up mah mind whether to try and lick you for what you was a-sayin' this afternoon and blow the club or whether ah was a-goin' to take it and stay." Hub paused and blew his nose with his fingers. "Ah can't afford to blow the club, so ah guess ah'll just have to take it."

"Aw . . . , listen, Hub . . . You ought to have seen enough of me by now to know that what I say in the heat of the game don't go. Now forget it. I didn't mean anything except I wanted to impress on you that when I tell you that you're the number two, you are to be in shape to step into the box at a second's notice."

Hub nodded.

When a sportswriter asked Hub what the brouhaha in the dugout was all about, the amiable bumpkin replied: "This Stallings man is some manager, and he treats his men right fine, but he ain't mah style. He's too all-fired strenuous. Why, he don't know what he's a-doin' when a game is bein' played. He just jumps around that there bench like a grasshopper and says anythin' and everythin'."

Hub continued. "Why, he'll walk right on you when you're a-settin' on that there bench. And man can he talk somethin' awful. Ah never seen no man who had such a flow of language." Pause.

"When ah first began to work for Gawge, and he done talked to me that way, ah told him, 'Now Mr. Stallings, you mustn't talk to me like that or we ain't a-goin' to get along. Ah ain't been raised that way.' But there was no use o' me a-talkin'. Gawge told me ah should ought not pay no attention to what he's a-sayin'." Pause. "But we sure does where ah comes from, and when he says somethin' that sounded right bad, ah'd get mad and ah'd call him down."

Aw-shucks Hub may have been good for a barrel of laughs, but his performances on the mound were no laughing matter for a manager with first-division aspirations.

The charley horse Charlie Deal suffered in spring training did not mend; he had difficulty reaching ground balls. Charlie couldn't give it his best. But he didn't complain. He showed up every day (hoping there would be some life in the leg) and dealt with the injury as best he could. Charlie was a sick man, more so than fans imagined. The acute charley horse was but one of his ailments. He was underweight—he'd lost 15 pounds—and his stomach constantly troubled him. The leg throbbed overnight. Each morning it was anybody's guess about how his ailing and bruised muscles would respond. It was always wait and see. Therapy didn't help. Extended rest was what was needed.

Burdened by ill health, Charlie slumped badly at the plate and in the field. He'd been reduced to practically standing on third base, taking throws and anything hit right at him. That was it. Maranville handled the area along the third-base line and ground balls wide of third base, and Evers shifted toward second base as a means of assisting Maranville. The "hot corner" weakened a once stellar infield.

Stallings envisioned acquiring more offense in a trade for a starting pitcher and resumed talks with the Cardinals, a potential trading partner, dangling Hub Perdue as his primary trading chip. Things fell into place quickly.

Miller Huggins, keen on snaring an experienced starting pitcher, expressed interest and indicated a willingness to let go of two utility players, "Possum" Whitted and Teddy Cather, in exchange for Hub Perdue. A three-player trade. It was the right time to swap Perdue for players capable of helping the team.

"The Whitted and Cather trade rounded out the club nearly to my satisfaction," Stallings said. "They improved our lineup and gave the club more balance and depth. It was good for both teams."

Having been traded from a third-place team—a pennant contender, six and a half games behind the league-leading Giants—Whitted was less than pleased to land on a club stuck deep in last place. "The Braves were not a great team," he later recalled. "They looked lousy. They were certain to wind up in last place."

Stallings was optimistic. His quest had been a success. He told Whitted he'd joined a pennant winner.

"I didn't believe him," Whitted said. "We belonged in eighth place."

"Whitted was lazy when he first arrived," Stallings said, "but, like other men who joined me who were supposed to have certain bad habits, he soon got over this and was full of ambition."

A multidimensional player, Whitted didn't have great numbers; his worth was in the intangibles. He was a strong defender who could spell

Charlie Deal at third base, stabilize the infield, and fill any other immediate need elsewhere in the lineup. With the Cardinals in 1913, the tough 31-year-old handyman willingly played in 122 games, wherever needed: 40 in the outfield (every position), 37 at shortstop, 21 at third base, seven at second base, and two at first base.

Teddy Cather (pronounced KAY-ther), though less experienced, was a hard worker, a rangy outfielder, a right-handed batter whose theory of hitting fit into the Braves' philosophy: if you wait long enough, the pitcher will give you the pitch you can hit best.

As a Cardinal outfielder the previous season, Cather was injured when he crashed into a fence while making a spectacular catch and was knocked unconscious, still clutching the ball. Thirteen weeks later, his first game back from the injury, he broke his leg sliding into second base in a game against the Cubs. Now that he'd fully recovered, the Braves anticipated an increase in production from him.

Still trying to solve the Braves' outfield problems, Stallings completed another trade a week later, this time with the Philadelphia Phillies on the third of July, sending utility infielder Jack Martin to the Phils in exchange for Josh DeVore, a 26-year-old left-handed-hitting outfielder.

"I'm mighty glad to be back with Stallings," DeVore told reporters. "I played for the Chief over in Newark before I broke in regularly with the Giants, and we used to get along first rate."

Even on bad days DeVore made others smile. Few could lay down a drag bunt the way Josh could. A speedy little fellow, the 5'6", 160-pound fly chaser batted .302 in 30 games for the Phillies during the first half of the 1914 season, and as a Giants regular in the outfield, he'd played in two World Series and covered the outfield "like a circus tent."

Though not overly ambitious and an in-and-out hitter, DeVore was a good money player. He did not get rattled in tight situations. Instead of getting nervous, he worked all the harder to get on base.

The Braves won 14 of 21 games at the end of June and compiled a winning 16–13 record for the month. Overall, they were 26–35 in the standings. Not bad, considering their horrendous start. They even managed to escape the cellar for a day, on June 25, but immediately fell back into last place after the visiting Giants swept them in a doubleheader at South End Grounds.

Hardly anyone noticed, though. That evening newsboys held up papers hot off the presses with screaming headlines: "FIRE SWEEPS SALEM" and "20,000 HOMELESS."

Bostonians were appalled and at the same time fascinated by the spectacle of a conflagration that threatened for a while to wipe out the entire city of Salem, Massachusetts. Spectacular pictures of the disaster chronicled a third of the town being burned to the ground, an area of two square miles. Since radio and television did not yet exist, newspapers were everywhere. They made life exciting. Bold-type headlines of catastrophic events sold out editions. People eagerly awaited updates from boys shouting headlines. "Extra! Extra! Read all about it!" Echoes of their strident voices filled the streets.

Three days later the big, bold, black type on front pages across America brought disquieting news from the Austro-Hungarian province of Bosnia. "ARCHDUKE FERDINAND SHOT BY SERB AUSTRIAN PRINCE AND WIFE KILLED."

Archduke Franz Ferdinand, heir to the Habsburg throne, and his wife Sophie were visiting Sarajevo in an effort to reduce the growing sentiment for an end to Austro-Hungarian rule in Bosnia-Herzegovina.

The royal pair escaped a homemade explosive thrown at their 1911 open Gräf & Stift touring car that morning, an attempt the prince alertly warded off with his arm. The hand-held fuse bomb bounced off the folded canopy on the rear of the car and exploded under the staff vehicle behind them, wounding three aides and several bystanders.

Despite the attempts on their lives, the archduke and his wife, known for their good manners and quiet dignity, continued the state visit. They were fearless.

After attending a reception at city hall, the royal couple insisted on visiting the army hospital where the injured officers were taken. Unfamiliar with the altered itinerary, amid shouts of "Zivio, zivio" ("long live the heir"), the driver of the lead car of the imperial motorcade turned right into Franz Josef Strasse—the wrong street—a departure from the original route along the Miljăcke River. The entourage followed.

Recognizing the mistake and sensing the extreme danger to the archducal couple, the chauffeur of the royal limousine, the third car in line, immediately stopped, put the car in reverse, and attempted to back out of the street. The car stalled.

Standing at the curb was a member of the treacherous Black Hand organization, Gavrilo Princip, a mustachioed, 19-year-old student carrying a gun. He'd just walked out of Moritz Schiller's Corner Café to see what all the commotion was about and couldn't believe his luck. The crown prince, the man he and six other committed terrorists wanted to assassinate that day, was eight feet away. It was pure happenstance.

Princip stepped off the curb, raised his Browning semiautomatic pistol, and fired twice at point-blank range. The first shot severed the archduke's jugular vein; the second struck his wife Sophie in the abdomen. Minutes later both were dead. It was a little before 11:30 on Sunday morning, June 28, 1914.

The assassination triggered a catastrophe. "The Great War." World War I.

CHAPTER 26

YOU CALL YOURSELVES BIG LEAGUERS?

On the way to Chicago, the beginning of an 18-day road trip, the Boston contingent stopped off at Olympic Park in Buffalo for an exhibition game with the Buffalo Bisons, an eager troop of young bucks locked into a four-way battle for first place in the International League. The Buffalo front office billed the July 7 contest as a homecoming of sorts for four former Bisons, George Stallings, Hank Gowdy, Les Mann, and Fred Mitchell—favorites all.

Though it was steamily hot, 1,735 fans turned out to welcome the visitors and get a look at Johnny Evers, the Braves' celebrity second baseman, the once-proud centerpiece of the Chicago Cubs' famous "Tinker to Evers to Chance" double-play combination.

But it was Rabbit Maranville, the smallest player on the field, who drew the crowd's collective gaze. Fans could not get over how swiftly the little fellow flashed after pop-ups, how easily he settled under them—arms hanging at his sides, always at his sides—how quickly his hands came together at his belt buckle when the ball whisked by the visor of his cap, and how unerringly he made the catch.

Maranville's stature, already large in the minds of fans, had grown considerably. Brash and bratty, the attention-addicted Rab, eager for public esteem, was a crowd-pleaser, one of a kind, a fast-talking merrymaker whose natural ebullience aroused genuine enthusiasm. He always acted as if he were about to be photographed. Despite his penchant for playing the role of court jester, the little fellow was one heck of a ball player, perhaps the best defensive shortstop in baseball history.

Rabbit talked nonstop to anyone. To everyone. It didn't matter who, the batboy, Evers, fans in the stands, the base runner, the third-base coach; a day seldom went by when he didn't engage an umpire in a tongue-in-cheek conversation. The dialogue usually began on a serious note and more often than not ended with the umpire scarcely able to keep from laughing.

Glib, funny, exceedingly self-confident, with an exhilarating craziness, the little guy might start by asking about a called strike, or a close call at second base, or whether or not a runner ran out of the baseline. If nothing else worked, there was always the umpire's eyesight. That never failed to get things going.

Rab was mischievous, not mean. His infectious gaiety and sweet, goofy charm allowed him to get away with all kinds of crazy antics, unlike Johnny Evers and Ty Cobb, who went bananas over every little thing and argued with umpires, no holds barred.

Maranville picked his spots. Made his moves when umpires least expected them. It might be when the arbiter was distracted by another player, or an incident on the field, or while he was bending over brushing off home plate. Before the man in blue realized what was happening, Rab would skitter around behind him, turn and face the grandstand, incline his head in the umpire's direction, and make a face. And Rabbit was some face-maker.

As the crowd got into the spirit of things, Rabbit would shake his rear end at the stands in a slightly naughty imitation of a Parisian can-can dancer at the Folies Bergère, and people would split their sides laughing. Few could resist the guy when he meant to charm them, and he meant to charm them most of the time.

When an umpire started getting after the little fellow, out would come a pair of spectacles kept hidden in a pocket for just such emergencies. He'd give the umpire a big grin and drop his voice into a hoarse whisper that sounded like Popeye talking to Wimpy a city block away, and say, "Here. Put these on. Maybe they'll help you a little bit. You can't see a damn thing out here today."

Off the diamond, Rab, a Peter Pan who never grew old, had a glorious time raising all kinds of hell, usually after a great deal of elbow-bending in some seedy bar.

His escapades were marked by excitement, daring, and adventure. One night in St. Louis he dived fully clothed into a water fountain.

"There's a nasty fish in there," he said as he climbed out. "It bit me."

"What did you do?" a spectator asked.

"I bit him back," he said. And spat out half a goldfish.

Rab's teammates didn't really appreciate having him around when they had a card game. He simply wouldn't take things seriously. On one of these occasions—a stormy evening at the Majestic Hotel in Philadelphia—they locked him out of the room and hurt his feelings. So he went down the hall, entered another room, and stepped out of a window onto a ledge in the driving rain. Soaking wet, he crawled along the ledge until he reached the cardplayers' room. When his teammates looked up and saw him in the window making faces at them, they were terrified. You see, the ledge the kid was standing on was six stories above the street.

Several years after the Miracle Season, the Braves were in New York, comfortably settled in the Ansonia Hotel, and the boys were in a happy mood after taking a couple of games from the Giants. They celebrated. A beery scene filled with the smell of booze and bad air. And the whoopie kid was at his best entertaining his drink-happy comrades.

Swaying backward and forward, the little runt was playfully teasing Jack Scott—an Appalachian country boy—challenging him to a wrestling match. Jack was almost a foot taller than Rab and outweighed him by at least 50 pounds, and was cockeyed drunk himself.

"Stay away from me, Rabbit," he kept saying. "I don't want to rassle you. I might hurt you."

Rab, feeling no pain, couldn't have cared less. He put a chokehold on the big guy who, understandably, reacting instinctively, broke free and wrenched Rabbit's neck violently. The little guy crumpled to the floor, unconscious.

The alcohol-fogged Jack left the room, saying, "I didn't want to hurt that boy."

When Rabbit regained consciousness, he and a couple of his boozehounds cooked up an insanely cruel and sadistic practical joke.

The misfit adolescents smeared white powder all over Rabbit's face and arms and laid him out on a bed. Then, gleefully, one of the guys dashed downstairs and told Jack that the violent neck-wrenching he'd given Rab was fatal. The little guy was dead as a doornail.

Filled with dread, Jack rushed up to the room, and sure enough, there was Rabbit, laid out on the bed, lifeless. Jack fell to his knees and prayed, as the cast of dim bulbs looked on.

"Lord," Jack pleaded, tears streaming down his cheeks, "you know I didn't mean that boy no harm. Don't have him die, Lord. Put the breath of life back in him. Please, Lord. Have mercy. Let little Rabbit live."

Rabbit lay as still as death. And his miscreant pals took in the scene with nary a hint of intrigue on their gloomy faces.

Jack walked out in a daze, his mind filled with thoughts, a welter of thoughts, and went down to the lobby and waited for the police to pick him up on a murder rap. He sat there all night, in bottomless despair, his heart aching, his mind in turmoil.

Having taken the bait, he was still there early in the morning, in an unending panic, when the elevator door opened and Rabbit stepped out, and smiled brightly: "Hiya, Jack, you're up early, aren't you?"

Bison fans filed out of Olympic Park with happy smiles on their faces that afternoon. They'd seen a good show, capped off by a satisfying victory. The hometown boys had trounced the win-a-few-lose-a-few Boston Braves by a 10–2 score.

George Stallings was not the least bit amused by the way the Braves had gotten whipped. His club did little more than go through the motions, settling for three hits off Johnny Verbout, a minor-league lifer, the kind of player for whom the term "journeyman" was invented. At the same time, manager Bill Clymer's hungry Bisons raked Paul Strand and Gene Cocreham for 10 hits, and ran pell-mell around the bases with cheerful and deliberate malice, much like Donald Duck's nephews, Huey, Dewey, and Louie.

The Big Chief was upset. Terribly upset. His anger came on like a battering ram. Shoddy play was unacceptable even in meaningless exhibition games, and his grim, ornery, foul-mouthed postgame explosion scared the players half to death. That evening they skulked out of Buffalo on a New York Central Pullman, their tails between their legs.

The Braves' manager was so filled with bad humor that he boarded the train much earlier than the rest of the party, alone and with little civility. "Once you lose," he said, "you want to get out of there and start thinking about tomorrow. No well-wishers. No good-byes. No interviews. No nothing. Just get out of there."

There wasn't a lot of talk among the boys when the train left Buffalo. Empty gazes stared through unwashed windows at the darkening sky as the train rocked along the south shore of Lake Erie. Damp with perspiration, swimming in heat and the stink of tobacco, the men ate stale sandwiches, flipped through magazines, smoked cheap cigars, drank a beer or two, and read the paper, anything to pass the time. Gamblers among them shuffled decks, dealt hands, smacked down cards, and raked in winnings. Someone strummed a mournful guitar.

Les Mann, sitting by himself, leafed through a dog-eared edition of Edgar Rice Burroughs's latest bestseller, *Tarzan of the Apes*. Another book lay at his side: Price Collier's *Germany and the Germans*. And nearby George Davis was studying a book of poems he'd just picked up at the Harvard Coop, *A Boy's Will*, the work of a young New England poet by the name of Robert Frost.

George Stallings sat alone at the end of the car, submerged in ruminations, listening to the familiar rhythm of the rails, an expression of disgust on his face. Every now and then his head moved from side to side. He'd click his dentures, scowl and curse the dirty rotten luck plaguing the team, thinking how he'd worked so hard to keep the club functioning in the dark days of April and May. Now this.

The team was breaking apart, backsliding into mediocrity. They'd lost five straight in the first four days of July (they were 15 games behind the first-place Giants) and made a nightmarish 21 errors in those five games... 21 errors. What happened to pride? he wondered. Did it crash and burn? A grunt of frustration boiled out of his throat. Somehow the team had to be shaken up and put back on track.

When it came time to retire, the Big Chief rose to his feet, his eyes bulging, his mouth pursed, his chest heaving, and walked up and down the aisle. Tremors of rage ran through his body. (The players knew the look.) As he walked, he stopped and stared at each player and moved on. Three times he walked up and down the aisle. Some of the boys turned their heads away, averted their eyes, tried to avoid his glare. They dared not look up.

Stallings stopped short when he reached his compartment door, turned brusquely, and looked fixedly down the long Pullman, his angry, swarthy face bathed in sweat. A sarcastic smile parted his lips: "Bah!" he snarled, in a voice like an arctic wind. "You call yourselves big leaguers, huh? Why you—" He broke off. There was a distressful pause. "You goddamn bums couldn't whip a girlie team in petticoats."

"His grunt of disgust cut us to the quick," Maranville said. "I don't think we were ever hurt more."

When Stallings's stateroom door slammed shut, Johnny Evers, leaning his shoulder against a window, intuitively alert to what was going on, put on a pretense of reading a newspaper while keeping an eye on each player's reaction. Most stared at the door, their feelings in turmoil. The Pullman lapsed into silence. No one spoke.

Maranville's shoulders gave an involuntary shrug, his brow wrinkled in furrows. He pulled a crumpled pack of Chesterfields out of his shirt pocket, shook a cigarette loose, lit up, and inhaled a lungful. Smoke filtered slowly from his nostrils. Rab was not without blame, in spite of some sensational performances. Afternoon games left the restless young man free for an evening of pleasure, and the hormonally unhinged Rabbit seldom went to the library. Getting tanked up and picking up a Broadway showgirl or a chick out for kicks was a lot more fun. Singing and dancing and whooping it up in saloons until four or five in the morning left him besotted and hardly ready for action the following afternoon.

Smoke wreathed Maranville's head. He waved it away, cleared his throat, and broke the silence. "John," he called across the aisle, "can you play better ball than you've been playing?"

Evers, bent over a copy of the *Chicago Tribune,* looked up irritably and thought for a minute before answering. "Yeah, I think I can." He removed a dead cigar from his mouth, bit off the end, spit it out, relit the cigar, and added, "Hell, I know goddamn well I can."

"I can certainly crank it up a couple of notches," Rab replied.

This gave the guys within earshot a bit of a start. What an admission. Two of the league's brightest stars, Evers and Maranville, admitting they were not doing as well as they could day in and day out. Working in perfect harmony, the Crab and Rab inspired salvos of applause wherever they went. Their play often changed the swing of a game. They were the fastest double-play combination in all of baseball: marvelous theater, fun to watch, fluid and natural, the ultimate sideshow.

On the road, Stallings assigned Maranville to room with Evers, thinking that the arrangement might keep the kid out of trouble. If anyone could straighten out Rabbit and give him a little polish and stability, Evers was the man to do it.

Johnny lived and breathed baseball every waking hour of the day. He knew what to do, how to do it, and when to do it, and it seemed like he remembered every play and every situation, as well as the strengths and weaknesses of the players he'd faced in the 1,400 major-league games he'd played in, information he willingly shared with Maranville and the others.

Rabbit asked questions, listened attentively, disagreed occasionally, and when he won a point, silence usually followed.

"Evers was the old pro," Rabbit said, "the brains and everything else of the club. His effect on me was tremendous. We would sit in the room at night, him reading the newspaper and me walking up and down smoking

Chesterfields. Every now and then I'd interrupt and ask, 'How do you play this guy?' or 'What does this guy pitch?' John wasn't much of a talker. He'd look up at me, answer in a few words, and go right on reading the paper."

Maranville handled more chances in the field that season than any shortstop in baseball history. His combined total of 1,046 assists and putouts in a single season is a record that stands today.* Johnny Evers was right there at his side, all season long, shouting encouragement, giving directions, applauding or scolding, on every play.

Kinetic energy picked them up. Made them better. Evers attributed his own success of hitting the heights within himself to working alongside Maranville. "I suddenly realized I had to hustle to keep up with him, raise the level of my game." After a short pause he said, "Just think about it for a minute. For years I played next to one of the greatest shortstops there ever was, Joe Tinker, and thought Joe was the last word. But I changed my mind."

Maranville absorbed and grasped plays quickly, plays the average infielder took two or three months to master. That made him an almost instant success when he joined the Braves. "I figured I was pretty well-rounded in baseball knowledge," Evers said, "but contact with Rabbit proved me wrong. I can still learn something from him."

And this was coming from a seasoned warrior, a ferocious, stomping, clattering, swaggering, ego-driven ball player, the kind opponents can't stand. Nobody liked him. The guy even annoyed his own teammates. "He'd make you want to punch him in the nose," Maranville said. "But you knew you were playing alongside a winner and you didn't. You listened, because Johnny was a brain, smart and tough, and you knew he was thinking of the team."

Evers was tough all right. For years he went without speaking to Joe Tinker, his partner at shortstop on some of the great Chicago Cubs teams. "With good reason," Evers said. "Tinker was arrogant and had a chip on his shoulder. One day the bastard threw me a ball real hard [like a catcher throwing to the second baseman]. He did it when he was right on top of me, threw the goddamn ball so hard it broke my finger. I swore at him. He laughed. That did it. I'd had all I could take of that son of a bitch."

Though they played alongside each other for years afterward, they never spoke to each other again. Once in a while they'd have a fistfight on the field; they often traded punches in the clubhouse and went through

---

* Rabbit Maranville is also major-league baseball's all-time leader at all positions in career assists with 8,967. Dave Bancroft of the New York Giants tied Maranville's record in 1922.

two World Series without uttering a word to each other. Other than that, they got along pretty well.

"What a guy thinks about another guy on a ball team doesn't mean a goddamn thing," Evers said. "That's a personal affair. What a guy thinks about the team as a whole is something else. Tinker and myself. We hated each other. So what? But we'd come close to killing people for the team."

"But John," someone said, "how about the time you and Tinker trapped Ty Cobb off second base in the 1907 World Series? You guys must have been talking to each other then?"

"No, we weren't," Evers said. "I remember the incident very well. We were playing Detroit. We took signs from each other but we didn't speak. Cobb was on second and Johnny Kling was our catcher. I think Kling was the first Jew in the majors."†

"Cobb took a lead off second and Tinker said to him, 'Don't get too far off the bag, Ty, or the Jew will get you.' With that Tinker gave me the signal to take the throw. Cobb, a self-taught antisemite, turned and snarled something at Tinker as I rushed over to cover the bag. Kling fired a perfect strike. We caught Cobb by a good two feet. The play helped us win the ballgame and the series."

The maniacal Evers was the gasoline and steering wheel of the ball club. He relished the big stage and had a front-runner's sense of determination, a relentless drive for perfection, and a penchant for headbutting. Defeat crushed him. If he got four hits in a game, and the team lost, the four hits didn't matter; he was downcast, miserable, and more than a little sarcastic.

Johnny Evers was just plain hell.‡

Here they were, Evers and Maranville, baseball's regular Pac-Men of the diamond, seated on a Pullman headed for Chicago, acknowledging loud enough for others to hear them that they could play better baseball.

Quite a few of the Braves had not been performing up to the level of their ability for some time. Their poor attitude preyed on Evers's mind. Win or lose, Captain Johnny expected a total effort. Nothing less. It was the only

---

† Lipman Pike was the first Jewish athlete to play baseball professionally in the majors; he was one of the leading names of the game between 1866 and 1887.

‡ During an interview with Betty McGinnis, Rabbit Maranville's daughter, I asked about Johnny Evers. "Oh," she said, "I loved him like an uncle. He was nice to me." "Was he a nice man?" I asked. "No," she replied.

way to play the game. What these guys needed was a jolt, something to snap them out of their ennui, something to spur them on, something to make them play more consistently at a high level.

The train gave a long whistle and shuddered as an eastbound express thundered by.

Suddenly there was a blast of mockery from one end of the Pullman to the other. "Some of you guys aren't playing at the intensity you have to play at to win," Evers shouted. "We've got to have commitment. No more lackadaisical play. We've gotta change the pattern. Change our luck."

Cursing and making tight-lipped acid comments, he demanded an all-out effort and moved down the aisle, swaying, his jaw set like a rock, a flash of anger in his eyes. "Put aside thoughts of individual accomplishments and personal statistics. Promise you'll play your heart out for the team when you're not a hundred percent," he said, his blue eyes snapping.

He moved from player to player. No one escaped, regular or benchwarmer. If a man hesitated or sat poker-faced, Evers challenged him, got in his face, eyeball to eyeball, and was even more indomitable. Blunt words were exchanged. He would work himself into a frenzy and refuse to move until he extracted the response he wanted. And he made each player shout it out for everyone to hear.

"We can still make the first division. We're a first-division ball club. You know it. I know it. Winning's about chemistry. About cohesiveness. About what we do together. Call it what you want. I don't give a good goddamn what you call it. We gotta do the little things. We gotta make the effort. We gotta change."

Evers turned to James and Rudolph and Tyler. "You guys," he said, an accusatory tone in his voice, "underperforming disappointments. That's what you are." They knew his meaning. "You gotta do better. You know that. You've got to make the commitment. We're counting on you."

"It was at this point that Stallings's psychology began to function with effect," Hank Gowdy recalled. "We didn't know it at the time, but a startling transformation had begun to take place. Johnny got us thinking that we could still salvage the season . . . in spite of our revolting start. It sounded good. But could we do it? The only way to find out was to try, and that's what we decided to do."

CHAPTER 27

THE CRAB AND RAB

The moment the Braves stepped onto the field at West Side Grounds in Chicago, George Stallings sensed a change, a certain intensity, a new cohesiveness, an emotional eagerness, not anything he could actually put his finger on, not exactly. It was more like a feeling of stepped-up concentration, increased sharpness, greater determination.

Nothing much bothered the boys in their second swing through the league's western cities. If someone booted a ball and it cost the team a run, so be it; they bounced back, scored, and made up for the mistake.

As good as they looked, it was not good enough for Johnny Evers. "I guess I gotta do it all myself," the ball-busting Crab told a reporter. "If nobody else can't do nothing, I guess I gotta do it." John felt the guys were not sprinting fast enough or sliding hard enough or playing smart enough.

Evers and Maranville were maddeningly good around second base. Wherever they played they were terrific. Their animated brilliance started and stopped all kinds of rallies. And they performed with so much gusto, their teammates extended themselves in an effort to keep up with them. Everybody played better ball.

"Shorty led off the second," the *Chicago Tribune* reported, "beating out a hit. He stole second and fussed so, Hippo Vaughn, the pitcher, tried to pick him off and threw wildly into center field. Maranville went to third. He saw Tommy Leach, the center fielder, loafing on the play, and kept right on going, easily beating Leach's throw home."

Nothing came easily, though. They scuffled. They fought. They won. They battled for everything. In Chicago they took advantage of the Cubs' poor fielding and careless baserunning to win three of four games. They'd now defeated the Cubs seven out of nine times, something they hadn't done in years. The boys were doing the little things well, things they'd been doing poorly in the past, and the breaks were evening out.

The stop in St. Louis was no different. The Braves buried the Cardinals under an avalanche of runs, 12–5, in the first game of the series, a Sunday game that Maranville sat out because of the death of his younger brother, John, who passed away in Springfield, Massachusetts, after a long illness.

Knowing how close Rabbit and his brother were, Stallings told the heart-heavy Maranville: "Get yourself packed and go home," even though the team was halfway across the country. "Take all the time you need."

Rabbit refused. "The team needs me," he said. "I'll go to church, though . . . if you don't mind . . . and I'll be in the lineup tomorrow."

A devout Roman Catholic and former altar boy at the Sacred Heart Church in Springfield, Maranville attended early morning Mass, as they say, religiously. His belief in the Almighty was a lifelong habit, and he counted among his friends many members of the clergy.

Rabbit dipped his fingers in the cold marble basin, made the sign of the cross, and slowly walked down a side aisle, the mingled scent of candle wax and incense filling his nostrils. He stopped in front of a bank of flickering votive candles and lit two of them, one for his brother, John, the other for his mother, Catherine, whom he'd lost when he was a boy of eight. Rab then knelt quietly on a padded riser in one of the oak pews, hands clasped in prayer, his lips moving silently, and said Our Fathers and Hail Marys for the souls of the two people he loved most. Silently he dedicated the next day's game to his brother John.

"That marvelous little fellow was back today," J. B. Sheridan wrote in the *St. Louis Globe-Democrat,* "and what a wonderful afternoon he had. He made some miraculous stops, catches and throws, got two doubles and a single, scored three runs and cut off as many Cardinal runs as the Boston team made."

"The Cardinals will never win another ball game from the Braves," a writer for the *St. Louis Republic* said, "unless somebody chloroforms Maranville. He isn't bigger than a flea," but he made "plays that were nothing short of highway robbery. It can't be done is not in Maranville's repertoire. He can do anything."

Although an even break was all the Braves managed in St. Louis, they exhibited a lot more grit and tenacity than they'd ever shown before. Each man playing a role. They were smart, aggressive, and brassy. There was no dawdling or fooling around. And Johnny Evers never looked better.

Bill James exhibited eye-catching control in the opener at Cincinnati. His spitter was breaking in all sorts of puzzling ways. He dominated the Reds until the sixth when, suddenly, he got sick on the mound. Shifting uneasily from one foot to the other, then back again, his mouth contorted; he looked like he was about to disgorge the contents of his stomach.

Umpire Mal Eason stopped the game and called for a doctor. James waved him off and made strange motion toward the Braves' bench. Manager Stallings, sitting in the corner of the dugout with what looked like a pound of tobacco in his cheek, knew exactly what was wrong. He stood up, bowed low, hat in hand, passed a colossal chaw of tobacco into his lucky fedora, and sent the chaw, from his own mouth, out to Bill James. Happiness spread over Bill's face.

The umpire could not believe what he was witnessing. "Look here, you," he said, reproachfully, "did you stop this game to get a chaw?"

"Well," Bill said, wiping brown spittle on his sleeve. "What was I supposed to do? I swallowed mine."

The umpire was not amused.

Nor did he see any humor in Rabbit Maranville's cleverly contrived attempt at outwitting him, a ruse the boss encouraged.

With the Braves leading 1–0, a fastball ticked Maranville's bat and may have hit his hand as well. Rab let out a terrible squawk. Jumped around in great distress. Threw the hand in the air. Gave it a nervous flutter and, using the index finger of his other hand, indicated where the ball hit him. "Damn . . . that hurt," he said, shaking his head and looking at his hand as he took a step toward first base.

Umpire Mal Eason ripped off his mask and snarled. "Ain't that too bad. Get back up there and hit. If your hand's injured, it was injured shaking dice last night."

The Braves didn't get away with a whole lot of gonzo tactics, but their penchant for nasty, aggressive deception did give them an adrenaline rush. Tricks also put a good deal of pressure on opponents and umpires. And Johnny Evers's sarcastic verbal prods and infectious passion kept the adrenaline flowing at a high level. Johnny, the club's necromancer, also mixed an occasional pat on the back among his harsh comments. A pat coming from Evers was a rare and beautiful thing. It really gave a player an emotional boost.

Though nearly crippled after being spiked (Evers's right shin was heavily swathed in bandages), Johnny performed remarkably well both at bat and in the field, relying on his experience and guile in leading the Braves' march to get out of last place. His spectacular one-handed grabs and sharp line drives gave the team a much-needed lift. That week he batted .579, the best week ever in 13 big-league seasons.

On the nineteenth of July (a Sunday), after taking Friday and Saturday contests from the Cincinnati Reds, the Braves, going for a sweep of the series, found themselves in a deep hole. They trailed 2–0 with two on and two out in the ninth inning. But they didn't quit. They fashioned a minor miracle instead, exploding for three runs that turned a certain defeat into a glorious victory.

And what a victory it was.

The win over the fourth-place Reds lifted the Braves out of last place, one percentage point ahead of the Pirates, whom they were about to play in a five-game series at Forbes Field in Pittsburgh. The Braves had shaken off their early-season torpor. Great pitching and a tight defense sparked the turnaround, and they roared into Pittsburgh and beat the Pirates four times in five games, 1–0, 6–0, 1–0, and 2–0, despite practically no hitting. Tyler pitched two of the shutouts, Rudolph and James the other two.

The Buccaneers didn't roll over and just die. Wilbur Cooper was brilliant in the final game of the series. He scattered three hits and didn't allow a run as the two teams grappled and struggled in a scoreless tie. It seemed like the Braves' hitters were hoping for hits instead of producing them.

"I'd been up to the plate a couple of times," Rabbit recalled. "Cooper was unconscious. I couldn't buy a hit. There was nothing I could do except watch his pitches go by and flip my bat in the direction of the dugout."

Stallings called Rabbit aside as he was about to take another crack at Cooper. "Come on, Rabbit. Do something," he said in a low voice. "We gotta have this game . . . It's a big one."

"Yeah. Yeah. I know . . . I know. But I can't hit this guy today. He's impossible."

"You know what McGraw's players do in situations like this, don't you?" Stallings said, dropping his voice to almost a whisper. "You know . . . where they just need a run to win . . . Guys like Grant . . . Fletcher . . . Snodgrass . . . they stick out their arms and get hit on the sleeve."

"Yeah. I know. But McGraw had long sleeves made for them . . . So they can do that . . . We don't have long sleeves."

"What the hell difference does that make?" Stallings snarled, acting offended and making a gesture of disgust. "Well, goddamn it," he blustered. "I don't care what you do . . . Just go out there and get on, somehow."

Feeling a tinge of guilt for letting the boss down, Maranville shrugged noncommittally and offered the Chief a sheepish smile. A thought popped into his mind as he headed for the plate. "Why not try it? Why don't I at least try sticking my arm out a little bit?"

"I stuck my arm out on the first pitch and failed to get hit. To my surprise, the umpire said, 'Ball one.' Well, I said to myself, I guess I'll stick my arm out again on this next pitch. A little farther this time." It missed again. "Ball two."

Stallings, bellowing something unprintable from the dugout, urged Rabbit on.

Maranville pulled at his jersey, loosened it, gave Stallings a confident look, took a deep breath, and this time quietly dug in, much closer to the plate. Almost leaning over it.

Cooper gave Rabbit an angry stare. He knew exactly what the little guy was up to. Coop rocked back and forth and delivered one high and tight, a nasty rising fastball. The pitch seemed to come out of nowhere.

Thonk.

It slammed into Maranville's forehead, right between the eyes. Rabbit lay unconscious for three minutes. Maybe four. He was only barely alert when he finally came to. A vein throbbed like mad in his temple. Pain stabbed through his head. The impressions from the seams of the ball were visible on his forehead.

Cy Rigler, the umpire behind the plate, looked at him severely. He shook his head with displeasure, sighed deeply, and said, "Rabbit . . . I'll tell you what . . . if you can walk to first base, I'll let you get away with it." Rabbit made it to his feet and hobbled out of the batter's box, still dazed. About three-quarters of the way down the first-base line, some big dumb Irishman in the grandstand stood up and shouted: "That's putting the wood on it, Rabbit."

The game remained scoreless until the ninth inning. Hank Gowdy was sent up to bat for the pitcher, George Tyler. One man was out and the bases were loaded. The count went to three and two. Cooper let fly a fastball, a sizzler, just off the plate. Gowdy swung. Held up. Too late. He'd gone too far around. Up came Rigler's right arm. Instinctively, Gowdy turned, half in anger, half mad at himself, about to argue, and saw Rigler pointing at first base.

"Take your base," he said. The ball four call forced in the go-ahead run, the improbable winning run. (The Braves went on to score another run in the inning.) Infuriated, the Pirates, screaming in rage, charged the umpire, challenging him. But he did not budge. The decision stood.

Bill James came in for Tyler in the last half of the ninth and set down the Pirates in one-two-three order, and, as we have seen, the Braves walked off the field with a 2–0 victory.

The boys were beginning to believe in themselves. Their upbeat sentiment grew. They played each game as if it were part of a movie of a game they'd won the previous day, confident about the way it would turn out. Because breaks played such an important part in a number of victories—other teams called their sudden burst of excellence "luck"—critics felt that they'd soon suffer a letdown and fall back into the pack. And it certainly looked that way when they lost a heartbreaker, a game they had all but won. But the boys bounced back with a vengeance after the loss and won nine in a row.

They were formidable now, 23–5 since the sixth of July. The turnaround lifted them to within six and a half games of the league-leading New York Giants.

The charging Braves were big news in Boston. But the headlines in newspapers throughout the nation focused on something far more earthshaking than baseball, the deepening crisis in Europe:

WAR

EUROPE AFLAME

AUSTRIA HURLS ARMY INTO SERBIA

CHAPTER 28

WITHOUT CHARGE

The sports world watched the streaking Braves with interest. They were a ball club different from anything fans had seen before, a team built on camaraderie, fraternity, and friendship, whose mindset had shifted from hoping to win to expecting to win. Winning became a habit. They were humming right along, doing their best diamond work to date.

Would they stay competitive or break under the strain? The question lingered.

Grantland Rice played up the Braves' potential. "They have shown a vast superiority over the Cubs and Cardinals over the past six weeks," he said. "They are close enough to be in the running. Now it depends on what they do in hand-to-hand combat with the Giants."

The next day's *Evening Sun* characterized Rice's comments as "nonsense" and went on to remind its readers that Stallings's machine would be well worn down by the first of September and probably fade back into the pack.

Excitement crackled on the streets of Boston on the fourth of August. The Braves, 47–45, were making a run at the Giants, closing the gap, putting themselves squarely in the picture, and it seemed like everyone in the Hub City was Braves crazy.

Though some pundits may have considered the possibility of the Braves overtaking the Giants a joke, John McGraw was not taking the threat lightly. And rightly so. The Giants had been playing only a shade better than .500 ball for weeks and were showing no signs of snapping out of their long spell of listlessness. "I'm not looking forward to the games at the Polo Grounds with any great amount of enthusiasm," McGraw said. "Stallings is liable to play my team off its feet."

As the mania set in, the crowds grew dense at South End Grounds. The crush was terrific. Sellouts were the norm. Thousands were turned away. Aware of the Braves' loss of precious revenue, Red Sox owner Joe Lannin congratulated Jim Gaffney on the success of his ball club and offered the use of the much larger Fenway Park for the remainder of the season—without charge.

It was an overwhelming show of goodwill. Gaffney thanked Lannin profusely for his graciousness and said, "Boston needs two pennants. Let's go after them."

The success of the Braves lifted spirits everywhere; the war news from Europe seemed secondary in importance. From Maine to California newspaper headlines told the story:

Boston is excited and Germany's declaration of war pales into insignificance alongside the announcement that George Tyler will pitch today.

Cardinal players claim that in all their experience on the diamond, they never have encountered a luckier club than the Braves.

Umpire Byron was hit on the head with an empty bottle in Boston today . . . There was no harm done, both being empty.

CHAPTER 29

THE BAD BOY

George Stallings spent a good deal of the day at South End Grounds when the Braves were at home, and seeing visiting Pittsburgh out early for extra batting practice before the opening game of the homestand, he ambled over to the batting cage to see what the Pirates' manager had to say for himself. The batter in the cage, Max Carey, lashed a liner down the left field line, glanced at Stallings, winked, moved to the other side of the plate, and banged a line drive into short right field.

"Not bad," Stallings said, trying to start a conversation. No response. "He's swinging the wood pretty good," Stallings said, pulling a slab of tobacco out of his pocket and handing a piece to Fred Clarke before pressing some into his own cheek.

The Pittsburgh manager nodded. "He can hit them there slow ones, but get a fella out there who puts a little giddy-up on the ball and the son of a bitch can't hit nothin'." (Carey was suffering through the throes of a dreadful season.)

"Have you and Barney thought about trading him?" Stallings asked. "We'd sure like to have him." Clarke ignored the question and focused on Hans Wagner stepping into the cage.

"He ain't available."

"How about Mowrey? The papers say you ain't too thrilled with him."

"The guy's a disaster."

"We'd take a chance on him."

"Well, you better hurry. Barney's talking to Charlie Ebbets right now. Ebbets is all hot and bothered about Mike."

"Brooklyn???"

"Yeah. Robby needs a third sacker. Smith's way out of hand. Robby can't handle him."

Within 15 minutes, Stallings was on the phone with Jim Gaffney, telling him what he'd just learned. "See if you can get Red Smith," Stallings said. "We sure as hell can use the guy."

"You sure? A lot of talk around town. The guy's a bad actor."

"Yeah . . . yeah . . . I know. But, damn, he's a hell of a hitter, the best third baseman available."

"When he has a mind to be," Gaffney replied.

"I can handle him, Jim . . . Don't worry. I can handle him . . . Red can be special."

Charlie Ebbets welcomed Gaffney's call but insisted on players in exchange for the bad boy. Gaffney stood firm. Ebbets was in a tight spot and Gaffney knew it. Red wouldn't go anywhere he didn't want to go. Red wanted to join a contender. If he didn't get his way, he'd jump to the Feds. When Ebbets hesitated, Gaffney sweetened the pot; he made penny-pinching Charlie an offer he couldn't refuse.

Stallings immediately wired Smith a welcoming telegram and asked if he'd mind joining the Braves at once; the crucial series with the Giants was fast approaching.

This suited Red just fine. He was ready to get out of Brooklyn. He didn't have many friends there anyway. Red caught an early train out of Grand Central, arrived in Boston on Sunday, the ninth of August (no game was scheduled because of Sunday blue laws), and hurried over to the Braves' offices on Tremont Street.

Smith didn't know Big George, other than to say hello. They'd never really talked. But he'd seen the big fellow in action. The Big Guy was not to be trifled with. Gaffney was a mystery. Red knew the name. He'd seen it in the papers. He was a big shot. That's all he knew.

I suppose they're going to read me the riot act, Smith thought to himself as he took a seat opposite the two men. Well, they've got another think coming. I'll set 'em straight.

Years later, Smith would smile and shake his head with amused satisfaction while recalling what took place that afternoon.

"As soon as I reported, Manager Stallings began using psychology on me: '"Red,"' he said, 'I'm raising your salary.' Well, you can imagine my surprise. It was darn good psychology."

Red smiled to himself and thought about the meeting for a long few seconds. "Then, with Mr. Gaffney looking on, the Big Chief got up and walked over to me, his mouth parting in a wide smile, and placed a hand on my shoulder: "Red," he said (now pay attention to this—this is the good part). "Red," he said, "you're the man we've needed on this club. You're the man who's going to win the pennant for us."

Recalling the conversation, Red said, "I didn't know what to say. I was excited. I felt like a million bucks."

Jumping to his feet, a broad smile on his face, Red shook hands with Stallings and Gaffney and thanked them profusely. "See you at the ball park tomorrow afternoon," he said, starting for the door.

"Tomorrow morning," Stallings said. "Morning practice."

Red stopped short: "Morning practice? You guys still hold morning practice?"

"We kind of like it," Stallings said, his voice overflowing with warmth.

Smith glanced from Stallings to Gaffney, shrugged, and walked out.

CHAPTER 30

I SEEN IT DONE

The Braves continued to torture the visiting Pirates beyond understanding. Rudolph was unhittable in the series opener, stopping the Pirates 1–0 on two scratch singles. The only batter who gave him any trouble was little Jimmy Viox, the Pirates' second baseman. Jimmy fouled off seven balls in the eighth inning, four onto the New York, New Haven and Hartford tracks beyond the third-base stands, and drew a walk, the lone base on balls given up by Rudolph all afternoon.

"Goddamn hitting," Fred Clarke muttered. "They were knocking the hell out of the ball in April and May. What the hell happened?" He shook his head. "Never saw the likes of it. Nothin' like this."

The Pittsburgh players cursed their luck, pointed fingers at one another, blamed anyone and everyone: the umpires, the cold, the rain. They were especially distressed by their inability to knock the ball out of the infield when it counted. The big bashers—Hans Wagner, Max Carey, and Ed Knoetchy—were a bust. There was no bite in their toothless bats.

"That's it. That's it," one of the players on the Pirates' bench said excitedly. "It's the balls."

"What the hell are you jabbering about?"

Someone laughed. "His brain's overheated."

"It's the balls. Don't you see, guys? Those bastards are screwing around with the balls."

"Aw ... Come on."

"No, no. Wait. Listen to me ... Remember back in June? The last time we were here? The day Hub came to bat with that telegraph pole?"

"They swept us. So what?"

Above left: George Stallings, manager, Boston Braves, 1914 (Baseball Hall of Fame, Cooperstown, NY)

Above right: James E. Gaffney, owner, Boston Braves, 1914 (Author's collection)

Left: Ban Johnson, president of the American League (Collection of John Rogers)

Above: Manager Connie Mack (*center*) and Captain Ira Thomas (*right*) of the Philadelphia Athletics, conferring while the Boston Braves were walloping Chief Bender's delivery to all corners of the lot in Game One of the 1914 World Series (Author's collection)

Right: Rabbit Maranville, Boston Braves, 1914 (Author's collection)

Above, from left: Bill Sweeney, Johnny Evers, and Hub Perdue of the Boston Braves, spring training, Tampa, Florida, March 1914 (Author's collection)

Left: Dick Rudolph, Boston Braves, 1914 (Author's collection)

Joey Connolly, the speedy left fielder of the Boston Braves, 1914 (Author's collection)

Above left: Josh DeVore, Boston Braves, 1914 (Author's collection)

Above right: Hank Gowdy, Boston Braves, 1914 (Author's collection)

Left: Charlie Deal, Boston Braves, 1914 (Author's collection)

Fans cram the rooftops on Twenty-First Street beyond the right-field fence at Shibe Park to watch Game One of the 1914 World Series (Author's collection)

Left: Leslie Mann, Boston Braves, 1914 (Author's collection)

Below: Shibe Park, Game One of the 1914 World Series (Author's collection)

"Don't you see? Think about it. Klem tossed out a lot of balls that day. Remember? A couple of dozen—maybe."

"So?"

By this time others had perked up their ears. "He did, didn't he?" someone said. "That son of a bitch Stallings would do anything to get an edge."

"Yeah," another fellow said. "The gink's a slippery bastard."

"Sure is," three or four others chimed in.

Pirate manager Fred Clarke pushed forward, frowned slightly, narrowed his eyes, and thought about the player's theory. "Screwin' around with the balls? Hmm. Sounds far-fetched," he said, "but maybe you guys are on to somethin'. I'm gonna have a talk with Billy."

Clarke signaled for time and approached Billy Hart, the umpire calling balls and strikes behind the plate. Hart listened, nodded, and considered Clarke's complaint. Scuffed balls? Dirty balls? He shifted his weight from one foot onto the other and back again. "You might have something there. Some of them do look pretty bad."

"They do it all the time," Clarke said. "There's a gang of kids out on the tracks. You've seen 'em, Billy. They chase foul balls. Bring 'em back filthy, covered with coal dust, gravel, mud, and soot. The Braves put them back into play when we're at bat. Always when we're at bat. Not when they're at bat."

Billy Hart heaved a sigh of weariness, turned, and walked toward the Braves dugout. Several Pirates players following closely in his footsteps.

Stallings got up and met the umpire. "What's eatin' at you, Billy?"

"George, I don't want no more dirty balls thrown into the game."

"You fucking with me, Billy?"

"You're supplying balls, aren't you?"

"Yeah . . . "

"Well, what I'm saying is, if you supply the balls, you are responsible. No more discolored balls."

"You don't know what the fuck you're talkin' about."

"Somebody's paying those ragamuffins out there."

"You accusing me, Billy?" Stallings said, the heat rising in his face. "Those sooty-faced youngsters want a free ride into the ballpark. That's all. Nobody's paying them."

The Big Chief waved his arms in exasperation, a stricken look on his face. "You tellin' me we're doctoring the balls? That's crazy, Billy. You know me better than that. I wouldn't do no such thing. No sirree. These guys are a bunch of bellyachers. That's all. They're soreheads looking for an alibi . . . because they can't beat us."

"Maybe so, George. But I'm tellin' you. No more dirty balls or you're outta here."

"That ain't the half of it," one of the Pirates protested. "They're using frozen balls."

"Aw . . . for Chrissake," Stallings said, shaking his head. "First it's dirty balls. Now it's frozen balls. What the hell are they going to come up with next?"

"Put me wise on that, will ya?" Hart said.

"When we're batting," the Pirates' manager said. "That's what they're usin'. Frozen balls. We're being fucked over."

"The guy's a fruitcake. Any fool knows you can't freeze a baseball. The next thing he'll say is that I'm responsible for this lousy weather. Well, I'm tellin' you right now, Billy, I ain't."

"Wait a minute, boys, wait a minute," Hart said. "Not so fast, calm down, all of you." He paused until he was certain he had everyone's attention.

"I seen it done. Frozen baseballs. It ain't so strange as it sounds. I seen it with my own eyes down in the minors. They act funny. That's all. They're hard to control when you hit 'em. And you can't hit 'em far neither."

"This ain't winter, Billy. You can't freeze a fucking baseball in the summertime. It ain't possible."

"Yes, it is, George. You can put 'em in an icebox. Leave 'em in for twelve hours. And bingo. They freeze. I tell you, I seen it done. They stay froze a long time. All you gotta do is keep them in a cool place. In a box or somethin'. They don't swell up none or nothin'."

The umpires inspected each ball put into the game after that. They were damp and cold, but so was the weather, and Hart and Rigler decided that the atmosphere was probably responsible, not an icebox, as the Pirates claimed.

The incident was good copy, though. Pittsburgh's sportswriters needled the Pirates and poked fun at their latest excuse for losing.

"The Pirate crew of heavy hitters came up with another new alibi yesterday," L. G. Boggs told readers in the Food for Fans column of the *Pittsburgh Press*. "And this one is a pip: They imagined the Braves were using frozen baseballs when the Pirates were at bat. Yes, sir, folks. Frozen baseballs. Your eyes aren't playing tricks on you. That's what they claimed. Frozen baseballs. The umpires examined the balls and found them okay and our boys went on to lose another one. If the cause of the Pirates' slump is frozen baseballs, I guess all the teams in the league must have big ice bills this summer."

❖❖❖

Years later, Gabe Paul, the baseball executive who put together pennant winners at Cincinnati in 1961 and several championship teams for George Steinbrenner's New York Yankees in the late 1970s, told how George Stallings gave him his start in baseball (as a batboy for the hometown Rochester Red Wings) and how Stallings (the then Rochester manager) conspired to give the home team an edge.

Whenever the Red Wings were ahead late in a game, Stallings sent young Gabe Paul or his brother Sam Paul out to a grocery store behind the left field seats, where baseballs were stored in an icebox. The youngsters got the balls and slipped them, deadened by the cold, into the umpire's supply for use during the visiting team's final at bats.

George Stallings was far from alone in employing the surreptitious tactic, though, mysteriously, the names of the other practitioners are seldom mentioned.

A nineteenth-century statistician, George L. Moreland, author of *Balldom: The Britannica of Baseball,* told about a deceptively self-effacing young playing manager from the Smokey City who was also Pittsburgh's catcher. He was known for engaging in all kinds of underhanded tricks.

"There was an icebox in the Pittsburgh office," Moreland recalled, and the young playing manager "got the idea of freezing baseballs. . . . It really deadened them. He'd work a frozen ball into play in the late innings while the visiting team was at bat, and substitute a normal ball when his own team was at bat."

Fifty years later, Fred Lieb, the catcher's biographer, asked the now famous Hall of Famer, the very image of dignity and respectability, if Moreland's story were true. An amused twinkle came into the old man's blue-gray eyes.

"Well," he said, "we had to use a lot of tricks to win games in those days . . . and maybe that was one of them."

The old-timer's name was Connie Mack.*

---

* Connie Mack and his early Philadelphia Athletics teams also froze baseballs. But he was not alone. The 1920s Pittsburgh Pirates kept an icebox in their offices and froze baseballs overnight; manager Art Fletcher of the Philadelphia Phillies admitted that his ball club froze balls used in a two-hitter by one of his hurlers; and manager Eddie Stanky froze baseballs in support of his good-pitching, weak-hitting Chicago White Sox teams of 1966 and 1967.

CHAPTER 31

A CHANGE IN STRATEGY WAS UNTHINKABLE

The Braves were on a wave, a tidal force traveling fast, riding it hard for all it was worth, too fast, some said, predicting a fall. Some writers thought Stallings was taking foolish risks using only three starters as the pennant race heated up. It was unheard of. Critics second-guessed the strategy.

Stallings understood the debate. His young pitchers were on uncharted waters. But he saw no alternative so long as Rudolph, James, and Tyler kept on winning. A change in strategy was unthinkable. He would not settle for less. "I don't care what anybody says, it's strictly my business, and my business is winning ball games."

"You'll ruin them, George," a writer said, in the lobby of the Hotel Somerset the night before the opening game of the crucial three-game series against the Giants. "You're putting your most reliable starters at risk."

"No, no," Stallings said. "You fellows don't understand. My boys aren't being called upon to pitch any more often than they can stand." He gestured toward Rudolph, James, and Tyler across the lobby, almost hidden by a palm. "Look at them. How do they look to you?" He paused. "I've worked those guys in rotation for over a month now. They're no worse off for it. I'll tell you something else: They'll keep pitching phenomenal ball the rest of the way. You'll see. I firmly believe it."

The writer excused himself and strolled across the lobby toward Rudolph, James, and Tyler.

"McGraw says you guys are ready to crack," the writer said.

Rudolph wasn't biting. No sense in riling up the Giants. "We'll see," he said.

"You ready for them?"

"We'll show up."

"How's the arm?"

"Great."

"How about the pressure? Is it getting you guys?"

"Naw."

"Pitching every three days isn't getting to you?" the writer asked, incredulously.

"You gotta be in shape," Rudolph said. "That's all. If you're not, well..." he smiled and shrugged, "I guess it will kill you, or get you in shape pretty damn fast." They laughed. "Hell, Bill's stuff has never been better. Right, Bill?"

James nodded in agreement. "And Lefty here has been hooked up in some real battles lately. Look what he did yesterday. A nothing-nothing tie. He didn't give up a run in thirteen innings. His control is the best it's ever been. Too bad the guys didn't get him a run. He deserved a win."

"You starting tomorrow?"

"That's his call," Rudolph said, nodding toward Stallings, who was surrounded by reporters.

"George," an oversized fellow asked, "what happens if one of these guys buckles? You know, cracks. Falls to pieces?"

"Aw, come on, guys. Give me a break, will you? You know that won't happen."

"It happens."

The risk was that Stallings would flog his horses so hard they would pull up lame in September.

"Well, I'll tell you something," Stallings replied. "If anything goes wrong, anything at all, I've got one of the best youngsters in the league, George Davis. He's almost as good as Rudolph, James, and Tyler. In fact, I've been thinking about starting him against the Giants."

Everybody laughed.

George Davis owned the best stuff on the staff. A sensation out of Williams College, Davis got rave notices from scouts, most of whom believed he had all of the ingredients to become one of the stars in the game. A half dozen clubs scrambled to get his name on a contract, but his father, a well-to-do judge in Buffalo, would not hear of it. "Complete your education first," he said. That was before Yankees owner Frank Farrell dangled a $5,000 signing bonus in front of them (twice the amount most ballplayers earned in a season).

The hotshot pitching prospect signed with the Yankees in July. All that was needed now was an adjustment here, another there, cut down on the wildness, smooth out the rough edges, and Davis would be ready.

Harry Wolverton mismanaged the Yankees that season, the worst season in franchise history, and mismanaged Davis as well. The 24-year-old rookie heard a lot of talk about having the best stuff on the staff and thought he was supposed to be perfect, dominate hitters every time out. And he struggled between being brilliant and clueless.

Frank Chance, the Cubs' "Peerless Leader," replaced the hapless Wolverton at the Yankees' helm in 1913 and liked what he saw of Davis at spring training. Everything went well until a few days before the ball club was scheduled to leave Bermuda for the mainland. Davis requested a week's leave of absence to get married. He could not wait. Chance was not sympathetic. "Stick to the game," he said. "Marriage can wait."

Davis wouldn't listen. Starchy and repressed, and consumed by thoughts of pretty Georgianna Jones, he sailed for the mainland without asking permission, saying he did not have to play ball for a living. He got to church on time, honeymooned for a week, and rejoined the Yankees in New York.

Chance immediately farmed him out to Jersey City of the International League. Bad attitude. Too independent. Doesn't take baseball seriously enough.

Almost recessively shy, the moody and cerebral Davis disliked the minor leagues, and his working-class teammates disliked his boiled-milk personality. You can imagine what they thought of his habit of spending a good deal of his free time in solitude translating French and Latin. It seemed that he got a lot more enjoyment out of the company of dead Roman poets—Horace, Ovid, and Virgil—than he did from hanging around with the boys.

Most outings at Jersey City were like the lottery: full of tantalizing promise, rare in payoffs; he finished the season with a 10–16 record.

But strengths and limitations aren't always measured by statistics. George Stallings saw the ability, the raw power, the special arm. Thinking that he could remedy the flaws in the youngster's makeup, he bought his contract and placed the young man's future in the hands of Fred Mitchell.

Mitchell stressed fundamentals, arm extension, body and leg thrust, flicking the wrist, focusing on the plate, not the batter. They talked about the importance of attacking the strike zone, jumping ahead on the count, moving the ball up and down in the strike zone, and keeping pitches down.

After a while, Mitchell wore out Stallings's ears, suggesting that he give Davis a start. "The Buffalo boy is ready," he would say. It was welcome news, of course, but Stallings waited. "I want conditions just right for him," he said. "The right psychological moment."

With Stallings at the helm the Braves seldom had trouble getting up for games. The Big Chief was an inveterate schemer, something of a cross between Notre Dame's celebrated football coach, Knute Rockne, and Kansas City third baseman George Brett, a commanding influence, the kind of leader who makes a player believe that he can do anything. Stallings preached morning, noon, and night. No matter where the team was.

"Come out smoking. Attack. Take control. Jump the other guys before they jump you. Put the pressure on. Grab the lead. Never let up. They will make a mistake, and when they do, climb all over them. Make them pay."

Between July 6 and August 12 (the day before the big series with the Giants opened), Braves pitchers shut out opponents 11 times. They won six of those games by scores of 1–0, won five of them in the ninth inning, and won six of them in extra innings. A remarkable record.

Did the hard-charging Braves have a chance of catching the Giants? Most people didn't think so. They'd certainly made up a lot of ground, but the strain would soon catch up with them. John McGraw wasn't panicking. "Their pitchers are sure to crack," McGraw said. "You might see it at the Polo Grounds."

The Giants were a self-assured, experienced, and talented team of veterans accustomed to performing like champions when menaced. They outdueled the Cubs in 1911 and won by seven and a half games; pushed aside the Cubs and the Pirates in 1912 and won by 10; and turned back the preseason favorite Pirates in 1913 and won by 10. The boys from "the Big Town" were certain they would destroy the Braves, just as they had taken down threats in seasons past.

CHAPTER 32

HE DID NOT CROSS THE LINE

August 13. Braves versus Giants. Polo Grounds. New York City.

Brow damp, cheeks burning, nerves on edge, "Rube" Marquard flicked his right foot high into the air, spun, and whipped a wicked curve into "Chief" Meyers's waiting mitt.

Thud. The familiar sound split the air.

"That's the stuff," Meyers growled through clenched teeth.

Rube smiled.

"Get your hand out of your ass," a bullhorn voice bellowed above the lazy hum of the crowd. The Braves' wrecking crew was already at work. "You ain't got it no more, Rube. We're gonna bust your balls. D'ya hear?"

Rube slammed his fist into his glove, spat a stream of tobacco juice into the grass, turned so quickly that dust rose under his feet, and unleashed a verbal attack of his own.

The Boston bench howled with glee.

"Don't pay them no nevermind," a voice behind Rube said, as home plate umpire Bill Klem thrust his face mask into the air and cried, "Play ball!"

Shoulder to shoulder, the Braves huddled around George Stallings in the Boston dugout, joined hands, looked each other in the eye, and in one voice shouted, "Let's go get 'em."

In a bold display of mental belligerency, Teddy Cather, leading off for the Braves and brandishing a black bat, waved the big stick in Rube's direction as the Giants' left-hander leaned forward and studied the catcher's sign. "Up your alley," Cather snarled. Marquard flipped Cather an obscene hand gesture. For a brief moment the two stared hot-eyed at each other. Theirs was a shimmering enmity, a kind of winner-loser thing. I'm a winner, you're a loser. There would be no lollygagging at the Polo Grounds this afternoon.

Marquard's first pitch, his trademark curveball, buckled Cather's knees. Then, with the count one ball and two strikes, Cather ripped a line drive over the bag at third, sending up a puff of white chalk where the ball nicked the foul line, and cruised easily into second base. A standup double.

Johnny Evers, tight-lipped, gaunt with fatigue, a hated figure at the Polo Grounds, approached the plate, hauling heavy personal baggage. Instead of booing the Crab, as they normally did, Giants fans spontaneously applauded in a generous show of sympathy for the terrible loss Johnny and his wife had suffered the week before: the sudden death of their three-year-old daughter, Helen, after a few hours of illness with scarlet fever.*

After taking two strikes, Johnny popped a high twisting foul ball toward the seats, off first base, and watched it settle into Fred Merkle's glove for an easy out. Johnny turned and slammed the bat into the ground and disappeared into the dugout.

Joey Connolly was the next scheduled batter. Stallings normally hid Joey when a left-hander faced the Braves. Not today. Stallings was playing a hunch, and Connolly made the boss look good. He chopped a high bouncer between first and second, just beyond the first baseman's outstretched glove; Cather dashed home with the first run of the game.

With one down in the second inning, Les Mann crushed a full-count fastball into left-center. The drive seemed to rise over Bob Bescher's outstretched glove, and after several bounces and a long roll, it caromed off the concrete barrier 445 feet away. Bescher, chasing after the ball, had all kinds of trouble picking it up. By the time he did, Mann had crossed the plate standing up for an inside-the-park home run. The Braves led 2–0.

Laughing teammates spilled out of the dugout and pounded Les on the back. For a minute or so, it looked like they might carry him right out of the ballpark, but after each one of the 28 Braves shook his hand—the batboy included—the happy gang decided they'd stay around and finish the game.

After giving up the home run, Marquard settled down and went on to pitch efficient fourth and fifth innings, showing flashes of his past brilliance. But after Connolly singled in the sixth, things again began to unravel.

---

* Johnny Evers carried a gun, and in a fit of rage he shot off his wife's toe after learning that she'd taken their two little children, John Jr. and Helen, to a circus during a highly infectious scarlet fever epidemic—a leading cause of death among children. A few days later three-year-old Helen contracted the deadly disease and did not survive. Recorded interview with Betty McInnis, Rabbit Maranville's daughter, January 9, 1999. "Everybody knew it at the time," Betty remarked.

Maranville dumped a well-placed bunt along the first-base line. Rube rushed over, scooped up the ball, and tagged Rabbit using the hand without the ball. Realizing his mistake, he made a desperate backhand flip of the ball and watched it sail over Fred Merkle's glove at first base. Both runners were safe.

The next batter moved the two base runners into scoring position with a sacrifice bunt. After Red Smith popped out, Marquard breathed a sigh of relief, that is, until he saw the on-deck batter, Les Mann. Rube looked into the Giants' dugout for instructions. Two men out. Two runners in scoring position. First base open. What would it be? Put Mann on? Or pitch to him?

McGraw gave the sign: pitch to Mann.

Les watched two balls and a strike go by. Marquard, thinking he might fool Mann, tried an off-speed pitch that hung over the outside corner of the plate; the Braves' center fielder did a good job of finding a hole in the right side of the infield, blistering a sharp single through the gap. Connolly and Maranville sprinted home, giving Boston a 4–0 lead.

Bewilderment filled the eyes of McGraw's players. The Giants may have been the defending National League champions, but the Braves were the classier outfit. They ran out to their positions, made no defensive mistakes, and handled every play with poise, confidence, and élan.

The *click, click . . . tap, tap, tap* sounds of the telegraph and typewriters up in the press box drifted over the stands. Something big was happening. Sportswriters traded glances and scribbled notes.

Sam Crane, confident of a Braves victory, pecked away at his Smith Corona, polishing up a story for the late edition of the *Evening Journal.* "The fire the Braves put into their work is in direct contrast to the Giants," he wrote. "They make the champions look slow, lazy, and heavy. Rube appears to be on the mound to earn his salary, while Dick looks like he's out there because he loves to pitch."

John McGraw, carrying a potbelly on his belt, stomped around the third-base coaches' box, waved his stubby arms, pounded his fist into the fielder's glove he kept handy, and ranged in and out of the chalk lines and back and forth, like an angry hornet, trying to upset the pitcher.

Once he so infuriated Phillies pitcher Ad Brennan that Brennan boiled over and went after the little potbellied son of a bitch. Just what McGraw wanted. Before the players could get between the two men and pull Brennan away, Brennan knocked his tormentor cold with one punch. And he got in a few good kicks as well, while McGraw lay unconscious on the ground.

♦♦♦

The Giants were a solid team. They kept jabbing away and eventually got to Rudolph. Art Fletcher stretched a single into an extra-base hit when a ball trickled through Joey Connolly's glove. The next batter, Fred Merkle, saw Smith playing deep at third, five or six feet off the line, and laid down a bunt. Both runners were safe. Chief Meyers singled Fletcher home from third for the Giants' first run of the game, and a big inning appeared likely. The score was 4–1, Braves.

"Sandy" Piez ran for Meyers.

Evers called time and jogged over to the pitching mound, planted both feet in front of Rudolph, and peered into his eyes. Gowdy and the Braves infielders crowded around.

"You okay?" Evers asked in a sharp, curt voice.

Rudolph assured him he was fine with a nod and a slight smile. "They just got a little lucky, that's all."

Evers looked at Gowdy. "Well? What do you say?"

"He's not lying, John. He hasn't lost a thing."

"You sure?"

"I'm telling it straight, John. The ball's moving good."

Evers looked back at Rudolph. He could see the answer in Dick's face. Dick wanted the ball; that was half the battle. Evers lifted his cap, smoothed his shiny brilliantined hair, took a deep breath, and sighed.

"Okay, then," he said, reaching out and lightly touching Rudolph on the arm. "You stay. But let's stop the sons-a-bitches right here. Understand? Put one in his fucking ear if you have to. Scare the hell out of him." Evers turned toward the dugout and gave Stallings a confidential nod. Stallings agreed. Keep him in there.

McGraw bellowed "Time." He called back the batter, Milt Stock, and motioned for "Harvard Eddie" Grant, a good man in the clutch. "Get up there, Eddie," he said. "You can hit this guy."†

Eddie poked around for a while selecting a bat, making Rudolph wait, started for the plate, stopped, picked up a resin bag, and stared into the grandstand.

"Get up there and hit," Rudolph shouted from the mound.

Bill Klem, the home plate umpire, was no more successful in moving things along. Grant started an argument. McGraw charged down the base

---

† A 1904 graduate of Harvard, Grant would later lose his life in action during the Meuse-Argonne offensive of World War I while leading an attempted rescue of the "Lost Battalion" trapped behind enemy lines.

line and joined in. The irritated umpire scratched a line in the dirt with his spikes and turned his back on McGraw. Everyone knew what the line meant: cross it and you're out of here.

Klem was the voice of authority, an arrogant little autocrat who lost few verbal battles. Before he came along umpires were often hired because they were big and handy with their fists. The general feeling was that umpiring was only for broken-down ballplayers and rowdies who couldn't earn a living any other way; umpire-baiting was an accepted part of the game. Players swore at them, stepped on their toes, and roughed them up.‡

Bill Klem changed all that. He made umpiring a respected profession. The dynamic little thunderer became a symbol of authority in baseball officiating. He set the standard for excellence and was credited with major innovations such as the jerk of the thumb, the signal that indicated a runner was out; the palms-down gesture showing he was safe; straddling the foul line and pumping one arm or the other indicating a ball was either fair or foul.

One day, a sudden attack of laryngitis prevented him from bellowing out balls and strikes, so he improvised. For a strike, he shot his right hand above his head so everybody in the ballpark understood the pitch was a strike, and for a ball he kept his hand at his side so they knew it was a ball. The spur-of-the moment change became the custom.

While Grant and Klem went at it behind home plate, fans craned their necks. What would McGraw do? Would he challenge Klem? Would he cross the line?

In the back of his mind, Bill Klem had a fleeting image of McGraw in

---

‡ McGraw made umpire Bob Emslie's life on the diamond so miserable, publicly humiliating him on a daily basis, criticizing his eyesight and visual judgment, and shouting "You blind robber" at him every chance he got, that Emslie could stand it no longer.

One day he showed up unexpectedly at a Giants' practice carrying a .22 caliber Winchester rifle, a menacing glower on his face. The situation had every appearance of trouble. Big trouble. Emslie looked at no one. Nodded at no one. Spoke to no one. Wary of his intentions, every one of the Giants kept away from him and gave him plenty of room, especially McGraw.

"What's he up to?" "The crazy bastard." "Stay out of his way."

Emslie took his time. Looked around. Anxious eyes followed his every move while he placed a dime on the pitching rubber. He then walked slowly behind home plate, stood there for a moment, turned, raised the rifle as the players scattered for safety, aimed, and fired a single shot. The coin went spinning into the outfield.

McGraw never again challenged Emslie's eyesight.

his face. And yet when he turned around and faced him, McGraw was still behind the line yapping like a pit bull about to bite someone. He glowered hatefully. Kicked up dust. Shouted. But he did not cross the line. He knew if he did, a not-so-mysterious force would slap him down like a gnat. The crowd hooted. It was great theater.

The question now was: Could the Giants come back? Had McGraw succeeded in changing the momentum of the contest? Was the opposition sufficiently poisoned?

Rudolph worked carefully, made good pitches, brushed the corners of the plate, and on a pitcher's count, Grant grounded a ball into the hole at deep short. Maranville darted over, backhanded the ball on the edge of the outfield grass, turned, jumped into the air acrobatically, and threw the ball low and a trifle wide of first base. Butch Schmidt stretched for the throw, keeping his foot on the bag, and dug the ball out of the dirt. "Fast Eddie" Grant was out by half a step.

Both runners advanced into scoring position. McGraw called time and made his way toward the plate. He pointed toward the dugout and motioned for "Long Larry" McLean to pinch-hit for the pitcher. McLean, big, brutish, hot-tempered, with tree-trunk legs and a head too small for his 6'5", 230-pound body, was the first really tall catcher in major-league history.

Long Larry was a bad actor. A real bad actor. A terror when drunk. Larry claimed he drank only when he needed one. Unfortunately he always needed one, and his beer-battered 33-year-old body left a trail of barroom brawls in its drunken wake, the last of which ended when a Boston saloonkeeper shot and killed him.

The Boston infield set up for the double play. Rudolph's first pitch missed outside. He then poured over two quick strikes. The crowd was on its feet cheering noisily. Working quickly, Rudolph fired a belt-high fastball in on the hands. McLean got a piece of it and bounced weakly to Evers, allowing Merkle to hustle across the plate, cutting Boston's lead to 4–2.

Right-hander Art Fromme replaced Marquard in the eighth. The Giants were not finished yet. But Fromme had difficulty finding the plate. Seeing this, Rabbit Maranville sat back and drew out the count. Rab called time with the count 3–2 in an attempt to further disrupt Fromme's rhythm.

McGraw jumped on the top step of the dugout, shouted encouragement at his pitcher, and took the opportunity to motion Bescher over toward right-center field. Bescher edged over four or five steps.

Maranville, looking for a fastball, got one, and drilled a low liner deep into left-center, exactly where Bob Bescher had been standing a moment before. The ball bounced and rolled 447 feet from home plate, a little to the left of the bull pen. Maranville stopped at third with a stand-up triple.

McGraw grumbled. It wasn't his day.

Minutes later, Rabbit scored on a single through the middle off the bat of Red Smith. The Braves led 5–2.

In the bottom of the ninth, after two men were gone, Merkle doubled and Grant singled, making it a 5–3 game. The sound of hope rose from the stands. With one man on, all it would take was one swipe of the bat to tie the score, and the man stepping up to the plate, Long Larry McLean, could easily send one into the seats.

The strategy was obvious: hit away. But Long Larry just stood there, his bloodshot eyes instinctively staring at McGraw, one of those what-shall-I-do looks on his face.

McGraw gritted his teeth and snarled, "Hit one into the stands, you goddamn dope."

Larry smiled, his untroubled mongrel smile, and asked, "Which seat, Mac?"

Rudolph got two quick strikes on McLean, then teased the big goon with a bad ball. Larry took the bait, lunged, and dribbled a slow roller at Evers, forcing Grant at second. The game was over. The mighty Giants had been humbled, 5–3.

Visibly shaken after the game, McGraw's men sat quietly in the dugout, a glum-looking bunch, too numb for words. McGraw leaned forward, cheerlessly, elbows on knees, a gritty hard look on his face, mulling over what he'd just witnessed. He glanced over his shoulder at several of the players and said, "To tell you, frankly, I didn't imagine they were as good as they looked today." His players returned silent nods.

Shocked into the realization that the rampaging Braves might sweep the series, McGraw made a serious effort to slow down their remarkable run. When the Braves strolled into the Polo Grounds Friday afternoon for the second game of the series, the skinned part of the infield around shortstop was soaked, actually muddy. Stallings went into an Evers-like rant and a nice kerfuffle ensued. McGraw explained: he was sorry, but "the grounds crew left on the sprinklers too long; there was nothing he could do about it." It was baseball gamesmanship. That's what it was. And no one doubted that the wet ground was an attempt on McGraw's part aimed at shutting down Maranville.

But McGraw's artful dodge didn't bother the slick-fielding shortstop. He was just as comfortable playing on the edge of the outfield grass as he was on the infield, and the Braves pounded the Giants, 7–3, with plenty to spare.

"In a slam-bang battle the champions were simply overpowered," Bozeman Bulger reported in the *Evening World*. "The Braves . . . showed as much superiority in class as they did the day before. Playing as they did, no team in the world could have beaten them."

The question now was: could the Braves sweep the series?

CHAPTER 33

A MAN WHO CAN DO ANYTHING HE SETS OUT TO DO

The delicious aromas of bacon and eggs, buttered toast, and steaming coffee teased the nostrils of subdued voices in the crowded dining room of the Somerset Hotel. High on a shelf a fan thrummed and swung back and forth in a slow languid arc. Outside on 47th Street, amid the trembling sound of engines and the clippety-clop of horse-cabs, taxis honked and a fire wagon clanged impatiently in stalled traffic.

George Stallings pushed aside his plate, lifted his cup to his lips, sipped coffee, put the cup down, wiped his lips on a napkin, unfolded the morning paper, and read the headlines:

PANAMA CANAL OPENS FOR FIRST BIG LINER TODAY
Steamship *Ancon,* 10,000 tons, will go through to Pacific with full cargo

1,000,000 MARCH ON BRUSSELS
CZAR RUSHES 2,500,000 TO BORDER

COCAINE PEDDLER WHO HAD GIRL AIDE SEIZED
James Wilson, a cocaine salesman with a society clientele, saved himself by working with a pretty girl in blue.

Leaning back in his chair, Stallings considered the news and ignored the faint clatter of plates and the clink of spoons and forks and the enervating chatter at tables nearby, though not entirely.

"I'm tellin' you, Harry, if you want to show the broad a good time, take her to a *pitcher* show."

"I dunno . . . Maisie's the cultured type. She kinda has her heart set on seein' a live show. Music. Dancin'."

"How about Rectors? . . . Right over here at Forty-Eighth and Broadway. They got it all: cabaret, dinner, dancin' . . . It'll cost you a bundle, though."

"I know. I know . . . There's something about her . . . I kinda like this girl."

"It's your dough, pal . . . Hey . . . I know. How about 'Peg O' My Heart?' At the Opera House. Thirty-Fourth and Eighth. Papers say it's played more than six hundred times. Elsa Ryan is starrin' in it. She's some looker. I seen her *pitcher* in the paper."

Stallings turned to the entertainment section. Glanced at an advertisement for the "Tango": a split-skirt mesh bag. "Very nobby and all the rage, only $4.00." It was the year of the tango, a dance fad of sensual abandon for the fashionable, at least at first. Now couples tangoed in dance halls across the country, even in the sand at Coney Island.

Stallings's eyes skipped across the paper to a sidebar on the right-hand side of the page, a producer's blurb about Miss Pearl White starring in the ninth episode of the new movie serial, *The Perils of Pauline*. "Pauline flees to the shore, persuades a hydroplane pilot to take her to safety. As they soar aloft, he lights a cigarette, flicks away the match, which lights on one of the wings, and in a few minutes the machine is in flames. Coward that he is, the pilot grabs the only parachute and leaves Pauline to her fate."

"Hmm," Stallings murmured and smiled. "All that and more for only five cents," he said to himself. "That's some bargain." At that moment he heard a waiter say: "Right over there, miss." The waiter motioned toward the window. "I don't see . . . ?" "The gentleman with the newspaper."

"Oh, yes. Yes, that's him. Thank you. Thank you so much." She walked over and introduced herself. "Mr. Stallings. I'm Zoe Beckley from the *Evening Mail* . . . " She looked at him expectantly.

Stallings acknowledged her with a polite nod and struggled to his feet, part of the paper spilling on the floor as he got up. He flashed his teeth.

"Nice to meet you, Miss Beckley." He walked around the table and held the chair for her. "Please sit down."

"How kind of you." She gave him a sleepy smile.

"Will you join me in some breakfast?"

"I've already had mine, thank you . . . A little coffee might be nice, though," she said, as she took a notebook out of a large, sensible handbag.

He signaled the waiter.

She smiled and glanced at the headlines as he bent over to pick up the newspaper. "Isn't the news awful?" she said. "The slaughter. So many men.

They say a woman was forced to undress in front of soldiers. Then shot. Children trampled by German cavalry and tossed aside with bayonets. Wounded men killed as they begged for mercy."

"A lot of ocean between us," he said.

"People say we'll be pulled in."

"I don't think there's much chance of that. Let them fight their own battles."

"You have a military background. Don't you, Mr. Stallings?"

"Yes . . . Yes, I do. My daddy, William Henry Stallings, fought the Yankees in the War of the Recent Unpleasantness. One of the first volunteers. A first lieutenant in Blodgett's Company, the Georgia Flying Light Artillery. My momma and daddy named me after my uncle—George E. Stallings. The Yankees killed Uncle George at the Battle of Monocacy Junction the year before the war ended."

"And you?"

"My schooling was military. Started at Richmond Academy. [It's called St. Patrick's now.] Then I attended Virginia Military Institute."

That's it, she thought. He's accustomed to command. Ramrod straight. His back and shoulders show military training. The days at VMI when he was a slim youth from an old fighting family. She studied his face as he spoke: dark, clean shaven, nice hair, brown eyes, pleasant lines around the eyes from either sun squints or smiles, maybe both, regular features, teeth even and white, suggesting a bulldoggish grip on things, and a chin with a dimple chaperoned by a scar.

The two chin marks, she thought. They hold the key to the real Stallings. The dimple shows he's human. The scar shows he's strong. When under the auspices of the scar, the chin mark is at its loudest and scathingest. The men may smart, but they know when the game is over the dimple will still be there.

"How," she said aloud to Stallings, who was patient with her, though some of her questions were a bit strange, "how did you manage in five or six months to make that collection of tailenders of yours start working together like a well-turned-out machine?"

"Now you sound like a sportswriter," he said through gleaming white teeth.

She colored a little.

"There is no sense in trying to fool you, Mr. Stallings. I've never seen a baseball game in my life. I don't know a hit from an out. Our sportswriters,

I believe you know them, Harry Schumacher and Grantland Rice, gave me some ideas, and four office boys helped me rehearse my questions."

He smiled.

"My boys aren't tailenders," he said, his voice tolerant. "They're young at it, that's all. They're all good fighting stuff." Pause. "I will tell you a little story that may answer your question. Out at the American Can Works where a friend of mine is manager, the five great steam boilers stopped one day. Completely shut down. Business came to a standstill. Nobody could find out what was wrong."

"Oh, my."

"My friend got ahold of this little old gink from the other side of town. The little guy was a genius at mechanics. He took a hammer, rapped a couple of times here, tapped a couple of times there, tightened a nut somewhere, threw the switch and everything started up. They asked him how much. And he replied, a hundred dollars. My friend the manager almost fainted when he heard that. It's a lot of money. So he insisted on an itemized bill. This is what the old gink wrote:

To fixin' biler, 1 nut	.50
To knowin' how	99.50
Total	$100.00

"What a nice story." She sipped delicately from her cup, and they continued to discuss the mighty affairs of baseball.

"Every manager has a system," he said. "McGraw likes players who are like him, very aggressive and cocky. Connie Mack favors college types, like Jack Barry and Eddie Collins. (Collins is a Columbia man, you know.) And Eddie Plank and 'Chief' Bender. They all went to college."

He paused and sipped more coffee. "Now, if I know how to make the boys into a good fighting machine, it's because I get them working together. Give me a ball club, I always say, with only mediocre ability, and if I can get the players in the right frame of mind, they'll beat the world champions."

"So that's it," she said. "You make them believe. A mind-over-matter thing. One heartbeat. That sort of thing. The same pulse. All for one and one for all. And it won't work if somebody's off someplace."

"That's right. Every ounce of spirit in my body goes into my team and my work when I'm on the field. I am my team. I eat baseball. I sleep baseball. I breathe baseball. I think baseball. I live baseball. The boys have the same spirit. If you want the reason why we succeed, why we haven't cracked, that's it."

The sound of traffic out on the street was constant. Out of the corner of his eye, Stallings caught sight of a fat-to-busting load of hay as a horse-drawn wagon lumbered past the hotel, and he watched it long enough for her to suspect that he'd made a wish.

"They say you're superstitious?"

"Me . . . oh . . . well . . . They say that, do they?" He looked at her and smiled amiably. "Well . . . in baseball you can't keep it out altogether. I'd hate to break a mirror next week. Or have flowers sent to me. But if I should meet a load of empty barrels coming toward me, that's fine. Means base hits."

They laughed together.

"Seriously, Miss Beckley, there is very little luck in baseball. Everything is thought out, though it often looks like luck from the stands. The man who uses his brains, stays alert and thinks quickly, can pull off things fans attribute to luck. A bonehead player, no matter how strong he is in the arms and legs, is a bad investment."

"So what you're saying is, you don't believe in bad luck?"

He looked at the floor, shook his head slightly, and sighed. A peculiar little smile ran over his lips. "Well, I don't like two-dollar bills. I never take them if I can get ones instead."

"Why is that?"

"I've had a lot of rough luck when I've been carrying two-dollar bills . . . Of course, you come in contact with some two-dollar bills during the season. When I do, I fold them over and tear off the corners."

"The two-dollar bills?"

"Just as soon as I get one. You have to tear off the corners to kill the jinx. So if any of your readers come across a two-dollar bill with the corners trimmed off, they'll know it circulated somewhere on the Boston club." Pause. "My players got to doing it too. And our luck changed. We started winning ball games, regularly, as soon as we began to play the two-dollar-bill jinx off the map."

"You've been awfully generous with your time, Mr. Stallings. I know you have to get to the Polo Grounds."

"Yes. We have morning practice."

"Even on the road after beating the Giants two in a row?"

"Especially after beating the Giants two in a row."

"Think you can make it three? They tell me Matty's pitching today."

"Well, all I can tell you is the stars are all in alignment."

She watched him walk across the hotel lobby. "What a handsome man. At Broadway and Forty-Second Street," she said to herself, "you'd take him for a matinee idol. In a ballroom every pair of feminine eyes would be focused on him, I swear, upon his face and figure." In the Somerset Hotel he was simply "a very tall, very well-built, very well-dressed, very businesslike, very handsome man."

"George Stallings," she wrote, "is a man who can do anything he sets out to do, and he can do it with sheer spiritual force."

CHAPTER 34

MATHEWSON WAS BRILLIANT

After the two stylish victories over the Giants, the Braves demanded attention. The teams were evenly matched, but the Braves played just a little bit better. Now thoughts of a three-game sweep did not seem like idle dreaming.

The weather was a summery 81 degrees for the third and final game of the series, a perfect blue-sky day, and 33,000 fans turned out to see if New York could stop Boston. It would not be easy. The Braves were tough. But McGraw had saved his best for last: "Big Six," the great Christy Mathewson, already a 19-game winner on the season.*

Impressive looking, college-educated, a gentleman among hooligans, "Matty" was the man most admired and respected among members of the team. He was an icon. A national hero. In the words of sportswriter Bill McGeehan: "The incarnation of all those virtues with which we endow the ideal American."

Few players had the tools or knew as much about the game as Mathewson. He did not waste pitches; he threw strikes; he rarely made a wild pitch; he fielded his position well; and he avoided giving up bases on balls. Through 312 innings in 1914, "Matty" walked 23 batters, and once pitched 68 consecutive innings without allowing a base on balls.

---

* The nickname "Big Six," meant to honor Mathewson, was the result of a huge mistake perpetrated by sportswriter Sam Crane, who had no idea what he was talking about when he gave Mathewson the nickname in an article. "Big Six" was a shamefully fraudulent group of firefighters, organized in 1848, as Station no. 6, on the Lower East Side of Manhattan, by Tammany's notoriously corrupt Boss Tweed. Its members were so out of control, they frequently brawled with rival fire companies over who was going to put out a fire while the building burned down. Critics and reformers dubbed the infamous gang of thugs the "Big Six Company."

But it was intelligence more than control that made Mathewson's work outstanding. His memory file was filled with the strengths and weaknesses of every batter he ever faced, and he adeptly mixed subtle variations of speed and curves while pitching (and occasionally his famous fadeaway pitch), delivering them exactly where he wanted them. And he was still bagging opposing batters after 14 seasons in the big leagues.

Mathewson's brilliance led American poet Ogden Nash to write this about his favorite ballplayer:

M is for Matty,
Who carried a charm
In the form of an extra
Brain in his arm.

Tyler and Mathewson matched each other pitch for pitch. They were never more effective. Tyler was working on a streak of 13 scoreless innings, and, as he set Giants down without a run in inning after inning, his fired-up teammates chanted, "That's another one, George. That's another one."

Neither team mounted a serious threat through the first six frames. In the Giants' half of the seventh, with George Burns on first base, Fred Snodgrass, the Giants' cleanup hitter, rammed a terrific smash toward third base, the hardest kind of liner (seven feet off the ground), a sure double, maybe a triple.

Nobody thought third baseman Red Smith had a chance. Red, in the habit of playing deep, threw his body into the air, twisted his gloved hand backward across his chest, and somehow snagged the ball. The force of the blow spun him around, but he recovered quickly and doubled Burns off first base, ending the potential threat.

With his legs crossed and one foot wiggling in the air at all times, Stallings's eyes were everywhere at once. And his acid wit, never meant to hurt, dominated the dugout. He suffered through every play, hectoring, badgering, and bellowing like a lion roaring just to hear himself roar. Fans who had never before heard his yawping kept asking friends: "What's wrong with the guy? Is he out of his mind or something?"

"One minute he'd be praying," Charlie Deal said, "the next minute cursing. But he was a grand man."

John McGraw and Connie Mack made it a rule never to criticize a player while a game was in progress. Not George Stallings. He was the hardest taskmaster in the game. Yet he wasn't unpopular. It was just that profanity was the lubricating oil he used in putting together a winning combination.

Stallings stalked the dugout in a vigilant prowl and yelled "Bonehead" every time one of his players made a misplay. The players did too. And, not surprisingly, they had great affection and a not-so-secret pride in their leader's flights of eloquent profanity. One of them boasted about a series earlier in the season when the Braves played poorly: "Stallings swore steadily for four days and never repeated himself once."

Goose egg after goose egg appeared on the scoreboard. It was the top of the eighth and still a 0–0 tie. Big Six was brilliant, a regular strike-throwing machine. The efficiency with which he dispatched the Braves was extraordinary.

After one out in the eighth, Gowdy, casual and loose-jointed, faced Mathewson for the third time that afternoon. He was one for two in his previous at bats (a single in the second inning). Gowdy tapped the dirt off his spikes, tugged at his uniform, pulled at his cap, and cocked the bat.

Sportswriter Hugh Fullerton, a longtime observer of the game, provided us with the one verifiable description we have of the verbal exuberance Stallings regularly displayed in the dugout. He acted like a sane madman. And it's worth repeating here for posterity:

"That's the boy, Hank!" Stallings shouted from the corner of the dugout, his voice flying out over the field. "Get in there and wait him out. Make him pitch to you. You're the boy. Now if you pinheads only had half the baseball brains Hank Gowdy has . . . Watch him up there. Get a lesson from him. See him look 'em over and wait. That baby never takes a swing at a bad one."

Ball one.

"That's waiting, Hank, that's waiting. You've got him worried."

"SHUT UP, DEVORE—" (Josh DeVore was constantly shooting off his mouth.)

"Attaboy, Hank. Make him come over. Don't waste anything . . . Look at that third baseman creeping up. Old Hank has an eye on him. He'll bust one over there so fast—"

Stee-rike!

"What? Strike? Why, that blind burglar back there. Never mind, Hank, old boy. Make him pitch to you. You're the baby. Watch him wait—"

Strike two.

"What? Did he take that one? That sparrow-brained fool hasn't sense enough to pound sand into a rat hole. Right across the middle of the plate and he took it? Did you fellows see that? I'll trade him to Wappinger Falls for a one-armed scarecrow. He never could play ball. I don't see why the hell I ever allowed him to borrow a secondhand uniform in the first place, taking a strike like that."

"SHUT UP, DEVORE. If I hear any more of your yawp, I'll send you where you belong. You're in the same class as Hank. If ten like you would sell your brains to a rabbit, he'd be half-witted."

Ball two.

"That's the boy, Hank. Great waiting! You always could play this game. You fellows watch Hank and you'll learn how the game is played. Two and two. He'll bust one if Matty dares put it over."

Foul ball.

"What? What did that ivory-skulled idiot bonehead mean by fouling that one off? It was a foot outside the strike zone. And he swung at it. Forgets everything I tell him as soon as he gets up there."[†]

"SHUT UP, DEVORE."

"Attaboy, Hank. Make him put it over. If some of you guys had Hank's brains and nerve, you'd be good ballplayers."

"Tyler is up next," Stallings said, commenting to no one in particular. "If Gowdy gets on I guess I'll let old ivory head take a crack at pinch-hitting for him." He got up, scratched his leg, tugged at his belt, turned with a scowl toward the players on the bench, and considered his options. "You, bonehead," he barked, "get your fucking bat. You're hitting for Tyler." Five guys jumped off the bench and grabbed a bat and began loosening up. They eyed each other awkwardly. But nobody laughed. Not in front of the Chief. They didn't dare.

Every member of the team was eager to help. They meshed together, their talents complementing one another. It seemed like every player at one time or another did something that won a game. "There isn't a lazy man in the bunch," Stallings said. "The men encourage one another and there is no jealousy." To a man, they literally put the team ahead of themselves.

Foul ball.

"WHAT THE HELL? He fouled that one . . . He'll never be a ballplayer. He hasn't sense enough to make water run downhill."

"SHUT UP, DEVORE—you laughing hyena, or I'll plank a fine on you that will starve you to death this winter, as you ought to be."

THWOCK. A satisfying crack of the bat. Matty jerked his head around and followed the flight of the ball with his eyes.

"Whoo-ee! See that baby hit," Stallings shouted. "Spanked it right between the seams."

[†] The infamously abusive Stallings called his players a lot of names during his dugout rants. No one was bothered by them. Les Mann was "Stone Head," Gene Cocreham was "Leather Face," and Hank Gowdy was "Feather Brain." Others had similar labels.

The ball shot deep into left-center, drawing a window-rattling roar from the crowd, struck the wall a foot from the top, and bounded away from the outfielders. Gowdy cruised into third with a stand-up triple.

"Best young ballplayer in the world," Stallings said. "I've been saying it for years; he's the best and smartest player in the world, and he's bound to be a winner. I wouldn't take twenty-five thousand dollars for him today." It was one of the few times the Braves developed anything resembling a threat against Mathewson.

Due up next was George Tyler, the pitcher. "Lefty" was a good hitting pitcher, averaging .202 for the season. Stallings second-guessed himself and went with Tyler instead of one of the five pinch hitters who were ready. Mathewson quickly exploited the move, zipping fastballs past the overmatched Tyler, and struck him out on three pitches. Stallings smashed his hat on the dugout floor and you can bet nobody laughed.

Gowdy was on third, there were two outs, and Josh DeVore was the next batter. "Get up there, DeVore, and lay into one," Stallings yelled. "You're the baby. More brains and nerve than any of them."

Matty kneaded the stained baseball in his hands, pulled out a handkerchief, and mopped his sweaty forehead, making DeVore wait. Matty put the handkerchief back into his pocket, got the sign, and delivered a strike. He followed it with a ball high and away, and then another ball. Pitches high and out of the strike zone, especially by the 34-year-old Mathewson, were the sign of a tiring pitcher.

Matty slowed down a bit and gathered his wits before the next pitch: a curveball that danced. DeVore hacked at it. Hit a comebacker right back at Mathewson. He gloved it, examined the ball, and threw to Merkle for the out. The inning was over.

The game remained a scoreless tie.

After one man was out in the Giants' half of the ninth, Mathewson drew a walk. He represented the winning run. The Giants' center fielder, Bob Bescher, followed with a single, moving Big Six into scoring position at second base. A hit would give the Giants the game. Larry Doyle, the next batter, watched two pitches go by before bouncing a ball between first and second, where Johnny Evers, ranging far to his left, gobbled it up. Evers's only play was at first base; Mathewson and Bescher advanced on the play. Now there were two outs and the winning run was 90 feet away from home plate.

Pitching carefully around George Burns, the Giants' leading hitter, Tyler ran the count full before losing him, loading the bases. This brought up the right-handed-hitting Fred Snodgrass who'd been robbed of an extra-base hit in his previous at bat.

Lefty was in trouble, and he knew it. He hitched up his pants, drew his sleeve across his forehead, cleared off the summer sweat, and considered the situation. It was a pressure-packed moment. He quickly jumped ahead on the count with two strikes and no balls. One more strike and he would be out of it. One swing of the bat could cost the Braves the game. What would it be?

Snodgrass slashed the third pitch between third and short. It looked for a second like the ball might get by Maranville. But the Rabbit, ranging far to his right, snagged the ball with a diving stop and, from his knees, threw out Burns, sliding into second base, retiring the side. The Braves were still alive.

It was time to ratchet up the pressure on the tiring Mathewson. Stallings spread the word: "Attack. Don't wait. Attack early in the count." Following orders, Red Smith opened the 10th inning with a drive just beyond George Burns's reach in left field. A sacrifice bunt moved Smith into scoring position. Hank Gowdy, the man swinging a hot bat, was next up. Full of confidence, Hank stepped into the batter's box, rocked his knees, and squeezed the bat.

Sweat trickled from Mathewson's hatband into the corners of his mouth. He wasn't invincible when it came to giving up hits, but he usually kept hitters on the defensive and seldom allowed two hits in the same inning, especially when the game was on the line. He studied the sign, shot a brief glance at Smith on second, went into his stretch, and delivered. The ball stayed up in the strike zone, the sound of the bat striking the ball unmistakable.

Gowdy drove a liner into deep center. Bescher turned and darted back; the hearts of Giants fans sank as the ball bounced twice and struck the tarpaulin in left-center.

Smith held up between second and third until he was certain Bescher would not make the catch, then he bolted home. Gowdy slid into third base far ahead of the throw. It was his second triple of the day. The Braves had taken the lead, 1–0.

The extra-base hit was a heartbreaker for Mathewson. Now, with the pitcher at bat, he did something few fans had ever seen him do in a tight situation: he uncorked a wild pitch. It ran up and off the catcher's mitt and bounced away and ended up against the backstop. Gowdy trotted home with the much-appreciated insurance run, giving the Braves a 2–0 lead.

Mathewson recovered his poise and struck out Tyler and got DeVore on an easy pop foul to the first baseman.

Though the Braves were only three outs from sweeping the series, the players on the Giants' bench remained limp and lifeless, resting on their wallets. McGraw's cheek muscles worked up and down. Shouting didn't work. They tuned him out. Anger reddened his face. "You can't just keep going through the goddamn fucking motions," he shouted. "Wake up. Do something. Challenge them."

The boys responded with aggressive lethargy. McGraw tugged at his cap, looked at the ground, shook his head, let out a deep sigh, and trotted out to the coach's box at third base for the bottom half of the 10th.

The Giants' leadoff hitter, shortstop Art Fletcher, tapped a bouncing ball toward the left side of the infield, right at Maranville, a routine play.

"Son of a bitch!" McGraw screamed, then he stopped cold, mouth open. Smith cut in front of Maranville and fielded the ball on an in-between hop. The ball struck his glove, twisted out, and rolled a few feet away. Red pounced on it, scrambled to his knees, and gunned a low throw across the diamond. Too late. Fletcher was across the bag. Safe.

"Hah, hah, hah!" McGraw hollered. "You fucked up good, redneck. No wonder they run you outta Brooklyn."

Smith's lip curled. He said something and spat in McGraw's direction.

"Hoo, hoo, hoo. Ain't we touchy today."

"Kiss my grits."

It was Fred Merkle's turn now. Giants fans were on their feet, cheering wildly. "Pickle one, Fred." "Give it a ride." "Poke it out of here." (It was only 257 feet down the foul line in right field at the Polo Grounds.) Sure enough, Merkle put a charge into the fourth pitch and sliced a shot to the opposite field past third base on one bounce. Smith was playing five or six feet off the line. His bare hand flashed out and snared it. The ball spun away. He scrambled after it. Picked it up . . . looked around . . . no play.

Fans whistled, stomped, and let out savage war whoops. Cries of "Chief," "Chief," "Chief" rang out from the cheap seats. John "Chief" Meyers was on deck, rhythmically swinging a couple of bats. Meyers, the Giants' second leading hitter, represented the winning run. The broad-shouldered, 5'11", 200-pound Cahuilla Indian was not a savage and disliked Indian nicknames and war whoops. He was Dartmouth educated, a gentleman.

"I liked playing ball," Meyers later said. "It's a lot of fun and I was good at it. But I do wish I had finished my education at Dartmouth."

Meyers, struggling along on battered legs and playing with badly swollen fingers, came into the game hitting .287. He was considered dependable in the clutch, an athlete who would die for the team.

Tyler floored him with a high, tight pitch, moving him off the plate. Meyers got up, brushed off some dirt, glared at Tyler, and moved back into position, still crowding the plate. They eyed each other distastefully.

Tyler came in tight on Meyers again; this time a fastball caught the Chief flush in the ribs. You could feel the sting in the grandstand. You could also feel the momentum of the game changing. Lightning-fast Dave Robertson came in to run for Meyers.

The inning, filled with so much promise for the Braves minutes before, was turning into a nightmare, a no-outs, bases-loaded nightmare.

Milt Stock was the first Giant to bid for glory. He stepped in batting .258. The count reached three balls and one strike, a hitter's count. Tyler was disgusted. He thought he should have made better pitches. It was a crucial at bat. He had to get Stock.

Dry spit covered Tyler's tongue. He peered in at the sign. A perplexed look came over his face as if to say, "You want me to throw that?"

Gowdy trotted out toward the mound, his gear clanking as he ran. Tyler reached for the resin bag. Slammed it on the ground.

Evers came over. "What's goin' on?" he asked.

Tyler shrugged.

"You're hurrying your delivery," Evers said. "Relax. Throw strikes. Don't worry about nothin'. Go hard, and let us catch the ball."

Tyler tugged at his cap and stared at the ground.

"Yeah," Gowdy said. "Slow down. Tie your shoes. Give yourself a breather. Make him wait."

Again the count ran full, three and two. Tyler removed his glove, rubbed up the ball, and glared at Stock. Stock shifted uneasily, set himself, cocked the bat, and waited. Tyler cut loose a fastball. Gave it all he had. The runners were moving. Stock swung, got under the ball, and lifted a soft pop fly over the left side of the infield. Red Smith moved under it and gathered it in for out number one.

"Red" Murray, a dangerous veteran, was sent in to pinch hit for Mathewson. Murray led the league in home runs in 1909, averaged .273 as a Giant regular through 1913, and averaged 45 stolen bases over six seasons. Murray was a tough out. The count ran to three and one, the gut-clutching suspense building. Giants loyalists were hanging on the edges of their seats, standing up, sitting down, and standing up again. This was it. This was it. Murray would give Tyler the works. They were sure of it.

Murray whipped the bat menacingly. Tyler fired. Murray took a big rip. Missed again. Strike two. A full count. It was nail-biting time again.

Gowdy offered Tyler a target. The payoff pitch was on its way. It sizzled up and darted into the strike zone, sudden and quick.

"Stee-rike," Bill Klem bellowed. "Yer outta here." The big second out. The capacity crowd booed.

Murray stared, speechless, then slammed the bat down in front of the plate. He knew it had been a good pitch, a very good pitch. He did not argue.

Now the ballgame was in Bob Bescher's hands.

Tyler worked the corners and battled for control. Unbelievably, the count once again ran to 3–2. Tyler was on the slipperiest of slippery slopes. The game was on the line. He walked around the back of the mound, bowed his head, and took several deep breaths.

Bescher spat on the ground, dug in, waved the bat aggressively, his anxiousness held inside. The bases were full, two outs. The runners danced away from the bags. They would be running on the pitch.

Tyler went into the stretch and blazed away. Bescher swung, couldn't quite handle it, and dribbled a slow roller toward Johnny Evers. Johnny fielded the ball easily and threw Bescher out at first for the final out of the game. It was in the books. A 2–0 shutout.

The Braves had swept the Giants, something no team had done all season. George Tyler, the pride of Derry, New Hampshire, was the hero of the day. He'd humbled the powerful front-runners in the face of disaster. Not bad for "Slats," a slender lefty, whose 168-pound body in a bathing suit wouldn't attract a second look from the homeliest girl on Nantasket Beach.

Tyler sprung off the mound, raised his arms, and whirled in a glorious leap. The Boston players threw hats and bats in the air and swarmed around Tyler, banged him on the back, and wrung his hand. The lanky lefty had been lucky. Very lucky. And he knew it. The game could have gone either way.

It was Tyler's fifth shutout in 26 days, an almost unbelievable achievement. For the proud Braves, it was their 19th victory in 22 games.

George Stallings watched quietly from the dugout, satisfied, smiling happily, nodding, thanking well-wishers, shaking hands, his white teeth flashing. He took off his hat, ran his fingers through his hair, and looked at Fred Mitchell. "Well, if Matty and the Giants can't stop us, who is there in the West who can? Beating Matty is like giving us pennant credentials."

The taciturn Mitchell smiled and nodded.

The Braves' fortunes now hinged on how well they did in their swing through the West.

CHAPTER 35

BRAVES WATCHERS WERE EVERYWHERE

Winning three of four in Cincinnati, the first stop in their swing around the circuit, kept the team on track. The future looked bright. Carried along by their own momentum, it seemed like they came up with big plays and big innings whenever they needed them. In describing their performances, the only word writers used more often than "character" was the word "team." One happy family without any semblance of a faction, spontaneously throwing bats and caps in the air and doing snake dances after pulling out a victory.

Three games separated the top four teams. The winning percentage of the league-leading Giants was .551; the Braves, .550; the Cardinals, .539; and the Cubs, .518. St. Louis was considered the most dangerous of the four contenders. They'd been the most consistent, their pitching was deep—five seasoned starters—and they worked together in perfect harmony.

But it was the Braves who touched the hearts of people across the nation. Their sensational climb from last to second in the standings, in such a short time, produced Braves watchers everywhere. Crowds in Cincinnati, Brooklyn, Philadelphia, and Pittsburgh cheered Boston rallies, actually hoping the Braves would beat the home team. This was unheard of, a response considered disloyal by some locals. Still they cheered.

Seeking improvement in his "tramp" outfield for the sprint down the stretch, Stallings purchased Herbie Moran from the Cincinnati Reds, a fly chaser he'd been after for over a year. A stellar fielder with top-of-the-order batting skills, Moran was extra fast, owned an exceptional arm, and could easily handle the vast expanse of right field at Fenway Park, a difficult place in which to play.

Moran hit .276 and .266 for Brooklyn in 1912 and 1913 while playing every outfield position in an almost flawless manner. Few outfielders were better at turning batted balls into outs. Fast on his feet, a base runner who forced breaks, he delighted in catching passive fielders off guard, and scored from second base on infield outs several times during the 1914 season, once coming all the way home from first on a single. Stallings's new acquisition was, in short, much better than the statistics indicated.

John McGraw tried desperately to jump-start the Giants and shake them out of their lethargy. From time to time, he took each man aside for a heart-to-heart talk. Nothing worked. Even when they were together they seemed apart, and the club lumbered along without enthusiasm.

Boston and New York were in a virtual tie for first place when the Braves arrived in the Windy City on the twenty-fourth of August. Intent on seizing the lead from the Giants, Stallings started his ace left hander George Tyler against the Cubs, but the Cubbies drove "Lefty" from the mound after two innings of work. Dick Rudolph replaced him with the Braves trailing 4–2 and pitched effectively. Eventually, his teammates rallied and tied the score. It was anybody's game.

Animosity boiled over on the field in the bottom of the fifth after third baseman Red Smith made a spectacular stop of a hard smash off the bat of Frank Schulte. Runners were on first and second at the time, and "Heinie" Zimmerman, a two-bit psychopathic bully, realized he'd be out going from second to third on the play. In a brazen act of barbarity, the dim-witted narcissist went out of his way to slam into Red Smith and send him sprawling head over heels. Zim's unchecked malignancy was so flagrant, thousands rose from their seats and unceremoniously hissed the beast. They hissed and they hissed. For minutes on end, hisses pulsated from the stands: *ss-ss-s, ss-ss-s, ss-ss-s, ss-ss-s, ss-ss-s.*

Knocked unconscious in a crumpled heap, Smith looked for a minute or two like he might be seriously hurt, but he eventually came around, recovered, and remained in the game.

Rudolph's chances of picking up his 12th victory in a row were looking better and better as the game wore on, that is, until the eighth inning, when Chicago hits began falling like raindrops. The Cubbies scored four runs in the inning and ended Rudolph's personal winning streak at 11 straight games.

Critics thought Boston was suffering the luck of a longtime loser: they were finding it impossible to get over the hump into first place.

The next day the Braves came right back at the Cubs behind "Big Bill" James and tied the series at one game apiece. Stallings again called on Tyler in the third game. This time Lefty pitched brilliantly and lost 1–0 to Larry Cheney of the Cubs, who hurled a one-hit shutout.

The hard-fought contest was marred in the seventh inning by an ugly fight after Vic Saier homered into the right field bleachers. The next batter, bully-boy Zimmerman, attempted to stretch a single into a double, but Joey Connolly's perfect throw had him by 15 feet. The easiest kind of play. Johnny Evers waited for Zim to slide into the tag, and slide in he did, a clenched fist swinging at the ball, trying to knock it out of Evers's hand.

The punch missed the ball and struck the most tender part of Evers's anatomy, the last place a man wants to be hit. Evers retaliated by jamming the ball into the face of the chest-thumping lowlife, dazing the brute. Johnny smashed him again, this time behind the ear. The two scrambled to their feet and squared off, the lead-fisted Heinie intent on inflicting bodily damage, Evers circling warily as the lamebrain pressed forward.

Afraid Evers might get the worst of a gloves-off confrontation (Zimmerman outweighed Evers by 40 pounds), Rabbit Maranville tried getting at Zim from the side. "I finally backed up about five feet," Rabbit said, "and with a running start, jumped into the air with my fist closed and landed a surprise punch on Heinie's jaw. Down he went." The sucker punch split Zimmerman's upper lip. Blood crawled scarlet across his mouth. He had no idea who hit him.

Nobody knows exactly what happened next. Raw emotions boiled over. Dugouts emptied. Players swarmed onto the field. Confusion reigned. Men shouted and shoved in a babble of hostile confrontations. Witnesses saw all kinds of action through clouds of dust, fists flying, few landing; Zimmerman and Evers and Maranville in a rough mix-up behind second base; Schmidt grappling with Zimmerman; Zimmerman breaking away, yelling, "Lemme at him"; umpire Mal Eason restraining Zimmerman's right arm and several Cubs teammates holding Zim's left arm. It was the worst brawl the big leagues had seen in years. After order was restored, the umpires banished Zimmerman, Evers, Maranville, and Schmidt, and issued several warnings.

Though separated by an umpire and a Cubs player, Evers and Zimmerman continued bickering on the way to the clubhouse. Their words got more and more contentious. "I know who hit me," Zim said. "And I'll get him. It was either Moose Whaling or Butch Schmidt."

Maranville sidled over and soothed Zimmerman with small talk. "Butch didn't hit you," Maranville said in an effort to dissuade him. "I hit you."

"The hell you did. It was Schmidt or Whaling. No shrimp like you could knock me down."

Much like a slavering, ferocious dog, Zimmerman snarled at Schmidt, fists up. Butch, maintaining he'd never thrown a punch, lost his composure and went after the dunderhead. Teammates had to restrain them. Then Evers and Zim went at it again, this time arguing. Evers reminded Heinie with sharp words that he had a few things on him that might make it hard for him if they were made public. Zimmerman, a dim bulb at best, stopped in his tracks and stared at Evers in disbelief. He muttered obscenely under his breath and said no more.

It was several days before Zimmerman's teammates convinced him that it really was Rabbit Maranville whose surprise punch had knocked him down. Zim blew his top. "If I'd known the little bastard did it, I'd of killed him."

The underlying cause of the episode was the long-standing jealousy between Evers and Zimmerman. Mutual displays of animosity were commonplace while they were teammates in Chicago. Johnny was known as the brainy one and Heinie as the smirky rogue, an arrogant bully with a mean streak. And Evers's popularity in Chicago did not sit well with Zimmerman.

Zim's major-league career came to a sorry end when he connived with gamblers and got caught. He was suspended for throwing games—charges he denied. He did admit, however, to having acted as a go-between in a betting scam, telling teammates they could make "a little change" for themselves if the team lost a certain game.

Zimmerman also had underworld connections. His brother-in-law, Joe Noe, a bootlegger, allegedly the partner of racketeer "Dutch" Schultz, died a violent death in 1928, riddled by bullets in an ambush outside a speakeasy, the Chateau Madrid at 230 West 54th Street in New York City. Heinie later became Dutch Schultz's partner in a speakeasy and was among those named in a tax-evasion case against Schultz in 1935.

Enduring the indignity of losing key players through suspensions in the middle of a pennant race was something the Braves could ill afford. Stallings immediately telephoned Jim Gaffney in New York. The two men conferred for about 15 minutes. Stallings described what happened and urged the Braves owner to personally visit Governor Tener at the Metropolitan Tower (the league offices) and present the facts, as the Braves saw them, pointing out that "it was wholly Zimmerman who was responsible. It was not the Braves' fault."

Tener's ruling required ingenuity. Suspensions could tear holes in the Braves' infield and hurt the Cubs' chances as well, though not as severely, giving the Giants and Cardinals the upper hand in the pennant race, a public relations disaster that would provoke a cascade of complaints from sports fans.

Governor Tener did what good politicians do: he straddled the issue. Instead of handing out suspensions, he fined Zimmerman, Evers, and Maranville, and absolved Schmidt of any blame in the matter. Everyone was relieved.

In St. Louis, the next stop on the Braves' road trip, optimism was boundless. The prospects of the Cardinals' pennant chances excited fans. Interest was at fever pitch. The Cards captured the opening game of the series, a come-from-behind 3–2 victory over the Braves on a mist-cloaked afternoon. It was Boston's second loss in as many days, their fourth in six games, something they'd not endured since the Fourth of July weekend. Was the law of averages catching up with them? It certainly looked that way.

"The turn in the Braves' fortunes has arrived," W. J. O'Connor wrote in the *St. Louis Post-Dispatch*. "Dick Rudolph has lost his last two decisions and is tiring under the strain."

"Nonsense," George Stallings said, a bit annoyed. "They're still playing good ball and there is no sign of a slump. No team can maintain a near perfect momentum forever."

The big fellow was correct. The Braves bounced back and swept the next three games of the series, winning the last one, 2–1, despite managing only one hit against lefty Dan Griner.

The schedule gave them a breather, two days off, a much-needed rest, before they tackled the always difficult Philadelphia Phillies in the City of Brotherly Love. A train wreck on the Main Line delayed their arrival in Philadelphia until seven o'clock Monday morning, yet most of the boys took in the Athletics game at Shibe Park that afternoon, a game in which the Mackmen destroyed Cleveland, 16–3.

"They certainly can sting the ball," Stallings said. No one disagreed.

Two days of rest did the Braves a world of good. They played demonic ball in a doubleheader, looked like champions, and sank the Phillies 7–5 and 12–3. Five of Connie Mack's players scouted the Braves that afternoon—Chief Bender, Rube Bressler, Jack Lapp, Wally Schang, and Amos Strunk—and thought the boys from Boston a "bush league" outfit. They went away unimpressed. "They're a bunch of bushers," Bender told Mack.

George Stallings accepted compliments in his modest off-the-field manner after news spread that the Giants had lost and the Braves had tied the

Giants for first place in the standings. He pointed at his players as they rushed toward the clubhouse, hats and bats flying in the air, their chemistry palpable. "They are the fellows you want to praise," he said. "They have accomplished what two months ago baseball critics believed impossible."

The race was touch and go. The Phillies rallied and beat the Braves the following day behind Grover Cleveland Alexander, but Stallings's boys came right back and made it four victories in five games, taking the final two contests of the series. Boston and New York ended the week deadlocked for first place.

The stage was set for a Monday showdown in Boston. A Labor Day doubleheader.

CHAPTER 36

IT WAS THE SPIRIT OF THE TEAM

The Braves were at the top of their game, the hottest team in baseball. Now the question was: could they maintain the momentum?

McGraw didn't think so. "The Braves took my boys by surprise in August," he said. "It was a great blow to suddenly realize that another team had pulled even with them. My boys have gotten down to business now. And you all know they play their best when challenged."

But the Giants' war cry rang hollow. More than a few pundits maintained that the tabloids were playing up the Giants' aging stars—in newsprint—as a championship team, when in reality they were no longer a steady, first-rate, big-league ball club. They viewed the New Yorkers as having one foot on a banana peel.

September 7. Labor Day. Game One. Fenway Park. Boston. The Braves, behind Dick Rudolph, took an early lead in the morning contest, pushing over a run in the first and another in the fourth. The Giants answered with a run in the second and three in the fifth, jumping ahead 4–2, behind the incomparable Christy Mathewson.

Time after time, baseballs soared into roped off areas for ground-rule doubles, often pushing Mathewson and Rudolph to the brink of disaster. But they made adjustments, mastered the sorry field conditions, and got better as the game wore on, particularly Matty. One Braves batter followed another into the dugout as the Giants ace blazed unharmed through the fifth, sixth, and seventh innings. The future Hall of Famer wasn't just unhittable, he was untouchable, allowing only one scratch hit in the three innings.

Rudolph, though not quite as effective over the same three innings, pitched well enough to keep the Giants in check.

Mathewson moved majestically out to the mound for the bottom of the eighth and went to work. Six more outs and the game was his. Nervous faces were everywhere. Time was running out. This was an important game. A Boston victory would put serious pressure on New York.

A loss?

Well . . . use your imagination.

The Braves put two men on with two outs in the eighth inning: Joey Connolly on third and Butch Schmidt on first. Could they cash in? That was the question. Matty was at his best in tight situations; he always had been.

Big Six stood quietly on the mound, burrowed his chin into his chest, his eyes bent toward the ground. He was the only pitcher remaining in the National League who'd pitched in 1900, the year he broke into big-league baseball. Matty had outlasted them all. But he was losing his athleticism, and there were questions in his own mind about how long he could maintain his effectiveness.

Matty fed a fastball to Red Smith. Timing it perfectly, Red smacked a golf-like shot into the crowd behind the ropes in left field for a ground-rule double, driving in Connolly and cutting the Giants' lead to 4–3. Suddenly, and unexpectedly, the game was on the line. The tying and winning runs were in scoring position. The SRO crowd sprang to its feet. Fans banged tin pans, rang cowbells, blew horns, sounded bugles, pounded on the backs of seats. An incredible orgy of excitement.

A solid base hit and the Braves might take the game away from the Giants. Could they do it?

Rabbit Maranville, the number seven hitter, crossed himself, dug in, and got set, knowing there was a lot riding on the at bat. Fans whistled and stamped.

The Giants' ace broke off a curve on the outside corner for a strike, then came right back with the same pitch seconds later, a curveball in the dirt. Rab started his swing. Checked it. Too late. The umpire ruled, "Strike two." Rabbit questioned the call.

Guessing on the next one, Rabbit looked for the express and got the local, a good off-speed pitch. Luckily for the Braves, Rab got a piece of it and fouled the ball back into the seats.

It was cat and mouse now. One ball, two strikes. A pitcher's count. Big Six challenged the Braves' "Mighty Mite" with a fastball. And missed. He tried a curve. Missed again. His pitches were flying up and out of the strike zone. The crowd roared. The count reached 3–2. It seemed that Matty's uncanny control had deserted him.

The Giants' catcher set up on the inside corner for the payoff pitch. Matty delivered a jam shot. Maranville, trying to punch the ball into right field, hit a bouncer toward second baseman Larry Doyle. Doyle gobbled it up for the inning-ending out.

Thousands of Boston fans stared blankly at the field, shook their heads, and said little, slowly sagging into their seats, a mood of grim doubt intruding into their thoughts.

Rudolph kept the Braves within striking distance, pitching a scoreless ninth.

With defeat staring them in the face, the Braves returned to the dugout for their final at bats in the last half of the ninth, shouting things like, "This is it, guys." "Let's stick it to them." "This is where we take them." It was amazing. You'd think they'd just cornered the Giants. They hadn't. They were trailing by a run. Three more outs and the game would be over. And the great Christy Mathewson was on the mound. Nothing was sacred now. Mouths let loose a string of obscenities. A torrent of gutter talk.

"You think you can stop us, Matty? Not a chance." The dugout wrecking crew poked fun at his knock-kneed posture. His age. His recent losses. Talking and squawking, they babbled outrageous nonsense and generated a lot of noise, inventing adrenalin-laced language as they went along. They were a crazy bunch of guys, yet, at the same time, there was something oddly endearing about them.

The crowd rose in expectation and applauded Hank Gowdy, the first batter of the inning. Hank smashed the second pitch he saw into the hole between short and third, a sharply hit ground ball. Art Fletcher gloved it, and his feet went out from under him. Down he went. The Braves jumped for joy. But Art recovered quickly and threw out Gowdy, the first out of the inning.

"Aaaaaaaaargh!" Stallings cried out, raging like a wild man, his face distorted, his eyes bulging, his teeth flashing. He paced in front of the bench. He sat down and shot a look at Josh DeVore, the sunny, good-hearted oddball, who always wore a silly-looking grin on his face. The next scheduled batter was pitcher Dick Rudolph. "That Matty is smart," Stallings said to no one in particular. "The only way to offset brains is with a bonehead." Rudolph was on his way to the plate.

Stallings glanced at DeVore again, clicked his teeth, rubbed his chin with his right hand, thinking, and nodded to himself. "Sure. Why not?" The Chief had a hunch. Felt it in his bones. DeVore was one of those lucky players, a doltish dodo who always seemed to come up with a big play in an important game.

Stallings jumped to his feet and called Rudolph back.

"Josh. Get up there."

A frisson of excitement flashed down Josh's spine. He'd show them. A feast-or-famine hitter, Josh was currently on a hunger strike. His robust .302 average with the Phillies had plummeted to a barely eating .240 with the Braves.

But the brash and breezy DeVore was something of a good luck charm. Stallings knew it. He'd schooled the little bastard in the Eastern League (now the International League) and made a ballplayer out of him.

As little Josh left the dugout, Stallings growled, "Take a crack at one, Josh. Maybe if you close your fucking eyes when you swing, Matty will hit your bat." Josh hid a smile. No sense irritating the Chief.

Stallings was not only playing a hunch, he was also playing the percentages, sending a swift, left-handed batter up against a tiring right-handed pitcher.

Working quickly, Mathewson got two quick strikes on Josh, putting the little fellow into an 0–2 hole. The Giants' ace then offered a wicked curve over the inside corner. The pitch jammed Josh. He made imperfect contact, merely got enough of the ball to send it spinning crazily down the first-base line, directly at Fred Merkle. The Boston crowd let out a groan.

As Merkle moved in to make the play, the ball jumped up, struck him on the shoulder, and spun a few feet away. He quickly pounced on it and made an underhand toss to Mathewson covering first. A close play. DeVore crossed the bag. He wassssss . . .

Safe!

The crowd went wild.

The deafening sound swallowed the next batter, Herbie Moran, a dangerous line-drive hitter who took a lot of time digging in, his hands moving all over the bat.

Mathewson waited impatiently. Just as he was about to go into his stretch, Moran called time and once more disrupted Matty's rhythm. Herbie stepped out of the batter's box, tapped his right foot and then his left foot with the barrel of his bat, and stepped back in.

Big Six powered a fastball over the inside corner.

Thwack. Moran caught it squarely and hammered a missile into the right field corner, right down the foul line. Fair or foul?

Mathewson held his breath. So did everyone else.

Fair ball. DeVore scored from first base on the play. But umpire Bob Emslie signaled a ground-rule double: the ball had bounced into the roped-off crowd. DeVore was ordered back to third base.

The tying run was 90 feet from home plate, the winning run 180 feet away. There was one out. And Giant killer Johnny Evers was walking toward the plate, wearing an intense-concentration-before-an-at-bat face. According to the morning papers, Johnny had come into the game batting .289.

The bleacher crowd started a chant. "Come on you Johnny Evers. Come on you Johnny Evers." It was not long before the entire ball park joined the chorus. "Come on you Johnny Evers. Come on . . . " You could feel the excitement, the energy, the karma.

Evers knew what to expect: the big right hander's bread-and-butter pitch. A fastball.

Sure enough, in it came.

Stee-rike!

Evers laid off of it and turned on Bill Klem, the home plate umpire. "What are you, blind or somethin'?" Klem ignored him.

Using all of his wiles, Big Six fired another pitch, desperately striving to get out of trouble and save the day for his team. Evers wouldn't bite. He took it for a ball. The count was one and one. Matty peered in for the sign, took a deep breath, checked the runner on third, and spun in a breaking ball. The pitch dived through the strike zone.

Evers went after it, an inside-out swing, and looped a low liner into short left field, the opposite field. Left fielder George Burns came crashing in at full speed, knowing full well that this could be the game one way or the other. The ball skipped under his glove, found the grass, and rolled into the crowd, a ground-rule double. The Giants' four-leaf clovers had lost their juju.

DeVore trotted home from third base and coach Fred Mitchell waved Moran home. It was all over. The Braves had won a stunning 5–4 come-from-behind victory.

Evers rounded first, saw the ball disappear into the crowd, pulled up, turned, and raced for the safety of the dugout. His teammates ran every which way, jumping around like so many bucking broncos, exchanging handshakes and bear hugs, whacking each other on the shoulders until they exhausted themselves. Hundreds and hundreds of straw hats were tossed above the crowd—panamas, leghorns, milanos, mackinaws, sennits, shinkees, splits.* Even a police helmet. All kinds of stuff filled the air. Anything. Everything. Cushions, biscuit boxes, eggs, sandwiches, programs, ticket stubs, wads of newsprint.

An excited, shifting, swirling mass of people milled around the Braves' bench and prevented manager Stallings from leaving for the dressing room. Every face in the happy throng seemed to echo the beat of an impromptu cheerleader who danced on the roof of the Braves' dugout while the crowd sang the praises of the miracle worker trapped inside. They cheered him for 10 minutes. A blur of cheers. They cheered until they could cheer no more.

---

* Lamson & Hubbard of Baltimore manufactured most of the straw hats sold in the United States in those days.

CHAPTER 37

JUST AN OLD-FASHIONED NOSE-THUMBING

The holiday mood of the morning game carried over into the festive sunshine of the afternoon contest, and more than 41,000 fans packed Fenway Park for the matchup between Jeff Tesreau and George Tyler. The two games attracted a record-paying crowd of 74,183, a truly remarkable number when you consider that in 1914 the population of metropolitan Boston was 750,000. (It's an estimated 4.7 million today.)

Ferocious, ornery, and confident, Tesreau was a hard thrower, an assertive presence on the mound, one of the top hurlers in the National League. A 21–8 won-loss record and a 2.37 ERA at this point in the season chronicled his effectiveness.

Though somewhat overshadowed by his teammates, "Lefty" George Tyler (13–12 to date) also managed a high level of consistency, winning nine consecutive games in July and August, an extraordinary feat when you consider that the guys behind him scored only 15 runs in those nine games.

Tyler struggled in the game's early going and simply could not find his groove. Defensive gems by Maranville, Smith, and Evers were the only things that kept him from being driven from the mound.

The Giants finally caught up with the slender left hander after two were down in the fourth. George Burns walked and stole second. Art Fletcher also walked. Burns stole third when Hank Gowdy, holding the ball, argued the ball four call with the umpire. "Red" Murray then doubled into the crowd in left, driving home Burns and sending Fletcher to third. The Giants led 1–0.

The Braves looked helpless once Tesreau settled in. Throwing easily and confidently, the "Ozark Mountain Bearcat" watched his pitches dance around the Braves' bats. He'd get two strikes on a batter, then, playing gotcha, put the poor fellow away with a lethal breaking ball.

Stallings kept his fingers crossed and waited for an opening, possibly a lucky break, all the while trusting that Tyler's savvy would keep things close. And for a while it looked like sound strategy. The score was 1–0 after five innings; the Braves were very much in the game.

But things began to unravel after one man was down in the sixth. Fletcher lifted a towering pop-up into the swirling wind above the mound. Tyler gave way as Gowdy and Schmidt converged on the ball. Schmidt called for it. Then Gowdy. Then they both backed off, doing a fine imitation of the popular vaudeville act of the day, "Alphonse and Gaston," an extremely polite and indecisive comedy routine.

At the last split second Gowdy stuck out his glove and watched the ball drop untouched for a base hit. Tyler sighed in dismay. He knew he didn't have much left to throw at the Giants—except his glove.

Taking advantage of the misplay, Murray singled just beyond Maranville's reach, and Grant walked to load the bases. Now, with one down and runners on the corners, Fred Merkle slammed a ball into deep left-center. Really gave it a ride. Moran, a fleet outfielder, turned and dashed back fast, glanced at the wall, then at the ball, leapt and hauled it in a couple of steps from the fence. Fletcher tagged after the catch and scored easily, standing up. It was 2–0, New York.

Murray advanced to third. Grant on first, thinking the ball had been hit deeply enough, took off for second. But Moran's glove-to-glove throw was there waiting for Harvard Eddie as he came sliding into the bag.

Tyler let out a yelp. A double play. The pitcher's best friend. He pumped his fist in the air, pounded his glove, and headed for the Braves dugout. Suddenly he stopped. Frozen. Bob Emslie, the umpire on the bases, raised his hands—palms down. "Safe!" A burst of ear-splitting profanity showered down on Emslie. A lot of one-finger waves too, the middle finger. Evers had plenty to say as well. Words flung like fists. It was aural mayhem.

Long Larry McLean, the next batter (McLean was catching both ends of the doubleheader because Chief Meyers was sidelined with a split finger), doubled down the right field line, driving the two base runners home, making it 4–0 Giants.

Jeff Tesreau added to his cause, singling "Lumbering Larry" home with the fifth run of the game, and taking second on the throw home. Gowdy, thinking he might have a chance of cutting down Tesreau at second, fired the ball into center field.

Breathing heavily down his nostrils, Tyler stood at the rear of the mound twisting the rosin bag, obviously exhausted, his eyes casting hostile looks here and there, fatigue following him like a shadow. And there was Fred "Snow" Snodgrass, the eighth man to bat in the inning, standing near the batter's box, a toothy grin on his face, carrying on a chatty, cocky, sniggering conversation with his pals on the Giants' bench, sharing derisive guffaws. The veins of Tyler's temples swelled and the lines of his mouth hardened.

Snodgrass rocked back and forth on the balls of his feet in the batter's box, his smiling eyes measuring Tyler. (We are still in the sixth inning.) Tyler was anything but calm. He stretched and rotated his arms over his head, trying to loosen the muscles in the back of his neck. Over on third, Tesreau's eyes darted from Tyler to Snodgrass and back at Tyler again. Tesreau studied Tyler's eyes and thought to himself: "Uh-oh. Snow is about to get tattooed."

Sure enough, a fastball whistled toward the plate. Snodgrass screamed. The crowd gasped. A brushback. It was close. That's all.

"You son of a bitch," Snodgrass yelled, shouting a string of four-letter words at Tyler. He also thumbed his nose at Lefty, twittering his fingers as if he were playing a piccolo, forgetting for the longest time to take his thumb away from his nose. Boos rained down from the stands.

A glint of anger filled Tyler's eyes. He leaned in, got the sign from Gowdy, and showed Snodgrass the heater again, this time upstairs and inside. The ball just did tick the blowsy part of Snow's sleeve at the shoulder. He let out a barbaric squawk, yowled and danced and put on an all-around good show. Bill Klem motioned: "Take your base."

Tyler popped off the mound and pointed at the plate, yelling at Klem that Snodgrass had leaned over the plate. "He does it all the time."

Halfway down the line Snodgrass stopped and taunted Tyler. Challenged him: flipping him the bird.

Tyler did not say a word.

The two combatants were at it again a few minutes later, mouths flapping, swapping insults. Tyler tossed the ball a few feet into the air and purposefully let it bounce off his glove and drop to the ground, a reminder of Snodgrass's dropped fly in the final game of the 1912 World Series, an error that enabled the Red Sox to steal the championship from the Giants. An amused titter ran through the crowd.

Larry Doyle stroked a routine fly ball into left field, ending the inning. When Snodgrass trotted out to his position in center field, the crowd, lined up 12 deep behind the rope, gave him a warm reception: rows and rows of faces, all booing. The working stiffs, the men in overalls, standing and squatting on the steep incline, were particularly nasty.

Snodgrass wasn't intimidated. "As I approached the crowd behind the ropes out there," he later recalled, "booing and yelling at me, I just thumbed my nose at the whole bunch of them. Just an old-fashioned nose-thumbing. That's all. To let them know what I thought of them. That really set them off."

The crowd went berserk. Something glistened in the waning sunlight: a pop bottle. Pop bottles came showering down. Snodgrass ducked and dodged and didn't get hit. No one really wanted to hit him. Men and boys just threw the bottles in his direction to let the Giants' center fielder know that they didn't like him. Snow calmly walked around, picked up one or two bottles, and held them in the air so the umpires could see what was happening.

Bill Klem called time and Larry Doyle—handling the team for McGraw, who'd been ejected for the day during the morning contest—and Art Fletcher and Fred Merkle hurried out to help clean up the mess. Before they could get out there, however, Snodgrass further inflamed tempers, turning toward the crowd and feinting a throw of a pop bottle at them.

The bozos behind the ropes went mad. All kinds of missiles hit the grass: beer, peanuts, pop bottles, sausages, hot dogs, scorecards, cushions. Anything they could lay their hands on. Doyle ordered Snodgrass to stop baiting them and tried to ease the tension by gathering a half dozen empty bottles in his arms and carrying them over to the edge of the crowd. Just as he was about to deposit the bottles in a pile, a pop bottle came whizzing past his ear, barely missing his head.

The young fan who threw the bottle laughed. The Giants' second baseman plunged into the crowd after the kid and was about to bash him in the mouth when Fletcher and Merkle and a policeman pulled him away. Garbage rained down.

Suddenly the crowd parted as five mounted policemen galloped onto the field and rode back and forth, forcing the angry fans back behind the ropes while Fletcher and Merkle led a very upset Larry Doyle toward the infield. Snodgrass stood right there, glaring at the fans, hands on hips, as defiant as ever, even though the crowd was still after him, calling for the umpires to "get him out of the game."

Things began to quiet down and play was about to resume when a tall, dark figure in a stylish ice cream suit and a panama hat jumped the railing near the Boston dugout and walked toward umpire Bob Emslie, who was chatting with Giants' first baseman Fred Merkle on the collar of the infield.

The man spoke excitedly. "I won't tolerate that kind of behavior," he said, pointing at Snodgrass in center field. "Put that rowdy out of the game. He has insulted the good people of Boston."

Emslie was bewildered. "Huh? What?"

"You heard me. Get that man out of here."

"Who the hell are you?"

"Don't get wise with me, mister. I'm the mayor of this city. Can't you see my star?" he said, throwing open his jacket.

"Sure. And I'm the king of England. Beat it, Buster."

"Honest to goodness. I'm the mayor."

"Look, buddy. You ain't got no business out here. Now be a good guy and get out of here. Go back to your seat."

The mayor summoned a nearby police lieutenant from the Sixteenth Precinct. "That man in center field is insulting the good people of Boston. He's inciting a riot. Remove him from the game." Not knowing what to do, the police lieutenant shrugged helplessly and pleaded no jurisdiction.

Dissatisfied and getting increasingly agitated, the mayor turned to Bob Emslie again.

"Don't look at me," Emslie said. "I can't help you. Nothing in the rule book says a man can't thumb his nose." With this, Emslie drew up his coat and marched out to the middle of the diamond amid a mixture of boos and cheers.

Not knowing the mayor by sight, Larry Doyle took His Honor for some crazy who had wandered out of the stands. "Hey, asshole," Doyle barked, tapping the mayor on the shoulder, "Whaddya think you're doing out here? Beat it!"

Surprised, the mayor gave Doyle a hard look and did not respond.

"Look, you bug, get the hell out of here or I'll knock your block off."

"Don't talk to me like that, you—you uncouth—"

Doyle cut him off. "Uncouth? Uncouth?" he sputtered. "You better find yourself a hole and crawl in before I bust ya one." Then, in angry frustration, Doyle looked at the police lieutenant. "Why don't you fuckin' cops keep pests like this in the stands?"

"He's the mayor."

"Gwan."

Art Fletcher, acting as a peacemaker, got between the two men and said in the most diplomatic voice he could summon: "You'd better get back to your seat, mister, so we can get the game going. Larry doesn't mean anything. That's just the way he talks . . . that's all. He's a good guy. Just blowing off steam." Fletcher was doing quite well and the mayor was nodding agreeably.

"Oh, I know, he's not a bad man. Doyle is a good Irish name. I just wish he hadn't hollered so loud when he charged me. Kinda makes me look bad in front of the people."

At which point Doyle shouted over Fletcher's shoulder: "Look bad. Look bad. They won't recognize you when I get finished with you. I don't give a rat's ass who you are."

The mayor was buoyed by volleys of applause and cheers when he first walked out onto the field. Now there was more ridicule than applause. It was time to get out of there. He straightened his tie, snapped down the brim of his panama hat, threw back his shoulders, and, with all the dignity he could muster, walked back to his box seat in the grandstand.

Police scattered throughout the overflow crowd finally ended the bottle throwing in the highly charged atmosphere and the din gradually died down. The crowd discovered that the New Yorkers were not neophytes who could be intimidated. The Giants' brass got a little worried just the same. Acting manager Larry Doyle sent Bob Bescher out to center field in place of Fred Snodgrass for the last of the ninth inning and arranged for Snodgrass to walk back to the visitors' dressing room through a tunnel under the stands. Snodgrass was then taken by taxi back to the team's hotel under a police escort while still in uniform.

Announcers using megaphones walked along the edge of the crowd, informing the irate fans of the change in the lineup; police took up positions around the visitors' dugout and prevented any further outbreak of violence.

The Braves avoided a shutout in the seventh when Joey Connolly and Red Smith doubled to make it a 5–1 game. Ordinarily a four-run lead wouldn't be insurmountable, but the way Tesreau was mowing down batters, only the most fanatical Braves fans held out hope of a sweep of the doubleheader. And that hope swiftly vanished. The Giants pushed over three more runs in the eighth and the contest quickly ballooned into a 10–1 blowout.

Reporters surrounded Larry Doyle in the lobby of the Copley Plaza Hotel the evening after the game, and they weren't the only ones asking questions. Larry had a few himself.

"Is this man, Mayor Curley, touchy?" Doyle asked. "If I thought he took offense easy, I'd send him an apology."

"It would not be a bad idea," one of the scribes told him. "The mayor isn't a man to trifle with."

◆◆◆

Twice a congressman and a jailbird, condemned in the newspapers as a political rogue, and disparaged from the pulpit as a scoundrel, James Michael Curley bucked party bosses, terrified enemies, thrilled the masses, and won the hearts of voters as the ultimate Boston politician, an Irish Catholic Democrat.

"Mayor of the Poor" was the title he cherished most.

Left fatherless at the age of 10 and trapped in the sordid slums of Roxbury, Jim Curley and his brother John rummaged around in the local dump for coal to heat the family's cold-water flat and sold newspapers to keep the family together, while their mother worked her fingers to the bone as a scrubwoman in downtown Boston.

"Life was grim on the corned-beef-and-cabbage Riviera in those days," Curley recalled in his autobiography, and with only a seventh-grade education he turned to politics, because the prospects of getting ahead anywhere else were remote. Running for office as an underdog candidate against entrenched ward bosses, Jim Curley trumpeted about crooked deals, wooed the Irish vote, and got himself elected, first as a ward boss, then as a member of the Boston Common Council, and then as a state legislator, all of this before being carted off to the Charles Street jail for taking a civil-service exam for a friend.

From his cell, Curley read all the books in the jail library, wrote speeches, campaigned, and was reelected alderman.

Before the first meeting of the Board of Aldermen (meetings were held on the second floor of city hall), Curley asked the president of the board if he planned a motion to oust him. The president said that that was his intention. "Well," Curley replied, "if you present such a motion, you will go out head first through that window over there." That settled the matter. Curley kept his seat on the board.

He was elected to Congress in 1910 and 1912, and he ran for mayor of the city of Boston in 1913 when the incumbent, John F. Fitzgerald ("Honey Fitz"), the maternal grandfather of President John F. Kennedy, announced that he would vacate the office. But Honey Fitz reneged on the promise.

Politics is a blood sport, and the enraged Curley went after his opponent and took flesh. Several weeks into the election campaign, Curley scheduled a series of public lectures, one of which promised to be extremely popular. It was titled "Great Lovers: From Cleopatra to 'Toodles,'" the reference being to Elizabeth Ryan, a 23-year-old blond cigarette girl at the Ferncroft Inn in suburban Boston, a young woman Honey Fitz knew quite well.

One afternoon, not long after the announcement of the public lectures, a black-bordered envelope arrived at the Fitzgerald residence, addressed to Mary Fitzgerald, Honey Fitz's wife. Her daughter Rose (the future Mrs. Joe Kennedy) was at her side. The writer of the black-bordered letter described in detail her husband's affair with Toodles Ryan, the juiciest kind of tale.

Honey Fitz later told a friend that that evening was "the worst moment of his life."

Two weeks before the election Honey Fitz, claiming poor health, withdrew from the race, saying he was acting on doctor's orders.

Pretty soon a popular little ditty was on the lips of everyone in Boston:

A whiskey glass
And Toodles' ass
Made a horse's ass
Of Honey Fitz.

Mayor Curley made political points by telling the press his office was going to look into the Snodgrass/Doyle matter. But nothing came of it.

CHAPTER 38

AN UNAPPEASABLE HUNGER

There was an air of expectation among the 17,000 fans streaming into Fenway Park Tuesday afternoon, most of it kindled by speculation about the pivotal battle for first place. But sentiments were not all warm-hearted and devoted. Cynics were convinced that destiny had not chosen Stallings' rag tag band of also-rans to become champions. They insisted that it wouldn't happen.

Cocky and nasty and accustomed to winning, the Giants were nonetheless wary of the boys from Boston. McGraw felt they had to be stopped, and they had to be stopped now, and he placed the task of turning back the troublesome challenger in the capable hands of Rube Marquard, a veteran left hander who had pitched well lately.

Could the Braves' unappeasable hunger for victory be denied? Stallings didn't think so. Alive with anticipation and eager to seize sole possession of first place, he called on "Big Bill" James, the ace of his staff, to bring home the prize. Big Bill hadn't lost since the Fourth of July and was still adjusting to all the attention coming his way.

But Stallings's fireballer got off to a shaky start. Fred Snodgrass, the first batter of the game, walked on five pitches. Bill then walked Larry Doyle on four pitches, all fastballs. Ears smoking, eyes flashing, the big guy looked like a pitcher primed for a roughing up, and the Giants' toughest out, George Burns, approached the plate, whipping a bat around with conviction. A high heater arrived in the vicinity of Burns's head, sending him sprawling. He sprang right back up, hopping mad, and exploded with a barrage of obscene curses. After getting set once more, Burns swung at the next pitch and hit the ball imperfectly off the end of his bat. James fielded the bouncer cleanly, spun, and attempted to cut down Snodgrass at third base. The throw was late. The bases were loaded. There were no outs.

The macho New Yorkers burst out of the dugout, flung bats and sweaters in the air, and mocked their opponents: tough-tongued insults, rough words, lots of "bleeps." Red Murray, the on-deck batter, waved three bats above his head, and three teammates swung bats in front of the visitors' dugout, leaving no doubt in James's mind what they expected to do to him.

Coaching at third, McGraw prodded Bill James with his savage tongue, claiming that the Braves' starter wasn't keeping his foot on the rubber before letting go of the ball. "He doesn't have it today," McGraw howled. "He's got a yellow streak." Fans shouted, "Take him out."

Paul Strand was up and throwing in the Boston bull pen.

Johnny Evers, the Braves' captain, displeased with the way things were unfolding, called time and trotted over from second base to offer encouragement, reminding James of the weaknesses in Art Fletcher's swing, while Fletcher, the Giants' cleanup hitter, known for his ability to drive in runs, waited at the plate.

It was a predicament that had to be resolved. Fletcher got the hit sign from McGraw and, being a bit overeager, chased a bad pitch and fouled it off. Big Bill then cranked up his effort and blew the next one right by Fletcher for a swinging strike, his best pitch of the day. After having waved at two pitches, all the Giants' cleanup hitter could do was send a routine pop-up above the right side of the infield. Evers moved under it, pounded his glove, waited, waited, and pulled it in for the first out of the inning.

Red Murray, a formidable threat, went after an off-speed breaking ball and tapped a clunker between the mound and first base. James lunged for it, knocked it down, and alertly nailed Snodgrass charging for home. Things were looking up for the boys from Boston.

With two outs and runners at second and third, Harvard Eddie Grant stepped into the batter's box. A .326 hitter coming into the game, Grant was on a roll: eight hits in his last 19 at bats. James went right after him and, in his eagerness, threw a darting, diving spitter that tipped Gowdy's mitt and skipped back to the grandstand (a passed ball). Doyle scampered home. It was 1–0, New York.

The Braves lost no time in launching a far more aggressive attack of their own when they came to bat, producing hits and runs at a lively pace. They would not be denied. Led by Johnny Evers, Stallings's boys pushed over six runs after two men were out, two of the tallies coming on bases-loaded walks. The overmatched Marquard lasted just four innings.

What began as a contest ended as an 8–3 rout, a rout that enabled the Braves to take over sole possession of first place and, at the same time, expose for all to see the imminent obsolescence of the New York Giants.

The Braves were on top now. Respectable. Sensations of the moment. With gutsy determination, they had taken over the lead, something a lot of people thought they would never see. And for the first time in years, they were winning routinely, particularly when it mattered. Now, the question on everybody's lips was: "Can they maintain the momentum?"

CHAPTER 39

KID'S GONNA BLOW SKY HIGH

Wednesday afternoon, the first-place Braves played host to the always dangerous Philadelphia Phillies in a crucial doubleheader at Fenway Park, the first of 11 twin bills scheduled for the next five weeks. The weather was dirty. A lisp of rain darkened the sky. Thunder boomed on the horizon. Flags shivered and whipped above the grandstand.

"This goddamn wind goes right through you," an usher grumbled, his shoulders scrunched up against the chill.

"Thermometer outside the window read forty-eight degrees this morning," a fan said, the breeze rattling the scorecard in his hand as he spoke.

"Can't be more than sixty now," the usher said. "Too early for winter to be comin' on."

"Sixty-one," the other man said. "Weatherman blames it on sun spots."

"Sun spots? . . . What the hell are sun spots?"

"Doesn't look like the 'Miracle Man' thinks it's cold," another man said, with a nod over his shoulder. "Look at him, sitting up there in his lucky seat. I'd be in the clubhouse where it's warm if I was him."

"The Phillies hit the ball hard. He needs all the luck he can get; ain't got no pitching today," a man with a big cigar said.

"Who's gonna pitch?"

"I don't know. 'Baldy' Rudolph, maybe . . . in the first one. The second game? Who the hell knows? Won't be James, that's for sure. He went yesterday. And Tyler's all played out. He ain't strong enough to pitch on two days' rest. Especially after what the Giants did to him on Monday. Besides, the Phillies murder lefties."

Stallings often sat at the top of the grandstand an hour before game time, the last row. Always the same seat. Was it another of his superstitions? Writers thought so. And in a way, maybe it was. They would mention the lucky seat, and he'd give them that great big wonderful George Stallings smile, and shrug, and they would chalk it up to superstition.

But the Big Chief was a man with a purpose, a Georgia country boy, something of an amateur weather expert. The gravid smell of earth filled his nostrils. It seemed like he could hear the enormous breathing of rain miles away. Sitting there, he scanned the horizon, studied the clouds and gauged the wind, mulling over the chances of rain. When showers were a possibility, as they were on days like this, particularly in the early innings, he'd start one of the second-line hurlers: Cocreham, Cottrell, Crutcher, Hess, or Strand. Then, if the clouds started spitting rain, one of his three regular starters would not have been wasted.

The fifth-place Phillies were a powerful lot, led by "Gavvy" Cravath, the home run king of the dead-ball era, and Sherry Magee, a former batting champion. Cravath, baseball's all-time slugger until 1921, won the National League home run title six times and set the marks that Babe Ruth would break in 1920.

Stallings, reluctant to send a southpaw against the powerful Philadelphians, selected 23-year-old Gene Cocreham, pronounced C-o-r-r-y-ham, a rookie right-hander, to face Philly ace Grover Cleveland Alexander ("Old Pete") in the first game of the doubleheader.

Old Pete was almost unbeatable when right, and Boston had no chance against him that afternoon. The Phillies broke the game wide open in the first two innings, scoring seven runs, and soundly thrashed the Braves, 10–3. The slaughter of the home team was partially offset by news of the out-of-town games posted on the scoreboard. The Dodgers had hammered the Giants 9–3 in New York. If the Braves lost both ends of the double bill, they would still be in first place, a half game ahead of the Giants in the standings.

"Stallings's got to be worried," the fan said, a cigar clamped in the side of his mouth. Just then a murmur went through the crowd. A light-haired well-built right-hander with a Douglas Fairbanks mustache was walking toward the mound.

"Who the hell is that?" one of the men asked.

"Stallings must be nuts," the man with the cigar said, taking it out of his mouth and spitting. "That's Davis. The guy can't hit the side of a barn with a paddle when he's standing next to it."

"Where'd they get him from?"

"I don't know . . . off some scrap heap somewhere."

"Give him a *chanct,* bub, give him a *chanct,*" a third man said.

Davis looked like a rejuvenated pitcher in the initial stages of the game, a pitcher who had rediscovered his early speed and the tools that brought him to the major leagues in the first place: a good curve, an outstanding spitter, and an exploding fastball.

He buzzed through the first four batters in the Philadelphia lineup untouched, until a wicked foul tip off the bat of second baseman Bobby Byrne struck home plate umpire Ernie Quigley in the throat, just above the collarbone, below the Adam's apple.

Quigley staggered like a man shot in the chest. He reeled and, hands hanging helplessly at his sides, fell face first and lay helpless on the ground. Voices in the crowd fell to a murmur. Fans shook their heads. An inkling of tenseness hovered in the air. Blank faces stared. Players crowded around.

Deathly pale, looking as if the breath of life had been knocked out of him, Quigley looked like he was finished. A call for a doctor brought three physicians out of the stands; they worked over the fallen umpire but couldn't get a response.

More than 10 minutes passed in the clubhouse before the injured arbiter, suffering from shock and unable to move, regained consciousness. Though numb, he did not demand pity for himself; he kept insisting that he was all right. And, indeed, a half hour later, the mentally and physically tough Quigley was back on his feet, adamant about feeling well enough to go back to work. His umpiring partner needed him.

The unpleasant incident not only shook up the crowd but also unsettled the inexperienced Davis. When play resumed, the shaky-kneed youngster had trouble finding home plate. He walked the very next batter on four straight pitches. Mouth tight with disapproval, Davis turned, blew out his cheeks, stood with his back to home plate, head down, a hand on his hip, shaking his head.

Mitchell paid him a visit.

Davis regrouped, got accustomed to umpire Mel Eason's call of the strike zone, and worked his way through the Phillies' lineup without further damage.

"He ain't so bad," the man with the cigar said, after Davis set Philadelphia down in order in the third.

Just as he completed the sentence, cheers of approval became appreciative applause when umpire Ernie Quigley reappeared on the field. His throat wrapped in an icepack, the courageous man in blue slowly walked out to his position beyond first base.

"Gotta admire the guy's guts," the man with the cigar said, "even if he is an umpire."

Boston picked up two runs in the second off Philadelphia starter Ben Tincup, a full-blooded Cherokee—sometimes referred to as the "millionaire Indian," because he owned 500 acres of oil-lease land in Oklahoma—and two more runs in the fourth, when rookie right fielder Pat Hilly bobbled George Davis's clean single. Smith and Maranville, the two Boston base runners at the time, scored, giving Boston a 4–0 lead.

All young Davis had to do was hold the lead. But in the top half of the fifth he suddenly began acting as if home plate were not stationary. His pitches seemed to dance around it, inside and outside, up and down. Bobby Byrne walked. "Dode" Paskert walked. Jack Martin walked. No one had touched the ball and the bases were loaded.

Davis took deep breaths and stared in at the five-sided slab of white rubber that was causing him so much trouble. He adjusted his cap, fiddled with his belt, and kicked at the dirt.

"The kid's a false alarm," the man with the cigar said. "He's gonna blow sky high."

But as quickly as Davis lost his control, he found it, striking out catcher Ed Burns with a sizzling fastball for the first out of the inning.

The threatening sky began to close in; a few drops of rain fell; and Charlie Dooin, the Phillies' manager, decided to go for the knockout punch, right then and there. He called on his hard-cursing, hard-nosed, tobacco-chewing bruiser, "Cactus" Gavvy Cravath, to pinch-hit for the pitcher. Cravath was being rested in the second game of the doubleheader.

The prickly Cravath dug in and motioned at Davis in a menacing manner. "Okay, Joe College, show me what you got." Cravath was hitting .283.

Davis showed no signs of emotion. A fine cold mist touched his face. Every now and then he'd paw at the dirt, moisten his lips, and blow on his fingers.

Cravath was thinking curveball. Davis was thinking curveball. Davis gave him a wicked one. Cravath made contact and rocketed a shot right at Maranville. Rabbit fielded the ball on one hop and turned it into a Maranville-to-Evers-to-Schmidt double play. An impressive escape act.

"Pretty lucky," the talkative man with the cigar said. "But you have to admit, the kid's good."

The story line unfurled inevitably after Davis again closed the doors on hitless Philadelphia in the sixth; the bundled-up crowd sensed the possibility of a no-hitter.

Opening the top of the seventh, Bobby Byrne popped one up a mile high above the infield. Red Smith and Butch Schmidt drifted over to within a few feet of the mound, their spiked shoes leaving footprints on the wet grass. Red called for the ball. Butch stepped aside. Red punched his glove once, twice, waited, waited . . . and dropped the ball. The game had a goat.

Davis, acting like a veteran who had been through this before, appeared unruffled. He ignored the slip and kept doing his job. It was three up and three down; it seemed like he found a little extra fire somewhere when he needed it.

Fenway was electric with excitement. Only six more outs to go. Second-string catcher Ed Burns, leading off in the eighth, stepped into the batter's box. On the third pitch, Burns reached across the plate and drove a sinking liner toward right field. "Possum" Whitted retreated a couple of steps, realized he'd misjudged the ball—the wind was holding it back—and quickly changed direction. Too late. (It was only the second time in seven innings that the Phillies managed to drive the ball out of the infield.)

"The cards is gummed," the man with the cigar said. "The kid ain't got no luck."

In a last-second all-out effort, Whitted threw out his glove, made a desperate dive, and speared the ball as he skidded along on his chest on the soggy turf. The crowd went wild. The no-hitter was still intact.

Pinch hitter Bill Killifer, the second batter up in the eighth, carrying a .245 average, knocked the dirt off his spikes, set himself in the batter's box, and sneaked a look at Red Smith, playing deep at third base. "Reindeer Bill" was not the fastest player on the field, and everyone was caught by surprise when he bounced a ball toward Smith, hoping the unexpected challenge would earn an infield hit.

Forced into rushing his throw, Red sailed a ball low and away on one bounce and pulled Schmidt off the bag. A bang-bang play. Tantalizingly close. It was anybody's call. Thousands of pounding hearts waited for the official scorer's decision.

The official scorer ruled the play an error. The no-hitter was still intact.

Now, with one on and one out in the eighth, Davis went to work on Hans Lobert, a dangerous man on the base paths. The speedy Lobert once raced a horse around the bases and, after leading most of the way, lost by a nose at home plate. (He would have won, too, he later insisted, if the horse hadn't cut him off between second and third.) The guy could run.

Swinging away, Lobert slashed a two-hop liner at Rabbit Maranville. Rab fielded the ball cleanly and shoveled it to Johnny Evers for an easy 6–4–3 double play, smothering the threat.

The entire Braves bench greeted Davis and Whitted en masse as they approached the dugout, everyone thinking "no-hitter," but not one mentioning the two words.

Going into the top of the ninth inning, the Braves held a 7–0 lead. George Davis was three outs away from a place in the record books.

Beals Becker, batting .322, was the first Philadelphia batter Davis faced in the ninth. Beals was a good hitter, fast, a thinking manager's ballplayer, a thinking manager's ballplayer . . . because the manager had to think for him. Beals wasn't very good at it. Twice in one season he stole third base only to look up after the dust had settled and discover that the base was already occupied. "Look," his manager said. "Leave me do the thinking. It takes equipment."

Davis got Becker on a ground out for the first out of the inning. Now only two outs remained.

This brought up Sherry Magee, the most difficult out in the Philadelphia lineup. Davis, blowing on the fingers of his right hand and tugging at his jersey as the temperature rapidly plunged into the fifties ahead of a weather front, pumped fastballs over both sides of the plate. There was a little extra adrenaline going for him now.

With the count no balls and two strikes, Magee went down swinging. The big second out of the ninth inning.

The man with the cigar swore Davis was the best pitcher in the league. Fans were on their feet. Cheering. Pleading. Praying.

Pat Hilly, a raw rookie, unmentioned in scouting reports, therefore unknown and dangerous, was the batter. With the count even at one and one, Hilly smacked a ball into the hole between third and short. Rabbit Maranville went deep into the gap, gloved it on the second hop, and threw to Butch Schmidt at first for the final out of the game.

Davis's 7–0 no-hitter was the first ever thrown at Fenway Park, the home of the Boston Red Sox, and the first thrown by a National League pitcher in two years.

CHAPTER 40

SOLID IVORY

Virtually every sportswriter in the nation thought the Giants would prove themselves masters in the end. "As things are going," a reporter known as Herbert wrote in the *New York Tribune,* "it is quite likely that Stallings and his men will draw out a bit and force the pace for a time, but eventually the class of the Giants should tell."

The schedule looked as if it might give the Chicago Cubs an opening. Most experts considered the gang from the Windy City more dangerous than the Braves. Johnny Evers called the Cubbies "the best team in the National League," perhaps Johnny's way of embarrassing his successor Hank O'Day. "They have five good pitchers," Evers said, "and every man on the team is a player."

But West Side Grounds on Polk Street was not a happy place. Manager Hank O'Day had lost control of the club, and internal warfare raged in the clubhouse. The general public did not know of the sad state of affairs until a Tuesday afternoon in mid-August, during a game at Ebbets Field in Brooklyn.

The visiting Cubs were leading the Dodgers 2–0 in the fourth inning, when the Dodgers filled the bases after one man was out. Zack Wheat (hobbled by an injured leg) was the runner on third, Hy Myers and Dick Egan were the runners on first and second, and Otto Miller was the batter.

Swinging at the first pitch, Miller scorched a fastball on one hop right at third baseman Heinie Zimmerman, playing wide of the bag. Zim fielded the ball five feet off the bag, and instead of going for the force at home on the limping Zack Wheat for the easy double play (the catcher would then throw out Otto Miller at first base for the second out), Zim scrambled over and touched third for the force on Hy Myers, then hurried a throw to first base and winced as the ball sailed high above Vic Saier's outstretched glove and rolled to the stands.

Wheat scored easily, and Egan scampered all the way home from first on the error, tying the score. The Cubs eventually lost the game 3–2, largely because of Zimmerman's blunder. But it was worse than that. The knucklehead's mental mistakes were responsible in part for Cubs losses in two of the three previous games.

"Ain't he a bonehead?" a Brooklynite observed.

"Solid ivory," his pal replied.

Roger Bresnahan, the Cubs' catcher, radiating competitive fire, rushed halfway up the third baseline and bawled out Zimmerman for his stupidity.

Heinie shouted back. Curses echoed across the field.

Once the inning was over, the air on the Cubs bench was foul. Bresnahan kept after the "lunkhead" and didn't let up. He leaned forward and threw out snarling jibes. "You're the best third baseman Brooklyn's ever had."

Zimmerman's face went scarlet. Like a rabid dog, he hurled himself at his tormentor with animal ferocity. The big goon was out to destroy Bresnahan. Put him out of existence. Zim landed a roundhouse right on Bresnahan's jaw and wrestled the catcher to the ground.

Spectators in the stands were astonished by the violence of the clash. They gaped at the two combatants. It was no-holds-barred. Bresnahan reacted quickly and fiercely, battering the big German with a broadside of body blows. One pit bull attacking the other. Manager Hank O'Day of the Cubs glanced over at the two men brawling in front of the dugout, sighed, shook his head wearily, and flapped an indifferent hand in their direction. And in a dull, even voice O'Day remarked that he "hoped someone would lose, someone who wasn't Irish."

In spite of the discord, the Cubs were still close on the ninth of September, three games out of first place, close enough to win the pennant. A few breaks here and there, a string of victories, less fighting among themselves, and they might still capture the flag.

CHAPTER 41

THE MOST SPIRITED TEAM I EVER SAW

It was onward and upward for the carefully retooled Braves. Optimism hovered over them. They kept getting better. Began to pull away. Ran off winning streaks of four, eight, and nine games, and built a three-game comfort level for themselves in the standings. Bragging and laughter boosted their confidence. You never heard the word "lose" in the excitement of their chatter, always the word "win"; one player or another was repeatedly saying, "We will win today and we will win tomorrow too."

But warnings of a possible collapse appeared in the Braves' makeup. They committed seven errors in a game against the Dodgers before wiggling through to a lucky 4–3 victory. The young pitching arms were showing signs of being sapped. Rudolph and Tyler looked ragged in their starts, Tyler in particular. Stallings was at the end of his tether. A collapse was in the making.

On Saturday, the nineteenth of September, the Braves, looking flat and playing poorly, made more mistakes than they'd made in a week and trailed Pittsburgh 3–1 after five innings. The three runs looked immense the way Bucs southpaw Wilbur Cooper was pitching. Stallings's gut boiled with anxiety. He buttoned and unbuttoned his jacket, then buttoned it again. He crossed his legs, uncrossed them, and crossed them again, the upper foot always bouncing as he slid up and down the bench, muttering abuse and throwing angry glances at the players. The boys gave him plenty of room.

Cooper was cruising along unharmed in the bottom of the sixth; there was one out and Butch Schmidt was the batter.

Stallings drew a ragged breath and squinted with displeasure as his eyes followed a tiny piece of paper lightly bounding over the grass toward the Braves' dugout. Instinct warned him: bad luck. He bent over and caught the paper in his fingertips at the very instant that Schmidt drove a smoking line drive at second baseman Jimmy Viox. The ball exploded off Viox's glove and Schmidt reached first safely. Bent over double, the superstitious Stallings did not move; his eyes followed the action. Smith and Maranville walked, filling the bases.

Hank Gowdy then launched a tremendous drive into deep left-center. It bounced off the embankment, just short of the wall, a two-base hit. A jubilant explosion rocked the stands. Gowdy's blast cleared the bases; the Braves led, 4–3. Stallings's face was heavily beaded with perspiration, but he did not move from his stooped position.

Oscar Dugey, batting for the pitcher, singled up the middle, scoring Gowdy; Dugey took second on the throw home. The Pirates replaced the left-hander with a right-hander, and the Braves switched from a left-handed to a right-handed hitting outfield. Herbie Moran and Joey Connolly replaced Les Mann and Ted Cather. There was no letup in the cheering when Herbie flied to center, because the crowd knew Johnny Evers was due up next. Johnny didn't disappoint them; he dumped a single into left field, and Dugey reached third.

Joey Connolly then drove a shot at Viox, who knocked the ball toward the right field foul line; Connolly got a two-base hit on the play. Dugey scored and Evers stopped at third. Then, somehow, in the excitement of it all, Connolly blundered. He forgot Evers was on base ahead of him and took off for third on the pitch. Possum Whitted, batting for the second time in the inning, alertly saved Connolly from embarrassment by smashing a shot over second base, driving in Evers and Connolly. Seven runs scored in the inning. The bones in Stallings's head hurt. He offered a pained smile. But he did not move.

The scoring ended when Whitted was thrown out attempting a steal of second. Nobody really cared except George Stallings. The Braves had iced the game, 9–3.

Slowly, almost reluctantly, Stallings straightened up. It had been a good half hour. A grimace of pain covered his face. The strain on his muscles had been too much. The boys, smothering nods, rib pokes, and grins, helped him back into the clubhouse, where trainer Jimmy Neary applied hot towels and eased the Big Guy's discomfort.

By the twenty-first of September only two teams were still in the pennant race, Boston and New York. Since the Braves had not collapsed, they had the advantage. But they faced the unenviable prospect of playing three doubleheaders in four days, nine games in six days, a grueling schedule. There could be trouble ahead.

Stallings was in a constant fret. When well-wishers approached him about a George Stallings Day, he graciously told them how honored he was but asked that they not proceed with the plans. "I'm a bit superstitious," he said, with total sincerity. "I wouldn't for the world do anything or make any move that would indicate that I expect to see our team win the pennant." If the Braves did not make it, he pointed out, he would always attribute the loss to the day the fans honored him. He even refused requests for photographs. Another superstition.

Sure enough, the predicted collapse came. But it was not the Braves who collapsed; it was the Giants. McGraw had placed his bets on Tesreau, Mathewson, and Marquard, and hurled them as often as he could at opponents in August and September. Mathewson won three of nine starts and Marquard lost all of his starts.

In looking back at the season, Stallings told magazine editor F. C. Lane: "I have seen a half broken, wild, spirited saddle horse take the bit in his teeth and for a time nothing in the world, save dynamite, could stop him. It was just that way with the Braves."

Umpire Bill Klem, when elected to the Baseball Hall of Fame, was asked to name the most spirited team he'd ever seen during his 70-odd-year career in the major leagues, both on the field and as a supervisor of umpires. Without the least bit of hesitation, the Old Arbiter paid tribute to manager George Stallings's 1914 Braves: "They were the most spirited team I ever saw."

PART III

CHAPTER 42

REJOICING IN BOSTON

On September 29, 1914, the Kaiser's army drove the retreating French across the Marne, 30 miles from Paris: the outlook for the Allies was not promising. But it was a time of great rejoicing in Boston. The Braves had clinched the pennant. Fans and well-wishers sang and danced around George Stallings and his players as they left the field.

Late that afternoon, at Back Bay station, the players gathered around their euphoric leader before boarding a train for New York. The big fellow smiled broadly. "Well, boys," he said in his friendly southern drawl, "we've won the championship." He looked from one to another. "It was a long fight and we didn't crack.... Tonight you can ease off a little.... Do as you please. I'll be blind to what time you get in.... But tomorrow I want to see you all in my room at noon, for a talk."

Three hours later at Grand Central a large crowd of New Yorkers welcomed the Braves' party, and Stallings told a surprised group of journalists: "I will work my regular lineup in the five-game series against the Giants and in the final four games of the season against Brooklyn, just as if we were not sure of anything. I'll ride them harder, if possible, to keep them on the edge they've been on the past two months."

"Do you think you can beat the Mackmen?" Joe Vila of the *Sun* asked.

"On the Fourth of July nobody believed we had a ghost of a chance of winning the pennant, but we've got the flag clinched now."

Johnny Evers couldn't stay out of it. He jumped in and assisted the boss: "We'll keep winning when we meet Connie Mack's team," he said. "Don't you worry. We're going to surprise those Quakers."

At the noon meeting the following day, Stallings positioned himself in the middle of the room, hands in the pockets of his Norfolk jacket, observing each man as he straggled in. He kept nodding his head. Maranville appeared, walking stiffly, carefully, eyes haggard, face pale, suit crumpled, a whiff of cigarettes and stale beer on his clothes. Stallings arched an eyebrow and kept nodding.

"This place smells like a beer wagon," he said, the tone of his voice leavened by a hint of understanding.

"Then Stallings surrounded us," Maranville said.

"We got some deep talkin' to do, suh," Stallings said. "Do you know who we play in the World Series?"

Of course they knew. Everybody knew. The Philadelphia Athletics, a ball club bulging with talent, winner of the pennant with comparative ease, a team that compiled a phenomenal 39–6 record between July 11 and September 1, a period in which the Braves made an electrifying 33–10 run of their own. No one said a thing.

"Well," Stallings said, "we play the greatest team of all time. Connie Mack's champions, a team that pulverized regular-season competition."

"I take exception to that." There was a spluttering of laughter. Johnny Evers considered his former team, the 1906 Chicago Cubs, the greatest team of all time.

Stallings would not be sidetracked. "All right . . . all right . . . let's not get into that right now." He began again. "I don't mind getting beat," he said soberly, "but I hate being laughed at."

"Good Lord!" someone said. "Everybody's calling you the 'Miracle Man' . . . right this minute."

"That makes it all the worse. . . . Do you know the wise guys [the bookmakers] are betting ten to one against us?" This of course was a terrible exaggeration. No one responded.

Stallings turned toward Evers for affirmation. "Johnny, do you have any ideas of how we can wipe up the earth with a team that's supposed to be ten times better than we are?"

Evers rolled his cigar from one side of his mouth to the other and considered the question. Everybody stared at him. Johnny puffed on his cigar, blew out a stream of smoke, and puffed again. "We can't overpower them," he said. "That's for sure . . . We've got to put them out of step in some way, right from the beginning. . . ."

He stared at the tip of the cigar, thinking. The boys stared and waited.

"I'll tell you what we'll do. We'll accuse them of stealing signals with a telescope hidden in some house outside the park."

"Good," Stallings said. "Any more ideas?" . . . He looked around. Waited. No one spoke up. "Okay, then . . . Johnny's idea is a good one. It will work wonders. It'll upset them. Put them in a bad position, trying to win by unsportsmanlike work."

"Let's start by getting the goods on those bastards," Evers said. "All the dirt you can dig up . . . I've got lots of stuff in my black book. You guys start writing friends who played with the A's. Ask for any dope you can get on them."

CHAPTER 43

IT WAS A BAD SCENE

By mutual agreement the Braves and Dodgers moved up Wednesday's scheduled game at Ebbets Field, normally the closing day of the season, and played the contest as part of a Tuesday doubleheader. It was a way of giving Stallings's men an extra day of preparation for their meeting with Mack's juggernaut.

Pennant-winning managers generally rest starters in meaningless games after the league championship has been decided, allowing the second-stringers and late-season call-ups an opportunity to show their stuff. Not George Stallings. The Chief played his regulars.

The single exception was the club's mainstay catcher, Hank Gowdy, whose recent subpar performances, particularly against the Giants—two wild throws and three errors in one game—indicated the necessity of a badly needed rest.

George Davis started for the Braves in the first game of the doubleheader against "Big Jeff" Pfeffer of the Dodgers. "No-Hit" Davis was good that afternoon. Very good. But Big Jeff was better. The Braves trailed the Dodgers 3–2 after eight innings of play, their tallies coming on home runs by Johnny Evers and Joey Connolly.

After one out in the ninth, Butch Schmidt singled, and the Braves got to thinking that they might still pull this one out. The on-deck batter, Red Smith, was dangerous in clutch situations. Displaying a brand-new pair of spikes he'd just purchased for the World Series, Red stepped into the batter's box.

Bronx cheers and catcalls shattered the air. Hoarse voices spit out cruel taunts. A noisy chorus baited and provoked Red. He took the bait. Spat in the direction of the stands and made a below-the-belt gesture.

Schmidt, the runner on first, got the white teeth sign from manager Stallings, confirming the hit-and-run. Smith, normally a dead left field pull hitter, drilled a low liner over the second baseman's head. Schmidt, off at the crack of the bat, rumbled around second and headed for third, challenging right fielder "Casey" Stengel. Stengel picked the ball off the wall and made a strong throw across the diamond as Schmidt raced for third. Seeing this, Red rounded first, pumping his fists and shouting, and sprinted for second. The third baseman took stock of the situation, realized he had no play at third, but thought he might get Smith at second. He cut off the ball and snapped a throw to George Cutshaw covering the bag.

Smith slid in heavily just ahead of the ball, his ankle twisting awkwardly beneath him, the momentum of the slide carrying him past the bag. Cutshaw tagged him, turned quickly, and made sure that Schmidt on third wasn't going anywhere. When Cutshaw glanced back at second, Smith was pointing at the bag. Cutshaw jumped all over umpire Cy Rigler: "He's out, I tell you . . . I got him . . . He was off the bag when I tagged him."

Just then, Smith rolled over like a wounded animal, his face a ghastly white, his scorching pain unmistakable. Cutshaw and Rigler saw blood spurting from Red's right ankle and a bone protruding from his stocking. Rigler called for a doctor.

Red's body trembled from throbs of pain as players from both teams crowded around. Smith looked up at Evers and Maranville hovering above him: "I guess this lets me out," he said. Meaning the injury had knocked him out of the World Series.

Over in the Boston dugout George Stallings threw his hands in the air and let them drop helplessly at his sides, feeling betrayed and limp. "Goddamn it," he growled. "I knew this would happen . . . It's the Brooklyn jinx . . . The jinx waited for Red to come back in a Boston uniform . . . I wish I could get my hands on that jinx. I'd fix him. I'd fix him good."

The spikes on Smith's new shoes were longer than those he'd been wearing earlier in the season. The momentum of his slide carried him past second base. The heel of his right shoe caught the corner of the bag and stuck, and the bone snapped.

Urgent calls for help from the Swedish Hospital were futile. Both ambulances were out. Dodger pitcher Ed Reulbach volunteered his automobile:

"My machine is parked right across the street, John. We can take Red to the hospital ourselves."

"Let's go," Evers replied.

Evers, Reulbach, and Kid Elberfeld, a Dodgers coach, rushed Smith to St. Mary's Hospital, where X-rays revealed serious damage. Since the leg was not badly swollen yet, the attending physician, James C. Kennedy, a specialist in fractures, set the bones. Dr. Kennedy then prepared a statement for the press: "Red Smith has suffered an anterior dislocation of the ankle joint of the right leg and a fracture of the fibula [the small bone of the leg] three inches above the joint. There is also a fracture of the tibia [the large bone of the leg] near the external malleolus [the knuckle of the fibula], and ruptures of the external and internal lateral ligaments of the ankle joint."

"I guess what you're telling us, Doc, is Red's hurt pretty bad?" a reporter said.

"The injury is just as severe as it sounds," the physician replied grumpily.

Smith broke down and wept when doctors told him how badly he was hurt. "Damn it," he said. "I've dreamed of the series ever since I broke into baseball, now this—" Tears of heartbreak ran down his cheeks.

The freakish turn of fate in the ninth inning of the final day of the regular season shattered any hope the Braves had of winning the World Series. It was a telling blow.

CHAPTER 44

THE BOYS ROCKETED OUT OF THEIR SEATS

George Stallings was in a surprisingly cheerful mood when the team sat down for dinner at the Hotel Somerset that evening. He visualized a new future for the Braves, a different scenario unrolling for them. Now they were going to win with good old-fashioned defense.

His eyes swept the room. The usual good-natured badinage was missing. No whoops of youthful exuberance. No locker-room jokes. Just talk in low voices. He didn't like the gloominess of the room. They had come too far to let themselves get sidetracked now. He stood up, looked at his hands, and thought for a minute. A library hush fell over the dinner tables.

"Boys," he said, his voice at a low register, "I want to share some thoughts with you." He paused, to be certain he'd engaged everyone's attention. "At first I thought Red's loss would put a big hole in the team. Now I'm beginning to think otherwise. Red's a mighty good hitter, one who can line out long drives and clean the bases. No question about it. His ability to come through in critical situations will be missed."

He paused again. "But don't forget about Charlie Deal over here. Charlie was our regular third baseman. He knows the bag. And he can hit some."

The players nodded at one another.

Stallings gradually raised his voice. "You all know we lost Johnny during the season . . . for quite a while. And of the fifteen or so odd games we played while he was out of the lineup, we lost only two or three."

Stallings's voice grew stronger. "Charlie here played half the season with a charley horse that made every step he took painful. He was almost a cripple, forced to play on a lame leg when he should have been home in bed. That's all changed now."

Suddenly, it seemed like an electric current was emanating from Stallings's person. The players sat transfixed. The spell was working. Stallings pulled out all the stops.

"Charlie is healthy now," he said in a bold voice. "And we are mighty lucky to have him around to put in Red's place. Think about it... We are strengthened in the field. Charlie can do anything Red has ever done on defense; he is vastly superior in handling bunts and slow bounders toward third."

With firm conviction he loudly proclaimed, "We will show the Athletics pitching the Giants couldn't show them." He was shouting now. "Red's absence won't hit us as hard as some people think."

The boys rocketed out of their seats and cheered. The shouts grew louder and louder. The Big Chief had rallied the boys in the way he'd rallied himself. They had a job to do. And by God they would do it.

All the sentimental stuff was left behind when they boarded the 8:52 train to Philadelphia that evening.

Though the Braves arrived at a late hour Tuesday night, two dozen reporters were on hand in the lobby of the Majestic Hotel, asking what Smith's loss meant to the team. George Tyler and Possum Whitted expressed confidence in Charlie Deal: "I look for him to do great things," Tyler said. "He's steady, calm, and nervy, and while he's not as strong at bat as Smith, he's no laggard with the stick either."

About a dozen reporters waited for manager George Stallings to appear. "I suppose Smith's loss is a great blow?" several said.

"Yes, it may well prove that way," Stallings replied.

"It may serve a good purpose though," a scribe said. "It may make them fight all the harder."

"Oh, I don't think it will. I don't think the boys can fight any harder than they have already. They're the gamest club in the country." Stallings continued. "While the accident has unquestionably weakened our hitting, I still think we'll take the big end of the purse."

CHAPTER 45

NOT YOUR RUN-OF-THE-MILL MASCOTS

No one escaped the warm glow of publicity, not even Willie Connor and Louis Van Zelst, the team mascots. Scholarly looking and well read, Willie Connor, the Braves' batboy, carried a book wherever he went. If a reporter happened by, Willie hurriedly put on wire-rimmed glasses, opened the book, ordinarily one of the classics, and acted as if he'd been reading it all along.

This impressed hard-boiled sportswriters, a well-educated fraternity, for the most part, who'd seldom if ever seen a 14-year-old mascot doting on anything other than the funny papers: "Little Nemo," "Hairbreadth Harry," "The Yellow Kid," "Krazy Kat," "Mutt and Jeff."

But Willie was not as cerebral as most people thought. Hidden beneath the brainy veneer was something else altogether, a fun-loving, mischievous youngster who fantasized about becoming a big-league ballplayer.

"What about the glasses?" a reporter asked.

"Glatheth?" Willie said, taking them off and placing them on the book. "I can get along fine without my glatheth. I only wear them to threngthen my eyeth. I won't need glatheth in another couple of yearth." Willie had a lisp and it was not funny.

The Braves needed luck back in early June. A great deal of luck. They were in desperate need of a winning streak to snap them out of the doldrums. Shortly after the team returned from its first swing through the West, a disastrous 8–17 road trip, Johnny Evers noticed a clean-cut good-looking boy among the swarm of tough-talking roughnecks seeking autographs near the players' entrance.

"What's your name, son?" Johnny asked.

The boy's eyes opened wide behind his glasses. "Willie, sir. Willie Connor."

"Irish, is it?"

"Yes, sir. My parents are from Ireland."

Evers eyebrows raised slightly. "Are they now?"

Evers cast a look at the players' entrance, pursed his lips, and silently mulled over a knotty issue that had troubled him for weeks. "Maybe an Irish kid would change our luck. The club's Swedish mascot is a nice kid. A real nice kid. Not lucky, though. Hmm . . ."

Evers unconsciously moved his head up and down and said loudly enough to be heard, "Sure, why not?" He turned toward the boy. "Tell you what, son. Why don't you come with me? Maybe we can use you today."

Boston won that afternoon. They won again the following day, and the day after that. Willie Connor got the job. The Braves reeled off five consecutive victories before losing a game, then started winning all over again. They won more than they lost. Suddenly they were riding a wave of success. Within six weeks, they'd climbed out of last place and slowly moved up in the standings. Sixth. Fifth. Fourth. Third. Second. It was a miracle. George Stallings was full of happiness.

Working for the Big Chief was not what one might call easy. Emotionally driven, the Braves' manager tended to bowl over people; he demanded a lot from them. And there wasn't a more superstitious man in all of baseball. He was forever on the lookout for bad omens and saw bad luck everywhere: black cats, a card dropped on the floor during a card game, lighting three cigarettes from a single match, walking under a ladder, the number 13.

Encountering a cross-eyed person was the unluckiest sign of all. But if a man acted quickly, he could remove the jinx by spitting into his hat. Ballplayers spit a lot. Spitting was good. It canceled out all kinds of bad luck.

What made George Stallings such a slave to superstition? The answer may well lie in the loving care of a Black nanny whose apron strings little George clung to as a child in the family's Georgia home. Perhaps, in an effort aimed at scaring the unruly little hellion into behaving himself, the well-meaning woman might have recited all kinds of primitive mumbo jumbo.

"You better mind me, Mister George. You hear? Or that mean old bogeyman gonna get you. Oh, yes, he come in the night. He big. All black. With festering bloody eyes. Rotted hands. You better listen or you be in big trouble."

The good woman might have unwittingly planted aboriginal beliefs in little George's mind that stayed with him for life, a faith in native superstitions and a fear of African and Caribbean sorcery. Favorable omens too: the potency of a rabbit's foot, lucky pennies, elephants' hair, all talismans said to produce miraculous results.

Birds were the most malignant omen of all. If a flock of sparrows rose from the rafters of the grandstand and swept down onto the field and hovered in front of the Braves' bench or on top of the dugout, Stallings, fighter that he was, almost gave up hope of winning that day. He went mad at the sounds of beating wings. He shouted, clapped his hands, and kicked at the avian marauders. If this did not terrorize the birds, he hurled bats at them or had Willie Connor or Oscar Dugey or one of the other players shoo them away.

The very thought of birds wheeling and flapping around and around overhead and keeping up a desperate chatter preyed on his mind. He declared war on them. He'd fix the little bastards. No more halfway measures. No sir. Not anymore. He hired a bird chaser who guarded the dugout and threw stones at any winged creature that so much as thought about landing in the area.

The day before the World Series opener, a writer from the *Evening Bulletin* spotted Willie and a bellhop pitching pennies on the sidewalk in front of the team's hotel. "William," the reporter said, in a good-natured chummy voice, "what does this mean?"

"Ahh, gwan," Willie said, feeling somewhat undone. "This town's slow. A guy's gotta do somethin', ain't he?"

Then, with a display of boyish defiance, he blurted out the truth about himself. "I been pitchin' pennies ever since I caught on with this club. I play pinochle too. An' twenty-one. And I shoot craps. And once in a while I smoke a cigarette. See?" He held up his fingers and showed the reporter a tobacco stain. "So what?"

"But the books?" the reporter protested. "Carlyle? Dante? Macaulay? I don't understand."

"Ahh . . . them classics are all right . . . I read parts of them when my teachers made me. Dickens, Macaulay, that kind of stuff. But now I'm tellin' them teachers to give me Johnny Evers's *Baseball in the Big Leagues* and

Christy Mathewson's *Pitching in a Pinch*. That's the kind of stuff I wanna read when I get back to school. Not all that old-fashioned crap."

Louis Van Zelst, the Philadelphia mascot, was a mixture of modesty and openness, a trusted member of the Athletics' family. Whenever reporters asked questions about the team, thinking perhaps they might catch "Little Van" off guard, he would look at them pleasantly and say, "Better ask Mr. Mack, then you will have it officially." He would then smile pleasantly, bow, and go on about his business.

Louis was instantly recognizable on the field, even with no number on his uniform, from the way he picked up a bat, the way his shoulders swayed as he carried it back to the dugout, and the way he skipped with uncommon agility and positioned himself near the players' bench. So far as Philadelphia fans were concerned, the Athletics had the best mascot in baseball.

Before joining the Mackmen, "Little Louis" was a fixture on the sidelines at Franklin Field in Philadelphia, home of the University of Pennsylvania's intercollegiate track and football teams; his presence always seemed to bring the Quakers luck. The students loved Louis. And he was a special favorite of Mike Murphy, the legendary Olympic track coach, originator of several of the most remarkable contributions to the art of sprinting in modern times.

Louis's lively, animated, and energetic ways attracted Rube Oldring's attention. Rube liked what he saw. The young man was intelligent, blessed with a charismatic personality, and perhaps best of all, he was lucky, very lucky. When the Athletics needed a mascot, Oldring thought of Louis.

The little fellow's mouth fell open in awe as his eyes involuntarily swept the stands the first day he walked onto the playing field at Shibe Park and stood before Connie Mack. It was a magical moment.

"Might bring us luck, Mr. Mack," Oldring said, with a wink of an eye, putting a special accent on the word "luck."

Connie Mack lifted his straw hat, wiped the moisture from his forehead with a handkerchief, and gazed down at the little fellow's animated eyes and agreeable face. Connie squeezed Louis's hand and greeted him warmly. Something about the childlike, near-saintly awe in the bright, intelligent eyes looking up at him tugged at Connie's heartstrings.

Half mesmerized, Louis tottered and stared; his chest heaved, his heart thumped, his throat so tight he could hardly form words. Through quivering lips he finally managed to say something in a pale voice: "I'm lucky, Mr. Mack. Real lucky. I wonder if maybe you don't want someone to mind the bats or something?" Silence followed.

Like most baseball men, Connie Mack was superstitious. He lifted his straw boater, scratched his head, and cocked an eyebrow in Oldring's direction. Mack's eyes flicked from Oldring to Louis and back again.

The little fellow standing before him was one of God's poor, an odd-looking dwarf, a hunchback whose head was thrust down into his shoulders, one of those unfortunate afflicted souls who glowed with a saintly inner warmth. Having a hunchback around was considered good luck in those days, and touching a hunchback's hump was considered luckier still.

The seconds glided by. After a bit, Mack reached out and gently ruffled Louis's hair. "Sure, son, let's give it a try."

An expression of wonderment passed over Louis's face. He let out a gasp of joy and thanked Mr. Mack repeatedly. That afternoon, Louis Van Zelst took charge of the bats and the Athletics won.

"Why don't you come around again tomorrow," the kindly Mr. Mack said, "and mind the bats again?" Louis's face lighted into a big grin, his blue eyes aglow.

The following day, Louis's good karma worked again, and the day after that, and, serendipitously, the day after that. It worked six days in a row.

Louis's presence in the dugout gave the Athletics the big lift they needed, or that's what so many of them thought. Connie Mack was grateful. He named Louis the official team mascot, and the A's settled into a surprising run for the pennant in 1909, finishing three and a half games behind the first-place Detroit Tigers.

The following spring, Connie Mack presented Louis with a custom-tailored, regulation, Philadelphia Athletics uniform, put his name on the club's payroll (a rare thing in those days), and on the fifteenth and thirtieth of each month, the A's manager handed the little fellow a paycheck, just as he did other members of the Athletics family. Louis was one of the boys now, and his open face and gentle manner made him a favorite among fans as well.

Little Van had a way with children. They called out to him; they stopped for handshakes and hugs; they besieged him for autographs, and obtained them. Opposing players liked Louis as well. They kidded and saluted him. The tough guys did. Guys like Ty Cobb, Hughey Jennings, and Big Ed Walsh.

Louis was a clever mime. His deft portrayal of pitcher Eddie Plank on the mound was etched on the memory of all the fans who saw his performances. Wisely observant, Louis had Plank's body language and peculiar traits down pat, the somber face, the way he hitched his belt and turned and glanced at the outfielders, the tug of the cap, the careful concentrated look at the catcher's sign, the way he slowly inched one foot forward and then slowly, very slowly, pulled it back again, before going into a rocking-chair motion, designed to drive batters crazy.

Sometimes he would rock two or three times. Often four or five times. And then, finally, he would whirl his arm in a side-wheel motion and throw the ball. Louis was highly entertaining. Most fans considered the act better than vaudeville.

Once the game got under way, Louis was all business. Very professional. He moved to a position five or six steps out from the player's bench, dug two holes in the ground for luck, using the cleats of his right shoe, much the same as a pitcher does when he first takes the mound, then placed his feet in the holes, adjusted his cap, and, resting one haunch on the heels of his cleats, watched every move on the playing field, just as if he were managing the team. He seldom budged from the spot while the game was in progress.

"Stuffy" McInnis steps into the batter's box. Two on. Amos Strunk on third, Eddie Collins on second. McInnis flashes the double squeeze sign, baseball's most exciting play. Louis's heart beats wildly. He knows what's coming. Strunk steps off third, Collins edges off second, taking a big lead. McInnis's eyes are glued on the pitcher. The pitcher checks on Strunk at third, and delivers. McInnis shortens up and bunts. The infield charges in. Strunk breaks for home. Collins flies toward third. The bunt is perfect. It rolls past the pitcher's glove and within a hair's width of the first baseman's glove. The crowd is on its feet. A silent prayer passes Louis's lips.

Strunk scores standing up. Collins cuts the inside of the bag at third and streaks for home. The second baseman scoops up the ball and fires a strike at the catcher just as Collins starts his slide. The ball and Collins arrive simultaneously. The catcher lunges in a cloud of dust and makes the tag as Collins's left hand sweeps across the plate.

The crowd waits breathlessly . . .

"Safe!"

Louis slowly turns his head and glances at Connie Mack seated in the corner of the Philadelphia dugout, and grins when he sees the flicker of a smile cross Mack's lips.

Louis never hesitated in giving a slumping hitter encouragement. Like an eager puppy, he would smile warmly at someone like Eddie Murphy as he walked toward the plate, and chirp in his meek, sweet, effervescent voice, "Better rub me for a hit this time." Murphy would return Louis's smile and give him a soft pat on the shoulder, and somehow the harmless ritual relaxed Murphy. It helped him unbend a little.

On the road, Jack Barry and Jack Coombs looked after Louis and helped him over the hurdles. They acted as special guardians, seeing that Louis was in bed early, that he did not miss meals, and that he attended Mass every Sunday.

Early in 1913, Coombs came down with a severe case of typhoid fever, a highly infectious, life-threatening disease. He was hospitalized for weeks. Louis dutifully visited the hospital each day and sat at his pal's bedside for an hour or so, reading and chatting in his animated way. After a while, it seemed like he was part of the hospital family. The nurses adored Louis's cheerful eyes, lopsided smile, and sunny disposition, and they too looked forward to his daily visits.

Five months after the final game of the 1914 World Series, Louis himself was hospitalized. It was St. Patrick's Day, a Wednesday. Violent, pulling, shooting pains wracked his tiny body. At times the pain was more than he could bear. He prayed to die, and his doctors gave up hope and stood helplessly by.

With his last words, Little Louis thanked his mother and father for all they had done for him and begged them not to cry. He told them he had had a good life. He was glad to die. They would be together again in heaven.

On Sunday, March 21, 1915, an undertaker placed a white crape on the door of the little brick row house at 3717 Spruce Street. Little Louis Van Zelst was dead. He was 20. The cause of death: heart trouble complicated by Bright's disease. The faces of his many fans visibly melted when word of his passing spread through the city. A writer for the *Philadelphia Inquirer* expressed the feelings of Louis's thousands of admirers in mourning when he wrote, "Imprisoned in that misshapen little body was one of the greatest souls that ever lived."

CHAPTER 46

JUST KEEP QUIET AND LISTEN

Baggy-eyed, esophagus aflame, head aching, the Big Chief sat staring blankly at a spot on the carpet Thursday morning, his false teeth making a clicking sound.

"You about ready, Dad?" George Jr. asked.

"What? . . . Yeah . . . In a minute, son," he said in a detached voice, his eyes unseeing, his thoughts focused inward. The years flashed in front of his eyes. He could not help thinking about how he'd hungered for a shot at the World Series. Told himself he didn't care if his team won or lost. He just wanted to be there, to be part of the big show. Now that wasn't enough. Now he wanted it all. The whole shebang: he wanted to take the championship away from Connie Mack's perennial overdogs, the talent.

Stallings recalled how the Mackmen had made fun of him and knocked him when he was managing the Yankees . . . the bastards . . . He'd show them . . . if only he could get some kind of edge on them.

Most barstool pundits had already counted the Braves out. Writers too, he thought. "Like Mack's pal . . . what's his name? . . . Isaminger . . . Yeah . . . Jimmy Isaminger. That fat son of a bitch."

"Skull practice at ten, Dad. The guys are waiting."

"I know, son. I know." Stallings gave an impatient wave of his hand. An idea was taking shape in his mind. His head moved slowly up and down. He held a brief debate with himself. "Yes," he said, absorbed in thought, "yes, that might do it . . . Yes . . . Yes . . . That'll do it."

"Do what?"

"Never mind. Just keep quiet and listen."

Stallings grabbed the phone. "Operator. Gimme Diamond seven-two-five-zero. That's right . . . seven-two-five-zero."

"Hello? Hello? Yeah. Lemme talk to Connie Mack . . . What? What do you mean he's not taking calls? Tell him it's me, George Stallings. Tell him—My name? I just told you my name . . . Stallings . . . George Stallings . . . Manager of the Braves. Yeah . . . Yeah . . . That's right. He'll take the call."

Seconds passed.

"Yes, George."

"Connie," Stallings said, hoarsely, slipping the index finger of his left hand inside a collar that was suddenly a little too tight. "How're ya doin' this morning?"

"Fine, George, fine. And yourself?"

"Say, Connie . . . " Stallings cleared his throat. "My boys want to use your ballpark this afternoon. Wanna work out against the sun . . . specially the outfielders . . . so they can see what it will be like at game time tomorrow?"

Mack gave a sort of laugh and fell silent. After a brief pause, he said with evident annoyance, "I don't understand you, George. We talked about this yesterday. My boys decided on a two o'clock practice. I told you that. They wanted to take it easy this morning—sleep late. You know how it is . . . and work out in the afternoon. You seemed to understand. You—"

"Don't give me that crap. All I want is a couple of hours in the ballyard, so my boys can get a line on how the ball comes out of the shadows. They've heard how tough it is to see the ball at Shibe."

"George . . . be reasonable. How can I contact twenty-six men at this time of morning? Twelve of them live in the suburbs. Use your common sense. Most of them are on the way to the ballpark by now . . . I can't reach them."

"Three dollars' worth of telegrams will do it."

"Oh, George . . . "

"Don't you go 'Oh, Georgeing' me," Stallings said in a huff. "If your boys weren't familiar with Fenway, and you asked me to practice there this afternoon, you'd be welcome. You know you would. We'd go out of our way to be hospitable."

Mack sighed. "Look, George . . . we went over this yesterday. You told me you understood. You were satisfied. You had no objections." Mack paused. "I told Mr. Schroeder, my groundskeeper, to make the field available to the Braves at ten this morning . . . If only you called me before you left New York—"

Stallings cut him short. "That's no good. It will throw my players off their routine. It's unsportsmanlike." Stallings fulminated. "That's what it is. You're double-dealing." He sucked in his cheeks and shouted, "Let me tell you something else: You'll get yours. Right up the ass. Where the sun don't shine."

"Oh, George. Why do you always have to be such a dub?"

"Whazzat? Dub? Dub? You callin' me a dub? . . . Why, you lousy bastard . . . You're probably showing off for some fucking ink-slingers sittin' there listening to you call me down. Well, you can just tell them for me that I'll give you fifty bucks to say that to my face. I'll punch your fucking head off. That's what I'll do. I'll punch you senseless . . . You tell them that."

When push came to shove, Connie Mack could cut a man down with the best of them. "Why are you getting so upset, George?" he said. "Even if your club did use the park at two, it wouldn't make any difference. The series is already over. You haven't got a chance."

The sting went deep. One word led to another. Things were said that shouldn't have been said. And Connie Mack finally blew a fuse. "I've always tried to think you were on the level, George. Now I know you're not. You never have been . . . You big boob."

"Who you callin' a boob?" Stallings was so intense his body quivered. "You prissy fucking bastard. I'll flatten your fucking nose."

The Big Chief banged down the receiver, snatched up his Norfolk jacket, rammed his arms into the sleeves, slammed on his hat, and wheeled out the door. "Come on," he said to his son. "And don't you say a word when we get downstairs. You hear?"

CHAPTER 47

THE DR. JEKYLL AND MR. HYDE OF BASEBALL

A host of reporters engulfed Stallings as he stepped off the elevator, mouths rattling like Gatling guns, firing a barrage of questions at him. "Who you gonna start in the opener?" "Did you scout the Mackmen?" "How long you think the series will last?" "Ty Cobb says Mack will have the easiest series in history." "They say the Athletics can't hit left-handers."

Stallings's eyes raked the crowd. He nodded agreeably, tilted his hat, and began to speak. "Don't have any idea who I'll pitch in the opener. We'll see who looks good warming up." He paused and smiled good-humoredly. "This is how I'll decide." Without batting an eyelash, he pulled out a 50-cent piece and flipped it into the air. Everybody laughed.

"Have you scouted them?"

"Nope. Don't have to. I know Mack has a good club. I watched them play for years. Hell, they deserve all the praise they're getting." Pause. "I tell you what, though. I have a good ball club too. Before this thing is over, you'll agree with me."

Young George watched his father in amazement. Minutes before, the man had been an erupting volcano. Now he displayed an ingratiating calmness, working the crowd like a soothsayer, putting on a brilliant performance.

Stallings continued. "We refuse to admit the Athletics are our superiors in any aspect of the game. If they prove us wrong, that's fine with me. We'll take our hats off to them. But they're gonna have to beat us before we admit it. Remember! We've got pitchers as good as they have. And hitters. And fielders."

An electric horseshoe sign caught the big fellow's eye; a smile broadened his face. He jerked his head toward it. "I'm not planning on luck to win the championship," he said with a gesture of his head toward the horseshoe, "but I'll tell you boys one thing, that's a good sign."

A bellhop tapped Stallings on the arm. "Excuse me, Mr. Stallings. This is the morning mail," he said politely, thrusting a stack of envelopes in the Big Chief's hand. "Mr. McCarthy, the hotel manager, told me to give these to you." Stallings thanked the boy, gave him a half dollar, and handed the pile of paper to young George. "Go through this for me, will you."

While his father sparred with the reporters, young George opened envelope after envelope. Everything imaginable fell out, lucky pennies, four-leaf clovers, good luck charms, advice on how to beat the Mackmen.

"Here's one from Red," the young man said, excitedly, handing the letter to his father.

Necks craned. Eyes strained. "What's Red say?"

"Says he'll be with us in spirit," Stallings replied, handing an outstretched hand the letter. "Red's a good man. Shame he's going to miss it all . . . but we'll overcome his absence. The club's spirit is unbeatable."

"One more question, boys, one more, then I gotta go. Yes . . . Yes, you in the rear. What's that?" He cupped a hand around his ear and leaned forward to hear. "You're asking me how many games the series will go?" He smiled. Looked up at the ceiling for a second. "Well . . . I'll tell you what . . . I predict a Boston victory in four straight."

Then he waved a hand and left, nodding and smiling and shaking a hand here and there as he walked through the lobby. George Jr. followed closely on his heels.

The Braves players, talking idly near a bank of telephone booths, where club secretary Herman Nicholson had asked them to gather, appeared relaxed and confident as they gesticulated and jabbered away. There was a remarkable swagger and bluff about them. By golly, one of them was saying, arms outspread, waving both hands to make a point. "You can make lotsa money on the ponies. Lotsa money. All you gotta do is figure out what the horse is gonna do."

The big Friday night fight in New York also drew a good deal of attention. "What are you, crazy or something? 'Gunboat' Smith knock out 'Battling' Levinsky? No way . . . Levinsky's gonna look old Gunboat straight in the eye and say, 'You're dead!' and then he's gonna deck him."

Some juicy gossip was in the air: "Did ya hear about Jeff Tesreau?"

"What about him?"

"He's in big trouble."

"That a fact?"

"Yeah. Some gal back home in Perryville, Missouri, slapped him with a breach of promise suit. Says he broke her heart to pass the time away. She showed the papers Jeff's love letters. He kept his pitching arm in condition practicing bear hugs on her all winter. Asked her to sign up for life. Then good old Jeff took off for spring training and the next thing the little girl knew, he'd gone and married some cute little tootsie from the city."

Everything was happiness and fun. Maranville was as giddy as a schoolboy. Rubbing elbows with fans. Pleasing autograph seekers. Spinning yarns.

"Is Rabbit tellin' stories again?" Stallings asked, a pleasant smile breaking over his lips as he approached. "Or is he doing his imitation of me?"

The comment provoked a round of laughter.

Stallings greeted the gang, shook hands with several of them, and buoyantly announced, "Boys, we're going to work out at Shibe Park this afternoon. Two o'clock. You'll see what the sun field is like."

Eyes darted back and forth, heads nodded, casting notes of approval.

"I'm calling up Connie Mack right now . . . to confirm it." Mouth set in a cold line, he squared his shoulders, tugged at his trousers, went into a pay phone booth, left the door ajar, and dropped in a nickel. George Jr. watched open-mouthed, wondering what was going on.

Stallings spoke firmly, talking much louder than was necessary. Before long, curt angry phrases were audible. Eyebrows went up. Smiles turned into frowns. The players exchanged quizzical looks.

"The Chief sounds sore," someone said. "Mack must've changed his mind."

Stallings threatened to paste Mack one.

A hush fell over the lobby.

"That's what I said. I'll punch your face for you."

Silence.

"You can't talk to me like that."

More silence. He was quiet for a moment, listening.

"You won't win no championship if I meet you—"

Reporters scrambled over to find out what was going on. "Who's the Big Fellow hollering at?" someone asked.

"Connie Mack."

"You gotta be kidding."

"Nope. It's Mack all right."

The reporter yanked out a notepad and began scribbling.

Stallings was raising a rumpus now. His voice booming. The players were the perfect audience.

Suddenly, Stallings slammed down the receiver and, before anyone realized what was happening, he was standing in front of them, covered with perspiration, a maniacal expression on his face.

"That man Mack tried to tell me I was satisfied when I left him yesterday," Stallings said, his eyes flashing with indignation. "Tried to roast me. Belittle me. Tried to tell me he did not say I could use the grounds this afternoon. I told him he lied. Told him he was a poor sport."

He glanced around the lobby, color burning in his cheeks, his huge chest rising and falling. "I told the low-down skunk to come down here and tell me I was satisfied. Tell me to my face. I told him 'I'll punch you so hard you won't be able to tell which team wins the series.'"

Stallings made a big hit with the boys. All thoughts centered on destroying the Athletics. "They are a fine crowd of sports," one of the players said. "They've played in Shibe Park in seventy-five games this year, so of course they need this afternoon to get used to it."

Connie Mack was taken aback when reporters told him of Stallings's public accusations of unsportsmanlike conduct. Connie resented the innuendo heaped on him in such a barefaced manner. "George said what?" he asked, obviously puzzled. "You sure? . . . Tell me again. I need to be clear in my own mind." The reporter repeated everything.

"I can't believe George said those things." Pause. Mack reflected. "It was a misunderstanding. That's all. If George had come to me earlier, he could have had the grounds for the asking. Anytime he wanted them."

The notion that Stallings intentionally caused a ruckus with Mack generated an avalanche of speculation in the papers; accounts of the confrontation and statements by Stallings and Mack were hopelessly confused. What was said, and what was not, was on every sports page in the nation.

Had Stallings used his sharp elbows to gain an advantage over an opponent, as he was wont to do? The big fellow was known as a fanatical schemer and master manipulator, and his players were unusually susceptible to the power of his formidable personality. Was this simply another way of motivating them?

Damon Runyon thought so. "Stallings is the Dr. Jekyll and Mr. Hyde of baseball," Runyon wrote, "and some astute baseball men believe he intentionally lashed himself into a fury over the Mack refusal, for the effect it would have on his men. He wanted the Braves to go into the game feeling furious toward the Athletics, and that is certainly their feeling."*

---

* Long after the Big Chief had passed from the scene, George Stallings Jr. revealed exactly what happened in the celebrated wrangle between his father and Connie Mack. "My father faked the call, holding the receiver hook down, unseen by the players. . . . He put on such a good show that when he came out of the telephone booth, all the players felt just as burned up about Mack's attitude as my father did."

CHAPTER 48

ROYAL ROOTERS

Boston's Royal Rooters—architects, bankers, doctors, editors, engineers, grocers, lawyers, politicians, salesmen—exulted in the success of the Braves. Applications and checks for the World Series excursion to Philadelphia poured into the organizing committee from all over New England.

A letter from Boston's former mayor, John F. Fitzgerald, was in the first batch of mail. "Just add my name to the list," the mayor told the organizers. "I want to be with the rank and file this time. With no official dignity to hamper my actions, you can count on me to make as much noise as anyone in the party."

In 1903 the boisterous Royal Rooters backed Boston's American League champions in baseball's first World Series, when they faced the most powerful team in baseball, the Pittsburgh Pirates, proud possessors of three consecutive National League pennants. Pittsburgh, led by Hans Wagner, was an odds-on favorite to take it all. The Pirates looked invincible at the outset, winning three of the first four games of the best-of-nine series, practically dismantling Boston in the process. But the Bostonians pulled themselves together, dug in, and cheered on by the Royal Rooters (the song "Tessie" was on their lips at all times), won four straight and captured baseball's first World Series.

In 1912 the Royal Rooters were at it again, giving another potent World Series performance, and the Red Sox won a world championship for a second time. The Boston players agreed, to a man, that "Tessie" was responsible, at least in part, for their success.

The Braves' front office promised the Royal Rooters 200 reserved seats, but the tremendous demand for tickets exceeded the supply. More were needed. Red Sox owner Joe Lannin sent Honey Fitz a telegram: "Bring along all those Rooters who don't have tickets. I'll get tickets for them. If I can't arrange for tickets through the National Commission, I'll buy them myself. And if I can't get them seats, I will pay all the expenses incurred by them."

Thursday, shortly after five o'clock in the afternoon, at South Street Station, Barrington-Sargent's Ninth Regiment band serenaded Boston fans on track 17 as they boarded the Royal Rooter's Special. Security was tight. Every member of the party entered the train through a single door of the rear car. All of the doors and windows of the three parlor cars, the five day coaches, and the baggage car were locked. This kept out the "rat-faced" element: card sharps, crapshooters, thimbleriggers, three-card monte players, and other grifters who, in 1912, slipped onto the train unnoticed and almost cleaned out the unwitting Rooters on the way to the World Series in New York.

The lighthearted music of Barrington-Sargent's 25-piece band was suddenly shattered by a roar from the crowd. The two Johnnys, Keenan and Killeen, and Charlie Lavis, the group's organizers, arrived escorting a smooth, genial, fashionably dressed gentleman in formal attire: silk top hat, tails, boiled shirt, cufflinks, studs, the works. The gentleman was none other than Boston's popular former mayor, Honey Fitz Fitzgerald, his mouth working every second, while he shook hands, waved at friends, and kissed the ladies.

When bandleader Barrington-Sargent recognized His Honor, he interrupted the medley, and the band smoothly dropped into a chorus of "Tessie."

> Tessie, you make me feel so badly,
> Why don't you turn around,
> Tessie, you know I love you madly,
> Babe, my heart weighs about a pound,
> Don't blame me if I ever doubt you,
> You know I wouldn't live without you,
> Tessie you are the only, only, only.

Smiling and confident, Little Fitzie paused for flashlight photographs before entering the coach, then turned and raised his top hat and waved goodbye in the midst of a barrage of cheers, just as the shrill whistle of the engine announced the train's departure. The big locomotive hissed and shuddered and thumped and clanked and slowly moved out of the train shed, bound for Philadelphia and the opening game of the 1914 World Series.

Honey Fitz and his good pal John Feeny got right down to business, circulating through the coaches and parlor cars in a display of expansive good humor, words tumbling from their mouths. The former mayor was everywhere, always the center of attention, discussing the ticket mix-up, Boston's future as a city, prospects for revitalizing the New England economy. And, when given an opening, he drummed up a little business for himself, inviting everyone to visit his haberdashery: "Stop and see me sometime at Oak Hall," he would say. "We're on Adams Square. I've got a fine stock of worsteds and cashmeres. All sizes. I'd like to show you some."

At New London, a six-minute stop, most of the Rooters stepped off the train. Honey Fitz, egged on by his barkeep pal, "Nuf Ced" McGreevy, a five-foot stump of a man, took a bashful young lady by the elbow and coaxed her into dancing with him as the band tooted its way through a catchy melody. Together, singing and dancing, they led the party off the station platform onto a busy street, blocking traffic, though none of the locals seemed to mind.

Word of the Royal Rooters' planned stop in New Haven sent a ripple of excitement through the community. A group of Yale students, accompanied by townies from Louis' Lunch, prevailed upon the much-admired Johnny Mack, Yale's football trainer and track coach, to join them in welcoming the boys from Boston. When the Special pulled into New Haven, Yale voices could be heard singing above the brassy clanging of the band the school's popular fight song written by Cole Porter, a member of the Yale class of 1913:

Bulldog! Bulldog!
Bow, wow, wow,
Eli Yale.

It was half past 11 in the evening by the time the Special reached Grand Central Terminal in New York, the city's most recent symbol of progress. The boys, unrestrained by the lateness of the hour, were restless and fidgety as they formed in ranks four abreast, shoulder to shoulder, and filed out into the cool autumn night. Passing through shafts of light streaming down on 42nd Street from Grand Central's outsized windows, the "happy hour boys" greeted late-night New Yorkers with raucous cheers, shouting at the top of their lungs:

"Hurray for the Braves. Hip, hip, hooray. Hip, hip, hooray."

Several of the Rooters, watching with bright eyes, missing nothing, took a quick look up at Jules Coutan's famous sculptural group, *Glory of Com-*

merce, atop the terminal as they advanced along 42nd Street, and glanced at the New York Public Library, the city's newest neoclassical Beaux Arts gem, the nation's largest marble structure, ghostly white in the darkness, and smiled as they approached the bright lights of Times Square, the "Great White Way."

The drums went bang and the symbols clanged and the boys sang and sang and sang, running quickly through choruses of "Sweet Adeline," "Ruth," "Mulligan," "He's a Rag Picker," and "Tessie."

When the paraders reached the Times Tower at 42nd and Broadway (home of the *New York Times*), they turned north and basked in the vibrant, neon-drenched immensity of the entertainment crossroads of the world, saluting late-night amusement seekers and habitués of Times Square's noisy cabarets, while singing a joyful chorus of "Tessie" with all their hearts:

Tessie, you make me feel so badly,
Why don't you turn around,
Tessie, you know I love you madly,
Babe, my heart weighs about a pound.

At 45th Street, the merrymakers swung east toward Sixth Avenue. Lights appeared in the somber brownstones, curious heads poked out of windows, and sleepy-eyed people stepped out on stoops to see what all the racket was about.

Most of the marchers were ready to turn in when they disbanded in front of the Elks Home at 43rd Street and Sixth Avenue shortly after midnight. But a few of the more adventurous carousers had not yet seen enough. They drifted back toward Times Square, eager for a taste of nightlife and the naughty, bawdy, gaudy hot spots of the Great White Way.

Friday morning, the bleary-eyed revelers assembled in front of the Elks Home, grimacing and squinting in the harsh morning light, many of them in need of a quick pick-me-up. Somehow they managed to pull themselves together for the march down Seventh Avenue to Pennsylvania Station, where Irving Berlin's Serenaders, outfitted in authentic Indian headdresses and war paint, joined them for the nine o'clock departure of the Royal Rooters' Special.

A little before noon, the boys from Down East caught a glimpse of the red brick and cobblestone city of Ben Franklin, William Penn, and Betsy Ross. Minutes later, walking out of Broad Street Station, they passed Karl Bitter's magnificent bas-relief, *Spirit of Transportation,* and assembled once more on the street in ranks of four, this time sporting enough red, white, and blue regalia to outfit the entire cast of one of Florenz Ziegfeld's Broadway extravaganzas.

Beaming joyously from ear to ear while the Serenaders sang and the band played, Honey Fitz led the way, his walk wonderfully irregular, closely followed by a gigantic banner (inscribed "Baltimore 1897, Pittsburgh 1903, New York 1912, Philadelphia 1914") strung out between two boil-faced, impudent-looking Irishmen, whose beer bellies spilled over low-slung belts. Little boys skipped alongside and got in step as the marchers paraded down Broad Street, while the band pumped out chorus after chorus of "Tessie."

The brotherhood of men, their voices pounding the air, swept past the huge granite mass of City Hall (the loftiest masonry structure in the world unsupported by a steel frame), rising higher than all of the great cathedrals of Europe. Office workers appeared at windows. "That's him," a woman said, "the former mayor of Boston, the distinguished gentleman in the top hat and tails."

"Oh . . . isn't he wonderful?" another said.

Little Fitzie lifted his hat, waved, and acknowledged smiles and scattered applause from the patchwork crowd along the sidewalk. The procession moved along Market to Ninth Street, south on Ninth to Chestnut, and stopped in front of the Continental Hotel.

Without a moment's delay, Honey Fitz delivered instructions. "Grab a little dinner, boys," is the way he put it, for it was lunchtime, "or do whatever you have to do . . . They just told me that Horn and Hardart's Automat over here at 818 Chestnut is a good place to eat. Fast too. Self-service . . . There's another one a block away on Market, between Ninth and Tenth Streets. The north side. We just passed it. You'll like the food. It's in little glass compartments: chicken pot pies, baked beans, codfish cakes, Salisbury steak, rice pudding, pies . . . apple, cherry, pumpkin . . . the usual. You put in your nickel and you get what you see. They tell me the coffee's great . . . Free refills too . . . Remember now, get back here in thirty minutes, or you'll miss the automobiles and buses that are taking us out to the ballpark."

CHAPTER 49

A BOOM-BOOM VOICE

George Stallings was up before the break of day Friday, sleepy and nervous and at the point of exhaustion. He lay awake all night, fretting, worrying, scheming into the wee hours of the morning, leaving the bed sour and tortured. The moment he stepped off the elevator, a young reporter from the *Bulletin* intercepted him. It was a little after six.

"You're up early," Stallings said.

"Gotta work . . . You know editors . . . How about a story?"

"Why not?" Stallings said. He nodded toward the coffee shop. "Let's talk over breakfast."

The young man plunged right in. "I see where a colleague of mine, on another paper," he quickly pointed out, "says Maranville's a better shortstop than Barry, but Barry's smarter."

Stallings shook his head and allowed himself a half smile: "That Barry must have some brain . . . Maranville's one of the smartest players I ever saw." He jabbed a spoon into a half grapefruit. "Rabbit handles practice in an intelligent way, just like Cobb. And Rabbit has worked hard and made himself what he is today."

A squirt of juice got Stallings in the eye; he shoved the dish away. "Bring me an order of ham and eggs," he told the waiter. "Four eggs. Don't make them too runny . . . and lots of ham."

The Braves manager raised an index finger and pressed the point. "I've been in this racket a long time, a long, long time. I've seen 'em all, Jack Glasscock, Hughie Jennings, Herman Long, Hans Wagner, Bobby Wallace. All the old-time shortstops. They were great players. High quality. Every one of them.

"Wagner's the best all-around shortstop. No question about that." Stallings reached for the salt and pepper. "The Dutchman's got a great arm. He can hit. He can play any position. But he doesn't have Maranville's quickness or speed. Rabbit starts for grounders like nobody I ever saw. Nothing seems out of his reach. I don't think the kid's ever been equaled."

At that moment, Ty Cobb, in passing, stopped at the table, nodded briefly at the reporter, and turned toward Stallings. The two Georgians were off-season hunting pals. But Cobb was a hard-line, uncompromising American Leaguer, and there was a touch of disparagement in his voice when he asked, "What have you got to say about the series, George?"

Stallings appeared not to notice. "Nothing, Ty. Nothing. The experts already have us beaten. But we surprised the whole National League, didn't we?" . . . He waited for a response. There was none. "Well, don't be surprised if we repeat on the Athletics."

Cobb chuckled affably, slapped his pal on the back, and continued on his way.

The reporter renewed the interrogation. "They say your club can't hit southpaws."

Stallings puffed out his cheeks, breathed deeply, and exhaled. "Eddie Plank is a fine pitcher, but I don't think Eddie can hold us to less than three runs. And three runs will be enough if James, Rudolph, and Tyler are on their game."

"So you think you can beat Eddie?"

"I know we can beat Eddie. We are going to beat Eddie." Stallings drank more coffee. "Do you know that we've lost to only one left-hander since July?"

The brash young reporter did not ease up. "The general feeling is, the Braves are outclassed by the Athletics' star-stuffed lineup, especially after you lost Red Smith. The pundits are saying it will be the same old story: 'Philadelphia in a walk.'"

Stallings shook his head. "They say. They say. I don't give a damn what they say . . . My boys have a spirit that can't be shaken by the loss of any one man. They are going into this thing to win. They expect to win. I expect them to win."

The reporter tapped his pencil on the table and looked into Stallings's eyes. "What about this thing with Mr. Mack?"

Stallings's body stiffened. He stared at the man.

"You—er—I mean—you know—the disagreement," the reporter said weakly.

"Listen to me." Stallings waved a big paw in the man's face. "There's not going to be a row on the field, if that's what you're driving at . . . I've known the man for a good many years. He's cheap. That's what he is. Real cheap. And he has yet to do a sportsmanlike act."

"Aw, come on . . . Mr. Mack's all right."

"All right? All right?" Stallings voice sounded like a frayed wire. "Is that what you think? At least two tickets were supposed to be sent to each Boston player . . . Did the Athletics management send them any? Any at all? Well, did they? . . . Did they?"

The reporter shrugged, indicating he didn't know.

"They did not . . . not one ticket. They didn't send any tickets at all. The Athletics failed to observe what everyone in baseball considers common courtesy."

The reporter raised his hands deferentially, palms open, stood up, and said, "I've got to run. Thanks for talking to me. And, oh, thank you for breakfast."

Stallings nodded and said nothing.

Two hours later, while the team awaited ballpark transportation, Stallings sat cross-legged in a lobby armchair near the cigar stand, listening and soaking in the atmosphere as Rabbit Maranville entertained the boys. The room rocked with laughter and warm-hearted banter, until a boom-boom voice broke through the merriment. "Betcha any amount your team will lose." The slurred words came from a slab of beef as big around as a Japanese sumo wrestler. They were directed at George Stallings.

Stallings ignored him.

"I wanna lay a bet on the Athletics . . . How does two hundred bucks strike you?" the intruder asked in slow, inebriated words.*

"For Chrissake, can't you see I'm busy?"

"You don't look busy."

"Look, buddy, I'm minding my own business. Can't you mind yours?" Stallings's fingers drummed on the arms of the chair.

"So you're the 'Miracle Man,' are you?" the pest said, an imbecilic smirk on his lips. "'Mackerel Man' is more like it . . . ha, ha, hee, hee, hee."

The boys quieted and traded glances, eyeing the enormous fellow warily.

Stallings's eyes flared. His mouth tightened.

---

* Betting action was brisk. Gambling kingpin Arnold Rothstein, who became notorious as the man who fixed the 1919 World Series, bet $10,000 on the 1914 series, about $250,000 in today's dollars—and lost.

The mean, slow-witted nuisance went on giggling, oblivious of the half glances being sent his way.

"Get out of here, you big stiff."

"I've got confidence in the home team," the troublemaker said, then paused and knitted his brow. "Say, you called me a big stiff . . . same as Connie Mack." Pause.

"You can call Connie Mack a big stiff if you want to, and bluff punching him in the nose and get away with it, but you can't pull that stuff on me. No, sirree. Not on C. P. Callahan." The man then jostled Stallings's arm and tried to knock the Big Chief's hat off.

That did it. Excess testosterone got the better of the Braves manager. He lunged at the troglodyte and thumped him good. The sound of the fleshy smack spun heads around. A scarlet stream gushed from Callahan's nose. He staggered back against the wall and sagged to the floor. Stallings was all over him, both fists flailing away, pummeling his tormentor.

The house detective and several players pulled Stallings off the man. The detective quickly hustled Stallings into an elevator, and James, Schmidt, and Whaling dragged the big bozo outside and deposited him on the sidewalk, none too gently.

Eyes blinking wildly, Callahan moved his jaw from side to side, wiped the blood from his mouth on the back of his hand, and looked up at the three ballplayers.

"You tell your boss I'm going to beat the hell out of him. You tell him I'll beat him black and blue the first chance I get . . . I'll hound that bastard. I'll go to Boston if I have to."

"Suicide," a bystander said, matter-of-factly.

Summing up the ruckus, a man who witnessed the incident said, "George gave him what-for in the only way the big galoot understood. The guy deserved everything he got."[†]

[†] Forty-three years later, George Stallings Jr., who had been at his father's side throughout the series, wrote in an article published in *Baseball Digest*: "We found out later that the fellow was not drunk, and had deliberately tried to start a fight to get my father in trouble just before the game. It was assumed that this was a put-up job by the gamblers, trusting to any advantage that might accrue to them out of the incident."

CHAPTER 50

ROOFTOP SEATS

When "sold out" signs appeared on the bleacher gates, loud-mouthed barkers swung into action: "Rooftop seats," they hollered. "One dollar. Two dollars. Three dollars. Step inside. Better than the grandstand."

Twenty-First Street was the more desirable location: seats were only a few steps away from the right field wall (the roofs on Somerset beyond the left field fence were farther back, making large parts of the outfield impossible to see), and spectators took in the game from the perspective of the right fielder. For those lucky enough to find front-row seats, the outfielder seemed like he was just a long reach away.

Most homeowners removed second-floor windows, carted them downstairs, and stored them in the basement, frames and all. Only frayed pulley ropes remained. Paying customers sat on floors, benches, and windowsills. Small portable bleachers were built from floor to ceiling in front rooms. And quite a few men sat out on the edge of the porch roofs, feet dangling over the side without the least concern about what the dirt and tar were doing to their clothing. Others lolled around under the eaves, their backs against the clapboard walls.

The largest temporary bleacher, a massive rough-board affair, extended across the roofs of five houses and accommodated a thousand people. Smaller stands on the individual row houses took care of hundreds more customers. It's no wonder that the crowd inside Shibe began speculating about the possibility of the roofs collapsing under the strain.

The week before the opening game of the World Series, public safety officials expressed the same concerns, and fearing that casualties could be high if one or more of the roofs did give way, Ed Clarke, chief of the city's building inspectors, closed down the rooftop business. No permits were issued. That didn't slow down the homeowners. Work continued.

Clarke was furious. "It's illegal," he said, "a menace to society. If anything happens, the blame will fall on my head." He ordered the bleachers torn down and warned of stiff fines if the edict was not obeyed. Homeowners laughed and went about their work. It was a profitable business: they'd engaged in it for years. Why stop now? Clarke persisted, and found an ally at City Hall, a strong ally, an enforcer: George D. Porter, the director of public safety. Porter told the press a uniformed policeman would be stationed in front of each house when the World Series began. Their orders? Keep ticket holders from entering.

A howl went up from the homeowners. "They can't do that. Can they?" "Who the hell do they think they are, anyway?" "I'll see my lawyer." Attorneys advised them: "Go ahead. The police have no power over you."

With a legal battle in the offing, city officials approached solicitor Michael J. Ryan of the Department of Law for an opinion. The solicitor reviewed the relevant statutes and concluded there was nothing in any of them that could stop the sale of rooftop seats. Learning this, Porter countermanded the previous day's orders, and it was business as usual at the row houses.

Mothers inside houses urged children to "go to the bathroom, and hurry, before the strangers come in." Minutes later the treads of wooden stairs creaked under the weight of scores of ticket holders toiling up to the second floor. The man of the house directed them toward the bathroom where an extension ladder reached through a skylight, providing access to the roof.

Visitors ascended slowly, hand over hand, tensely gripping each rung, while burly men stationed at the top and bottom held the ladder steady. The climb was scary for some. One woman hesitated, took a deep breath, swallowed, and started up. A man above her smiled reassuringly and extended a helping hand, eventually pulling her over the edge of the skylight onto the roof.

The crowd moved upward in this way—thousands of people. The makeshift bleachers filled quickly. Those who couldn't find a seat made do with wooden folding chairs or straight-backed kitchen chairs or canvas beach chairs. A few pressed stepladders into service. Some just wandered around all afternoon. A number of men watched the ballplayers through binoculars, and a cute young lady, holding a colorful parasol, cuddled a pet bulldog she'd brought along.

Pretty soon, a puffing and perspiring street vendor appeared, offering chewing gum, peanuts, fritters, and soda pop. Homeowners made extra money too, selling hot dogs and lemonade. Their kids raced up and down ladders and out into the street, bought hot dogs from a vendor for a nickel, then scrambled back up to the roof and sold them for a dime. The spirit of capitalism in a homey atmosphere.

At one point the crowd heard a startled yell, then a dull thud.

"Oh my God, Harold," a woman shrieked.

Craning faces looked up from the street. "What was that?"

"A little doggy fell off the roof," a man reported matter-of-factly.

"Is he dead?"

"Nah. Fell on some guy's derby hat . . . That fellow over there. On the porch roof. The mutt's scared stiff, that's all."

"Poor little pup."

"Yeah, he's wobbly. He's okay. He's wagging his tail."

A few minutes later, a good-hearted soul carried the little fellow back onto the roof for a tearful reunion with the lovely young lady holding the colorful parasol.

CHAPTER 51

PUZZLED BY WHAT HE SEES

Garishly handsome, Shibe Park is an icon, an absolute gem, functional as well as beautiful, the perfect setting for the opening game of the 1914 World Series. From the steeply raked seats and the clifflike edge of the cantilevered concrete and steel upper deck of the grandstand, the panoramic view is breathtaking. A first impression inspires awe. The sightlines are excellent even from the nosebleed sections.

Fans take in the neatly manicured smoothness of the infield; the oceans of freshly cut outfield grass; the 400 blue-uniformed policemen ringing the playing field; the Stars and Stripes snapping, furling, and unfurling on the center field flagpole; and the wonderful mad chaos among the crowd atop row houses squeezed together beyond the outfield wall.

Spectators in the lower grandstand are right on top of the action, closer than ever before. The intimacy of the ballpark makes watching baseball a terrific experience. Not a column or post blocks the view. Those lucky enough to hold field-box tickets can practically reach out and touch the players, and sometimes do.

The scale of the playing field itself is enormous: 340 feet down the right field line; 378 feet down the left field line; and 515 feet in straight-away center field. Along the outer edge of the outfield the ground slopes up into a grassy terrace in front of a dark green wall—12 feet high and free of advertising—where 10,000 additional fans can sit or stand for regular-season games when the house is sold out.

Today, dark-suited men in gray fedoras and black derby hats, more than a few holding a lady by the arm, pause briefly on the concourse, eye the labyrinth of corridors around them, get their bearings, and make their way up the shadowed ramps and step out into the dazzling sunlight. Sharp claps like pistol shots greet them as weedy ushers, hustling for change, snap down steel seats, give them an insincere dusting, and stick out an indifferent hand for the obligatory tip.

Wearing blue asters, emblematic of Philadelphia hopes, white-gloved women dolled up in the latest "made in America" fashions, designed to showcase a military flair spawned in Europe—feminized field jackets, colorful capes, soldierly hats, abundant epaulets, brass buttons, the very squeak of chic—give the otherwise monochromatic crowd a dollop of color.

Seats fill rapidly. Fans awaiting the appearance of the players triumphantly wave tiny blue pennants stenciled with miniature white elephants (the Athletics' symbolic mascot) and welcome the band. People sing along with Tin Pan Alley song-pluggers who churn out novelty tunes from New York City's song-factory street.

Venders walking up and down the stairs hawk their wares. "Hawt Dawgs!" "Getchur hawt dawgs heeja!" "Soft drinks!" "Cokercola!" "Sasspriller!" "Moxies!" "Git y ice cold bottle, boys!"*

Eyes wander around the field. The first real cheer of the day goes up when Joseph Schroeder's ground crew runs the batting cage onto the field.

Arrivals thicken. Dignitaries settle into field box seats along the first and third base lines. Members of baseball's National Commission are forced to find their own seats. Ban Johnson is telling everyone how confident he is of an American League victory; Governor John Tener refuses to make predictions; Garry Herrmann does not appear to care one way or the other.

A few seats away, Clark Griffith, owner and manager of the Washington Senators, huddles with his star pitcher, Walter Johnson, and Johnson's bride of three months, the charming Washington socialite Hazel Lee Roberts. The celebrity couple stand out vividly in the crowd and graciously endure the intrusiveness of those seeking autographs or simply the opportunity of shaking the big fellow's hand, the ineluctable price of fame.

At precisely 12:25 P.M., Amos Strunk, the Philadelphia-born star who grew up just around the corner from the ballpark, places a foot on the top step of the dugout and casts an eye around the playing field. His gaze comes to rest on a brass band in the balding area behind home plate, performing John Philip Sousa's "Stars and Stripes Forever," music that reflects a nation at peace and proud of it.

---

* *The World* (New York), September 24, 1914.

Seeing Strunk, the bandleader stops abruptly and launches into the strains of "Hail the Conquering Hero" as the star center fielder, bat in hand, steps onto the field. The crowd roars its approval. A hundred cameras focus on Strunk and snap pictures. Seconds later, "Rube" Bressler, "Wickey" McAvoy, Rube Oldring, Herb Pennock, and J. Weldon Wyckoff join Strunk, looking washed and ironed in their pillbox caps and brilliant white flannels (in those days players wore no numbers on the backs of their uniforms) emblazoned with a large blue A. Minutes pass before the quick-tick sounds of spikes on concrete announce the arrival of Eddie Collins, "Home Run" Baker, "Stuffy" McInnis, and the rest of the ball club. They too display an aberrant nonchalance.

Unsmiling though confident, and strangely listless, the regal-looking Mackmen stretch, preen their overgrown egos, play pepper ball, and shag flies, methodically going through the motions of an unhurried warm-up. Several lean on bats and rest and look like they are in need of a cold shower. Not Eddie Collins or Wally Schang. They bounce around with a good deal of liveliness. Rube Oldring provides a few seconds of excitement when he slams a pitch into the left field bleachers.

George Stallings is puzzled by what he sees. The Athletics act like they are bored, like playing in the World Series is a waste of time, like they just want to get it over with.

Les Mann, the first Boston Brave on the scene, hearing a commotion in the stands, sticks his head around the corner of the visitors' dugout for a quick peek and is surprised by the friendly welcome he receives from one of the men in blue. The other Braves soon make an appearance, dressed in the same shopworn, stained, linty, moth-eaten uniforms, probably unwashed, they wore throughout the regular season.

Compared with the exquisitely tailored Athletics, Stallings's motley band of warriors look like a different species, like ragamuffins garbed in some fashion designer's mistake. Subtle red pinstripes try to enliven dark blue jerseys and knickers; horizontal red stripes decorate blue stockings; and a skimpy dirt-stained cap, characterized by Damon Runyon as "a piece of homeliness," rounds out what is an altogether dreary costume.

Behind home plate, song-spinners from Tin Pan Alley belt out the lyrics of Harold Atteridge's well-loved "By the sea, by the sea, by the beautiful sea," and so captivate the men in blue stationed around the field, that no one notices George Barlow, a boozehound from Trenton, filled to the gills with liquid glee, when he sneaks his wobbly belly over the low restraining wall and stumbles into the Philadelphia dugout. The Mackmen are taken aback when the drunk insists on shaking hands with each one of them.

At a quarter past one, the boys from Boston, oozing self-assurance, tumble onto the field, aglow with vitality, laughing and kicking up their heels like so many little kids just let out of school for summer vacation.

Dick Rudolph, Bill James, and Lefty Tyler, Boston's trio of starters, take turns in the batting cage, a Stallings gambit intended to keep the Mackmen guessing about who will be the Braves' starter.

Pumped up for glory, the Braves appear more comfortable than nervous. Several shadowbox and joust and joke with one another and act as if they are there just to have fun. "They defied all logic," Irwin Howe wrote. "Johnny Evers and Josh DeVore were the only ones with World Series experience. How could they be so confident, knowing they were going against a foe heralded as unbeatable on a field on which they had never before played? And yet, here they were, treating the game as an everyday affair."

Right-handers Tom Hughes and Fred Mitchell and left-hander Ensign Cottrell feed the boys batting practice fastballs. Batters step smartly in and out of the cage and sting the ball time after time. This is particularly true of Hank Gowdy. The ball seems to jump off Gowdy's bat. With one of his swings, he lashes a wicked liner into the left field bleachers several rows beyond where Rube Oldring's drive landed a few minutes before.

The air is full of baseballs. Otto Hess and Gene Cocreham, swinging specially designed fungo bats, spend most of the session hitting balls high in the air so outfielders can accustom themselves to tracking the ball against the stands. In most ballparks an outfielder can take a few steps before picking up the ball. Not against the background at Shibe Park. Outfielders must keep their eyes glued on the ball from the instant it leaves the bat.

As Fred Mitchell raps ground balls to the infielders, the play of Johnny Evers and Rabbit Maranville astonishes the crowd. Going to the right of second, going to the left of second, going into the air, Evers and Maranville grab everything that comes their way. American League fans had heard about their brilliant play but had no idea they were this good. Spectacular is what they are. Nothing seems beyond Maranville's reach. People applaud appreciatively.

Charlie Deal's play around third base is another story. Charlie unleashes two wild throws (exactly what the Braves feared); instead of settling down as the drill wears on, he becomes more agitated.

Stallings is more concerned than he lets on. When Charlie returns to the dugout, the Big Chief slaps him on the back and gives him a big "We're in this together" smile. "Cheer up, Charlie," the Big Chief says. "You know you're better than that. Don't worry about it. You've got it out of your system now. And that's great." With his irresistible charm and gutsy reputation,

Stallings is a master at getting a guy to believe in himself. Charlie Deal understands. The Big Chief is behind him. That's all that matters.

When the Mackmen amble onto the field for infield practice, the bandsmen once again pump out their stirring version of "Hail the Conquering Hero," and adoring fans cheer wildly. Not surprisingly, the excitement expressed for the work of Evers and Maranville minutes before is nothing compared with the joyous cheers fans lavish on Jack Barry and Eddie Collins. They bring the crowd off their seats more than once, pulling off practice stunts no other players have ever performed.

Out in left field, Rube Oldring, radiating true movie-star panache, lopes across the grass, his hands and legs moving instinctively as he gathers in high fly balls near the bleacher wall.

"Now there's what I call a swell-looking guy," a young woman says, oohing and ahhing and turning to her girlfriends. "Ain't he something? I could darn his socks for life."

"Ain't he?" one of the others replies. "Don't he throw that ball swell?"

"Oh, wasn't that a swell catch?" the third says. "I just adore swell catches, don't you?"

"I'm crazy about them," the first says. "Wasn't that a love?"

"Wasn't it?"

"I guess that Oldring person ain't got no swell pair of shoulders."

"I guess maybe he ain't."

"Did ya see that? He's lookin' this way" (giggle, giggle). "I wonder if he sees us?"

"I betcha he does."

Fans keep asking, "Where's Chief Bender?" After all, it was Albert Bender who pitched the opening games of the 1910, 1911, and 1913 World Series, and the big Chippewa Indian is nowhere in sight. In Bender's place, Connie Mack has Eddie Plank and J. Weldon Wyckoff warming up near the grandstand.

Across the diamond, George Stallings is playing the same game, though a little differently. Bill James and Dick Rudolph, his two 20-game winners, are loosening up on the sidelines along with the veteran left-hander Otto Hess. After working up a light sweat, James sits down and Lefty Tyler takes his place. Since the Athletics sometimes find left-handed pitching troublesome, a start by Tyler looms as a possibility.

Though deeply disappointed in not being selected as the starting pitcher for Game One of the World Series, Dick Rudolph's preparation is obsessive. He does not let his ego get in the way. He is pleased, excited, and honored to be there. He is a great teammate. There is no "me first" attitude with Dick. He will be ready to go a few innings in relief if Stallings calls on him.

While most of the attention is focused on what's happening on the field, the sphinxlike Connie Mack, wearing a black derby, a white shirt, and a black suit, slips unnoticed into the corner of the Philadelphia dugout. As Mack's eyes play over the diamond, they meet those of George Stallings. A sudden look of distaste crosses Mack's face. He is decidedly frosty. At breakfast that morning the A's manager told intimate friends he would "try to crush the Braves in the first four games . . . to square accounts with Stallings."

Photographers ask Mack and Stallings for a picture of the two of them shaking hands, the traditional World Series handshake, the posed kind, where decorum obliges each man to wear one of those friendly "May the best man win" smiles. Both men excuse themselves, saying it would be inappropriate to appear on the playing field wearing street clothes.

Stallings believed new clothes brought luck to the man wearing them. Before leaving New York he went on a shopping spree. Everything on him was new: hat, suit, shirt, pants, bow tie, belt, handkerchief, socks, shoes. Even his underwear.

Noisy with talk, the expanded press box at Shibe Park is swarming with sportswriters from all parts of the United States and Canada, and a few from as far off as Cuba and Hawaii. (Newspapers requested press credentials for 500 sportswriters, an unprecedented number, and 300 were granted.)

Everyone of consequence is present. Bozeman Bulger, the crown prince of baseball writers, credited with having invented the word "fadeaway" to describe Christy Mathewson's famous "screwball" pitch; Bat Masterson, the balding old gunfighter turned reporter, still carrying his trusty six-shooter after all these years.

Ring Lardner is on hand. Lardner would later shift to literature and give life to the fictional baseball world of Jack Keefe in classic stories like "Alibi Ike" and "You Know Me Al." Lardner will also lend Hugh Fullerton support in bringing to light information about the infamous Black Sox scandal of 1919.

Not far away from them is the gentlemanly and well-liked Grantland Rice, whose reporting portrays the athletes he writes about as heroes, and the games they play as great dramas.[†]

[†] Grantland Rice was justly famous for his brilliant lead paragraph describing a great Notre Dame football victory over a strong Army team, 13–7, in 1923: "Outlined against a blue-gray October sky, the Four Horsemen rode again. In dramatic lore they are known as Famine, Pestilence, Destruction and Death. These are only aliases. Their real names are Stuhldreher, Miller, Crowley and Layden. They formed the crest of the South Bend cyclone before which another fighting Army football team was swept over the precipice at the Polo Grounds yesterday afternoon as 55,000 spectators peered down on the bewildering panorama spread on the green plain below."

He is keeping a close eye over his shoulder on "Wild Bill" Phelon, the practical joker from Cincinnati who likes to spring exotic pets on colleagues—lizards, squirrels, snakes (some of them poisonous)—and scare the hell out of them.

Then there is Damon Runyon, an unusual talent among sportswriters of the day. Whenever Runyon covers a sporting event he likes to focus on a single theme and develop it into a story.

And nearby, locked into a conversation several rows in back of Runyon is the contentious Taylor Spink, publisher of the *Sporting News,* a trade paper considered by those in the business "The Bible of Baseball," giving one of his minions a piece of his mind.

Two ballplayers, Ty Cobb and Christy Mathewson, are also in the press section, seated on either side of Jack Wheeler, the syndicate man, for whom they are providing "a player's impression of the game." Wheeler assists in helping them put thoughts into words. Matty, however, is distracted. He beat the Yankees in the opening game of the City Series at the Polo Grounds the day before, and he keeps excusing himself so he can get the latest teletype update on today's game.

Ghostwriters often penned newspaper articles for ballplayers in those days, among them, Jack Berry, "Home Run" Baker, Eddie Collins, Hughie Jennings, Rabbit Maranville, Johnny Evers, and Grover Cleveland Alexander. Unlike the others, "Ol' Pete" Alexander made no pretense of doing his own writing. He wasn't even at the game; he'd left for his Nebraska farm the night after the Phillies' final game of the season.

Anticipating the scramble soon to follow, writers not gossiping or checking notebooks busily pound away at battered keyboards, trying one tentative lead or another, seeing which one works best. Writers employed by the evening papers are particularly hard-pressed. They generally describe the early inning action in graphic detail, then yank the page out of the typewriter, quickly reread it, and hand it to a teletypist who sends it off to the paper minutes before the deadline.

A few reporters fabricate preposterous quotations to spice up stories (they call it inside dope) gleaned from what they cite as anonymous sources.

Life is a little less hectic for reporters on the payrolls of the morning dailies. They can finish stories in comparative leisure, then have them sent out in Morse code by the telegraph operators. (Film for photographs is forwarded by carrier pigeon.) Some of the local scribes deliver stories downtown by messenger, or hop on a trolley themselves and bustle into the office and self-importantly lay the pages on the editor's desk.

Stallings clamps one of his big paws on Dick Rudolph's shoulder after Dick returns to the dugout. "Rudy," he says, "you looked real good out there... Real good... I've changed my mind... You're my starter today."

An inward frisson of excitement shoots through Rudolph's body. His adrenaline surges. "If I don't pitch a strike all afternoon," he answers excitedly, "I'm not going to give them anything good to hit."

"Now, now, Rudy. Take it easy. Don't get too wound up." Stallings's grip closes tightly on Rudolph's shoulder. The diminutive pitcher winces. "Listen to me. You can't slip up and give these guys the lead. If you do, they'll get real aggressive."

Dick Rudolph has been Stallings's choice all along. The Big Chief made the decision weeks before and never wavered. The thing to do, he told himself, is make Rudolph believe that he was not going to start the opening game and keep him relaxed. The plan worked perfectly.

At a quarter to two, a cry goes up from the crowd. "Here he comes. Here he comes." Fans spring from their seats, strain for a glimpse of the Philadelphia dugout, and chant, "Chief, Chief, Chief."

Charles Albert Bender makes his way out of the shadows, chest first. The Chief appears to strut even when standing still. The uproar swells. Hats wave, eyes shine, hands applaud. One fan salutes him; another jumps up on his seat and shouts, "It'll be all A's today. I can feel it in my bones." The Chief throws out his chest a couple of inches more.

Relaxed and poised and displaying an overreaching sense of superiority, the big Indian moves through a light warm-up, throws effortlessly, and watches his pitches smack into the catcher's mitt. He pauses occasionally, turns and poses for photographs and gazes at faces hovering nearby in the stands, where grown men, like filings drawn to a magnet, lean over the railings of box seats, wave pens, pencils, and paper, and clamor for his signature. The Chief is a bit playful, it seems, because he tosses a few pitches underhand to second-string catcher Jack Lapp.

Talk about asking for it.

The Braves lean forward on the dugout steps and gape at Bender in disbelief, all talking at once. "What the hell's he doing?" "Trying to show us up?" "That no-good son of a bitch." "He'll get his." "Wait and see." "Right up the old keister."

Little do they know. The Chief is ready. More than ready. He'd warmed up secretly for 20 minutes under the grandstand before taking the field.

While Bender completes his warm-up, the gate in right field swings open. Ron Mulford Jr., chairman of baseball's Most Valuable Player selection committee, drives past Bender in a dazzling black 1914 Chalmers Light Six. Bender pauses, watches the car go by, his expression unchanging. He flicks his glove, the signal for a curve, and delivers one last pitch.

Admiring players from both squads crowd around the car, caps off, happily posing for photographs, the Braves on one side of the car, the Athletics on the other. A hush falls over the stands. Charles Chalmers, brother of Hugh Chalmers, president of the Chalmers Motor Company (sponsor of the award), steps forward and begins the presentation ceremony. Few in the stands can hear him.

"Eddie Collins," he says, "considered by John J. McGraw as 'the greatest baseball player in the world' . . . " (McGraw may have exaggerated, although, even today, most baseball people think of Eddie Collins as the greatest second baseman ever to put on a pair of spiked shoes.)

Collins looks pained standing there, the center of attention. He studies his shoelaces, shifts his feet, and runs his hand through his hair as the speaker drones on and on. At length, Chalmers pauses and beckons Collins. Thousands rise and applaud. Cap in hand, the abashed Collins smiles uncomfortably and shakes his head. The ovation continues for over a minute. Collins makes a gesture of thanks toward the rows of faces lined up before him. Then, turning quickly, he grins at Johnny Evers, the National League's most valuable player (Evers will receive his MVP award prior to the start of the third game in Boston), grabs Johnny's hand and pumps it up and down, and keeps on doing it. The warmth of Collins's gesture embarrasses the prickly Evers.

They pose every which way for photographers wanting to commemorate the moment. "Look here, Eddie." "Over here, Johnny." Evers's face reddens, he squirms, and then finally manages a sheepish smile. Collins shakes Evers's hand once, then again, then once more before the ceremony ends.

At the same time the other players take the opportunity to stroke the car's upholstery, fumble with the steering wheel, and kick the tires. All in all, the opposing players are in complete agreement on at least one thing today. Chalmers makes a superior motorcar.

At that very moment, horns toot, trumpets blare, trombones groan, and drums can be heard underneath the third-base pavilion. Heads turn and see a man in a top hat and tails step jauntily out of the portal. The crowd applauds. The man smiles, and with a showboater's natural instinct, he waves his hat cheerily and threads his way through the crowded aisle.

It is Little Fitzie, followed by Boston's Royal Rooters, the most vibrant congregation of fans in all of baseball. Once the "happy hour boys" seat themselves behind the Boston dugout, the band they brought along strikes up a few brassy, boisterous bars of "Dixie," inspiring more applause.

At 1:56 P.M., four umpires in brilliant blue uniforms step resolutely onto the field and pose for photographs. Bill Klem, the National League's best, will make the calls on the bases; two newcomers to the big leagues, Bill "Lord" Byron and George Hildebrand, will guard the outfield foul lines; and burly Bill Dinneen will call balls and strikes behind the plate. Dinneen, a former Red Sox pitching star, was the hero of baseball's first World Series, having won three out of four decisions against the Pittsburgh Pirates.

Dinneen summons the rival captains, Johnny Evers and Ira Thomas. Facing Thomas across home plate, the abrasive Evers starts an unpleasant fuss about the ground rules, and a window in a house beyond the center field fence. Thomas listens, frowns sourly, and interrupts at intervals. A wordy discussion follows, delaying the start of the game.

A short distance away, a man, lineup cards in hand, brings a megaphone to his lips. He is the announcer, the person who calls out information to fans in the stands. People strain to hear him. (It was all megaphones and lungs in those days. The public address system did not come into use until it was installed in Yankee Stadium in 1929.)

"Your attention please. Ladies and gentlemen. The *batt-ries* for today's game. For the Athletics, Bender and Schang. For Boston, Rudolph and Gowdy."‡ Joyful applause greets the news. Name by name, position by position, the megaphone man identifies the players. Each one takes a step forward, the Braves lively, bubbling with enthusiasm, the Athletics reserved, almost impudent in their nonchalance.

Seconds later a torrential ovation rumbles through the stands. Fans cheer, whistle, stomp. The Athletics are taking the field, their white uniforms radiant under the afternoon sun. The 1914 World Series is about to begin.

Oblivious of most of the pomp and folderol surrounding him, big, stoop-shouldered Albert Bender gets some last-minute advice from Connie Mack and walks with a strut out to the mound, primed to show fans around the nation why he is the best big-game pitcher in the business.

After going through the allotted warm-up pitches, the Chief leaves the mound and strolls over to the third base line, stopping halfway between third and home. Quietly, almost unnoticed by the throng, he drags the spikes of one shoe across the white chalk line, making a foot-long smudge that looks like a cross, a symbol of good luck. He then strolls back to the

---

‡ In baseball, the "battery" is the pitcher and the catcher.

mound, looking combative and lethal, and waits, all the while staring at the Braves' bench, like a hired assassin confident of his prey.

The announcements completed, Bill Dinneen dusts home plate and growls, "Let's get this thing started."

CHAPTER 52

IT WAS LIKE LOOKING DOWN MURDERER'S ROW

At seven minutes past two, Bill Dinneen raised his face mask and commanded: "Play ball"; the battle for baseball's highest honor was under way. One question hummed through the crowd: did the Braves have a chance, any chance at all, against the mighty Mackmen, a baseball machine in the heyday of its glory, the most fearsome lineup in all of baseball?

Out on the mound, Bender was doing a little gardening, digging a landing place for his spikes, paving the surface, grooming it to his satisfaction.

The Royal Rooters gave the full bells-and-whistles treatment to Herbie Moran, the lead-off batter for the Braves, as he approached the chalk-lined batter's box. Herbie paused before stepping in, the barrels of two bats resting at his feet, his gaze riveted on Bender, the pitcher the Braves had heard so much about.

The Chief, looking tall and dominant on the high mound, pulled down the brim of his cap, held his glove at his chin, and peered in for the sign, all business, ready to do what needed to be done. He nodded assent, and with a mighty sweep of his arms, he reared back, drove forward, and unleashed an eyeball-blistering fastball writers described as exploding, the kind that has a natural darting movement to it. *Whoosh*. The ball was in the catcher's mitt before Moran knew it. Not a good sign. Umpire Bill Dinneen put out his right fist. Strike one.

The home crowd loosened its lungs.

On the fifth pitch of the at bat, Moran lifted a harmless pop-up over the right side of the infield. Stuffy McInnis drifted over and took it just inside of foul territory for the first out.

Johnny Evers acknowledged the scattered applause of the crowd as he stepped into the batter's box and took a few practice swings. Bender waited and stared at Evers, the half smirk of a bully on the big Indian's face. Famous for his combative swagger, Evers glowered back.

Bender went right to work on Evers. Johnny swung at Bender's first pitch and raised a soft fly over the infield. Second baseman Eddie Collins retreated, pounded the pocket of his worn mitt, and gathered in the ball at the edge of the outfield grass, while Bender stood motionless in front of the mound drinking in applause.

"Bender started with terrific speed," Grantland Rice wrote, "and looked to be at his best. He was throwing with conviction, as if to say, 'I believe in my fastball and I don't think you can hit it.'"

Bender whipped over a quick strike on slugger Joey Connolly, whose active eyebrows acknowledged the nastiness of the pitch. Bender reared back again and shot another across the letters. Connolly fouled it into the lower stands. It was evident that the Braves were having difficulty putting the bat on the ball. The Chief looked powerful and in control, and put macho energy into every pitch.

"Datta boy, Chief, datta boy, gwafter 'im, gwafter 'im," a man with a voice like a bugle noised.

Connolly took a couple of practice swings, then took a big cut at a high fastball and heard it thump heavily into the pocket of Wally Schang's mitt. Connolly swore, turned away, and swiped at the air with his bat.

Bender strutted back to the dugout, his chest thrown out, an ornery grin on his face, the grin of a man who enjoys pulling wings off flies. The Athletics' star right-hander had toyed with the three best left-handed hitters in the Braves lineup, just as a cat might toy with a mouse. He'd thrown nine wince-inducing pitches, all of them fastballs. All but one a strike. And he seemed to be what is termed "right" in baseball slang.

Confident that Connie Mack's championship express would keep rolling, the Philadelphia faithful settled back in their seats, feeling they were about to witness the complete destruction of the National League champions.

When the Braves took the field, they acted like a gang of unruly toughs, foul-mouthed and smart-alecky, hurling volleys of insults at the Athletics, confrontational language, the worst imprecations imaginable, blunt, filthy, nasty barnyard epithets. "Give 'em hell, boys," Stallings roared.

Rudolph was about to follow his mates onto the field when the Big Chief grabbed his arm: "Remember, Rudy, don't throw the bastards a fastball, whatever you do. No goddamn fastballs. That's an order. They murder fastballs."

Rudolph grunted and made his way out to the mound, his emotions soaring, excitement raging within him. Struggling to keep from showing his nerves, he scraped the loam of the mound with his spikes, turned, looked at the grandstand towering above him, and listened to the formless sounds of the throng.

Eventually he got around to throwing a warm-up pitch, and almost tumbled off the mound. "What the hell?" He screwed up his mouth, chewed at his lower lip, and studied the ground. A forehead-slapping thought suddenly hit him. The goddamn pitching rubber was too high.

And it was.

The rule book called for the rubber "not to be more than 15 inches higher than home plate and the baselines," a requirement seldom enforced, it seems, before 1950. (The pitcher's mound today is 10 inches high.) The mound at Shibe Park was 20 inches high, the highest in baseball, a tactic used by Connie Mack to gain an edge on visiting teams.

"I had a hard time keeping my control," Rudolph said. "It kept me pitching very carefully." Perhaps as a result, he struggled in the first inning and wasn't his usual steady self.

With businesslike ease, Eddie Murphy, the leadoff hitter for Philadelphia, crouched and waited for Rudolph's first pitch. (Murphy was so fast, he hadn't grounded into a double play all season.) Working quickly, Rudolph spun in a slow curve that Murphy banged into center field for a base hit. A scream of delight went up from the Philadelphia faithful. They were certain the Braves were overmatched by the powerful Athletics, who were known for bombing visiting teams. The highly favored Mackmen would surely dismantle this motley crew.

Rudolph's battery mate, Hank Gowdy, ran out to the mound. "Keep Murphy close," he said. The wisdom of holding base runners close was almost a religion with the Braves.

Connie Mack ordered a bunt. Advance the runner. Anticipating the play, Evers positioned the Braves infielders in on the infield grass, while Stallings's snarly rowdies went to work on the batter, Rube Oldring, unleashing a storm of obscenities, cruel and abusive chants, gossip for all the world to hear, secrets of a secret life, information not found in the program.

Using Rube's fiancée's name freely, they tore up the air with unbounded energy and serenaded him with comments that bore into poor Rube like a wound. "Hey, limp dick, can't keep it in your pants, can you?" "Get a little slack in your alimony payments, did you?" "When did they let you out of the slammer?" (Oldring had indeed spent some time in jail earlier in the week.) "How many wives do you have, lover boy?" This was more than gee-whiz enthusiasm. It was eye-watering gutter brutality. Shocking four-letter words. Rabelaisian vulgarity.

Cheeks ablaze, Oldring, wincing under the vehemence of the barrage—his fiancée, Hannah Ann Thomas of Quinton, New Jersey, was seated in a field box nearby—shortened up and flicked his bat at a curve and dropped a pretty bunt out in front of the plate. Schmidt started in from first, realized he had no play, and scrambled back to cover the bag.

Gowdy was the only one who had a chance. Off came his mask. He leapt forward, bare-handed the ball, turned and fired off-balance to Schmidt, just as the big guy got back on the bag. The throw sailed high. Schmidt jumped. He strained every inch of his powerful frame, managed to snag the ball in the hinged thumb of his first baseman's mitt, and came down on the bag just in time to nip the speedy Oldring. Had the ball gotten by Schmidt, Murphy probably would have scored and Oldring might have gone to third.

"Hyper-alert, Stallings watched every move the Mackmen made," Tim Murnane noted in the *Boston Globe,* "and kept an eye on Connie Mack too, because he knew how foxy his opponents were. He knew they were looking for the Braves to tip off their pitches."

Rudolph was visibly jumpy when "Cocky" Eddie Collins stepped into the batter's box. The Mackmen were poised to strike and Rudolph knew it. So did George Stallings. The Big Chief ordered, encouraged, and scolded, bellowing like a gorilla. The wildest behavior people had seen outside of a zoo.

Third-base coach Ira Thomas, making all kinds of flourishes and gestures, touched the bill of his cap, his nose, his chin, his chest, pointed to his eye, tugged at his belt, clapped his hands, and waved his arms. It was a convincing act.

Rudolph spun around and screamed at Thomas: "If you can get our signs, you bastard, you are welcome to them." But Rudolph was worried. He was about to face three of the most feared batters in the American League, and he was unsure of just how good his stuff was. "To look down at that batting order for the first time was scary," he said later. "It was like looking down 'Murderer's Row' at Sing Sing. When they connect, they connect. Good night."

Working quickly, often taking no more than 10 seconds between pitches, Rudolph ran the count on Collins to 3–0. Rudy reached down for the resin bag, dusted his hand, leaned forward, and studied Gowdy's sign.

Collins called time, stepped out of the batter's box, and complained that umpire Bill Klem was standing directly behind Rudolph's pitching arm. This was a favorite ploy of the White Elephants. By stepping out of the batter's box while Gowdy was flashing Rudolph the sign, Collins allowed the first- and third-base coaches and the runner on second to get a peek at what Gowdy was calling for.

"Take your time, Dick," Evers hollered from second. "Wait till he gets back in the box."

The umpire refused to move.

Trying to be too careful, Rudolph lost Collins. Now there was one out, runners were on first and second, and one of baseball's most feared sluggers was striding toward the plate: "Home Run" Baker, coming off a .319 season. The appearance of Baker churned up a storm of enthusiasm. Fans stood and applauded. The A's had Rudolph cornered.

"Bake" scooped up a handful of dirt, let it sift through his fingers, wiped his hands on the sides of his pants, pulled on the visor of his cap, and handed two of the three bats he was swinging to Louis Van Zelst. And for good luck, he gave the hump on little Louis's back a gentle pat.

People stamped their feet. Cheered. Applauded. A man in a first-row box seat stood and imitated Baker's swing. "We'll get 'em now," someone shouted.

Rudolph and Gowdy knew every strength and every weakness of the A's hitters, though occasionally they could not get together on what to pitch them. Rudolph shook off Gowdy. Asked for something else. Gowdy talked to Rudolph, tried to bolster his confidence. Gave him another sign. Rudolph shook him off again. Gowdy sighed deeply, swiped at the ground with his hand, his jawbone working continuously.

Rudolph squinted, hesitated for a long few seconds, nodded, looked back the runner on second, took a deep breath, and delivered an off-speed pitch. It floated up to the plate like a balloon, slow and inside. "I had to risk it," Rudolph said. "It was like a man in a poker game who has raised the pot on a four flush and just naturally had to get that other heart or spade. If I put one over the middle, I knew he would send it for a ride. There was nothing left for me to do but take a chance."

Baker took a savage swipe at the ball, a home run swing, got under it and raised a monstrous pop-up that twisted over near the box seats in short right field, 30 feet off first base. Butch Schmidt, glove outstretched, went after it and managed to snatch the ball out of the hands of a fan at the restraining wall, making a difficult catch with his back to the infield.

Murphy and Collins were off and running the instant they heard the slap of the ball in Schmidt's glove. No one except Schmidt's teammates expected what Butch did next. The former pitcher whirled, planted his feet, and cut loose a perfect skidding strike to third base. Charlie Deal, ignoring the glitter of the shining spikes coming at him, took the throw, chest high, and put down the tag. All eyes turned toward third-base umpire Bill Klem. Arms outstretched, palms down, Klem signaled: "Safe!" Quaker City fans expressed their approval.

Then, much to their astonishment, Bill Klem reversed himself. He called Murphy out. The Athletics' bench emptied in a rush, the players surrounding the Old Arbiter: "Murphy was safe!" "Murphy was safe!" "He beat the tag!" Bill Klem, unruffled, nodded, displaying the confidence of a man who knew without question that he was right. "He was indeed," Klem said. "But your man overslid the bag. He was tagged twice. The second time they got him."

The words of "Tessie" rang out across the field.

The heads-up play by the Braves' burly first baseman stopped the White Elephants in their tracks. Schmidt's heroics opened the Mackmen's eyes. These Boston fellows were well schooled; they were not a "bunch of bushers." They were legitimate. They knew what they were doing, and they knew how to do it.

CHAPTER 53

THE BRAVES' BEST PITCHER WAS IN TROUBLE

Leading off for the Braves in the top of the second, Possum Whitted spat out a stream of tobacco juice and stepped into the batter's box. Following Stallings's maxim "Attack and destroy," Whitted put his mouth to work. He jabbered at Bender in a disagreeable tone, verbally assaulting the Chief with the usual four-letter words, blunt, nasty and brutish, making the field foul by his presence. Bender's nostrils flared.

Full of anarchy, loudmouthed and dirty-mouthed, the wild and aggressive Braves howled like coyotes, hooted and hollered, and indulged in ugly taunts, the human equivalent of a pack of snarling, snapping, feral dogs.

"Hey, old pitch-'em-heap," they brayed, "here's where we send you back to the reservation."

Cursing inwardly, umpire Bill Dinneen ripped off his mask, pointed at the gallery of ugly Americans on the bench, and issued a warning. But Dinneen's disapproval did not muzzle the ferocity of the boys in the loony bin. Dinneen warned them several times. It didn't matter. The half-deranged gang of hooligans ignored him. What could he do? Send the entire Braves squad to the showers? Eject Evers and Maranville, and manager Stallings? No way. And the Braves' bench jockeys knew it.

Bender pounded in a fastball, then another, and another, missing each time; falling behind on the count, 3–0. His control was betraying him. Now he had to come in with a strike. The ball sizzled up. "St-rr-rike!"

Whitted's head snapped around. He jabbed a finger at Dinneen. Waved his arms. Argued that the pitch was high. Demanded to know why Dinneen didn't see it the way he saw it.

Bender burned in another fastball.

"St-rr-rike tuh!"

"Strike???" Whitted shouted at Dinneen with piranha-like intensity. "You crazy or something?" Whitted wagged his finger at the umpire, screamed profanities, gestured in disbelief, and pounded his bat on the plate.

Boos rang out from the stands. "Git offa dat stuff. Wassa matta wid yu?" a fan yelled. "Yu dip. Back to yure lead pipe an' dark alley. Back to th' gang."

Dinneen, a commanding presence on the field, looked like he wanted to punch out Whitted. "Who the hell are you anyway?" he said, his voice heavy with sarcasm. Whitted ignored the question. He was too busy explaining the strike zone to Dinneen, openly using his hands, apparently unaware of the World Series code: you do not make an umpire look bad. Whitted did not shut up until Bender walked him on the 3–2 pitch. Animally happy, the Braves' hired gun sprinted down to first and started his aggressive talk all over again, chewing tobacco, spitting, hopping around, and taunting Bender.

Butch Schmidt's arrival at the plate was greeted by a warm ovation that acknowledged the big first baseman's heads-up play on Eddie Murphy minutes earlier. The warmth of the cheers and the applause made Butch feel like he was a native Philadelphian.

"Wait him out, Butch," Stallings barked from the dugout. "You can do it. Wait him out."

Bender reset his game face and fed Butch a curve in on the hands. A swing and a miss. Stallings raised an awful holler. "What the hell are you doing, Butch? Wait him out! Wait him out!" Butch didn't wait him out. Swinging on the very next pitch, he sliced a line drive to the opposite field—right at Rube Oldring. Stallings watched with disbelieving eyes. He let out an exasperated groan and muttered in a low growl: "Nobody home upstairs."

Hank Gowdy stood in next for Boston. Gowdy did not look like a ballplayer, but, somehow, he got the job done. Gowdy had his own particular routine at bat: he wiped his face with his hands, spread his long legs, rubbed his trousers, dropped his bat, picked it up, swung it once, waggled his shoulders back and forth, lifted his chin, and made faces at the pitcher.

Working the corners of the plate, Bender fell behind, 3–0, another deep count. The big guy seemed to have lost his rhythm. Worry took up quarters in the Philadelphia dugout. Baker at third kicked the ground. Collins at second glanced at Barry. A hint of unease passed between them. Without a good curve in the mix, Bender's speed was not going to stop the Braves for long.

A called strike brought the count to 3–1, a hitter's count. Gowdy waited patiently. He seldom chased bad pitches. Bender then made a huge mistake: he delivered the pitch Gowdy was looking for. A belt-high fastball over the inside corner of the plate. Gowdy murdered belt-high fastballs. "Hammering Hank" went after the appetizing pitch. Swung hard. And missed. Strike two. A full count, 3–2. Bender got away with one that time. But if he kept slipping into deep counts, sooner or later he was bound to get hurt.

A pitcher occasionally comes right back with the same pitch, thinking he can fool the batter. That's what Bender did. Reaching high with his glove, he sprang at Gowdy, fed him another fastball in the same location. This time the pitch got a little too much of the plate. Gowdy turned his hips and walloped a wicked liner up the alley in left-center, well placed between Oldring and Strunk. The ball bounced twice and rattled off the wall 420 feet from home plate.

Whitted, the runner on first, running hard, rounded second and was on his way to third when Jack Barry threw a handful of the infield dirt in Whitted's face. Dirt in the eyes didn't slow the Braves' center fielder one bit. He scored standing up, giving Boston a 1–0 lead.

Gowdy settled into second with a stand-up double and a broad smile on his face. Wonderfully pleased, the Boston bench spilled out of the dugout; players jumped up and down and celebrated. It was a key moment. You could sense a subtle shift in the momentum of the game.

The number seven hitter in the Braves lineup, Rabbit Maranville, was on deck, preparing for a one-on-one confrontation with the Chief. Devoid of fear and wearing a small, intent frown, Rabbit tapped the dirt from his cleats with the handle of his bat, stepped in, and crowded the plate. Bender scowled. The Chief believed the plate belonged to him. Not the batter. If a batter got too close, the Chief let him know it with a fastball under the chin. If that didn't do it, the Chief simply knocked him down with a high hard one behind the ear.

The two men eyed each other belligerently. The first pitch ran up and in and almost tore the button off the top of Maranville's cap. Down he went in a whirl of dust, arms, and legs. Rab sprang right back up like a jack-in-the-box, screaming "Asshole! Asshole!"

Waggling the thick bat at Bender, Rabbit reclaimed the disputed space. Stood rooted to the spot. The kid had nerve. You had to give him that. Bender appeared calm and intense. But his heart hurried. His eyes glowed like red-hot coals. And he came right back at Maranville with a fastball on the inside corner. Rab drew in his hands, swung, made enough contact to manage a ground ball up the middle, a base hit, driving in Gowdy and extending the Braves' lead to 2–0. Bender kicked his right foot at the mound and tried to stay composed.

Boston fans erupted. Pennants waved. Mock Indian yells rent the air. The Royal Rooters cut loose with a rousing "Three Times Three." They stamped their feet three times and shouted, "Bang! Bang! Bang!" And for emphasis they did it one more time, and sang "Tessie," while Mike McGreevy danced an Irish jig. The scoreboard operator put up a big fat "2."

Bender took off his cap and mopped the beads of perspiration standing on his brow and stared woodenly at the next batter, Charlie Deal.

Connie Mack flicked his scorecard. Shortstop Jack Barry moved three steps to his right, toward third base.

With the count 0–2, Deal turned on a fastball and grounded it hard right at Jack Barry. The A's shortstop gobbled it up and tossed to Eddie Collins covering second. Collins fired a throw to first, completing a 6–4–3 double play.

Though the twin killing snuffed out the rally, the Braves were elated. They were certain now that they would win the game. But you can never be certain in the game of baseball.

Back in Boston, stores across the city scrawled scores on plate glass windows with a bar of soap, and 12,000 Braves fans wearing suits and ties packed the pumping heart of the city, Washington Street, "Newspaper Row." The huge throng stretched from the Old State House, where the Declaration of Independence was first read to the citizenry, to the South Meeting House, from where Patriots set out for the Boston Tea Party.

The thickly crowded streets were all but impassable and, surprisingly, they were not noisy. People moved about. Voices babbled. And the air carried sounds of dots and dashes.

"It must be good news," someone said, anticipation apparent in his voice. "The Braves are batting." A telegraph operator standing in the crowd shouted. "Whitted scored for the Braves." Blank faces stared at him. Soon other telegraphers in the crowd joined in. They too understood the code and described what was happening to those around them. Word spread; people cheered, or parts of the crowd did. Most fans were puzzled. The bulletin board read 0–0.

Soon a man holding a megaphone materialized above the entrance of the *Boston Globe*. The sea of faces turned toward him. "The Braves scored twice in the top of the second," the megaphone man bellowed. The street exploded in cheers. Strangers shook hands and pounded each other on the back. Everybody was talking at the same time, clerks, fashionable society swells, working stiffs, and fresh-faced youngsters in newsboy caps. New arrivals always asked the same question: "What's the score?"

Rudolph's first six pitches missed the plate in the bottom of the second. He walked Stuffy McInnis and fell behind 2–0 on Amos Strunk. This excited Philadelphia fans. Rudolph was in a dicey position. Evers and Deal started over. Rudolph smiled and waved them back. "I knew then that Dick wasn't flurried," Evers said, "he just didn't want to give those sluggers a good ball to hit."

Not aware of this, Boston fans were plenty worried. They began asking one another, "How long can Rudolph hold them off?" "How long will it take the A's to drive him off the mound?" "Did he have a chance, any chance at all of surviving?" Rudolph himself was a little unsure of things. He just wanted to hold the White Elephants down and wasn't quite sure he could do it.

Battling to make good, Rudolph was throwing good pitches, trying to contain the White Elephants. And, of all things, he left one out over the middle of the plate just when he shouldn't have.

Strunk jumped on the pitch and lashed a sinking liner into shallow right. Herbie Moran, a tough little guy with a strong arm, tried to control the play. He charged, intending to keep McInnis from going to third, reached down, and thinking "throw" before he actually had the ball in his glove, allowed it to skip under the leather and roll all the way to the right field wall. McInnis legged it home. Strunk stopped at third.

Jack Barry stepped into the batter's box.

Speed at third, speed at the plate. Nobody out. One run in. Another run almost certain. Tying the score or forging ahead would change the complexion of the game. The Mackmen would gain a world of confidence and get very aggressive.

Jack Barry was a tough out when a hit meant a run. The count on Barry ran full, 3–2. Gowdy went into his catcher's squat, gave Rudolph the sign. Dick nodded, looked back at Strunk on third, took a deep breath, and fired. The ball broke sharply into the dirt. Barry chased it, missed it by a foot. "Striker out," Dinneen growled. (The veteran arbiter began his playing career in the 19th century when the word "striker" was in general use.)

There was talk of passing Wally Schang, a dangerous .287 hitter on the season, and pitching to Bender. Rudolph wouldn't hear of it. And he was right. All Schang could manage was a dribbler off his bat handle. The ball rolled just beyond Rudolph's glove between first and second. Strunk hesitated at third before breaking for home. Evers flew in at full tilt, scooped up the ball with his bare hand at the edge of the infield grass, and rifled a throw home. The 6'2", 182-pound Gowdy dropped to one knee, blocked the plate, and glanced at Strunk bearing down on him like an oncoming locomotive. A gritty, grinding, jarring collision followed. A blur of dust. Gowdy applied the tag. Dinneen waited to see if Gowdy had the ball. He did.

"Yer out!" Dinneen roared.

"It took lightning judgment on Evers's part to decide whether to whip the ball to the plate, or retire Schang at first," a reporter for the *Evening Bulletin* wrote. "Evers knew Strunk was the fastest man on Mack's payroll, and he cut him down anyway with a neat throw."

Bender then drilled a sharp ground ball to deep short. Maranville fielded it on a bounce above his head and tossed underhand to Evers for the force on Schang at second, ending the inning.

Showing great heart and great desire and great will, the Braves kept coming at the Mackmen. They did not waver. They were young guys who knew what they were doing. Rudolph settled into a rhythm and, time after time, baited the Mackmen into swinging awkwardly at low breaking balls.

"The war clubs that crushed the Cubs and the Giants, batted no runs across the plate," Grantland Rice wrote. "Rudolph varied a fastball, fired directly at the Mackmen's heads, with a slow tantalizing curve that wobbled up to the plate with a hesitation waltz attached to it, singing all the way: 'Swing, you sucker. Swing!' And they all swung. But their bats never touched the ball."

When Rudolph struck out Home Run Baker, it brought a huge laugh from the crowd. "Baker twisted himself into a pretzel," Tom Rice wrote in the *Brooklyn Daily Eagle*, "swinging vainly at a third strike, a ball so slow that it delayed the game."

Though the Braves led by a run, 2–1, there was no pressure on the Athletics. Experience had taught them that they would catch up with Rudolph and score some runs the second or third time through the batting order. It was a matter of time. That's all. And Bender was doing his job. Keeping the game close.

CHAPTER 54

IN THE SPIRIT OF GOOD SPORTSMANSHIP

Facing Hank Gowdy in the top of the fifth, Bender delivered a fastball that drifted over the middle of the plate. Gowdy put the fat part of the bat on the ball and sent a well-tagged drive into deep right-center. It bounced once and caromed off the scoreboard. Gowdy wheeled toward second and sprinted for third. Strunk scooped up the ball, whirled, and fired a strong throw toward the infield. Collins's relay looked like it had him, but the ball bounced a little up the line and Hank slid in safely with a triple. A great roar rose from the stands.

The cold reality of what was happening was unmistakable. The Braves were beginning to assert their dominance over the Athletics. Connie Mack pushed back his hat from his brow, a puzzled look on his face, and studied Bender standing on the apron of the mound, pulling at his uniform in several directions, his eyes betraying the chill of injured pride. The tremendous drive was a psychological surprise for the A's. The game wasn't anything like what it was supposed to be. Hank Gowdy had changed the context.

The afternoon light was beginning to angle as Rabbit Maranville approached the batter's box. The Rab received a nice hand from the crowd. Much like Wee Willie Keeler of "I hit them where they ain't" fame, Rabbit's hands were almost a third of the way up the bat. This gave him good bat control.

Managing calmly from the dugout, Connie Mack pulled his infielders halfway in for a play at the plate. A stir of uneasiness rippled through the crowd. The Chief stood atop the mound, rubbed the ball, looked for the sign, nodded, toed the rubber, and delivered a fastball low and away. Maranville made just enough contact to send the ball looping over the drawn-in infield—a base hit, giving the Braves a 3–1 lead.

J. Weldon Wyckoff was up and throwing in the Philadelphia bull pen.

The next batter, Charlie Deal, squared away for a bunt and missed. Charlie squared away again. This time he popped a soft fly directly into Bender's waiting hands. The Chief made the grab and doubled up Maranville who had taken off for second on the pitch. The double play seemed to buoy the Chief's confidence, and he ended the inning by striking out Rudolph on three pitches.

Bender glanced at Connie Mack as he stepped down into the dugout, aware that Mack was about to say something. "Good Lord, Albert," Mack said, "how did you come to hand Gowdy that fast one?"

"Was that Gowdy?" the Chief said. "I thought it was Deal." Here it was the fifth inning and he didn't know that Gowdy had been pushed up a rung in the Braves' batting order.

In the home half of the fifth, Jack Barry lifted a twisting flare into left field, near the foul line. A sure hit. Maybe good for two bases. Connolly raced in. Maranville instinctively sprinted after it. Deal turned and watched. That's all he could do. Every eye in the park was on the ball when Rabbit nailed it, his back to the infield, showing off his famous "vest-pocket" catch in the process. A shake-your-head-in-disbelief play. The kind fans talk about for years.

Barry, a great shortstop himself, didn't hesitate in heaping praise on his rival during an interview later in the day: "That was the most difficult play of the game," Barry said. "It didn't seem possible that Rabbit could reach the ball. But nothing seems hard for the little fellow." This was generous of Barry, because most everyone else in the ballpark thought it was Barry who made the most spectacular catch of the afternoon.

It happened in the top of the sixth inning. Herbie Moran lifted a high pop fly into foul territory back of third base. The ball looked uncatchable. Barry sprinted after it, darted across the foul line, flung his body forward, threw out his bare hand, and plucked the ball off the top of the grass, stumbling and reeling forward as he did, trying not to fall, and plunged into the waiting arms of a policeman who kept him from crashing into the low restraining wall in front of the grandstand. The play was as thrilling as it was plainly impossible before Barry made the catch.

The Royal Rooters jumped to their feet and cheered and shouted more loudly than the hometown folks in a generous display of good sportsmanship.

Following Barry's sensational catch, Evers cracked a scorching line drive up the middle right over Bender's cap, almost tattooing stitches on the Chief's forehead. The viciousness with which the ball was hit unsettled the big Indian, and he walked the next batter, Joey Connolly, on five pitches. The crowd squirmed uneasily. And rightly so. This brought up Possum Whitted.

After taking a pitch outside of the strike zone, Whitted blasted a fastball over Amos Strunk's head in right-center, a one-hop triple off the wall, scoring Evers and Connolly. It was 5–1, Boston. The Chief shook his head dejectedly; Barry and Collins came over to settle him down.

J. Weldon Wyckoff was ready and throwing hard in the bull pen, but Connie Mack made no move. He was staying with his ace.

Butch Schmidt came to bat when play resumed, and Mack's infield closed in for a play at the plate. With the second pitch of the at bat, Bender tried a breaking ball, something he'd not shown much of all afternoon. The ball had no bite. It hung, belt high. Schmidt swung and lashed a wicked shot at Barry's feet, sending up a puff of dirt. The ball was hit so hard, it was in left field before Barry could get his glove down. Whitted raced home and made it a 6–1 game.

Mack gave Ira Thomas the word: "Get him out of there." Thomas walked toward the edge of the mound and motioned to the bull pen. White Elephant fans, perhaps numbed by what they'd seen, watched in near silence.

Knowing he was heartbroken, teammates crowded around and gave the Chief a pat on the back and watched as the big Indian shuffled slowly off the field, gently guided by Ira Thomas. Instead of leaving as a hero, the Chief was leaving as an object of pity—deflated, diminished, defeated.

Heywood Broun of the *New York Tribune* described the scene: "Bender walked slowly by J. Weldon Wyckoff, a young Bucknell College man, who was entering a World Series for the first time. As Bender neared the bench, he raised his hands to his face. Then his hands dropped and he looked at the people in the stands who were cheering him. The Chief was not smiling. The Braves had knocked Charles Albert Bender from the box, and they had done more. They hammered away that grin."

Carrying his glove in his left hand, Bender shook his head as he climbed down into the dugout and flung his cap on the bench, then swiveled a glance at Connie Mack over in the corner of the dugout. Connie's face was livid. He did not conceal his disdain. "Pretty good hitting for a 'bush league' outfit, huh?" Bender looked down at his shoes and said nothing.

The rest of the game fell into the now-familiar pattern. The final score was 7–1.

The spell was broken. The top of the baseball pyramid had been shaken; the Athletics' aura of invincibility shattered. The A's were unstoppable, until they weren't. The Royal Rooters dominated the ballpark and cheered in one voice, 500 strong. They sang "Tessie" with so much emotion that their excitement seemed schoolboyish. And when the band played, they danced in the aisles.

Staring at the field, a poker-faced Connie Mack remained on the bench and watched the Braves celebrate, then he turned in silence and disappeared into the tunnel heading back to his office.

CHAPTER 55

HE WAS LOOKING AT HIS WORST NIGHTMARE

A day later things got a lot more competitive. The series was no longer looked on as a mismatch between the big bad Mackmen, the best team in baseball, and the pathetic Boston Braves, an upstart gang of unknowns just happy to be there. The American League champions had come to realize that they were in a street fight, a struggle for survival. There was no way they were going to run roughshod over the National League champions. It just wasn't going to happen. Connie's boys were going to have to ramp up their intensity and ramp it up fast, if they were going to win the high-stakes battle for the world championship.

Temperatures of 84 degrees warmed the stands, moving scorecards fanned the air; fans took off their hats, peeled off jackets, rolled up sleeves, got comfortable, and asked one another: Can the Mackmen right themselves and get back in the series? Sure they could.

The change in the hometown team was unmistakable. The bounce in their step and their high-voltage smiles were conspicuous features of the pregame warmup. They were no longer Connie Mack's wooden soldiers. Yesterday's puffed-up egos were gone. The smugness was gone. The ho-hum attitude was gone. They were enjoying themselves, certain in their hearts and minds that today would be different.

Staring in silence from the visitors' dugout, his eyes devouring everything around him, George Stallings watched and listened to the chatter on the field, the crack of the bats on balls, the smack of the ball in the glove, and silently said to himself: They look like champions today. But the big fellow's unyielding confidence in his boys remained unshaken. Victory had intoxicated his lunch-pail warriors. The working-class blood brothers had come into their own. And the omens were good.

Believing that his fashionable new clothes had something to do with the team's success, the Big Chief came to the conclusion that his boys would not lose unless something happened to his new wardrobe. He decided to wear the same fetish-worthy objects for as long as the Braves kept winning: the same brown fedora, the same Norfolk jacket, the same bow tie, the same white shirt, the same trousers, the same underwear, the same shoes, going so far as to put them on in the same order each morning.

Eddie Plank (15–7), a left-hander, started for the Athletics. At 39, the veteran old lion of Connie Mack's staff was still one of the stars of the game. Bill James (26–7), a 21-year-old right-hander, started for the Braves. The up-and-coming stud of George Stallings's rotation had compiled a remarkable record of 19 wins in 20 decisions during the second half of the regular season.

Several hours before the ceremonial first pitch, Ban Johnson, the meddling president of the American League, visited Connie Mack's office and urged the Philadelphia manager not to place the fate of the second game of the World Series in the hands of Eddie Plank. "He's too old," Johnson insisted. "His skills have diminished. He won't get the job done."

Mack wouldn't hear of it. He'd called on the unflappable Plank to pitch against the best the opposition had to offer so many times in the past that pundits rightfully pinned the tag "A Big-Game Pitcher" on "Gettysburg Eddie." Plank did not panic when things got tough: he'd been there before; he still had power, control, and intelligence behind his pitches.

President Johnson smiled at his former protégé (Connie Mack), exchanged handshakes, and accompanied him down to the sedate Athletics dressing room. Standing before the players, the president of the American League delivered a brief, intense, emotional pep talk, challenging the boys to bounce back. He implored them to "rise up and be better than you were yesterday." A few listened attentively, others drifted away.

The capacity crowd of 20,562 exploded in four solid minutes of thunderous applause when Plank took the mound, showering the old boy with a blizzard of affection. Cheers and whistles and foot stomping resonated throughout the ballpark.

"He's a piece of work," an Athletics rooter said.

"He sure is," a friend replied, "but he's an old man. How long can he keep it up? It's boiling hot today." More than a few writers voiced the same opinion.

The game turned into a thrilling pitchers' duel, a treat from start to finish, one of the prettiest contests of the season. The Braves so dominated the Athletics that it seemed to many of those present that they actually held the lead throughout the game. That wasn't what happened. Gettysburg Eddie kept Boston's hits well scattered and somehow managed to control the contest. Inning after inning the scoreboard kept growing zeros. Not once did he deliver a pitch without first going through a maddening belt and cap routine.

"Why," a frustrated Boston fan complained, "can't he get a belt that fits him? He's slowing down the game."

That was exactly what Eddie was trying to do. Slow down the game. It was all about timing and rhythm, rhythm and timing, disrupting the batter's adjustments, changing speeds, changing locations, working the hitters, being mentally tough, and staying one step ahead of the hitter. His work was as precise as that of an eye surgeon.

The Braves put runners on base often enough (every inning except the seventh) and hit Plank freely enough, but Eddie dictated play and kept Stallings's charges at bay, harmless all afternoon.

Boston's "Big Bill" James was even more impressive. Once Stallings's young lion got comfortable and found his groove, he looked like the greatest pitcher in the world. So feeble were the Mackmen's bats—flailing away at James's lively fastball and dazzling spitter—hitters seemed overmatched. Most of them looked like they were facing a major-league hurler for the first time. James set them aside at a brisk pace. He was loose and fast, and every pitch broke the way he wanted it to break. At times it seemed like all he was doing was playing catch with his battery mate, Hank Gowdy.

The Athletics were so baffled by Big Bill's prowess, they began to wonder if he might be tampering with the ball and closely watched his every move. They even went so far as to furtively examine the ball to see if the surface had been roughened. The Mackmen, it seems, had been warned that the Braves hurler might have used an emery ball during the regular season, and not a spitter as was generally assumed. (The emery ball had recently been banned as an illegal pitch.)

Bill was working so well that only rarely did the Athletics drive a ball out of the infield. He was, in fact, so deadly effective that he threw a tidy

77 pitches in facing the minimum of 24 batters in the first eight innings of the game. The zeros on the scoreboard were proof of his efficiency. Of the three batters who did reach base safely (Murphy walked in the first; Schang doubled down the left field foul line in the sixth; Collins managed a scratch infield single in the seventh), two were caught napping and one was caught stealing.

It didn't seem like either team could score a run before darkness settled over the field. Of the two starting pitchers, young James was tiring more quickly than his geriatric opponent, a pitcher old enough to be James's father. Plank's athleticism was striking. He somehow managed to grow stronger under the rays of the glaring sun, even after throwing 110 pitches in eight innings.

The enormous yellow sun was getting seriously low in the sky when Gettysburg Eddie walked out to the mound for the top of the ninth. It raked the field at an angle that turned the shadows of the players into Giacometti-like figures. Seemingly oblivious to the applause being showered on him for a job well done, Plank drew a sleeve across his reddened face, rubbed up the ball, turned in the direction of the scoreboard, and studied the two long rows of zeroes after the words "Visitors" and "Home." It was anybody's game.

Watching from the Philadelphia bench, his right hand clasping a program, Connie Mack made a quick hard motion, moving center fielder Amos Strunk over to his right a couple of steps. Not a word was spoken. A simple flick of the program was enough. Strunk, the sweetest, swiftest, surest center fielder in all of baseball, lifted his eyes, squinted into the late afternoon sun, screwed up his face, and scanned the ballpark. Then, rubbing his eyes to clear them, shifted his gaze to a distant figure standing in the shadow of the grandstand. It was Rabbit Maranville, leading off for the Braves in the top of the ninth.

Mentally gearing up, the Rab tossed his head back and forth, blessed himself with the sign of the cross, an unconscious gesture, stepped into the batter's box, scraped the soft earth with his spikes, tapped the plate, brought up the bat, flexed his knees, and took a couple of practice swings. Rabbit was working on a perfect day at bat.

The overworked lungs of the Royal Rooters implored Rabbit to "do something." Thoroughly revved up, they beat their palms and whooped it up and gave the popular Braves shortstop three rousing cheers. "Hooray for Maranville! Hip, hip, hooray! Hip, hip, hooray!" A big spirited grin shot across Rab's face.

Pouncing on Plank's first pitch, Rabbit lined a sharp ground ball past the outstretched glove of third baseman Frank Baker. Jack Barry, sprinting to his right, knocked down the ball where the infield meets the outfield grass, picked it up, and tossed an off-balance throw across the diamond, low and wide of first base. Though there wasn't a chance in a hundred of McInnis getting his mitt on the ball, much less catching it, the talented first baseman didn't give up on it. Extending himself as far as he could, he hooked his toe on the bag and fell forward, his glove slapping the ground the instant the ball arrived. And in some inexplicable way, he held onto it for the out. At long last, things were looking up for the Athletics.

With Maranville out of the way, the hometown fans exhaled a sigh of relief and sat back and relaxed. Why not? Charlie Deal and Bill James, the light artillery in the Braves lineup, were coming up next. They were nonfactors at the plate, the easiest outs in the batting order.

Slight, pale, and mostly anonymous, Charlie Deal, wearing a worried expression, trudged toward home plate, his steps leaden, as if he were walking up a hill to the gallows. Charlie, a batter who might as well have been nicknamed "Dead Meat," was hitless in the series, failing dismally with the bat, having hit into three double plays in the opening contest, and stranding five base runners in this, the second game, alone, three of the base runners in scoring position. He had yet to drive the ball out of the infield.

Honey Fitz rose from his chair, faced the happy hour boys, and jovially led the 500-odd Beantown boosters in a cheer for Charlie: "Hooray for Deal! Hip, Hip, hooray! Hip, hip, hooray!" and then they sang a song:

Deal! Deal! Deal!
Can't you wield the stick at all?
Can't you hit the bloomin' ball?
For Gawd's sake, hit a single, Mr. Deal.

Deal! Deal! Deal!
Can't you help us?
Can't you see the way we feel?
Hit. Summon all your grit. And deal us a hit.

Talk about putting pressure on a bundle of nerves. Mouth twitching uncertainly, poor Charlie struggled to control his emotions; dry thick spittle covered his tongue, and his knuckles turned white as his hands squeezed the handle of the bat.

Plank could not help but notice. The old master stepped back off the pitching rubber, knocked dirt from his cleats, pulled up his socks, unbuckled and buckled his belt, rebuttoned his shirt, repositioned his cap, and watched Deal squirm. Eddie then stepped back on the rubber, stared at the ball, rolled it around in his hand and—

"Throw the damn ball!" a frustrated Boston fan yelled.

Plank did just that. He tossed the ball to the umpire, asked for another, and repeated the same excruciating routine all over again. It was enough to give young Charlie Deal a nervous breakdown.

Charlie took a big cut at the first pitch, after it had gone by for a strike. He was overmatched. A chorus of groans rose from the crowd. "Take him out!" someone yelled. "Give him a broomstick," somebody else shouted. "He can't do nothin' with a bat." Plank smiled behind his glove.

Hoping to get Deal to swing at a bad pitch, Eddie ran the count to two balls and a strike. Deal didn't bite. Though he did hear a fan shout: "Oh, hurry up and strike out," and tried to ignore it.

Plank then uncorked the cross-fire fastball, his bread-and-butter pitch, the same pitch that had baffled the Braves all afternoon. Deal swung, met the ball near the end of the bat, and sent it soaring into center field, directly at Amos Strunk, an easy out. Staring upward into the laser-like sun, Strunk took a quick step in, changed his mind, retreated, put his gloved hand up to shield his eyes, and zeroed in on the ball a split second before it streaked out of the dark shadows cast by the towering grandstand.

Bedazzled by the bouncing light, Strunk was suddenly out of sync with his surroundings, the ball lost in the sun. He couldn't pick it up until he saw it arching high over his head. Racing back with all the speed for which he was famous, he made a frantic last-second effort to redeem himself. Too late.

Wild-eyed, the Boston crowd leapt to its feet and cheered joyously as Deal slid safely into second base, kicking up a cloud of dust.

Feeling alive all over, Charlie pranced off second base, back and forth, betraying a careless eagerness, taking more than an ordinary lead. The Boston crowd came alive, chanting: "We want a hit." "We want a hit." "We want a hit." This was an opportunity the Braves could not afford to squander.

"Plank was easy to get a jump on," Home Run Baker remarked. "Rarely would he throw to a base unless the runner had an enormous lead."

Anticipating a sacrifice bunt, catcher Wally Schang noted that Deal was too far off second base, so far off, in fact, that he was guilty of base-running stupidity. Smart base runners did not take that kind of lead on Wally Schang. He threw bullets from a crouch. And Wally signaled for a pitchout.

James squared away for a bunt. Plank didn't even bother looking the runner back. He quickly blazed a fastball across the letters—high and away—where he'd kept his pitches to James all afternoon.

Certain that James would put the ball in play, Deal strayed farther off second base.

Big Bill missed the pitch by a foot.

"Stee-rike," umpire Hildebrand snarled.

The moment Schang cocked his arm, Deal realized he was dead wood waiting to be cleared away. Desperation led to daring. Charlie broke for third, knowing full well they had him.

Open-mouthed Boston fans groaned as Schang shot a throw to Jack Barry, covering second base. A perfect peg. Barry turned to throw out Deal at third, but he just stood there, just held the ball, and watched Deal slide safely into third. The ballpark was dumbfounded. What fans didn't know was that Barry had failed to get a good grip on the ball. It popped out of his hand and ran up to the top of his fingertips. An accurate throw would have been impossible, given the circumstances.

Though Plank was having a hard time of it, he shook off Barry's misstep and went to work on Bill James, striking him out for the fourth consecutive time on three pitches.

The strikeout did not lessen the enthusiasm of the Boston fans. Honey Fitz led the constant cheering of the Royal Rooters. With two outs and a runner on third, it was up to Les Mann. Les had singled sharply to center in the fifth inning.

Collins called time. He and McInnis walked over to Plank. The A's second baseman made a slight nod toward Schang, Baker, and Barry, asking them to join the confab.

The crowd quieted.

When play resumed, Mann swung at the second pitch he saw and made enough contact to muscle a soft broken-bat fly ball into shallow right-center. Second baseman Eddie Collins turned on the dead run, leaped into the air, threw out his gloved hand, snared the ball for a split second before sprawling onto the outfield grass, and watched helplessly as the ball rolled off his fingertips for a base hit. He never had possession of it.

Deal slid across the plate, giving the Braves a 1–0 lead, sending the Boston crowd into a frenzy. Charlie was about the happiest man in the world when he got to his feet and brushed off his uniform. He let out a tribal yell and embraced everybody in his path. It was one of those rare intoxicating moments every aspiring young ballplayer dreams about and seldom experiences. The rarest of moments.

Greeting Deal with a standing ovation, the Royal Rooters exploded into euphoric singing, the most exuberant voice in the chorus belonging to the popular William Shea, better known as "Blooch," who seemed to be vying with Little Fitzie for the role of leading entertainer of the afternoon.

Victory was just three outs away. The way Bill James was pitching, there wasn't any way they could lose. Fans began to filter out of the ballpark, that is, until the previously invincible James walked Jack Barry, leading off in the last of the ninth. This kept the Athletics' hopes alive and quieted the crowd, many of whom realized that a base on balls issued to the first batter of an inning frequently leads to the scoring of a run.

James was fearless, though, and full of confidence in what he was doing, knowing full well that he threw the ball harder than almost anyone else in baseball. Making each confrontation personal, much like Bob Gibson, the St. Louis Cardinal great of the 1960s, James enjoyed attacking hitters, daring them to hit his fastball. I'll just hum it in there, baby, he seemed to say, and let's see who is better, you or me?

After almost twice picking Jack Barry off first base, Bill turned his attention to the batter, Wally Schang. With the infield creeping in, Schang laid down two sacrifice bunts; each of them rolled foul. Having failed to advance the runner with the two bunts, Schang set himself in the batter's box and swung away at the 0–2 pitch, slashing the air in vain at a mitt-popping fastball. Strike three. Gowdy dropped the ball, and Barry took off for second. Gowdy chased after it and unthinkingly fired a bullet to first base, forgetting that the batter was automatically out when first base is occupied. The official scorer credited Barry with a stolen base.

Connie Mack called on Jimmy Walsh to pinch hit for the pitcher.

Going against the conventional wisdom of never putting the winning run on base, George Stallings countered Mack's move by ordering an intentional pass. Four wide ones put Walsh on first and set up the possibility of a double play.

Eddie Murphy drew huge cheers from the throng. Batting with a sense of urgency, Murphy held his bat directly in front of himself, stared at it, focused on James, and waited, calm, grim, and resolved, intent on inflicting a crushing blow on the Braves.

Jack Barry took a cautious lead off second base. There was one out and Walsh, the winning run, took a step or two off first. Murphy dug in, tightened his grip on the bat, aware that in a minute or two he would be either a hero or a bum. Hearts beat faster. The pressure was withering, the uproar deafening.

Every Braves player was on the top step of the dugout, while manager Stallings, sitting cross-legged on the bench, raised his foot-beat to about 150 beats a minute, putting on his fedora, taking it off, and putting it on again, his expression laced with worry.

Captain Johnny Evers pulled the Braves infield into double-play depth, Charlie Deal positioned himself 10 feet off third, and Rabbit Maranville 15 feet off second.

"Kiddo," the pugnacious Evers called out in an abrupt authoritative manner, "you oughta play closer to the bag."

Maranville shuffled over a couple of steps.

Evers wasn't satisfied. "That's not enough," he said in a voice more barbed wire than honeysuckle. "Get closer."

Maranville moved over a couple more steps. ("I was eight feet away," he later recalled.)

The humorless Evers threw him a sharp look: "Get closer, goddamn it."

"What do you want? I'm almost standing on the bag right now," the rebellious Rabbit noised, looking at Evers and holding out his hands, palms up.

The battle-hardened Evers narrowed his eyes: "Maranville," he said, baring his teeth with snarling abruptness (the use of Rabbit's last name betrayed Evers's anger), "get right on it."

Rabbit bristled at the savagery in Evers's voice.

"Suppose he hits one in the hole?"

"He's never hit the goddamn ball to left field in his life . . . Now move."

Evers got his way.

Confidence sometimes falters in tight situations and so do mechanics. A thread of self-doubt crept into young James's mind. He was getting a bit anxious. Breathing heavily down his nostrils, he studied Gowdy's sign, nodded, checked Barry at second, took a deep breath, and unleashed a diving, darting spitter to the left-handed-hitting Murphy.

"Bo-ool one!" umpire Hildebrand growled.

James winced, his mouth drooping a little at the corners, his heart knocking in his chest.

The mounting bedlam in the stands was unreal.

Hank Gowdy popped up from his crouch, pumped his fist at James, and talked up a storm, a one-way conversation. The count on Murphy ran to two balls and two strikes. The big moment was approaching. Murphy called time, stepped out of the box, practiced a couple of swings, aiming downward, and stepped up to the plate with the look of a man who was about to do something big.

Trying to control his emotions and brandishing a tough-guy attitude, although the inner Bill James did not feel that way, the big right-hander stood atop the rubber, grabbed his scrotum and gave it a tug, aimed a spurt of chaw into the grass, leaned forward, his glove on his left knee, got the sign from Gowdy, straightened up, looked Barry back at second, took a deep breath, and started his motion. Sticking to his strength, he put a biting fastball in the part of the strike zone where Murphy was least likely to do any damage. A good pitch.

Thwack! The thrilling sound of Murphy's bat connecting echoed around the ballpark. A smoking liner shot through James's legs. The ball had center field written all over it.

Maranville instinctively darted to his left, lunged, and speared the ball an instant before his foot brushed second base, retiring Walsh. Turning his body, Rabbit pivoted, whirled into the air, and fired a throw to first base, a hundredth of a second before Walsh came crashing into him, taking him out of the play. Schmidt stretched, reached for the throw, gathered it in, and got the speedy Murphy by a full step.* The ball game was over. A 1–0 Braves victory.

Thunderstruck by the head-spinning play, Philadelphia fans sat back with withered looks and acted as if they'd just witnessed a horrible traffic accident, their roaring voices giving way to stunned silence. The Boston crowd was thrilled. "It was the best play I ever saw" was all you heard from them as they were leaving the ballpark.

Yet, if it hadn't been for Johnny Evers's knowledge of the game and his clever positioning of Maranville, Murphy's blow would have been a base hit, instead of a double-play ball, and there might have been a different outcome to the game.

Rabbit's teammates jumped up and down, and danced and hugged, unaware of a disaster in their midst.

"He's hurt! He's hurt!" someone cried out.

"Rabbit is down!"

The words registered on George Stallings's face. His head spun around. His eyes stared. His heart sank. He was looking at his worst nightmare. Rabbit Maranville down. An alarmed silence ended the celebration in the dugout. Everybody held their breath.

Cap askew, face drawn in pain, the Rab, mumbling to himself, struggled to get up and fell back down, his legs folding under him. A minute later,

---

* It was the first time Murphy had hit into a double play all season.

the scrappy Braves shortstop climbed to his feet once more, dazed, shaking his head, trying to clear it, a touch of grimness on his face. Though woozy and walking unsteadily—he tried not to limp, Rabbit slowly made his way back to the Boston bench.

The moment he reached the top step of the dugout, he collapsed into George Stallings's waiting arms. Anxious moments followed. But, as it turned out, Rabbit was not badly hurt. The stuffing was knocked out of him. That's all.

Once again, the Boston Braves had punctured Philadelphia's invincible aura and sent the stunned Athletics down to their second straight defeat. Philadelphia was far from beaten, though: "The series isn't over yet," a defiant Connie Mack said. "Not by a long shot . . . We expect things will be different in Boston."

But the Braves were a confident bunch. Making the most of the psychological moment, Stallings ordered the team's road uniforms, traveling equipment, and trunks taken back to Boston with the team. "We won't need our room reservations," he told Jim McCarthy, the hotel manager. "We won't be coming back. It will be over after the two games in Boston."

It was a shrewd emotional ploy.

CHAPTER 56

THE VOICES TOLD THE STORY

The Braves' chances of winning the World Series were far greater on Monday than they were three days earlier. The thinking now among pundits was: the unstoppable Boston juggernaut would send the Mackmen crashing down to a bitter defeat. Stallings's boys looked that good. They were totally focused on closing out the penultimate chapter of their enchanted season.

"Every man on my club believes we outclass Connie Mack's team in every way," Stallings said, "and in place of trying to put courage in their souls, I've had to try to make them believe that, although they are the better team, they still have a fight on their hands, even though the Athletics have not exactly covered themselves with glory."

The Mackmen were an angry team, a wounded team, a team that had done a lot of soul-searching. Armageddon was at hand. Their backs were to the wall, and they were extremely dangerous. They knew the time had come to pump themselves up and draw back from the precipice, or face the prospect of stumbling into the abyss of irrelevance.

Failures at the number two position in the batting order (Oldring) and the number four position (Baker), two of the A's most dangerous offensive threats, seriously weakened the team's heretofore potent offense. Oldring and Baker, the connecting links of the first five rungs of the lineup, just couldn't get untracked. To make matters worse, the A's learned on Sunday, a travel day, that Amos Strunk, their speedy center fielder, would be sidelined by an abscessed finger injured during batting practice the previous week. With Strunk out of the lineup, and Oldring and Baker not hitting, the Athletics were no longer the menacing force they once were.

Monday was an Indian summer day, mostly sunny and dry, the air crisp, the cool edge giving the setting just enough snap to remind the people of Boston that it was autumn.

General admission tickets at Fenway Park sold out quickly. Though shut out by the thousands, fans hung around anyway, clogging the streets outside of the ballpark, waiting patiently for accounts of the action, the details of which were cheerfully passed down from above by men and boys in the top-row seats. A squad of patrolmen and three mounted police from Station 16 were on hand to keep order, but their presence wasn't needed.

A jovial character with a gap-toothed smile, garbed in the costume of an early pilgrim, strolled up and down the aisles of the grandstand, a silly grin on his face, wearing a string of sausages around his neck, and another around his hat, and drew attention to himself by ringing a bell. The counterfeit Puritan carried a sign reading:

FOR SALE: BRAVES SAUSAGES.
MADE FROM CONNIE'S GOAT.

Shortly before two, a shiny Chalmer's Light Six, driven by Harry Pyke, entered the first-base entrance of the ballpark and came to a stop in front of the grandstand. It was a reward for Captain Johnny Evers, the National League's most valuable player. Speaking on behalf of Hugh Chalmers, the trophy's donor, who was recovering from surgery at the Mayo Clinic in Rochester, Minnesota, Ron Mulford Jr., chairman of the Most Valuable Player committee, made the presentation, after which Evers and a carload of his teammates were driven around the ballpark, much to the delight of the capacity crowd of 35,520.

Dick Rudolph, warming up in the right field bull pen, was everybody's choice as the starting pitcher for the Braves. James and Tyler joined Rudy, each throwing earnestly, all taking batting practice as well. The show of arms was in keeping with Stallings's blueprint for prolonging the Mackmen's uncertainty about his choice of a starter. The National League champions had their American League rivals on the run, and Stallings intended to keep it that way.

"Bullet Joe" Bush, the 21-year-old pitching sensation from the 1913 World Series, and Albert Bender, the Athletics' ace, who was charged with the loss in the first game, were warming up in front of the visitors' bench.

Stallings had settled on Rudolph as his starting pitcher. The Big Chief was convinced that Rudy could snuff out the Athletics a second time in four days, and just about ensure the world championship for the Braves. The other possible starter, Lefty Tyler, was "thought not to have the goods," Fenway being a troublesome place for left-handed pitchers, particularly with temporary bleachers having been built for the Royal Rooters in front of the left field wall.

Several of the Braves urged the boss to reconsider: "Think back to the regular season," they argued. "Lefty always came through in big games. He's rested, he's stronger than he's been in a long time, and his left-handed slants are sure to tame the Athletics."

Heeding the exhortations of the players, Stallings listened, thought about the appeal, retraced in his mind Tyler's clutch performances of the past season, weighed the evidence, reflected on it, deliberated, and, at the last minute, switched pitchers. He named Lefty Tyler to start Game Three of the 1914 World Series.

Cheering started before some fans were settled into their seats. Philadelphia's leadoff hitter, Eddie Murphy, smacked a 1–1 pitch, the third pitch of the game, down the left field foul line for an opposite field double. Showing renewed enthusiasm, Quaker City fans roared their approval, particularly the *Philadelphia Inquirer*'s "Famous Fifty," the paper's contest winners seated behind the Athletics' dugout.

The second batter of the game, Rube Oldring, attempted to advance Murphy with a sacrifice bunt. He deadened Tyler's first pitch and pushed the ball a few feet to the left of the mound, carefully keeping it away from Charlie Deal at third base. Tyler, fielding his position well, bare-handed the ball, fumbled it, recovered, and got Oldring by a half step at first. Murphy advanced to third on the play.

Carrying out a dicey maneuver early in the game, Captain Johnny Evers, the consummate pro and driving force behind the Braves' all-out effort, brought outfielders in a couple of steps, hoping for a play at the plate. Sure enough, Eddie Collins, Philadelphia's most dangerous hitter, looked for a curveball, got one, met it squarely, and drilled a low liner into left field, directly at Joey Connolly. In his eagerness to throw out the runner at home, Joey made a clean muff of the ball, an error that allowed Murphy to prance home easily from third base and give the Mackmen the early lead.

Home Run Baker, the cleanup hitter, smug in his self-confidence, flashed an ear-to-ear grin in Tyler's direction. It was not well received.

Though in a dangerous situation, "Slats" pulled himself together, took advantage of Baker's cockiness, and, careful not to let Bake extend his arms, got two quick strikes on the power-hitting third baseman. Lefty then laid a fast one in on the hands and struck out the big fellow, swinging. Bat in hand, Baker spun around, a pained theatrical expression on his face, silently screamed at the war club, and sent it flying in the direction of the Philadelphia dugout.

Tyler then allowed Stuffy McInnis to get away from him, walking the A's number five batter on six pitches. Now it was up to Jimmy Walsh.

On the bench, manager Stallings, nostrils expanded, his lips tightened, he mumbled words about taking out Tyler that had to fight their way through clenched teeth. He groaned in dismay with each pitch and jerked his head around and cast a glance at James and Hess throwing in the Braves bull pen. Sunburned faces along the bench kept an eye on the Big Chief. What would he do?

He stayed with Tyler.

After taking a couple of practice swings, Jimmy Walsh prepared to face the Braves' left-hander. Taking a big lead, Fast Eddie Collins wandered off second. Eddie was dangerous on the base paths. His speed alone could transform a close game into a victory. Noticing that Collins was all but ignoring him, Johnny Evers inched over behind second base. Tyler whirled and fired a bulletlike throw to Evers. A set play. In that crucial split second Tyler caught Collins leaning the wrong way. He was out. The pickoff ended what might have been a big first inning for the Athletics.

In the Braves' half of the second, Rabbit Maranville coaxed a walk from Bush and listened with a smile on his face as Fenway rumbled to life.

Hammerin' Hank Gowdy, the one Braves batter on a hitting spree, stepped into the batter's box. Hank tapped the end of his bat on the dish and readied himself. Taking plenty of time, Bullet Joe assessed the situation in front of him, forgetting about Rabbit Maranville leading off first base. Noticing Bush's inattention, Rabbit lengthened his lead. When Bullet Joe delivered, the Rab turned and was on his way, digging for second, his arms shredding the air. Gowdy swung and missed and watched Rabbit slide into second under Collins's late tag. The Athletics did not look good on the play.

Bullet Joe challenged Gowdy again, this time leaving a belt-high fastball over the heart of the plate. Gowdy pounced on it, connected, and lifted a high fly ball toward the temporary bleachers in left, an area normally part of the playing field. Oldring loped over, positioned himself in front of the four-foot-high fence, waited, waited, leaped for the ball, and missed the catch by a foot. The ball disappeared into the temporary seats. A ground rule double. Oldring stared after it and shook his head. The ball most certainly would have died in his glove had the temporary bleachers not been there. Gowdy, standing on second, smiled a long, deep smile of silent delight as Maranville crossed the plate with the tying run.

The cheering for Gowdy did not stop. It went on and on until it seemed like it would never end. And it didn't. Not until the inning ended.

To open the Philadelphia fourth, Eddie Collins lined out to Evers, and Home Run Baker froze on a groan-inducing third strike. Bake felt like he was living a bad dream.

"Nice eye, Bake . . . Nice eye," a fan shouted.

"You want them to roll them to you, Bake?" another voice rang out. "Is that what you want?" The voices told the story.

This brought up Stuffy McInnis, one of the best hitters in the game. When a Tyler pitch came in high and fat, Stuffy drove a towering fly down the left field line. Connolly backpedaled, extended his glove over the wall, jumped, took a stab at it, missed, and tumbled into the crowd. A ground rule double. Connolly's teammates stared, waited, and held their breath, transfixed.

Seconds later, up popped Joey, laughing, talking, beaming from ear to ear, evidently none the worse for the fall. Several Royal Rooters and umpire Bill Byron hoisted the popular left fielder over the low fence and back onto the field. The hometown crowd welcomed Joey's return with adoring cheers.

Though two men were out, the A's were dangerous. A man was in scoring position, and the always troublesome Jimmy Walsh was at the plate. Walsh, swinging away, slashed a sizzler past Charlie Deal's glove.

As McInnis rounded third, Deal tripped him, a tactic the Braves sometimes used in their take-no-prisoners style of play. Though Stuffy and third-base coach Harry Davis complained bitterly, umpire Bill Klem told them there was nothing he could do about it; McInnis had scored on the play, giving the Athletics a 2–1 lead.

With one out in the Braves' half of the fourth, Butch Schmidt poked a humpbacked liner over Bush's head into center field for a base hit and advanced to second on a ground out by Charlie Deal. Schmidt was now in scoring position.

Rabbit Maranville, batting from the right side, lifted a little looper into shallow right-center. Jimmy Walsh streaked in, dived, and came up empty. The Texas League single drove in Schmidt and tied the game at 2–2. Fenway roared full-throatedly.

The Braves' offense went stagnant after that, their bats remaining largely silent through innings five, six, seven, and eight, while the Athletics, perhaps tiring of getting their noses bloodied, made a lot of noise at the plate, inning after inning, hammering away at Lefty Tyler's deliveries. But they did not score. The game remained a 2–2 tie.

Though Slats's pitches showed good movement, he didn't have his best stuff, was not efficient, and labored constantly, often having to pitch his way out of trouble, something he did extremely well. When Lefty showed signs of becoming a casualty to the Athletics' bats in the top of the ninth, Rabbit Maranville saved him with a wonderful stop of a wicked grounder—talk about soft hands—and an acrobatic throw that cut down the runner at first base.

Home Run Baker then clubbed a heart-stopping double down the right field line, bringing up Stuffy McInnis, the number five hitter in Philadelphia's batting order. A good stickman, McInnis dug around the batter's box to make it just right.

Swinging at Tyler's third offering, McInnis smacked the ball on the nose and drove it into deep left-center, a high drive that looked like it would leave the ballpark and give the Athletics the game. But the wind held it back long enough for Connolly to track it down and make the catch.

Stallings ordered an intentional pass for Jimmy Walsh, preferring to take his chances on "Black Jack" Barry, the weakest link in the Athletics' lineup. Dripping sweat and looking fatigued, Tyler tugged at his damp, baggy jersey, studied the sign, nodded assent, and pounded a fastball inside for a strike. Next he showed Barry a slow curve that hung over the inside corner, and Barry ripped a bullet down the left field line, foul. This put Barry into an 0–2 count. But it was still a dangerous situation. All the Athletics needed was a base hit.

Tyler reached for the resin bag, dusted his hand, bent forward, got the sign, nodded, took a look at Baker leading off second, and delivered a high fastball in on the hands. A real thumb breaker. Barry thought it hittable, but all he could do was raise a pop-up into foul territory. Gowdy moved under it near the Philadelphia bench.

"You got room. You got room," Evers shouted from second base. Gowdy made the play while falling down the steps of the visitors' dugout, bringing the top half of the ninth to a close.

In the last half of the ninth inning, Joe Bush, the epitome of calm, retired the Braves in one-two-three order, silencing their bats for the fifth inning in a row.

The game would go into extra innings.

CHAPTER 57

IT WAS HIGH DRAMA TIME

Leading off for the Athletics in the top of the 10th, Wally Schang worked the count full. Tyler didn't like the calls. He kicked at the earth and unloaded his frustrations, his eyes throwing sarcastic sparks at umpire Bill Klem, calling balls and strikes behind the plate. When Lefty finally got around to delivering the payoff pitch, a fastball, it ran over the inside corner of the plate, and Schang, a switch-hitter, batting from the right side, smoked a hard-liner through the hole in the left side of the infield. The ball shot past Charlie Deal so fast, Charlie didn't even have a chance to wave at it.

Almost everyone in the ballpark thought Mack would pinch-hit for Joe Bush, but Mack stayed with his pitcher and ordered a sacrifice bunt. Bush, a good bunter, laid down a beauty, 20 feet up the third-base line. The ball twisted foul. Bush tried again. Same result. After twice failing to advance his speedy battery mate, Bullet Joe struck out swinging at a curve that broke so low it almost grazed his shoelaces.

With Eddie Murphy at bat, the Mackmen sprang a hit-and-run surprise on the boys from Boston. Schang bolted for second on Tyler's first movement. Murphy topped the pitch and sent a weak dribbler back at Tyler. The sensible play was at first. A certain out. But Tyler, thinking double play, ignored good sense, whirled, and pumped a throw to Rabbit Maranville, covering second base. Too late. Maranville's throw to first failed to catch Murphy, and for the first time in the series the Braves looked rattled.

"They sprang the hit-and-run on us," Evers explained, "when we weren't looking for it, one of the few plays in the series we had not been set for."

This brought up Rube Oldring, still hitless in the series. Jumping on the first pitch, Rube lined a one-hop shot off Tyler's glove. The ball bounded toward Evers. Johnny charged, bare-handed the ball on the run, and made a crisp side-arm throw to first, nipping Oldring by an eyelash. Schang and Murphy moved up a base on the play. Now there were two outs, and the Mackmen had two runners in scoring position.

With first base open and Eddie Collins, the American League's most valuable player, striding toward the plate, Stallings signaled: put him on.

After giving Collins an intentional pass, Tyler took a few steps off the mound, his face heavily beaded with perspiration, the tip of his tongue between his teeth. Whatever edge he might have had earlier in the game had been dulled by fatigue. Visibly worse for wear, he spit on the mound and ground it in with his toe, mopped his brow, and noticed the infielders closing in on him.

"You out of gas?" Evers asked.

"I'm okay," Tyler said, hiking up his belt. "I'm tired but I can get this guy out for you."

"This guy," as Tyler put it, the man standing outside the batter's box, twisting his head slowly from side to side and flexing his shoulders, just happened to be Philadelphia's imperial first baseman, the celebrated slugger, Home Run Baker, the home run hero of two previous world championship series.

Baker's black bat swung back and forth as he crouched over the plate. Tyler did not waver. Chin thrust forward, ready to do battle, he tugged the visor of his cap low on his head, held his glove high over his lips, narrowed his eyes, and studied Gowdy's sign. Slats started Baker off with a two-seam fastball, inside. Bake went after it and hooked a liner into the seats beyond first base—foul. Strike one.

After falling behind 2–1 on the count, Tyler tried running a curve in on Baker's hands and left it out over the plate. Bake unleashed a ferocious hack. The ball exploded off the big guy's bat, cruised over the infield like a projectile, and took a sharp hop near the outfield grass, 20 feet off second base. Johnny Evers made a marvelous effort to choke off Baker's bid for a hit and keep Schang from scoring, but the ball took a bad hop, struck John on the left shoulder, and fell dead several feet away. Johnny scrambled after it, picked it up, and dropped it, picked it up, and dropped it again. Schang scored, giving Philadelphia a 3–2 lead.

Evers was 100 percent hustle in every game, every day, from start to finish. This time he'd slipped up. Even the elite do. After mishandling the opportunity to cut off the winning run, Captain Johnny just stood there and hung his head, crestfallen, his self-lacerating disappointment intensifying into disabling anger.

Eddie Murphy, having advanced to third on the misplay, edged farther and farther off the bag, all while watching Evers. Suddenly, Murphy sprinted for home.

"Throw the ball! Throw the ball!" Maranville screamed. But Evers had a brain cramp. He didn't react until Murphy was across the plate, the rankest kind of misplay. The visiting Athletics were now up by two runs, 4–2.

Waving blue pennants with the image of a white elephant on them, Quaker City fans sang the praises of Schang, Murphy, and Baker. It looked like the Athletics were about to score again when Stuffy McInnis lined a shoulder-high fastball deep into to left-center. Hustling back and to his right, Possum Whitted sized up the towering drive, leapt high into the air, and made a nifty catch for the third out as he bumped into the wall with his glove hand.

Stallings did not let Evers's reputation stand in the way of a tongue-lashing when the star second baseman returned to the bench. And Evers took it like a man.

If ever a team needed inspiration, it was the Braves. The Royal Rooters did their best to rally the boys with a rhythmic pattern of drums—boom-da-da-da-boom-boom-da-da—and roaring brasses and the cymbal crashes, and the joyful singing of "Tessie." None of it helped.

Bullet Joe Bush was on the cusp of victory. What could go wrong? Nothing. The way he was smoking them in, the celebrated fireballer Walter Johnson didn't have anything on him. It was time to finish off the Hub City crew.

Hank Gowdy stepped into the batter's box. He'd just told his pal Rabbit Maranville that he was going to pull a surprise on Bush. "He's been trying to slip a fast one over on me every time on the first pitch," Gowdy told Rabbit. "If he tries it this time, I'm going to kiss it goodbye. You watch that ball fly."

Gowdy was greeted with a tremendous ovation.

Pitching with a two-run lead, Bush toed the rubber, let his right arm dangle and sway back and forth at his side, hunched low, stared at Schang's mitt, considered the sign, nodded approval, kicked his left foot high into the air, and whipped his right arm forward, catapulting a fastball inside to the right-handed-hitting Gowdy. The pitch drifted over the plate.

Thwock! The electrifying sound rent the air. Gowdy did not so much as make contact as detonate the ball, and he watched the prodigious blast as it soared deep into right-center. Jimmy Walsh chased after the towering drive and let out an anguished yowl when he failed to catch up with it. The ball took a huge bounce and deposited itself in the lap of a fan 10 rows up in the bleachers. A home run. (Balls bouncing into the stands in those days were counted as home runs.) The score was 4–3. The Braves now trailed by a run.

The crowd went into a frenzy. Cheering was just as enthusiastic on the rooftops of apartment houses and office buildings around Fenway. The titanic wallop put new life into the Braves.

Rabbit Maranville, manning the coach's box at first base, acted like a human whirligig, a perpetual motion machine. His mouth was working a mile a minute, his quick feet leaping high into the air; he turned cartwheels and hopped around in full live-wire mode.

The Mackmen viewed Maranville's madcap behavior as amateurish. They did admit, however, that it bothered Bullet Joe. Baker, Barry, Collins, McInnis, and Schang hurried over to the center of the diamond and pleaded with Joe to "settle down." "Stop them now." "Finish them off."

Seemingly relaxed and confident, Bush nodded and toed the rubber and went after loosey-goosey Josh DeVore, pinch-hitting for Tyler. Joe pumped a fastball over for a strike, daring Josh to hit it. No way. About all "Mister Swing at Everything" could muster was a weak foul tip. Josh couldn't catch up with the second pitch either. He ended up striking out swinging, and he walked back to the Braves' bench, dragging the bat behind him.

Herbie Moran, the next batter, wasn't hitting his weight either in the postseason series. Herbie had been an easy out at each of his plate appearances earlier in the afternoon. All Bush had to do was lay the ball in there. Put it over the plate. Let Moran try to hit it. It was as simple as that. But Bullet Joe's fastball sailed high and wide. He unexpectedly lost command. Moran seized the advantage, worked the count full, and walked. It was unintentional brinkmanship.

And who but Captain Johnny Evers of the badly botched play scenario was standing at the plate. A rush of exhilaration ran through the crowd. It was high drama time. Captain Johnny eyed Bullet Joe, bitterly, his lips snarling, his eyes fierce. There was an air about him that few people had seen before. He was determined to make up for his mistake.

Legions of fans chanted rhythmically: "Johnny! Johnny! Johnny!" They begged, they cajoled, they implored.

Evers and Bush glared at each other, their eyes blazing. Johnny filled his lungs with the cool autumn air and stepped into the batter's box, his body screaming concentration. It was the kind of moment when even hardened sportswriters couldn't help but keep the fan within them from taking over.

Bush understood the arithmetic. He needed two more outs and the game was his. A double play would do it.

The noise swelled.

Bush delivered. A blazing fastball. Evers swung through it and missed. He fouled off another. Strike two. The third pitch was wide. Ball one. Fenway throbbed with anticipation. Bush delivered again, and Evers foul tipped the ball into the waiting glove of Wally Schang. "Stee-rike three!" Hearts stopped—until the ball somehow skipped out of Schang's mitt, giving Evers a life.

Jaw tight, lips thin, face aflame, Captain Johnny glared at Bush, an angry feral stare—he was always a little angry. Instinct and guessing told him the next pitch would be a curve. The Braves captain waited. Bullet Joe came in with a sweeping curve. Evers slashed at the ball and sent it flying into the grass in right field—a base hit that spoke of his intelligence as a hitter. Moran moved into scoring position at third base. There was still only one out.

It was nail-biting time, the moment of truth. Could the Athletics keep the Braves from scoring? The entire ballpark seemed to quake with excitement.

Left-fielder Joey Connolly, the Braves' best hope, followed Evers in the lineup. The regular-season stalwart swung at the third ball pitched to him and crushed a high fly ball into deep center, 390 feet from home plate, the deepest part of the ballpark. Jimmy Walsh moved over, got under it, and gathered it in. His throw home didn't have a ghost of a chance of getting Moran at the plate. Herbie trotted home, tying the game, 4–4.

It was a pinch-me moment. The Braves had clawed their way back from a staggering blow. They had shown the Athletics that they could take a hit and battle back. They didn't panic, and they never stopped busting their tails. When they got a break, they took advantage of it. The inning ended in a 4–4 tie.

An inning later the last bit of light was getting used up. The ball was barely visible from the stands, and advancing darkness was softly rolling in over the field. For a moment, it looked like the umpires might call the game, but after many a glance at their watches and at the gathering dusk, Bill Klem and Bill Dinneen agreed on one more inning.

Leading off in the 12th, Murphy walked. The next batter, an overeager Rube Oldring, who, like the A's offense, had been wheezing for days, stepped up to the plate, a hangdog look on his face. ("What chance had I to play good ball," he later asked rhetorically, "when everyone in the ballpark was yelling at me that I deserted my wife?") Rube jumped on a bad pitch and hit a chopper off the plate. A Baltimore chop. James waited for the ball to come down and shoveled it over to first for the out. Murphy moved into scoring position at second.

Philadelphians seated behind the Athletics dugout sensed the possibility of a score. Collins, Baker, and McInnis were the scheduled batters: the heart of Philadelphia's "Murderer's Row." Pounding hearts watched and waited.

Eddie Collins, missing a grand opportunity to become a hero, popped up a 2–2 pitch and put a damper on the visiting crowd's enthusiasm. Charlie Deal took the ball in foul territory for the second out.

All was not lost, though. Not in the least. Wagging his big black bat, J. Franklin Baker walked toward the plate. Philadelphia fans stood and cheered. Bake could do it. They were certain of it.

Showing respect for Bake's reputation, the Braves manager ordered an intentional pass, a decision that provoked a broadside of jeering. This left things in the hands of Stuffy McInnis.

Danger lurked in Stuffy's fearsome bat. He was swinging the bat well. Calm, resolved, and determined, the A's first baseman stepped into the batter's box ready to do battle. Fans were on their feet. Runners took their leads. The tension mounted. The count ran to one ball and two strikes. Trying to make something happen, Stuffy barely got wood on the ball and produced nothing more than a weak bouncer toward Johnny Evers, an easy play, an easy toss, an easy out.

A wave of applause greeted Hank Gowdy, leading off for the Braves in the bottom of the twelfth. Bullet Joe Bush had thrown an astonishing 172 pitches in 11 innings. He was tiring and still trying to figure out a way to suppress Gowdy's power surge.

The Philadelphia ace rocked and fired. Gowdy, swinging freely, fouled the first pitch into the stands behind home plate. Another pitch, another fastball high and tight, moved Gowdy off the plate. Ball one. Taking advantage of the darkening sky, Bullet Joe wiped the sweat from his face, fingered the resin bag, looked up at the scoreboard, gave the fielders the once-over, scrubbed around the mound with his toe, and took his own sweet time.

Beyond the outfield fence an occasional light winked; electric signs flickered on. It was getting late. Very late. Bush challenged Gowdy with another fastball. Gowdy measured it. All he could do was raise a foul back into the seats. Ahead on the count, 1–2, Bullet Joe tried to catch Gowdy off guard. He changed speeds and delivered a slow backdoor breaking ball.

Gowdy uncoiled an all-or-nothing swing and slammed a line drive crashing high off the left field wall, behind the spectators in the temporary bleachers. The ball struck near the top of the fence, just missing a home run by inches, and bounced back among the Royal Rooters whose enthusiasm knew no bounds. A ground rule double.

Knowing that the failing light would not allow another inning, Stallings pulled out all the stops. He sent Les Mann in to run for Gowdy. The Braves' leader wanted Mann's speed on the base paths. Stallings also sent Larry Gilbert up to pinch-hit for the pitcher. The Mackmen countered by walking Gilbert, setting up the possibility of a double play or a force at third. Runners were on first and second. There were no outs. And the weak-hitting Herbie Moran stepped into the batter's box.

Stallings signaled for a bunt. Move the runners up. Moran would be followed by Evers in the batting order. Evers already had three hits in the game. After Evers came Joey Connolly, Boston's leading hitter.

Louder and louder the passionate throng cheered. You couldn't hear yourself think. Fenway was all noise. And building.

Moran squared away, jabbed at a high pitch, and pushed a weak pop-up between the mound and third base.

"Third! Third!" catcher Wally Schang yelled.

Bush lunged for the ball, couldn't quite make the grab, scooped it up on the half bounce, spun, slipped on the grass, and, while falling backward, flipped it to third—past Baker's outstretched glove—and watched the ball bounce into foul territory. A cringe-inducing error.

Screaming at the top of his lungs, third-base coach Fred Mitchell windmilled Mann home. Les scored standing up. The game was over. An amazing 5–4 come-from-behind victory.

Confusion reigned. The men who ran around the bases for the Braves were soon blotted out by the flood of people, most of whom wanted to congratulate Hank Gowdy.

The stunned Mackmen looked on thick with disappointment, their spirit crushed. The Braves were one victory away from the world championship.

Grimly studying a scorecard filled out by his own hand, Connie Mack, a man who lived many seasons, sounded more disappointed than angry: "I'm just about ready to concede that the Braves are a great ball club," Mack said in passing. "They played like the devil possessed. But they can't do it forever."

Boston fans tended to differ with the Philadelphia manager's assessment of the situation. "Four straight!" was the slogan of the day, words heard everywhere in the city.

"Today's game was the critical one in the series," Ty Cobb said. "The Braves showed they could take a hit and battle back . . . If the Athletics had won, they had a chance . . . That chance is gone now. I count them out as a beaten team."

It was baseball Darwinism. The last stand for the Philadelphia Athletics. The young, lusty, upcoming force prevailing over the once seemingly invincible, dominant force.

CHAPTER 58

LIGHTNING-BOLT TALENT

When the World Series opened four days earlier, the Philadelphia Athletics' star-studded lineup of superior players were seeking an unprecedented fourth world championship against the just-happy-to-be-there Boston Braves, a team of lesser players. Five days later, these same talented Athletics were seeking to avoid the humiliation that goes along with a powerful ball club losing four straight in a World Series to a bunch of rough-and-tumble misfits, whose greatest asset was their enthusiasm.

If the Braves emerged victorious, it would be the first four-game sweep in the 10-year history of the fall classic, and the thought of being humiliated by the take-no-prisoners Braves generated more than a little emotional voltage in the Athletics dugout. It was a must-win game. There was no tomorrow.

And there was optimism. A good deal of optimism. No opposing pitcher had beaten the Mackmen twice in the same World Series since Christy Mathewson shut them out three times in 1905. Connie's boys were certain they would come out on top this time. They were facing the winning pitcher of the first game, Dick Rudolph, and they were confident that Dick could not stop them a second time.

The weather was cold, the seats uncomfortable, the wind gusty. "Tessie" was there, ad nauseam, and so was "Sweet Adeline," pressing "Tessie" for popularity among the happy-hour boys. But the loyalty of the Royal Rooters was unwavering. They were not about to abandon "Tessie," the fair lady in the battle song who got them there, not even for lovely "Sweet Adeline," or any other pretty maiden for that matter.

◆◆◆

Dick Rudolph delivered the first pitch of the game, a nasty curve that dropped into Hank Gowdy's mitt for a called strike. Taking all the way, Eddie Murphy did nothing more than stare at the ball as it went by; the sellout crowd of 34,365 cheered in wild delight. They seemed to anticipate what was going to happen, long before it happened. A ball leveled the count at 1–1.

Murphy then poked a ground ball toward the hole on the right side of the infield. Evers glided over and shoveled the ball to Butch Schmidt for the out. Butch, following the tradition of tossing the ball around the diamond after an infield out, fired a wild throw over Evers's head, and Johnny didn't seem to mind. He turned and watched the ball roll into center field. Whitted retrieved it and did something odd with the ball (in the grass) before returning it to Maranville.

And what do you know? Rabbit dropped the ball. This surprised the crowd. Not the Royal Rooters. They'd seen this one before and considered it a neat trick. That of course depended on one's point of view. Maranville, kneeing the spirit of sportsmanship in the groin, bent down and picked up the ball and rubbed it into the loam of the infield, smearing the new baseball with dirt, then returned it stained and dirty to Dick Rudolph, who set the side down in order.

The weather was too raw for a start by the aging Chief Bender, Philadelphia's "money pitcher," and Connie Mack called instead on Bob Shawkey, 16–8, to carry the A's banner into battle. Knowledgeable fans questioned the move, but the 24-year-old Shawkey quickly convinced skeptics that it was the right move, retiring the first nine batters he faced. He was in command, breezing along, showing the baseball world that he was indeed ready for prime time. The White Elephants looked good. They played their game. They played it well. At last the most powerful team in baseball resembled the fearsome, well-rounded aggregation that had run roughshod over American League opponents all season.

They pounded Rudolph. Hit him freely. Made him struggle. For a while, it seemed that all Rudy was capable of doing was scrambling to survive, barely standing the Mackmen off. Yet whenever the man at the plate thought he had Rudy figured out, the poor guy learned he'd guessed wrong.

Meanwhile, Shawkey cruised along untroubled until the bottom of the fourth, when Johnny Evers, the first batter up, walked. Joey Connolly, batting third in the lineup, cracked a sharp ground ball at Eddie Collins, perfectly positioned to turn a fast double play. But the sure-handed Collins booted the ball, had trouble picking it up, and lost the chance of cutting down Evers at second. The greatest second baseman in the game had to be content with making the easy play at first base.

The next batter, Possum Whitted, smashed another ground ball at Collins, a solid shot. The ball took a bad hop, glanced off Eddie's glove, and rolled into short right for a base hit, and Collins went down in pain, having twisted his ankle going after the ball. Evers advanced to third on the play.

Rube Bressler, Herb Pennock, and Jack Wyckoff rushed out to the Philadelphia bull pen in left field while the A's trainer worked on Collins. Though in considerable pain, Fast Eddie insisted on staying in the game, and the admiring crowd gave the popular second baseman a big hand as he limped into position.

With one out and runners on first and third, the Philadelphia infield played deep, demonstrating a willingness to give up a run while guarding against a big inning. The next batter, Butch Schmidt, a contact hitter, chased a breaking ball out of the strike zone and slapped a slow roller toward short. Jack Barry rushed in, gloved the ball on the run, and threw off balance to McInnis at first for the out. Evers scored on the play. It was 1–0, Boston. The crowd's response was thunderous, and the Royal Rooters' band played a rousing rendition of "When Johnny Comes Marching Home."

Collins's unexpected breakdown had given the Braves a gift run, an unearned run, an all-important one-run lead. From then on, the keyed-up boys from Beantown cheered every good play by a teammate. They had the upper hand. They were confident. And they smelled victory.

The Mackmen came right back at them in the top of the fifth; Jack Barry sent a high bouncing chopper over the head of third baseman Charlie Deal. The elusive chopper was Barry's first hit of the series.

The next batter, the switch-hitting Wally Schang, batting from the left side, flashed the hit-and-run sign and grounded a curveball into the hole on the right side on the infield. Evers fielded the ball cleanly. Seeing that there was no chance of getting Barry at second, he made the play at first, nipping Schang by a step.

Shawkey then slashed a chest-high off-speed pitch past third—fair. The ball caromed off the side wall of the grandstand and bounded into the left field corner. Connolly backhanded it, spun, and threw toward third, as Barry scored. The pitcher's bat had tied the score, 1–1.

With two down in the Braves' fifth, Dick Rudolph lashed a ground ball up the middle for a base hit; it was only the Braves' second hit of the afternoon. Cocksure of everything, Stallings's stud brawlers went into action. The collection of reprobates yapped like howler monkeys, directing the brunt of their verbal assault at Shawkey, Oldring, and Collins.

"Hey, Shawkey! Who's in charge inside your head?"

"What do they need you for, Oldring? You're just taking up space."

What they did to Collins was cruel and abusive.

Maranville, coaching at first, spewed crude obscenities at Collins and extended his middle finger at him. "Being a kid," Rabbit admitted in later recountings, "I went out of my way to badger Collins and get his goat. Everybody did . . . Eddie, whose sum total of foolish plays in the regular season could be stuffed into a thimble, got pretty upset and had a poor series."

Told to attack early in the count, Herbie Moran put a charge into a low fastball and sliced a line drive into the gap in left-center, inches beyond Oldring's outstretched glove, and sped into second, just beating the throw. Rudolph held up at third. Two runners were in scoring position, there were two outs, and the score was tied, 1–1.

A sustained roar welcomed Johnny Evers.

Coaching at third, Fred Mitchell shouted instructions at the base runners.

The tough-as-nails Braves dugout stoked up the decibel level of their verbal attack.

"Make him pitch, Cap!" voices called out.

"Kill it!"

"It's got to be a hit."

Shawkey needed one more out. That's all. Just one more out. Using all of his wiles, he challenged Evers and tried to fool the Braves' field leader into going after a bad pitch. But Evers was about as easy to fool as a red fox. Shawkey dug himself into a 2–0 hole. John then swung through a 2–0 fastball for a strike and hacked away unsuccessfully at another, a sharp breaking curve. The count leveled at 2–2.

Baker and Collins shouted words of encouragement at Shawkey, something you seldom heard from the Athletics. Shawkey kept pounding away at the strike zone, forcing Evers into three consecutive defensive swings on 2–2 pitches. Johnny hung in there, iron willed. And he eventually worked the count to 3–2.

The Braves' captain then spat into the palm of his left hand, dug in his spikes, crouched slightly, readied himself, and met the next pitch squarely, drilling a whistler up the middle. Two runners scored. Evers clapped his hands on the way down to first base. It was 3–1, Boston.

The hit set off a crazed celebration in the Braves' dugout. Captain Johnny's teammates laughed and hugged and whooped it up in self-delighted giddiness. Caught up in the excitement of the moment, a deliriously happy Oscar Dugy ripped off manager Stallings's brand-new lucky brown fedora, threw it on the floor of the dugout, and danced on it—with his spiked shoes.

Hands on his hips, Shawkey sighed, shook his head, kicked at the air, gave a modest shrug, pulled off his cap, and turned away. He was finished. Herb Pennock, a left-handed side-armer, replaced Shawkey and pitched shutout ball the rest of the way.

In the top of the sixth, Eddie Collins, swinging at the first pitch, sent a scorcher up the middle. Maranville, showing the ardor of a boy who was playing for the pleasure of playing, went after a ball he didn't have a prayer of getting. Most shortstops would not have tried. Darting behind second base, where the infield meets the outfield grass, Rab shot out his gloved hand and somehow snared the ball, turned, transferred it to his bare hand, and, without looking at first base, made a quick, jerky throw in the general direction of Butch Schmidt. The ball bounced and looked like it would get by Butch, but the big, galumphing first baseman stretched the full length of his body and dug it out of the dirt in time to get the speedy Collins—an incredible play.

A mighty roar rewarded Rabbit, a gee-whiz wonder, "for making one of the most marvelous stops and throws ever seen on any diamond."

"Baseball has never seen a more spectacular play," a writer for the *Washington Post* remarked. "The reality of it was almost ungraspable."

Rabbit was great, all right. He had lightning-bolt talent straight from the gods.

After Baker fouled out for the second out of the inning, Stuffy McInnis drove a sharp ground ball past Charlie Deal. Rabbit Maranville, breaking to his right, scooped up the ball with his bare hand, spun around, set himself, and fired it across the diamond in time to get McInnis by an eyelash. It was Rabbit's second fantastic play of the inning. The capacity crowd went crazy. No team could succeed against that kind of defense.

Writers, managers, and coaches looked on in awe. All agreed: Rabbit Maranville was the best-fielding shortstop they'd ever seen.

The play had the impact of a gut punch. From that play on the Athletics were a beaten club. "Their attitude," Damon Runyon wrote, "told plainly that they had quit."

The Braves had outplayed the Mackmen from start to finish. They were the better team. Steady pitching, a ferocious defense, and timely hitting had driven a stake through the heart of the White Elephants. It was all over. The Boston Braves were about to be crowned baseball's new World Series champions.

When a throw by Charlie Deal snuffed out Stuffy McInnis at first, completing the last play of the 1914 World Series, captain Eddie Collins, Ira Thomas, and several other Mackmen rushed across the infield to congratulate Stallings, Evers, Rudolph, Gowdy, and the other victorious Braves.

A somber figure in ministerial black remained behind in the Philadelphia dugout, the corners of his mouth pulled down, staring glumly in front of himself, barely glancing in the direction of the Boston bench. The first four-game sweep in World Series history by a team managed by George Stallings embarrassed Connie Mack. The defeat sat heavily on his shoulders. Mack could not forgive the Braves manager for the way he attacked him before the series. "Stallings may be ready to forget now," Mack said, "but I'm not," something his body language made clear.

"It was in a period of sustained brilliance that the Braves beat the Mackmen four straight," Grantland Rice wrote, "and furnished the greatest upset in baseball history."

"Hereafter," Ty Cobb wrote, "George Stallings will have to be rated among the greatest managers that the game has ever produced.... He won the World Series Championship by beating what was considered to be the greatest team ever put together."

"The Mackmen are still a great team," Sid Mercer wrote. "You can't take that away from them. But they were defeated by a team that rose to greater heights than any team ever mounted in a World Series" and achieved the seemingly impossible.

ACKNOWLEDGMENTS

In the research and the writing of this project, I was blessed by the love, assistance, and faithful support of three lovely and intelligent women, Lisa Hankin, Jennifer Dicus, and Pam Bush, my daughters. Lisa and Jennifer offered loving encouragement, support, and commentary, and never lost faith in what they called "the book."

To avoid secondhand facts and the lazy and uninspired reporting of others, I relied almost exclusively on fresh, groundbreaking primary sources: tens of thousands of inches of newspaper articles, interviews, letters, reports, notes, court transcripts, and personal recollections that tell the human side of a story that pulls no punches about the lords of baseball.

Most of my research in newspapers was done over a period of six years in the Microfilm Room of the New York Public Library. I am indebted to the good folks at the NYPL, particularly Warren Platt and Philip Yokke, who facilitated my passage through the library's vast microfilm collection and assisted me with an enormous number of interlibrary loans.

My daughter Lisa Bush Hankin and I spent many rewarding hours on several occasions in the Research Department of the National Baseball Library and Archive at the National Baseball Hall of Fame in Cooperstown, where she readily assisted me in my research. Everyone thought she was delightful. Director Donald C. Marr Jr., Tim Wiles, Bruce Markusen, Scot Mondore, and Cassidy Lent made our visits memorable; they were always courteous, helpful, and upbeat, and seemed to genuinely enjoy assisting us. The library's copious files were an invaluable source of information.

The book owes its existence to Clara Totten. She read the manuscript when no one else would, loved the story, and made the publishing of it happen. I will always be grateful to her. My editor, Mary Young, has been great at every turn. I could not have been in better hands. I owe a special thanks to Christine Brooks for her exceptionally good cover and book design, and to Lori Rider for her acute and sensitive editing. The entire staff at the Press has been a delight to work with: their professionalism at every stage of the process made the production of the book a happy collaboration.

I am also obliged to the many librarians and archivists listed below, and to many others whose names I never knew. They were uniformly knowledgeable, helpful, and generous with their expertise and time: Aaron Schmidt, Boston Public Library; Chicago Public Library; Cara Curtis, Cumberland County Historical Society, Carlisle, Pennsylvania; Romie Minor and Michelle Williamson, Detroit Public Library; Historical Society of Pennsylvania, Philadelphia; Kansas City (Missouri) Public Library; Massachusetts Historical Society, Boston; Jessica Harden, Michigan State Archives, East Lansing; New-York Historical Society; New York Mercantile Library; New York Society Library; Philadelphia Public Library; Pat Morrison, director, Railroad Museum of Pennsylvania, Strasburg; Todd H. Christine, State Historical Society of Missouri, Columbia; the Archives of the Supreme Court of the State of New York, New York City; University of Iowa Library, Iowa City; Diana E. Kaplan, Yale University Library, New Haven, Connecticut; and Gary Urbanowitz, executive director, New York City Fire Museum.

Rabbit Maranville's daughter, the late Betty McInnis, supplied wonderful insights, anecdotes, and information, made no demands, and imposed no restrictions.

The editorial assistance, insights, and suggestions of my daughter Jennifer Dicus were invaluable, particularly her expert guidance in shaping the complex nature of the story. She saved me from many errors, and I owe her a deep debt of gratitude.

My friend James Lee Burke took time from his own busy writing schedule to read drafts of several chapters and offer valued advice.

Another valued friend, Mike Raia, a baseball historian, who very likely knows more about this period in baseball history than any living soul, contributed to the scholarship of the project in many ways. I am grateful to Mike for his comradeship and the innumerable hours of delightful conversation about baseball.

My sincere thanks goes to Ron Miller of Pittsburgh, whose research in the Pittsburgh newspapers on subjects largely ignored by others supplied me with wonderful insights and anecdotes of the era.

I owe a deeply felt debt of gratitude to my former wife, Jennie Gordon Peugh Bush, for allowing one-third of our apartment to be used as an office and an archive, and for generously putting up with my years of research and writing. Jennie was always a good sport about it.

My heartfelt thanks to Neel Stallings and Greg Stallings, who gave generously of their time and greatly contributed to the project, and became loyal and sustaining friends.

I'd also like to thank the late Dave Anderson, sportswriter for the *New York Times,* for his suggestions and assistance.

Scores of people helped in so many ways, and I offer my thanks to those listed below and those whose names I can no longer recall: Bill Alward; Mark Bartlett; Michael Brodherson; Michael Bruno; Gene Budig; Corey Busch; Donna H. Bushey; Steve Button; Ken Carlson; Major Jack Crance; Dipak Datta; Todd Dicus; John Dorsey; Philip Felig; Russ Gordon; Jordan Haines; Ted Hathaway; Herbert Hochman; Mathew Jones; Lyvia and Yaniv Larish; Mike and Vjollca Lekperi; Muriel Y. McDowell; Tom McInnis; Kay Marsh; Daniel B. May; Louis Meisel; Dane Neller; John O'Grady; Keith Olson; Joe Overfield; Gabe Paul Jr.; Sam Paul; Thorin Peugh; Mikey Rappucci; Bobby Rappucci; Mark and Gay Ritchey; John Rogers; Robert Seten; Max Silberman; Bryan Stevens; Clyde Sukeforth; Brian Taylor; Mary Kay Ward; Jonathan Warman; and Ruth Weichsel.

Nobody contributed more to this book than Steven and Lisa Hankin. I owe them a special debt of gratitude for their unstinting generosity and enduring thoughtfulness over these past few years. Without their assistance, this book would never have been completed.

A wholehearted word of thanks to my typists: my daughter Lisa Hankin, who got me started on this project; Elizabeth Kent; and especially Patty, Brian, and Tom Shannon, whose skill, efficiency, and professionalism allowed me to focus on completing it.

Without the assistance of my good friend and brilliant physician Murray R. Rogers, it would have been difficult to finish the manuscript. Murray enabled me to maintain my health and my spirit, as well as my confidence.

Needless to say, the shortcomings of the book are my own.

CHAPTER SOURCES

Please note: The following sources appear in their complete forms in the bibliography.

1. THE BEST MANAGER IN BASEBALL

Boston Traveler; Chicago Post; Dewey and Acocella, *Encyclopedia of Major League Baseball Teams; Evening Mail* (New York); James E. Gaffney Collection; *Globe and Commercial Advertiser* (New York); Lane, "Miracle Man"; Light, *Cultural Encyclopedia of Baseball;* John J. McGraw Collection; *New York Clipper; New York Tribune;* Reidenbaugh, *Baseball's 25 Greatest Pennant Races; Sporting Life;* George Stallings Collection; Fred Tenney Collection; Wright, *Southern Association in Baseball.*

2. THEY'D DELIVERED DISAPPOINTMENTS FOR YEARS

Ed Delahanty Collection; Nap Lajoie Collection; *New York Times; Philadelphia Inquirer; Philadelphia Press; Philadelphia Times;* Pietrusza et al., *Baseball; Sporting Life; Sporting News;* George Stallings Collection; Westcott and Bilovsky, *New Phillies Encyclopedia.*

3. ROGERS'S RULES

Cincinnati Post; Norman Elberfeld Collection; Jordan, *Athletics of Philadelphia;* Lieb and Baumgartner, *Philadelphia Phillies; North American* (Philadelphia); *Philadelphia Inquirer; Philadelphia Item; Philadelphia Press; Philadelphia Record; Philadelphia Times;* Pietrusza et al., *Baseball; Public Ledger* (Philadelphia); *Sporting Life;* George Stallings Collection.

4. THE NEWLY NAMED AMERICAN LEAGUE

Alexander, *John McGraw;* Axelson, *Commy; Cincinnati Enquirer;* Dewey and Acocella, *Encyclopedia of Major League Baseball Teams; Inter Ocean* (Chicago); Light, *Cultural Encyclopedia of Baseball;* Murdock, *Ban Johnson; Reach Official American League Base Ball Guide; Sporting Life; Sporting News;* George Stallings Collection.

5. SOMETHING'S WRONG HERE

Chicago Chronicle; Chicago Daily News; Chicago Times-Herald; Chicago Tribune; Norman Elberfeld Collection; *Sporting Life;* George Stallings Collection.

6. A MEMORABLE ERA IN BASEBALL HISTORY

Alexander, *John McGraw; Baltimore Sun; Boston Herald; Chicago Evening Post; Chicago Tribune;* Dewey and Acocella, *Encyclopedia of Major League Baseball Teams; Evening Star* (Washington, DC); *Kansas City Times;* Light, *Cultural Encyclopedia of Baseball; New York Herald; New York Press; Philadelphia Inquirer;* Seymour, *Baseball: The Early Years;* Shuld, "Charles W. Somers"; *Sporting Life; Sporting News;* Voigt, *American Baseball.*

7. HIS FOCUS WAS SOUND

Chernow, *Titan;* Hittner, *Honus Wagner;* Josephson, *Robber Barons; Kansas City Journal; New York Press; Philadelphia Inquirer.*

8. SELF-SERVING PRONOUNCEMENTS

Chicago Evening Post; Chicago Record-Herald; Chicago Tribune; Detroit Free Press; Sporting Life.

9. ROWDIES RUN RIOT

Baltimore American; Baltimore Sun; Evening Star (Washington, DC); *Sporting Life.*

10. A DEEP FREEZE DEVELOPED

Baltimore Sun; Detroit Free Press; Detroit Journal; Detroit News-Tribune; Evening News (Detroit); *Kansas City Journal; New York Times; Sporting Life; Sporting News;* George Stallings Collection.

11. EVERYONE'S DIRTY LITTLE SECRET

Barrow, *My Fifty Years in Baseball;* Dash, *Satan's Circus; Evening Mail* (New York); *Evening Sun* (New York); Ginsburg, *Fix Is In;* Graham, *New York Yankees;* Kohout, *Hal Chase;* Koppett, *Koppett's Concise History of Major League Baseball;* Lieb, *Baseball as I Have Known It; New York American; New York Herald; New York Press; New York Times;* Reisler, *Before They Were the Bombers; Spaulding's Official Base Ball Guide, 1890–1915; Sporting Life;* Stout, *Yankees Century.*

12. TRIED TO SHOW THAT HE BELONGED

Evening Sun (New York); Lieb, *Detroit Tigers; Reach Official American League Base Ball Guide; Sporting Life;* George Stallings Collection.

13. SURPRISING SUCCESS

Brooklyn Citizen; Detroit Journal; Evening Sun (New York); *Evening World* (New York); *Globe and Commercial Advertiser* (New York); Graham, *New York Yankees;* Light, *Cultural Encyclopedia of Baseball; Macon Telegraph; New York American; New York Evening Journal; New York Press; New York Times; New York Tribune; Reach Official American League Base Ball Guide;* George Stallings Collection; *Sun* (New York); *World* (New York).

14. THE PRICE THE YANKEE MANAGER PAID

Astor, *New York Cops; Boston Traveler;* Ty Cobb Collection; *Detroit Courier; Detroit Journal; Detroit News-Tribune; Detroit Times;* Dewey and Acocella, *Biographical History of Baseball; Evening News* (Detroit); *Evening Sun* (New York); *Globe and Commercial Advertiser* (New York); *New York Evening Journal; New York Press; New York Times; New York Tribune; Reach Official American League Base Ball Guide;* Ritter, *Glory of Their Times; St. Louis Post-Dispatch; Sporting Life;* George Stallings Collection; Steffens, *Autobiography of Lincoln Steffens.*

15. ALWAYS A TRUTH-BENDER IN THE CROWD

Chicago Daily News; Chicago Evening American; Chicago Evening Post; Chicago Record-Herald; Evening Sun (New York); *Evening Telegram* (New York); *Globe and Commercial Advertiser* (New York); *Inter Ocean* (Chicago); *Morning Telegraph* (New York); *New York American; New York Evening Journal; New York Post; New York Press; New York Tribune;* Ritter, *Glory of Their Times; St. Louis Globe-Democrat; St. Louis Post-Dispatch; St. Louis Republic; St. Louis Star; St. Louis Times; Sporting Life;* George Stallings Collection; *Sun* (New York); *World* (New York).

16. A STAND-UP GUY

Chicago Tribune; Evening Sun (New York); *Evening Telegram* (New York); *Evening World* (New York); *Globe and Commercial Advertiser* (New York); *New York American; New York Herald; New York Times;* George Stallings Collection; *World* (New York).

17. FULL OF INSINCERE SINCERITY

Chicago Evening American; Chicago Record-Herald; Chicago Tribune; Cleveland Leader; Cleveland Plain Dealer; Cleveland Press; Detroit Free Press; Evening Mail (New York); *Evening Sun* (New York); *Evening Telegram* (New York); *Evening World* (New York); *Globe and Commercial Advertiser* (New York); *Inter Ocean* (Chicago); *Gordon v. Farrell; Morning Telegraph* (New York); *New York American; New York Evening Journal; New York Herald; New York Press; New York Times; Reach Official American League Base Ball Guide; St. Louis Globe-Democrat; St. Louis Republic; St. Louis Times;* Seymour, *Baseball: The Golden Age; Sporting Life;* George Stallings Collection; *Sun* (New York); *World* (New York).

18. THE FIRST REAL GEM

Boston Globe; Boston Herald; Boston Post; Lane, "Dick Rudolph, Pennant Winner"; *New York Evening Journal; New York Tribune; Pittsburgh Post;* Bill Rariden Collection; *Reach Official American League Base Ball Guide;* Rhode Island State Archives; *Spaulding's Official Base Ball Guide, 1890–1915; Sporting Life; Sporting News;* George Stallings Collection.

19. HE TALKED HIMSELF OUT OF MORE BALL GAMES

Boston Herald; Chicago Record-Herald; Chicago Tribune; Dewey and Acocella, *Biographical History of Baseball; Evening Sun* (New York); *Evening Telegram* (New York); *Globe and Commercial Advertiser* (New York); Golenbock, *Wrigleyville; Kansas City Post;* Lane, "Sensational Evers Deal"; *New York American; New York Press; Reach Official American League Base Ball Guide; St. Louis Globe-Democrat; St. Louis Post-Dispatch; St. Louis Republic; Sporting Life; Sporting News;* George Stallings Collection; *Sun* (New York); *World* (New York).

20. DAMN THAT MAN

Boston Herald; Chicago Evening Post; Chicago Record-Herald; Chicago Tribune; Evening Telegram (New York); *Globe and Commercial Advertiser* (New York); *Kansas City Star; Kansas City Times;* Lane, "Sensational Evers Deal"; *New York Press; Sporting News; Reach Official American League Base Ball Guide; World* (New York).

21. A SYMBOL OF GREED AND SELFISHNESS

Boston Herald; Brooklyn Citizen; Chicago Record-Herald; Chicago Tribune; Cincinnati Enquirer; Cincinnati Post; Evening Mail (New York); *Globe and Commercial Advertiser* (New York); Golenbock, *Wrigleyville; Kansas City Times;* Murphy, *Crazy '08;* Charles Webb Murphy Collection; Ogden Nash, "Line-Up for Yesterday"; *New York Evening Journal; New York Press; New York Times; New York Tribune;* Seymour, *Baseball: The Golden Age; Sporting News; Sun* (New York); *World* (New York).

22. A WHIFF OF SCORE-SETTLING

Axelson, *Commy; Boston Herald; Brooklyn Citizen; Chicago Record-Herald; Cincinnati Post; Evening Telegram* (New York); *Globe and Commercial Advertiser* (New York); *New York American; New York Press; New York Tribune; Reach Official American League Base Ball Guide; Sun* (New York); *Washington Post; World* (New York).

23. A SELF-STYLED HAND GRENADE

Boston Herald; Boston Journal; Brooklyn Daily Eagle; Chicago Daily News; Chicago Evening Post; Chicago Record-Herald; Chicago Tribune; Cincinnati Post; Evening Mail (New York); *Globe and Commercial Advertiser* (New York); Lieb, *Baseball Story;* Murphy, "True Story of Why I Left the Game"; *New York American; Sporting Life.*

24. MISERY AND SUFFERING

Boston American; Boston Globe; Boston Herald; Boston Journal; Boston Post; Boston Traveler; Brooklyn Citizen; Chicago Daily News; Chicago Evening Post; Chicago Tribune; Cincinnati Enquirer; Evening Mail (New York); *Evening Telegram* (New York); Johnny Evers Collection; *Globe and Commercial Advertiser* (New York); Light, *Cultural Encyclopedia of Baseball; New York Herald; New York Press; New York Times; New York Tribune; Pittsburgh Press; Pittsburgh Sun; St. Louis Star;* Shatzkin, *Ballplayers;* George Stallings Collection; *World* (New York).

25. CONFIDENCE GREW STRONGER DAY BY DAY

Boston Globe; Boston Herald; Boston Journal; Boston Traveler; Ted Cather Collection; *Cincinnati Enquirer; Evening Mail* (New York); Holway, *Run, Rabbit, Run;* Light, *Cultural Encyclopedia of Baseball;* Rabbit Maranville Collection; *New York Tribune;* Hub Perdue Collection; *Pittsburgh Dispatch; Pittsburgh Gazette-Times; Pittsburgh Post; Pittsburgh Press; Pittsburgh Sun; Reach Official American League*

Base Ball Guide; Troy Times; St. Louis Post-Dispatch; Sporting Life; Sporting News; George Stallings Collection; *Sun* (New York); Possum Whitted Collection.

26. YOU CALL YOURSELVES BIG LEAGUERS?

Brooklyn Daily Eagle; Buffalo Evening News; Johnny Evers Collection; Golenbock, *Wrigleyville;* Hank Gowdy Collection; Rabbit Maranville Collection; Maranville, "Old or New, It's Still Baseball"; *New York Journal-American; Sporting News; Springfield Daily Republican;* Stallings Jr., "Life with Father's Miracle Braves"; Stallings, "When I Was a Miracle Man Myself"; George Stallings Collection; Wolf, *Amazing Baseball Teams; World Telegram* (New York).

27. THE CRAB AND RAB

Boston American; Boston Globe; Boston Herald; Boston Journal; Boston Traveler; Chicago Evening Post; Chicago Tribune; Cincinnati Enquirer; Holway, *Run, Rabbit, Run;* McGinnis interview; Rabbit Maranville Collection; *St. Louis Globe-Democrat; St. Louis Post-Dispatch; St. Louis Republic; St. Louis Star.*

28. WITHOUT CHARGE

Boston Globe; Boston Traveler; Evening Mail (New York); *Evening Sun* (New York); *Pittsburgh Post; St. Louis Post-Dispatch.*

29. THE BAD BOY

Boston American; Boston Globe; New York Herald; New York Times; Sporting News.

30. I SEEN IT DONE

Boston American; Boston Journal; Boston Traveler; Gutman, *It Ain't Cheatin' If You Don't Get Caught;* Klem and Slocum, "I Never Missed One in My Heart"; Lieb, *Connie Mack;* Light, *Cultural Encyclopedia of Baseball;* Macht, *Connie Mack and the Early Years of Baseball;* Connie Mack Collection; *New York Times;* Hank O'Day Collection; Sam Paul interview; *Pittsburgh Dispatch; Pittsburgh Post; Pittsburgh Press; Pittsburgh Sun;* Quigley, *Crooked Pitch; St. Louis Post-Dispatch.*

31. A CHANGE IN STRATEGY WAS UNTHINKABLE

Boston American; Boston Evening Record; Boston Globe; Boston Herald; Boston Traveler; George Davis Collection; *Evening Mail* (New York); *Evening Sun* (New York); *New York American; New York Evening Journal; New York Herald; New York Tribune;* Overfield, "The Other George Davis"; *Reach Official American*

League Base Ball Guide; Sporting News; George Stallings Collection; *Sun* (New York); Wallenstein, "1914 Miracle Braves"; *World* (New York).

32. HE DID NOT CROSS THE LINE

Boston American; Boston Herald; Boston Journal; Brooklyn Daily Eagle; Bill Klem Collection; Maranville, "Old or New, It's Still Baseball"; Larry McLean Collection; *New York Herald; New York Press; New York Times; New York Tribune;* Shatzkin, *Ballplayers; Sun* (New York); Ward, "Man Who Broke the Pitching Record—Almost"; *World* (New York).

33. A MAN WHO CAN DO ANYTHING HE SETS OUT TO DO

Buffalo Evening News; Evening Mail (New York); *New York American; New York Tribune.*

34. MATHEWSON WAS BRILLIANT

Boston American; Boston Globe; Boston Herald; Boston Journal; Boston Post; Boston Traveler; Chicago Tribune; Durant, *Baseball's Miracle Teams; Evening Mail* (New York); *Evening Sun* (New York); *Evening World* (New York); *Globe and Commercial Advertiser* (New York); *Kansas City Post;* Ring Lardner, "Matty"; Mathewson, *Pitching in a Pinch;* Chief Meyers Collection; Ogden Nash, "Line-Up for Yesterday"; *New York American; New York Herald; New York Press; New York Times; New York Tribune;* Ritter, *Glory of Their Times; St. Louis Post-Dispatch;* Red Smith Collection; George Stallings Collection; *Sun* (New York); Lefty Tyler Collection.

35. BRAVES WATCHERS WERE EVERYWHERE

Boston Globe; Boston Herald; Boston Journal; Boston Post; Brooklyn Daily Eagle; Chicago Daily News; Chicago Evening Post; Chicago Herald; Chicago Tribune; Evening Mail (New York); *Evening Bulletin* (Philadelphia); *Evening Sun* (New York); *Globe and Commercial Advertiser* (New York); Holway, *Run, Rabbit, Run; New York Evening Journal; New York Herald; New York Times; New York Tribune; North American* (Philadelphia); *Philadelphia Record; Public Ledger* (Philadelphia); *St. Louis Post-Dispatch; St. Louis Star; Sporting Life; Sporting News;* George Stallings Collection; *Sun* (New York); Heinie Zimmerman Collection.

36. IT WAS THE SPIRIT OF THE TEAM

Boston American; Boston Globe; Boston Herald; Boston Journal; Boston Post; Boston Traveler; Josh DeVore Collection; *Evening Mail* (New York); *Evening World* (New York); *Globe and Commercial Advertiser* (New York); *New York American;*

New York Herald; New York Press; New York Times; New York Tribune; North American (Philadelphia); *Pittsburgh Sun; World* (New York).

37. JUST AN OLD-FASHIONED NOSE-THUMBING

Beatty, *Rascal King; Boston American; Boston Evening Record; Boston Evening Transcript; Boston Globe; Boston Herald; Boston Journal; Boston Phoenix; Boston Post; Boston Traveler;* Cameron, *Rose; Cincinnati Enquirer; Evening Mail* (New York); *Evening Sun* (New York); *Globe and Commercial Advertiser* (New York); Goodwin, *The Fitzgeralds and the Kennedys;* John J. McGraw Collection; *New York Herald; New York Times; New York Tribune;* Ryan, "That Man Curley!"; Fred Snodgrass Collection.

38. AN UNAPPEASABLE HUNGER

Boston American; Boston Herald; Boston Post; Boston Traveler; New York American; New York Herald; New York Tribune; Johnny Evers Collection; John J. McGraw Collection; George Stallings Collection; *Sun* (New York).

39. KID'S GONNA BLOW SKY HIGH

Boston Herald; Boston Journal; Boston Traveler; Kavanagh, *Ol' Pete; New York American; New York Tribune; Philadelphia Inquirer; Philadelphia Press;* Shatzkin, *Ballplayers;* George Stallings Collection; Stallings Jr., "Life with Father's Miracle Braves"; Westcott and Bilovsky, *New Phillies Encyclopedia; World* (New York).

40. SOLID IVORY

Chicago Herald; New York Tribune; Sun (New York).

41. THE MOST SPIRITED TEAM I EVER SAW

Boston Globe; Boston Herald; Boston Journal; Boston Post; Brooklyn Citizen; Brooklyn Daily Eagle; Chicago Evening Post; Evening Mail (New York); Jones, "Miracle Manager"; Bill Klem Collection; *Pittsburgh Dispatch; Pittsburgh Press;* George Stallings Collection; Stallings, "When I Was a Miracle Man Myself"; *World* (New York).

42. REJOICING IN BOSTON

Boston Herald; Evening Sun (New York); Maranville, "10,000 Years in Baseball"; *New York Tribune; Reach Official American League Base Ball Guide; Sporting News.*

43. IT WAS A BAD SCENE

Boston Evening Record; Boston Journal; Boston Post; Boston Traveler; Brooklyn Citizen; Chicago Herald; Daily Standard Union (Brooklyn); *Evening Sun* (New York); *Evening Telegram* (New York); *Globe and Commercial Advertiser* (New York); *New York Tribune;* Red Smith Collection; *Sun* (New York).

44. THE BOYS ROCKETED OUT OF THEIR SEATS

Evening Bulletin (Philadelphia); *North American* (Philadelphia); *Philadelphia Inquirer; Philadelphia Press; Public Ledger* (Philadelphia); George Stallings Collection; Lefty Tyler Collection.

45. NOT YOUR RUN-OF-THE-MILL MASCOTS

Evening Bulletin (Philadelphia); *Evening Mail* (New York); Lieb, *Connie Mack;* Lieb, *Sight Unseen;* Meany, "King of Fidgets"; *New York Herald; New York Tribune; North American* (Philadelphia); *Philadelphia Inquirer; Philadelphia Press;* Eddie Plank Collection; *Public Ledger* (Philadelphia); *Pittsburgh Sun;* Reeves, "Michael C. Murphy"; *Sporting News;* George Stallings Collection.

46. JUST KEEP QUIET AND LISTEN

Boston Globe; Boston Journal; Evening Bulletin (Philadelphia); *Evening Mail* (New York); *Globe and Commercial Advertiser* (New York); Lieb, *Connie Mack; New York Times; North American* (Philadelphia); Ritter, *Glory of Their Times; Springfield Daily Republican;* George Stallings Collection; Stallings Jr., "Life with Father's Miracle Braves"; *World* (New York).

47. THE DR. JEKYLL AND MR. HYDE OF BASEBALL

Boston Globe; Boston Journal; Chicago Herald; Chicago Journal; Evening Bulletin (Philadelphia); *Evening Mail* (New York); *New York American; New York Evening Journal;* Rabbit Maranville Collection; *Philadelphia Inquirer; Public Ledger* (Philadelphia); *St. Louis Daily Globe-Democrat;* George Stallings Collection; Stallings Jr., "Life with Father's Miracle Braves"; *Troy Times; Washington Post.*

48. ROYAL ROOTERS

Boston Globe; Boston Herald; Boston Post; Chicago Herald; Evening Bulletin (Philadelphia); Lieb, *Story of the World Series; North American* (Philadelphia); *Public Ledger* (Philadelphia); *St. Louis Republic.*

49. A BOOM-BOOM VOICE

Ashenback, *Humor among the Minors; Boston Globe; Chicago Evening Post; Chicago Herald; Evening Bulletin* (Philadelphia); *Globe and Commercial Advertiser* (New York); *New York Herald; New York Tribune; New St. Louis Star; Public Ledger* (Philadelphia); *Sun* (New York); *Times Union* (Albany); *Washington Post*.

50. ROOFTOP SEATS

Evening Bulletin (Philadelphia); *North American* (Philadelphia); *Philadelphia Record;* Rooney, "Bleachers in the Bedroom."

51. PUZZLED BY WHAT HE SEES

Boston American; Boston Globe; Boston Herald; Boston Journal; Boston Post; Chicago Daily News; Chicago Evening Post; Chicago Herald; Chicago Journal; Chicago Tribune; Cincinnati Enquirer; Cincinnati Post; Daily Standard Union (Brooklyn); *Evening Bulletin* (Philadelphia); *Evening World* (New York); Hank Gowdy Collection; *Hartford Courant; Kansas City Post;* Light, *Cultural Encyclopedia of Baseball; New York Herald; New York Times; New York Tribune; North American* (Philadelphia); Okkonen, *Baseball Uniforms of the 20th Century; Philadelphia Record; Public Ledger* (Philadelphia); *Reach Official American League Base Ball Guide;* Rice, *The Tumult and the Shouting; St. Louis Globe-Democrat; St. Louis Star;* Shatzkin, *Ballplayers; Springfield Daily Republican;* George Stallings Collection; Stallings Jr., "Life with Father's Miracle Braves"; *Washington Post;* Whitcomb, *Irving Berlin and Ragtime America; World* (New York).

52. IT WAS LIKE LOOKING DOWN MURDERER'S ROW

Boston American; Boston Globe; Boston Herald; Boston Journal; Brooklyn Citizen; Chicago Evening Post; Chicago Herald; Chicago Tribune; Cincinnati Enquirer; Constitution (Atlanta); *Evening Bulletin* (Philadelphia); *Evening World* (New York); *New York American; New York Evening Journal; New York Times; New York Tribune; North American* (Philadelphia); *Philadelphia Record; Reach Official American League Base Ball Guide;* Dick Rudolf Collection; Stallings, "When I Was a Miracle Man Myself."

53. THE BRAVES' BEST PITCHER WAS IN TROUBLE

Frank Baker Collection; *Boston Globe; Boston Herald; Boston Journal; Boston Post; Boston Traveler; Brooklyn Daily Eagle; Chicago Daily News; Chicago Evening Post; Cincinnati Enquirer; Daily Standard Union* (Brooklyn); *Evening Sun* (New York); Johnny Evers Collection; *Globe and Commercial Advertiser* (New York); *New York*

American; New York Evening Journal; New York Herald; New York Press; New York Tribune; Philadelphia Press; Philadelphia Record; Springfield Daily Republican; George Stallings Collection; *Sun* (New York).

54. IN THE SPIRIT OF GOOD SPORTSMANSHIP

Boston Herald; Boston Journal; Boston Post; Chicago Daily News; Cincinnati Enquirer; Evening Bulletin (Philadelphia); *Globe and Commercial Advertiser* (New York); *Kansas City Post; New York American; New York Evening Journal; New York Times; New York Tribune; Philadelphia Press; Philadelphia Record; Springfield Daily Republican.*

55. HE WAS LOOKING AT HIS WORST NIGHTMARE

Boston American; Boston Globe; Boston Post; Brooklyn Citizen; Brooklyn Daily Eagle; Chicago Daily News; Chicago Herald; Chicago Journal; Chicago Tribune; Cincinnati Enquirer; Cincinnati Times-Star; Eddie Collins Collection; *Evening Bulletin* (Philadelphia); *Evening Mail* (New York); *Evening Telegram* (New York); *Evening World* (New York); *Hartford Courant;* Kaese, *Boston Braves;* Light, *Cultural Encyclopedia of Baseball; New York Herald; New York Journal-American; New York Times; New York Tribune; Philadelphia Inquirer; Philadelphia Press; Philadelphia Record; Public Ledger* (Philadelphia); *St. Louis Globe-Democrat; St. Louis Republic; Sporting News; Springfield Daily Republican;* Stallings Jr., "Life with Father's Miracle Braves"; *Sun* (New York); *Times Union* (Albany); *Washington Post; World* (New York).

56. THE VOICES TOLD THE STORY

Boston Globe; Boston Herald; Boston Journal; Boston Traveler; Brooklyn Daily Eagle; Chicago Daily News; Chicago Evening Post; Chicago Tribune; Cincinnati Post; Daily Standard Union (Brooklyn); *Evening Bulletin* (Philadelphia); *Evening Mail* (New York); *Evening World* (New York); *Hartford Courant; New York Herald;New York Times; New York Tribune; North American* (Philadelphia); *Philadelphia Inquirer; Philadelphia Record; Public Record* (Philadelphia); *Reach Official American League Base Ball Guide;* George Stallings Collection; *Sun* (New York); *World* (New York).

57. IT WAS HIGH DRAMA TIME

Boston American; Boston Globe; Boston Post; Boston Traveler; Brooklyn Citizen; Brooklyn Daily Eagle; Chicago Daily News; Chicago Herald; Chicago Journal; Chicago Tribune; Cincinnati Enquirer; Daily Standard Union (Brooklyn); *Evening Sun*

(New York); Johnny Evers Collection; *New York Herald; New York Press; New York Times; New York Tribune; Philadelphia Inquirer; Philadelphia Record; Public Ledger* (Philadelphia); *Reach Official American League Base Ball Guide; St. Louis Globe-Democrat; St. Louis Republic; Times Union* (Albany); *Sun* (New York).

58. LIGHTNING-BOLT TALENT

Boston Globe; Boston Herald; Boston Post; Chicago Daily News; Chicago Evening Post; Chicago Herald; Chicago Journal; Chicago Tribune; Cincinnati Post; Evening Bulletin (Philadelphia); *Evening Mail* (New York); *Globe and Commercial Advertiser* (New York); Lane, "Miracle Man"; Maranville, "Old or New, It's Still Baseball"; *New York American; New York Evening Journal; New York Times; North American* (Philadelphia); *Philadelphia Inquirer; Reach Official American League Base Ball Guide; St. Louis Globe-Democrat; Springfield Daily Republican; Times Union* (Albany); *Washington Post*.

BIBLIOGRAPHY

BOOKS

Alexander, Charles C. *John McGraw*. Lincoln: University of Nebraska Press, 1995.
———. *Our Game: An American Baseball History*. New York: MJF Books, 1991.
Allen, Lee. *The National League Story*. New York: Hill & Wang, 1961.
Apple, Marty. *Pinstripe Empire: The New York Yankees from Before the Babe to After the Boss*. New York: Bloomsbury, 2012.
Ashenback, Edward Michael. *Humor among the Minors*. Chicago: M. A. Donohue, 1911.
Axelson, G. W. *Commy: The Life Story of Charles A. Comiskey*. Chicago: Reilly & Lee, 1909.
Aylesworth, John S., and Benton Minks. *The Encyclopedia of Baseball Managers, 1901 to the Present Day*. New York: Crescent Books, 1990.
Barrow, Ed. *My Fifty Years in Baseball*. New York: Coward McCann, 1951.
Beatty, Jack. *The Rascal King*. Boston: Addison-Wesley, 1992.
Brown, Warren. *The Chicago Cubs*. New York: G. P. Putnam's Sons, 1946.
Cameron, Gail. *Rose: A Biography of Rose Fitzgerald Kennedy*. New York: G. P. Putnam's Sons, 1971.
Caruso, Gary. *The Braves Encyclopedia*. Philadelphia: Temple Univ. Press, 1995.
Chadwick, Bruce. *The Cincinnati Reds*. New York: Abbeville Press, 1994.
Chernow, Ron. *Titan: The Life of John D. Rockefeller, Sr*. New York: Random House, 1998.
Creamer, Robert W. *Stengel: His Life and Times*. Lincoln: Univ. of Nebraska Press, 1984.
Dash, Mike. *Satan's Circus*. New York: Crown, 2007.
Deford, Frank. *The Old Ball Game*. New York: Grove Press, 2005.
Deutsch, Jordan A., and others. *The World Series*. New York: Dial Press, 1976.
Dewey, Donald, and Nicholas Acocella. *The Biographical History of Baseball*. New York: Carroll & Graf, 1995.
———. *The Black Prince of Baseball*. Toronto: Sport Media, 2004.
———. *Encyclopedia of Major League Baseball Teams*. New York: Harper Collins, 1993.

Dickson, Paul, ed. *The Dickson Baseball Dictionary.* New York: Avon Books, 1991.
Durant, John. *Baseball's Miracle Teams.* New York: Hastings House, 1975.
Enders, Eric. *Ballparks: Then and Now.* San Diego: Thunder Bay Press, 2002.
Evers, John J., and Hugh S. Fullerton. *Touching Second.* Chicago: Reilly & Britton, 1910.
Evers, Johnnie, and Hugh S. Fullerton. *Baseball in the Big Leagues.* Chicago: Reilly & Britton, 1910.
Gallagher, Mark. *The Yankee Encyclopedia,* vol. 3. Champaign, IL: Sagamore, 1997.
Gershman, Michael. *Diamonds: The Evolution of the Ballpark.* New York: Houghton Mifflin, 1993.
Ginsburg, Daniel E. *The Fix Is In: A History of Baseball Gambling and Game Fixing.* Jefferson, NC: McFarland, 1995.
Golenbock, Peter. *Wrigleyville: A Magical History Tour of the Chicago Cubs.* New York: St. Martin's Press, 1996.
Goodwin, Doris Kearns. *The Fitzgeralds and the Kennedys.* New York: Simon & Schuster, 1987.
Graham, Frank, Jr. *The New York Yankees: An Informal History.* New York: G. P. Putnam's Sons, 1943.
Gutman, Dan. *World Series Classics.* New York: Penguin Books, 1994.
Hawkins, Jim, and Dan Ewald. *The Detroit Tigers Encyclopedia.* Champaign, IL: Sports Publishing, 2003.
Heilbron, Louis, ed. *Heilbron's Official Baseball Blue Book 1914.* Fort Wayne, IN: Louis Heilbron, 1914.
Hittner, Arthur D. *Honus Wagner.* Jefferson, NC: McFarland, 1996.
Holtzman, Jerome, and George Vass. *The Chicago Cubs Encyclopedia.* Philadelphia: Temple Univ. Press, 1997.
Holway, John, ed. *Run, Rabbit, Run: The Hilarious and Mostly True Tales of Rabbit Maranville.* Cleveland: Society for American Baseball Research, 1991.
Honig, Donald. *The National League: An Illustrated History.* New York: Crown, 1983.
Jordan, David M. *The Athletics of Philadelphia: Connie Mack's White Elephants, 1901–1954.* Jefferson, NC: McFarland, 1999.
Josephson, Matthew. *Robber Barons.* New York: Harcourt, 1934.
Kaese, Harold. *The Boston Braves: An Informal History.* New York: G. P. Putnam's Sons, 1948.
Karst, Gene, and Martin J. Jones, eds. *Who's Who in Professional Baseball.* New Rochelle, NY: Arlington House, 1973.
Kashatus, Bill. *Connie Mack's '29 Triumph.* Jefferson, NC: McFarland, 1999.
Kavanagh, Jack. *Ol' Pete: The Grover Cleveland Alexander Story.* South Bend, IN: Diamond Communications, 1996.
Kohout, Martin Donell. *Hal Chase.* Jefferson, NC: McFarland: 2001.
Koppett, Leonard. *Koppett's Concise History of Major League Baseball.* Philadelphia: Temple Univ. Press, 1998.
Lieb, Frederick G. *Baseball as I Have Known It.* New York: G. P. Putnam's Sons, 1977.
———. *The Baseball Story.* New York: G. P. Putnam's Sons, 1950.
———. *Comedians and Pranksters of Baseball.* St. Louis: Sporting News, 1958.
———. *Connie Mack.* New York: G. P. Putnam's Sons, 1945.

———. *The Detroit Tigers*. Kent, OH: Kent State Univ. Press, 2008.
———. *The St. Louis Cardinals*. New York: G. P. Putnam's Sons, 1944.
———. *Sight Unseen*. New York: Harper & Brothers, 1939.
———. *The Story of the World Series*. New York: G. P. Putnam's Sons, 1919.
Lieb, Frederick G., and Stan Baumgartner. *The Philadelphia Phillies*. New York: G. P. Putnam's Sons, 1953.
Light, Jonathan Fraser. *Cultural Encyclopedia of Baseball*. Jefferson, NC: McFarland, 1997.
Lindberg, Richard C. *The White Sox Encyclopedia*. Philadelphia: Temple Univ. Press, 1997.
Lowry, Philip J. *Green Cathedrals*. New York: Walker, 2006.
Macht, Norman L. *Connie Mack and the Early Years of Baseball*. Lincoln: University of Nebraska Press, 2007.
Mack, Connie. *My 66 Years in the Big Leagues*. Philadelphia: Universal House, 1950.
Mathewson, Christy. *Pitching in a Pinch*, reprint ed. New York: Stein & Day, 1977.
McGraw, John J. *My Thirty Years in Baseball*. New York: Boni & Liveright, 1923.
McNeil, William F. *The Dodgers Encyclopedia* (Champaign, IL: Sports Publishing, 1997.
Moreland, George L. *Balldom: "The Britannica of Baseball."* New York: Balldom, 1914.
Murdock, Eugene C. *Ban Johnson: Czar of Baseball*. Westport, CT: Greenwood Press, 1982.
Nash, Ogden. "Line-Up for Yesterday: An ABC of Baseball Immortals." In *Versus*. Boston: Little, Brown, 1949.
Nash, Peter J. *Boston's Royal Rooters*. Charleston, SC: Arcadia, 2005.
Okkonen, Marc. *Baseball Uniforms of the 20th Century*. New York: Sterling, 1991.
———. *The Federal League of 1914–1915: Baseball's Third Major League*. Garrett Park, MD: Society for American Baseball Research, 1989.
Pietrusza, David, Matthew Silverman, and Michael Gersham, eds. *Baseball: The Biographical Encyclopedia*. Kingston, NY: Total/Sports Illustrated, 2000.
Quigley, Martin. *The Crooked Pitch: The Curveball in American Baseball History*. Chapel Hill, NC: Algonquin Books, 1988.
Reichler, Joseph L., ed. *The Baseball Encyclopedia*, 7th ed. New York: Macmillan, 1988.
Reidenbaugh, Lowell. *Baseball's 25 Greatest Pennant Races*. St. Louis: Sporting News, 1987.
Rice, Grantland. *The Tumult and the Shouting*. New York: A. S. Barnes, 1954.
Ritter, Lawrence S. *The Glory of Their Times: The Story of the Early Days of Baseball Told by the Men Who Played It*. New York: Collier, 1966.
———. *Lost Ballparks: A Celebration of Baseball's Legendary Fields*. New York: Penguin, 1992.
Robinson, Ray. *Matty: An American Hero*. New York: Oxford Univ. Press, 1993.
Schneider, Russell. *The Cleveland Indians Encyclopedia*. Philadelphia: Temple Univ. Press, 1996.
Schott, Tom, and Nick Peters. *The Giants Encyclopedia*. Champaign, IL: Sports Publishing, 1999.
Selter, Ronald M. *Ballparks of the Deadball Era*. Jefferson, NC: McFarland, 2008.
Seymour, Harold. *Baseball: The Early Years*. New York: Oxford Univ. Press, 1960.

———. *Baseball: The Golden Age.* New York: Oxford Univ. Press, 1988.
Shatzkin, Mike. *The Ballplayers.* New York: William Morrow, 1990.
Simon, Tom, ed., with the Deadball Era Committee of the Society for American Baseball Research. *Deadball Stars of the National League.* Washington, DC: Brassey's, 2004.
Steffens, Lincoln. *The Autobiography of Lincoln Steffens,* vol. 2. New York: Harcourt, Brace, 1931.
Stout, Glenn. *Yankee Century: 100 Years of New York Yankees Baseball.* Photographs selected and edited by Richard A. Johnson. New York: Houghton Mifflin, 2002.
Stump, Al. *Cobb: A Biography.* Chapel Hill, NC: Algonquin Books, 1994.
Voigt, Quentin David. *American Baseball,* vols. 1 and 2. University Park: Pennsylvania State Univ. Press, 1983.
Ward, Geoffrey C. *Baseball: An Illustrated History.* Based on a documentary filmscript by Geoffrey C. Ward and Ken Burns. New York: Alfred Knopf, 1994.
Westcott, Rich, and Frank Bilovsky. *The New Phillies Encyclopedia.* Philadelphia: Temple Univ. Press, 1993.
Whitcomb, Ian. *Irving Berlin and Ragtime America.* New York: Limelight, 1988.
White, G. Edward. *Creating the National Pastime: Baseball Transforms Itself, 1903–1953.* Princeton, NJ: Princeton Univ. Press, 1996.
Wolf, Dave. *Amazing Baseball Teams.* New York: Random House, 1970.
Wright, Marshal D. *The Southern Association in Baseball, 1885–1961.* Jefferson, NC: McFarland, 2002.

PERIODICALS

Bobrick, M. A., and Napoleon Lajoie, eds. *Napoleon Lajoie's Official Baseball Guide.* Cleveland: American League, 1907.
The Reach Official American League Base Ball Guide, Annual Compendium (Philadelphia: A. J. Reach, 1890–1915). Information for this book was drawn from each of *The Reach Official American League Base Ball Guides,* 1890–1915.
Spaulding's Official Base Ball Record Guide, Annual Compendium (New York: American Sports, 1890–1915). Information for this book was drawn from each *Spaulding's Official Base Ball Guide,* 1890–1915.

PERIODICAL ARTICLES

Allen, Lee. "The Superstitions of Baseball Players." *New York Folklore Quarterly* 20, no. 2 (June 1964): 98+.
"Big League Superstitions." *Literary Digest* 48, no. 19 (May 9, 1914): 1151+.
Brown, Warren. "George Stallings Introduced Platooning." *Baseball Digest,* Feb. 1971, 76+.
Cary, J. R. "Charles Deal: The Man Who Made Good in the Pinch." *Baseball Magazine,* Feb. 1915, 53+.
Collins, Edward T. "Pitchers I Have Faced." *American Magazine,* July 1914, 23+.
Emslie, Robert D. "Ramblings of an Umpire." *Baseball Magazine,* Nov. 1908, 17+.
Evers, Johnny. "Confessions of an Old Timer." *Baseball Magazine,* May 1918, 150.

———. "The Greatest Second Baseman the Game Has Ever Known." *Baseball Magazine,* Feb. 1925, 386+.
Fullerton, Hugh S. "Flashback: Johnny Evers, 'the Crab.'" *Baseball Magazine,* June 1953, 24+.
Ghio, Joanne. "The 1914 Miracle Braves—50 Years Later! James Reveals Feud with Evers." *Baseball Digest,* Oct. 1964, 15+.
Greene, Lee. "Sport's Greatest Teams: The Miracle Braves." *Sport* 37, no. 11 (Nov. 1964): 38+.
"The Incomparable Hank." *Sports Illustrated,* Sept. 7, 1964, 19.
Johnson, Samuel M. "Good Natured Joe Connolly." *Baseball Magazine,* Feb. 1915, 25+.
Jones, Jimmy. "Miracle Manager." *The Mercerian,* Jan. 1972, 17+.
Klem, William J., and William J. Slocum. "I Never Missed One in My Heart." *Collier's,* Apr. 7, 1951, 30+.
Kofoed, J. C. "Fred Mitchell: The Comeback Cast Off." *Baseball Magazine,* Feb. 1915, 76+.
Lane, F. C. "Dick Rudolph, Pennant Winner." *Baseball Magazine,* Feb. 1915, 37+.
———. "The Miracle Man." *Baseball Magazine,* Feb. 1915, 57+.
———. "The Sensational Evers Deal." *Baseball Magazine,* Aug. 1914, 27+.
Lardner, John. "They'll Never Forget the 'Rabbit.'" *Sport* 10, no. 5 (May 1951): 70+.
Lardner, Ring W. "Matty." *American Magazine,* Aug. 1915, 19+.
Maranville, Rabbit. "Can Baseball Rebels Make Good?" *Liberty,* Aug. 1937, 24.
———. "Old or New, It's Still Baseball." *American Legion Monthly,* Oct. 1935, 55.
Maranville, Rabbit, with W. E. Deaton. "10,000 Years in Baseball." *Dime Sports Magazine,* Aug. 1936, 62+.
Meany, Tom. "King of Fidgets." *Baseball Digest,* May 1951, 25+.
Mitchell, Fred. "The Fighting Spirit of the Boston Braves." *Baseball Magazine,* Oct. 1921, 495+.
Murphy, Charles Webb. "The True Story of Why I Left the Game." *Baseball Magazine,* Feb. 1919, 205+.
Overfield, Joseph M. "The Other George Davis." *Baseball Research Journal* 18 (1989): 33+.
Reeves, D. L. "Michael C. Murphy as Known by an Intimate Acquaintance," *Anaconda Standard,* June 22, 1913, 26+.
Rice, Grantland. "The Miracle Club." *Collier's,* Oct. 10, 1914, 14+.
Rooney, John J. "Bleachers in the Bedroom." *Elysian Fields Quarterly* 17, no. 3 (Summer 2000): 33+.
Russell, Fred. "How Braves Were Psyched Up for '14 Series." *Baseball Digest,* Oct. 1974, 27+.
Ryan, Mike. "That Man Curley!" *Irish America,* Oct. 1989, 37+.
Sheldon, Harold. "The Miracle Braves: Golden Anniversary for Eight." *Baseball Digest,* Oct. 1964, 19+.
Shuld, Fred. "Charles W. Somers." In *Baseball Stars of the American League,* edited by David Jones. Dulles, VA: Potomac Books / Society for American Baseball Research, 2006, 393+.
Simons, Herbert. "The 1914 Miracle Braves: Stallings, Pitching and Demons." *Baseball Digest,* Oct.–Nov. 1964, 5+.
Stallings, George. "The Miracle Man's Own Story." *Collier's,* Nov. 28, 1914, 7+.

———. "When I Was a Miracle Man Myself." *Baseball Magazine,* Nov. 1919, 401+.
Stallings, George, Jr. "I Was Buddy-Buddy with the Rip-Roaring Players of My Dad's Teams." *Baseball Digest,* July 1957, 79+.
———. "Life with Father's Miracle Braves." *Baseball Digest,* Aug. 1957, 23+.
Wallenstein, John. "The 1914 Miracle Braves: At a 127-Win-a-Year Pace." *Baseball Digest,* Oct. 1964, 29+.

NEWSPAPERS

Baltimore American
Baltimore Sun
Boston American
Boston Evening Record
Boston Evening Transcript
Boston Globe
Boston Herald
Boston Journal
Boston Phoenix
Boston Post
Boston Traveler
Brooklyn Citizen
Brooklyn Daily Eagle
Buffalo Commercial Advertiser and Journal
Buffalo Courier
Buffalo Courier-Express
Buffalo Enquirer
Buffalo Evening News
Buffalo Express
Buffalo Morning Express
Buffalo Times
Buffalo Review
Cataract Journal (Niagara Falls)
Chicago American
Chicago Chronicle
Chicago Daily News
Chicago Evening American
Chicago Evening Post
Chicago Examiner
Chicago Herald
Chicago Journal
Chicago Record
Chicago Record-Herald
Chicago Times-Herald
Chicago Tribune
Cincinnati Commercial-Gazette
Cincinnati Enquirer
Cincinnati Post
Cincinnati Times-Star
Cleveland Leader
Cleveland Plain Dealer
Cleveland Press
Constitution (Atlanta)
Daily Cataract (Niagara Falls)
Daily Standard Union (Brooklyn)
Detroit Courier
Detroit Free Press
Detroit Journal
Detroit News-Tribune
Detroit Times
Detroit To-Day
Evening Bulletin (Philadelphia)
Evening Mail (New York)
Evening News (Detroit)
Evening Post (New York)
Evening Star (Washington, DC)
Evening Sun (New York)
Evening Telegram (New York)
Evening Telegraph (Philadelphia)
Evening World (New York)
Globe and Commercial Advertiser (New York)
Hartford Courant
Inter Ocean (Chicago)
Kansas City Journal
Kansas City Post
Kansas City Star
Kansas City Times
Macon Telegraph
Morning Telegraph (New York)
New St. Louis Star
New York American

New York Clipper
New York Evening Journal
New York Herald
New York Herald Tribune
New York Journal-American
New York Post
New York Press
New York Times
New York Tribune
New York World-Telegram
Niagara Courier
Niagara Falls Gazette
Niagara Falls Journal
North American (Philadelphia)
Philadelphia Item
Philadelphia Inquirer
Philadelphia Press
Philadelphia Record
Philadelphia Times
Pittsburgh Dispatch
Pittsburgh Gazette-Times
Pittsburgh Post
Pittsburgh Press
Pittsburgh Sun
Public Ledger (Philadelphia)
St. Louis Globe-Democrat
St. Louis Post-Dispatch
St. Louis Republic
St. Louis Star
St. Louis Times
Schenectady Union-Star
Sporting Life
Sporting News
Springfield Daily Republican
Standard Union (Brooklyn)
Sun (New York)
Times (Philadelphia)
Times Union (Albany)
Tribune Welland (Ontario, Canada)
Troy Record
Troy Times
Utica Observer-Dispatch
Washington Post
World (New York)

NATIONAL BASEBALL HALL OF FAME LIBRARY COLLECTIONS

Babe Adams Collection
Jimmy Austin Collection
Frank Baker Collection
Jack Barry Collection
Chief Bender Collection
Roger Bresnahan Collection
Three Finger Brown Collection
George Burns Collection
Joe Bush Collection
Ted Cather Collection
Frank Chance Collection
Hal Chase Collection
Fred Clarke Collection
Ty Cobb Collection
Gene Cocreham Collection
Eddie Collins Collection
Charles Comiskey Collection
Joe Connolly Collection
Jack Coombs Collection
Ensign Cottrell Collection
Dick Crutcher Collection
George Davis Collection
Charlie Deal Collection
Ed Delahanty Collection
Josh DeVore Collection
Bill Dinneen Collection
Larry Doyal Collection
Oscar Dugey Collection
Kid Elberfeld Collection
Johnny Evers Collection
Art Fletcher Collection
Russ Ford Collection
James E. Gaffney Collection
Larry Gilbert Collection
Hank Gowdy Collection
Eddie Grant Collection
Otto Hess Collection
Bill James Collection
Ban Johnson Collection
Bill Klem Collection
Johnny Kling Collection
Nap Lajoie Collection

Les Mann Collection
Rabbit Maranville Collection
Rube Marquard Collection
Christy Mathewson Collection
Joe McGinnity Collection
John J. McGraw Collection
Stuffy McInnis Collection
Larry McLean Collection
Fred Merkle Collection
Chief Meyers Collection
Fred Mitchell Collection
Herbie Moran Collection
Charles Webb Murphy Collection
Danny Murphy Collection
Eddie Murphy Collection
Red Murray Collection
Hap Myers Collection
Hank O'Day Collection
Rube Oldring Collection
Hub Perdue Collection
Eddie Plank Collection
Jack Quinn Collection
Bill Rariden Collection
Wilbert Robinson Collection
Dick Rudolph Collection
Wally Schang Collection
Butch Schmidt Collection
Red Smith Collection
Fred Snodgrass Collection
George Stallings Collection
Paul Strand Collection
Amos Strunk Collection
Jeff Sweeney Collection
Fred Tenney Collection
Joe Tinker Collection
Lefty Tyler Collection
Hans Wagner Collection
Bert Whaling Collection
Possum Whitted Collection
Heinie Zimmerman Collection

MISCELLANEOUS

Author interviews with Betty McInnis, Rabbit Maranville's daughter, in Lyons, New York, Dec. 10, 1998; recorded telephone interviews, Jan. 9, June 3, and June 22, 1999.
Conversation with Sam Paul, May 16, 1998.
Joseph Gordon v. Frank J. Farrell and the Greater New York Baseball Association, Nov. 20, 1911, Index No. 26242/1911. Supreme Court of the State of New York, New York County, New York, New York.

INDEX

Abbaticchio, Ed J., 20, 24
A. J. Reach Company, 42
Alexander, Grover Cleveland "Old Pete," 218, 237, 290
American Association, 45
American League: constitution, 45–47; corporate trust structure of, 46–47, 47n, 48; fan and game attendance statistics, 63, 85; inaugural season, 52–56; minor league status, 30–32; National League numbers comparison, 84–85; National League players signing with, 48–51; reorganization and expansion, 34–38, 39–47, 48, 52, 84–85; scandal coverups in, 76; Stallings's dissociation from, 69–70; umpires, 57–62. *See also* Johnson, Byron Bancroft; World Series (1914)
Anderson, Johnny, 54
Andrews, Ed, 8–9
Angus, Sam, 66, 69, 70
Associated Press, and free publicity, 41–42
Augusta Electricians, 10

Baker, J. Franklin "Home Run": ghostwriter for, 290; World Series Game One, 286, 299, 302, 306; World Series Game Two, 315, 317; World Series Game Three, 324–25, 326, 327, 329–31, 333; World Series Game Four, 339, 340; World Series performance, 322
Baker, William, 136
Balldom (Moreland), 185
Baltimore Baseball and Athletic Company, 43
Baltimore Orioles, 42–43, 50, 57–59, 62, 63, 155
Barlow, George, 286

Barrett, Jimmy, 53
Barrington-Sargent's Ninth Regiment band, 273–75
Barrow, Ed, 72
Barry, Jack: personal qualities, 263; Stallings's assessment of, 277; World Series Game One, 288, 302, 304, 305–6, 308–9; World Series Game Two, 315, 317, 318–19; World Series Game Three, 327; World Series Game Four, 338
Baseball in the Big Leagues (Evers), 259–60
baseballs (doctored), 182–85, 185n
batboys, 257–63
Baumgartner, Stan, 25
Beard, Ollie, 11
Becker, Beals, 241
Beckley, Zoe, 199–203
Bender, Charles Albert "Chief": scouting Braves players, 217; superstitions, 293; World Series Game One, 288, 291–92, 293–94, 295–96, 301–4, 306, 307–8, 309; World Series Game Three, 323; World Series Game Four, 337
Berger, Henry, 143
Berlin, Irving, 275–76
Berry, Jack, 290
Bescher, Bob, 191, 195–96, 208–9, 212, 230
"Big Chief." *See* Stallings, George Tweedy
"Big Six," 204, 204n. *See also* Mathewson, Christy "Matty"
Bischoff, Henry, 110
Bitter, Karl, 275
Boggs, L. G., 184
Boston Americans, 44–45, 63

365

Boston Braves: background, ix–x, 5–6; beginnings, 144–50; Buffalo Bisons exhibition game, 162–63, 165–66; Evers-Maranville bond, 167–70; financial issues, 154–55; game attendance statistics, 178; growth in confidence for, 151–59; league champions, 249–51; mascot, 257–60; pitcher strategy, 186–89, 237; players and management picks by Stallings, 115–21, 122–26, 139–40, 141–42, 179–81, 213–14; playing Brooklyn Dodgers, 144, 244, 252–54; playing Chicago Cubs, 171–72, 177, 214–17; playing Cincinnati Reds, 149, 151–54, 173–74; playing New York Giants, 120–21, 146–48, 186–87, 189, 190–97, 204–12, 219–24, 225–32, 233–35; playing Philadelphia Phillies, 217–18, 236–41; playing Pittsburgh Pirates, 148–49, 155, 174–76, 182–84, 244–45; playing St. Louis Cardinals, 172, 178, 217; sign-stealing rumors, 251; as "spirited team," 246; Stallings's first season managing (1913), 120–21; standings in 1914 season, 213, 214, 217–18, 235, 245–46; turning point for, 170, 177–78. *See also* Royal Rooters (fans); World Series (1914)

Boston Globe: on Boston Braves performance, 156; reporting on World Series score, 305; on umpire calls, 147

Boston Journal, on Maranville performance, 150

Boston Red Sox, 178, 272

Brennan, Ad, 192

Bresnahan, Roger, 150, 243

Bressler, Rube, 217, 286, 338

Britton, Schuyler, 136

Brooklyn Bridegrooms, 10

Brooklyn Daily Eagle, on Baker's performance, 306

Brooklyn Dodgers: Moran playing for, 214; player trades, 179–81; playing Boston Braves, 144, 244, 252–54; playing Chicago Cubs, 242–43; playing Philadelphia Phillies, 20; sign-stealing by, 86

Broun, Heywood, 309

Brush, John T., 133–34

Buccaneers. *See* Pittsburgh Pirates

Buffalo Bisons, 45, 115–18, 162–63, 165–66

Bulger, Bozeman, 197, 289

Bulletin, pre–World Series interview, 277–79

Burke, Jim, 53–54

Burns, George, 205, 208–9, 223, 225, 233–34, 239–40

Burns, James D., 31, 34–38, 64–70

Bush, "Bullet Joe," 323, 325–26, 327, 328, 330–32, 333–34

Bush, Donie, 90

Byrne, Bobby, 238–40

Byron, Bill "Lord," 178, 293, 326

Callahan, C. P., 280

Cantillon, Joe, 33–36, 83–84, 86

Carey, Max, 179, 182

Casey, "Doc," 58

Casey, Jimmy, 68

Cather, Teddy, 158–59, 190–91

Chalmers, Charles, 292

Chalmers, Hugh, 292, 323

Chalmers Motor Company, 292, 323

Chance, Frank, 79, 125, 134–35, 188

Chase, Hal "Prince Hal": as New York Yankee manager candidate, 72–73; as New York Yankee player-manager, 103, 104–5, 111, 112; personal conduct, 73–77, 80–81, 91–92, 93; and Stallings, 80, 87–90, 93–100, 105–7; throwing games, 99–100, 101–3, 108, 110–11, 112

Cheney, Larry, 215

Chicago Cubs: City Championship series, 126; Evers's contracts with, 122–23, 127–30, 131–32, 136–37, 138; Murphy's ownership of, 134–35, 142–43; O'Day as manager of, 123–24, 125–26; playing Boston Braves, 171–72, 177, 214–17; playing Brooklyn Dodgers, 242–43; reputation for fighting, 125; standings in 1914 season, 213, 242, 243; "Tinker to Evers to Chance" combination, 162, 168–69

Chicago Tribune: on Boston Braves performance, 171; on Evers's contracts, 128

Chicago White Sox: City Championship series, 126; doctored baseballs used by, 185n; fan and game attendance statistics, 63, 85; original name, 31; ownership of, 44n; pennant-winning season, 38; playing Detroit Tigers, 33–36; playing New York Yankees, 97–100; treatment of umpires by, 59–61

Cincinnati Reds, 149, 151–54, 173–74, 213

Cincinnati Times-Star, Murphy as sportswriter at, 132

Circuit Committee, 40

Clarke, Ed, 281–82

Clarke, Fred, 155, 179, 182, 183

Clarke, Tommy, 151–54

Cleveland American League team, 31–32, 63, 85

Cleveland Plain Dealer, fictional umpire account in, 29–30

Cleveland Spiders, 31–32

Clymer, Bill, 116, 165

Coakley, Andy, 92

Cobb, Ty: on Boston Braves performance, 334; on Chicago Cubs, 125; Detroit Tigers player, 50n, 90–91; personal qualities, 261; on Stallings, 144, 341; Stallings relationship with, 278; World Series (1907) player, 169; World Series (1914) spectator, 290
Cocreham, Gene, 165, 207n, 237, 287
Collins, Eddie: ghostwriter for, 290; Most Valuable Player award, 292; World Series Game One, 286, 288, 296, 298–300, 302, 304, 307, 309; World Series Game Two, 314, 317; World Series Game Three, 324, 326, 329, 331, 333; World Series Game Four, 337–38, 339, 340–41
Collins, Jimmy, 49
Comiskey, Charles, 28, 30, 31, 32, 35, 36, 38, 44n
Connolly, Joey: background, 120; hitting record, 155, 191–92, 220, 230, 252; as outfielder, 193, 215, 245; World Series Game One, 296, 308–9; World Series Game Three, 324, 326, 327, 332, 334; World Series Game Four, 337–38
Connolly, Tom, 58–59
Connor, Willie, 257–60
Cook, Frank C., 65
Cooley, Duff, 19, 23, 24, 25
Coombs, Jack, 263
Cooper, Wilbur, 174–75, 244–45
corporate trust, 46–47, 47n, 48
Corriden, "Red," 95, 150
Cottrell, Ensign, 237, 287
Coutan, Jules, 274–75
Crane, Sam, 192, 204n
Cravath, Gavvy, 237, 239
Crawford, Sam, 50n, 90
Criger, Lou, 95
Cross, Monte, 19–20, 24
Crutcher, Dick, 153, 237
Curley, James Michael (mayor), 229–32
Curley, John, 231
Cutshaw, George, 253

Daniels, Bert, 87, 96–97, 98
Davis, George, 166, 187–89, 237–41, 252
Davis, Harry, 326
Davis, Tom, 103, 104–5
Deal, Charlie: background, 121; injuries, 145, 156, 157–59; as Red's replacement, 255–56; on Stallings, 205; World Series Game One, 287–88, 299–300, 304, 305, 308; World Series Game Two, 315–19; World Series Game Three, 326, 328, 333; World Series Game Four, 338, 340–41
Delahanty, "Big Ed," 14–15, 16–17, 19, 23, 24, 25

Detroit Evening News, on Yankees management decision, 88
Detroit Journal, on Chase's performance, 89–90
Detroit Tigers: fan and game attendance statistics, 38, 63; financial issues, 63–70; playing New York Yankees, 83–84, 89–91, 94; sale of, 69–70; Stallings as manager of, 12, 27, 33–38, 52–56; and umpires, 58–59; winning seasons, 50n
Devery, "Big Bill," 91–92
Devlin, Art, 121
DeVore, Josh, 159, 206–9, 222–23, 287, 331
Dillon, "Pop," 54–55
Dinneen, Bill, 293, 294, 295, 301–2, 306, 332
doctored baseballs, 182–85, 185n
Dolan, "Cozy," 150
Donahue, "Red," 19
Donlin, Mike, 57
Donohue, F. L., 24
Donovan, "Wild Bill," 84
Dooin, Charlie, 239
Douglas, "Klondike," 19
Douglass, W. B., 24, 25
Doyle, Larry, 208, 221, 227, 228–30, 233–34
Dressen, "Chuck," 86
Dreyfuss, Barney, 50, 131–32
Duffy, Hugh, 49, 55, 61
Dugey, Oscar, 245, 259, 340
Dunkle, Ed, 24
Dunn, Jack, 59

Eason, Mal, 173, 215
Ebbets, Charlie, 179–80
Egan, Dick, 242–43
Elberfeld, "Kid": and Brooklyn Dodgers, 254; and Chicago White Sox, 34–36, 37; and Detroit Tigers, 55–56; and New York Yankees, 72–73, 78, 80; and Philadelphia Phillies, 19–20, 24, 25
Elkus, Abram, 109
Emslie, Bob, 147, 194n, 223, 226, 228–29
Evening Bulletin: on Boston Braves mascot, 259; on Evers performance, 306; on Rogers's rules, 23, 24
Evening Item, on Stallings, 24–25
Evening Journal, on Boston Braves performance, 192
Evening Mail, Stallings interview in, 199–203
Evening Sun: on Rice's comments, 177; on Stallings, 105, 111
Evening World, on Boston Braves performance, 197
Evers, Helen, 191, 191n
Evers, John, Jr., 191n

Evers, Johnny: *Baseball in the Big Leagues,* 259–60; batboy chosen by, 257–58; Boston Braves beginnings, 144, 145, 147, 149–50; Boston Braves–Chicago Cubs games, 171–72; Boston Braves–Cincinnati Reds games, 173–74; Boston Braves exhibition game, 162–63, 166–67; Boston Braves growth of confidence with, 151–54, 158; Boston Braves negotiation, 139–40, 141–42; Boston Braves–New York Giants games, 193, 195–96, 208, 211–12, 223, 225–26, 234; on Boston Braves performance, 249; Boston Braves–Philadelphia Phillies games, 239, 241, 245; Boston Braves–Pittsburgh Pirates games, 245; and Chicago Cubs, 122–26, 127–30, 131–32, 136–37, 138–40, 141–42; on Chicago Cubs performance, 242, 250; family life, 191, 191n; ghostwriter for, 290; homeruns, 252; Maranville's bond with, 167–70; Most Valuable Player award, 292, 323; on Murphy, 127–29, 136–37; personal qualities, 142, 142n, 169, 169n, 215–17, 226, 253–54; World Series captain, 293; World Series Game One, 287, 296, 297, 299, 305, 306, 309; World Series Game Two, 319–20; World Series Game Three, 324–25, 326, 327, 328–32, 333, 334; World Series Game Four, 337–41; World Series strategy of, 250–51

Farrell, Frank: and Chase, 76–77, 91, 104–5; and Davis, 187; Elberfield appointment by, 71–72, 73; and Johnson, 108–11; and Stallings, 78–80, 98, 99–100, 103, 105–7, 111–12
Federal League, 49, 116, 116n, 123, 137, 138–39, 141, 180
Fisher, Newt., 24
Fisher, Ray, 95
Fitzgerald, John F. "Honey Fitz" (mayor), 231–32, 272–74, 276, 292–93, 315, 317
Fitzgerald, Mary, 232
Fletcher, Art, 185n, 193, 210, 221, 225–26, 228–30, 234
Ford, Russ, 16, 87
Frank, Sidney, 43
Franklin, Jim, 45
Freedman, Andrew, 41
Fromme, Art, 195
frozen baseballs, 184–85, 185n
Fullerton, Hugh, 206–8

Gaffney, Jim: background, 3–7; on Boston Braves performance, 154–55, 178; and Evers, 124, 136–37, 139–40, 141; on Smith, 180–81; suspension interventions, 216; and umpires, 147–48
George Stallings Day, 246

Gilbert, Larry, 145, 155, 334
Gilmore, Jim, 139
Gleason, Kid, 53–54
Globe and Commercial Advertiser, recycled sports non-wisdom in, 99
Glory of Commerce (Coutan), 274–75
Gordon, Joseph, 108–10
Gowdy, Hank: background, 115–16; Boston Braves exhibition game, 162; Boston Braves–New York Giants games, 193, 206–8, 209, 211–12, 221, 225–27, 234; Boston Braves–Pittsburgh Pirates games, 175, 245; on Stallings, 170; Stallings's nickname for, 207n; World Series Game One, 287, 297, 298–99, 302–4, 305–6, 307–8; World Series Game Two, 313, 318–19; World Series Game Three, 325–26, 327, 329, 330–31, 333–34; World Series Game Four, 337, 341; World Series strategy for, 252
Graham, Frank, Jr., 85–86
Granger, Bill, 70
Grant, "Harvard Eddie," 193–96, 193n, 226, 234
Greater New York Baseball Association, 92, 109, 112. *See also* New York Yankees
Griffith, Clark, 49, 61, 71, 120, 285
Griffith, Tommy, 144, 145
Griner, Dan, 217

Halstead, Hurat, 28
Hanlon, Ned, 155
Hapgood, Walter, 136
Hart, Billy, 183, 184
Hart, Jim, 31, 134
Hartzell, Roy, 95
Haskell, Jack, 58, 60–61
Hawley, Pink, 54
Herbert (reporter), 242
Herrmann, Garry, 132, 135, 138, 285
Hess, Otto, 120, 155, 237, 287, 288
Hildebrand, George, 293, 317, 319
Hilly, Pat, 239, 241
Holmes, Ducky, 54, 55
Hooper, Harry, 74
Hough, Frank, 41–42
Howe, Irwin, 287
Hoy, "Dummy," 33
Huggins, Miller "Hug," 123, 124, 125, 158
Hughes, Tom, 287
Husting, Bert "Pete," 53–55

International League, 118–19, 121
Isbell, Frank, 34, 36

Jackson, Shoeless Joe, 49
James, Bill: background, 116–17; Boston Braves–Chicago Cubs games, 215; Boston

Braves–Cincinnati Reds games, 174; Boston Braves growth of confidence with, 156–57; Boston Braves–New York Giants games, 233–34; Boston Braves pitching strategy, 186–87; Boston Braves–Pittsburgh Pirates games, 176; chewing tobacco habit, 173; Stallings's assessment of, 278; statistics, 233; World Series Game One, 287, 288; World Series Game Two, 312–14, 315, 317, 318–20; World Series Game Three, 332; World Series pre–Game One, 280
Jennings, Hughie, 84, 90, 261, 290
Johnson, Byron Bancroft: American League player signings, 48–51; American League reorganization and expansion, 34–38, 39–47, 48, 52, 84–85; background, 30–32; on Chase game-fixing controversy, 108, 110–11, 112; on Detroit Tigers' financial issues, 65–70; on Farrell-Gordon legal dispute, 108–10; on Milwaukee game attendance, 63; ownership and financial stakes in ball clubs, 44, 44n; personal qualities, 40, 40n, 45–46, 48, 62, 70, 101–2; scandal coverups, 76; and Stallings, 50–51, 69–70, 78–80, 83, 84, 100, 101–3, 107–8, 111, 112; on umpires, 57, 61–62; as Western League president, 28–30; on World Series lineup, 312; World Series spectator, 285
Johnson, Walter, 71, 285
Jones, "Butch," 41–42
Jones, Davy, 89–90
Jones, Fielder, 49
Jones, Georgianna, 188

Kansas City Blues, 40, 43
Kansas City Journal, on American League structure, 48
Katoll, Jack, 60–61
Keeler, "Wee Willie," 72, 80, 82
Keister, Billy, 57, 59
Kelly, Joe, 119
Kennedy, James C., 254
Kilfoyle, John, 32
Killefer, Bill, 95–96, 240
Killilea, Matt, 38
Klem, Bill: Boston Braves–New York Giants games, 190, 193–95, 212, 223, 227–28; on Boston Braves performance, 246; World Series games, 293, 298–99, 300, 332
Kling, Johnny, 169
Knight, Jack, 87, 90, 94
Knoetchy, Ed, 182
Koppett, Leonard, 75–76

Lajoie, Napoleon "Larry," 14–15, 18, 19, 21, 24, 25, 49, 72–73

Lane, F. C., 246
Lannin, Joe, 178, 273
Lapp, Jack, 217, 291
Lardner, Ring, 289
Leach, Tommy, 171
Lieb, Fred, 25, 148, 185
Lobert, Hans, 240–41
Loomis, Clarence, 68

Mack, Connie: background, 41, 42; on criticizing players, 205; doctored baseballs used by, 185, 185n; scouting Braves players, 217; superstitions, 260–61; and Van Zelst, 260–62; World Series Game One, 289, 293, 297, 304, 307–10; World Series Game Two, 314, 318; World Series Game Three, 328, 334; World Series Game Four, 337, 341; World Series practice times, 265–66, 269–71, 278–79. *See also* Philadelphia Athletics
Mack, Johnny, 274
Magee, Sherry, 237, 241
Mann, Les: background, 116–18; Boston Braves exhibition game, 162, 166; Boston Braves–New York Giants games, 191, 192; Stallings's nickname for, 207n; World Series Game One, 286; World Series Game Two, 317; World Series Game Three, 334
Manning, Jim, 38, 40, 43–44
Maranville, Catherine, 172
Maranville, John, 172
Maranville, Rabbit: background, 120; Boston Braves beginnings, 144, 145, 149–50; Boston Braves–Brooklyn Dodgers game, 253; Boston Braves–Chicago Cubs games, 171–72; Boston Braves–Cincinnati Reds games, 173; Boston Braves exhibition game, 162–65, 166–68; Boston Braves growth of confidence with, 151–54, 158; Boston Braves–New York Giants games, 192, 195–97, 209–10, 220–21, 225–26; Boston Braves–Philadelphia Phillies games, 239, 241; Boston Braves–Pittsburgh Pirates games, 175, 245; Boston Braves–St. Louis Cardinals games, 172; career assists record, 168n; family life, 169n, 172, 191n; fight on field, 215–17; ghostwriter for, 290; post–pennant win celebration, 250; Stallings's assessment of, 277–78; World Series Game One, 287, 303–4, 306, 307–8; World Series Game Two, 314–15, 319–21; World Series Game Three, 325–27, 328, 330–31; World Series Game Four, 337, 339, 340
Marquard, Rube, 191–92, 195, 234, 246
Martin, Jack, 159, 239
mascots, 257–63
Masterson, "Bat," 289

Mathewson, Christy "Matty," 204–11, 204n, 219–23, 246, 260, 290
McAvoy, Wickey, 286
McCaffey, Jim, 119
McCarthy, Jim (hotel manager), 268, 321
McFarland, E. W., 24
McGeehan, Bill, 204
McGinnity, Joe "Iron Man," 49, 59, 61–62
McGraw, John "Muggsy": on American League structure, 48; ball club ownership advice by, 4; Boston Braves games, 192–97, 204, 210; on Boston Braves performance, 121, 177, 186, 189, 219; on Collins as Most Valuable Player, 292; on criticizing players, 205; ejected from games, 142n, 228; on Gaffney, 6; and Johnson, 42–43, 50–51, 61–62; management style, 214, 234; mistakes made by, 246; pool hall ownership, 73; and Rudolph, 118–19; umpire interactions, 57, 193–95, 194n; win-at-any-cost tactics, 174
McGraw's pool hall, 73–75
McGreevy, Mike "Nuf Ced," 274, 304
McGunnigle, Bill, 10
McInnis, Betty, 191n
McInnis, "Stuffy": World Series Game One, 286, 295, 305; World Series Game Two, 315, 317; World Series Game Three, 325, 326, 327, 330–31, 333; World Series Game Four, 338, 340–41
McIntyre, Matty, 90
McLean, "Long Larry," 195–96, 226
McNamara, James, 65, 68, 69
Mercer, Sid, 341
Merkle, Fred, 191–93, 195–96, 208, 210, 222, 226, 228
Meyers, John "Chief," 190, 193, 210–11, 226
Miller, Otto, 242
Milwaukee Brewers, 52–56, 63
Mitchell, Fred "Mitch": background, 115–16, 162, 212; Boston Braves base coach, 223; Boston Braves pitching coach, 188–89, 238; player recommendations by, 118–19; World Series Game One, 287; World Series Game Three, 334; World Series Game Four, 339
Moran, Herbie: background, 213–14; Boston Braves–New York Giants games, 222–23, 226; Boston Braves–Pittsburgh Pirates games, 245; World Series Game One, 295, 305, 308; World Series Game Three, 331–32, 334; World Series Game Four, 339
Moreland, George L., 185
Mulford, Ron, Jr., 291–92, 323
Murnane, Tim, 298
Murphy, Charles Webb: background, 132–35; on City Championship series, 126; Evers's contracts with, 123–24, 127–30, 131–32, 136–37, 142–43; financial irregularities of, 143; ownership of Chicago Cubs, 79
Murphy, Eddie: personal qualities, 263; World Series Game One, 297–99, 302; World Series Game Two, 314, 318–20; World Series Game Three, 324, 328–30, 332; World Series Game Four, 337
Murphy, Mike, 260
Murray, "Red," 211–12, 225–26, 234
Myers, Hy, 242–43

Nash, Billy, 20
Nash, Ogden, 137, 205
Nashville Seraphs, 12
Nashville Vols, 10–12
National Agreement, 31, 41, 49
National Commission, 80, 129, 131–32, 273, 285
National League: American League numbers comparison, 84–85; annual meetings, 123–24, 132–33; on Evers's contracts, 123, 129, 131, 136–37, 138–40, 142; player exodus to American League, 49–51; reorganization and downsizing of, 40–42, 49; rumored sale of Detroit Tigers to, 67, 68, 69; "territory" of, 31–32, 38. *See also* World Series (1914)
Neary, Jimmy, 245
Nelson, "Red," 96–97
Newark Sailors, 78, 159
New York American: on Chase, 98; on Stallings, 102; "Yankees" name, 71n
New York Giants: background, 41; DeVore playing for, 159; Murphy as press agent for, 133–34; playing Boston Braves, 120–21, 146–48, 186–87, 189, 190–97, 204–12, 219–24, 225–32, 233–35; and Rudolph, 118–19; standings in 1914 season, 159, 176, 177, 189, 213, 214, 217–18, 219, 235, 245–46; win-at-any-cost tactics, 174
New York Rustlers, 4–5
New York Times, on Philadelphia Phillies performance, 22
New York Tribune, 242, 309
New York Yankees: Chase as player-manager of, 103, 104–5, 111, 112; Davis as pitcher for, 187–88; Elberfeld as manager of, 72–73, 78; fans and game attendance, 83; Griffith as manager of, 71–72; name origin, 71n; sign-stealing rumors, 83–84, 85–86; Stallings as manager of, 71, 78–81, 82–86, 87–92, 93–100, 101–3, 104–7, 111–12
The New York Yankees (Graham), 85–86
Nicholson, Herman, 268
Nie (journalist), 99
Noe, Joe, 216

Northen, Hub, 95
Northwestern League, 116–17

O'Brien, Jack, 34
O'Brien, Joseph D., 45
O'Connor, Jack, 96
O'Connor, W. J., 217
O'Day, Hank, 123–24, 125–26, 242–43
Oldring, Rube: personal qualities, 260; World Series Game One, 286, 288, 297–98, 302, 303; World Series Game Three, 324, 325–26, 328–29, 332; World Series Game Four, 339; World Series performance, 322
Orth, A. T., 24
outfielder platoon system, 155–56

Padden, Dick, 33, 34, 35–36
Paskert, "Dode," 239
Paul, Gabe, 185
Pearson, Howard, 89–90
Pennock, Herb, 286, 338, 340
Perdue, "Hub," 120, 136, 138, 149, 156–58, 182
Pfeffer, "Big Jeff," 252
Phelon, "Wild Bill," 290
Philadelphia Athletics, 41–42, 45, 63, 85, 185n, 250–51, 260–63. *See also* World Series (1914)
Philadelphia Inquirer: and free publicity, 41–42; on Thompson's performance, 20; on Van Zelst's death, 263
Philadelphia Inquirer's "Famous Fifty," 324
Philadelphia Phillies: Boston Braves trades, 159; doctored baseballs used by, 185n; playing Boston Braves, 217–18, 236–41; Stallings as manager of, 13, 14–18, 19–26, 26n; Stallings playing for, 8–10
Philadelphia Record, on Philadelphia Phillies performance, 22
Piatt, Wiley, 19, 22, 24
Piez, Sandy, 193
pinch hitters, 155
Pitching in a Pinch (Mathewson), 260
Pittsburgh Pirates: doctored baseballs used by, 185, 185n; player roster, 50, 179–80; playing Boston Braves, 148–49, 155, 174–76, 179–80, 182–84, 244–45; World Series, 272
Pittsburgh Press, on frozen balls, 184
Plank, Eddie, 262, 278, 288, 312–17
platoon system, 155–56
Porter, Cole, 274
Porter, George D., 282
Postal, Fred, 43
Providence Grays, 121
Pyke, Harry, 323

Quigley, Ernie, 238–39
Quinn, Jack, 87, 98, 121

Rariden, Bill, 116, 120
Reach, Al, 13, 22–23, 25–26, 26n
reserve clause, 48–49
Reulbach, Ed, 253–54
Rice, Grantland, 10, 177, 201, 289–90, 289n, 296, 306, 341
Richter, Francis, 25
Rigler, Cy, 125, 146–47, 150, 175–76, 253
Roberts, Hazel Lee, 285
Robertson, Dave, 211
Robinson, Wilbert, 43, 57, 123
Robison, Frank DeHass, 32
Rochester Hustlers, 121
Rockefeller, John D., 47n, 48
Rogers, John, 13, 17, 18, 21–26, 26n, 41
rooftop seats for World Series, 281–83
Royal Rooters (fans): background, 272–73; traveling to Philadelphia, 273–76; World Series Game One, 292–93, 295, 304, 308, 310; World Series Game Two, 314, 315, 317, 318; World Series Game Three, 324, 326, 330, 333; World Series Game Four, 336, 337, 338
Rudolph, Dick: background, 118–19; Boston Braves–Brooklyn Dodgers game, 244; Boston Braves–Chicago Cubs games, 214; Boston Braves–Cincinnati Reds games, 174; Boston Braves–New York Giants games, 186–87, 193–96, 219–22; Boston Braves–Pittsburgh Pirates games, 148–49, 182; Boston Braves–St. Louis Cardinals games, 217; Stallings's assessment of, 278; World Series Game One, 287, 288, 291, 296–99, 305–6; World Series Game Three, 323–24; World Series Game Four, 336–39
Runyon, Damon, 271, 286, 290, 340
Russell, William Hepburn, 4–5
Ryan, Elizabeth "Toodles," 231–32
Ryan, Michael J., 282

Saier, Vic, 215, 243
Salem (Massachusetts) fire, 159–60
Salsinger, H. G., 88
Schang, Wally: scouting Braves players, 217; World Series Game One, 286, 296, 306; World Series Game Two, 314, 316–17, 318; World Series Game Three, 328–32, 334; World Series Game Four, 338
Schmalstig, Charles, 134–35
Schmidt, "Butch": background, 121; Boston Braves beginnings, 145, 146; Boston Braves–Brooklyn Dodgers game, 252–53; Boston Braves–Chicago Cubs games, 215–17; Boston

Schmidt, "Butch" (cont.)
  Braves–New York Giants games, 195, 220, 226; Boston Braves–Philadelphia Phillies games, 239–41; Boston Braves–Pittsburgh Pirates games, 244–45; World Series Game One, 280, 298–300, 302, 309; World Series Game Two, 320; World Series Game Three, 326; World Series Game Four, 338, 340
Schroeder, Joseph, 265, 285
Schulte, Frank, 214
Schultz, "Dutch," 216
Schumacher, Harry, 201
Scott, Jack, 164–65
Serenaders, 275–76
Seymour, Cy, 118
Shaw, Al, 35
Shawkey, Bob, 337–40
Shea, William, 318
Sheridan, Jack, 37
Sheridan, J. B., 172
Shettsline, Billy, 24, 26n
Shibe, Ben, 42, 45
Shibe Park, 284–85
Shugart, Frank, 60–61, 62
sign-stealing rumors, 83–84, 85–86, 251
Smith, "Red": background, 180–81; Boston Braves–Chicago Cubs games, 214; Boston Braves–New York Giants games, 192–93, 205, 209–10, 211, 220, 225, 230; Boston Braves–Philadelphia Phillies games, 239–40; Boston Braves–Pittsburgh Pirates games, 245; injured and sitting out World Series, 252–54, 255–56
Snodgrass, Fred, 146–48, 205, 209, 227–30, 233–34
Somers, Charles, 32, 38, 40, 42, 45, 49, 107–8
South End Grounds, 5
Sox, Chicago White, 185n
Spink, Taylor, 290
Spirit of Transportation (Bitter), 275
Sporting Life, on Stallings, 25, 78
Sporting News: on American League politics, 111; World Series coverage by, 290
Stahl, Jake, 72
Stallings, George E., 200
Stallings, George, Jr., 264, 266, 267–69, 271n
Stallings, George Tweedy: background, 6–13, 200; on Boston Braves standings, 217–18; Chase game-fixing controversy and, 111; Detroit Tigers and, 27, 31, 33–36, 37, 52–56, 63–70; dissociation from American League, 69–70; doctored baseballs used by, 182–85; Johnson's feud with, 50–51, 69–70, 78–80, 83, 84, 100, 101–3, 107–8, 111, 112; management style, 170, 177–78, 201–3, 205–8, 207n, 221–22, 255–56, 258, 271n; Newark Sailors owner-manager, 78, 159; New York Yankees manager, 71, 78–81, 82–86, 87–92, 93–100, 101–3, 104–7, 111–12; Philadelphia Phillies manager, 13, 14–18, 19–26, 26n; pitcher strategy, 186–89, 237; reputation of, 3–4, 6–7, 224, 246; sign-stealing rumors, 83–84, 85–86; superstitions, 20, 155, 202, 222, 237, 245–46, 253, 258–59, 268, 312; umpire interactions, 33–35, 61; World Series Game One, 287–88; World Series Game Two, 311–12, 319–21; World Series Game Three, 322–24, 327, 329, 330, 334; World Series Game Four, 341; World Series handshake with Mack, 289; World Series interview, 277–79; World Series strategy, 250–51, 252, 255–56, 264–66, 267–71, 271n, 278–79, 287. *See also* Boston Braves
Standard Oil Company, 47n, 48
Stanky, Eddie, 185n
Steffens, Lincoln, 92
Steinfeldt, Harry, 125
Stengel, "Casey," 253
St. Louis Browns, 32, 94–97
St. Louis Cardinals: formerly known as St. Louis Browns, 32, 94–97; players' lawsuit against Rogers, 21; player trades, 158–59; playing Boston Braves, 172, 178, 217; standings in 1914 season, 213, 217
St. Louis Globe-Democrat, on Maranville's performance, 172
St. Louis Post-Dispatch: on Rudolph, 217; on Stallings, 111
St. Louis Republic, on Maranville's performance, 172
Stock, Milt, 193, 211
Stone, George, 95
Strand, Paul, 165, 234, 237
Street, "Gabby," 73–75
Strunk, Amos: scouting Braves players, 217; World Series Game One, 285–86, 303, 305–6, 307, 309; World Series Game Two, 314, 316; World Series injury, 322
Sugden, Joe, 60–61
"suicide squeeze," 96–97
Sun, on Stallings's opinion on Boston Braves chances, 249
Sweeney, Bill, 120, 136, 138
Sweeney, Ed, 87
syndicate league, 48. *See also* corporate trust

Taft, Charles P., 132, 134–35, 142–43
Tammany Hall, 4, 5–6

Tener, John K.: background, 123; and Evers's contracts, 129, 131, 138, 142; on Evers-Zimmerman dispute, 216; on Murphy, 137; on umpires, 148; World Series spectator, 285
Tenney, Fred, 4
Tesreau, Jeff, 225–27, 230, 246, 269
"Tessie" (song), 272–73, 275, 276, 300, 304, 310, 330, 336
Thomas, Charlie, 125–26
Thomas, Hannah Ann, 298
Thomas, Ira, 293, 298, 309, 341
Thompson, Sam, 14–15, 20
Tincup, Ben, 239
Tinker, Joe, 123, 125, 141, 168–69
Tin Pan Alley, 286
Toronto Maple Leafs, 118–19
Tribune, on sign-stealing rumors, 85
Truesdale, Frankie, 95
trust (corporate), 46–47, 47n, 48
Tuthill, Harry, 84, 85, 86
Tyler, George "Lefty": background, 120; Boston Braves beginnings, 144, 146; Boston Braves–Brooklyn Dodgers game, 244; Boston Braves–Chicago Cubs games, 214, 215; Boston Braves–Cincinnati Reds games, 174; Boston Braves–New York Giants games, 186–87, 205, 207–12, 225–32; Boston Braves–Pittsburgh Pirates games, 175–76; Stallings's assessment of, 278; statistics, 225; on World Series chances, 256; World Series Game One, 287, 288; World Series Game Three, 323, 324–25, 326–27, 328–29, 331, 334

umpires: bad calls and rowdy responses to, 29–30, 33–37, 57–62, 125, 146–48, 150, 175–76, 178, 194n, 226; hand-signal custom, 194; Maranville's approach with, 163; Rogers's Rules on, 17; standard for excellence, 193–95; for World Series, 293, 295

Vanderbeck, George, 27, 31
Van Zelst, Louis, 257, 260–63, 299
Vaughn, "Hippo," 95, 171
Vaughn, Irving, 128
Vaughn, Jim, 87, 89, 96
Verbout, Johnny, 165
Vila, Joe, 249
Viox, Jimmy, 182, 245

Wagner, Hans, 49–50, 49n, 179, 182, 277–78
Walsh, "Big Ed," 71, 261
Walsh, Jimmy, 318–20, 325, 326, 327, 330–32
Walsh, John R., 134
Ward, John Montgomery, 5–6

Ward brothers, 137
Washington Post, on Maranville's performance, 340
Washington Senators, 43–44, 59–61, 63, 83
West, Melville, 156
Western League, 28–30
Whaling, Bert "Moose," 116–17, 146–48, 215, 280
Wheat, Zack, 242–43
Wheeler, George L., 24
Wheeler, Jack, 290
Whitted, "Possum": background, 158–59; Boston Braves–Philadelphia Phillies games, 240–41; Boston Braves–Pittsburgh Pirates games, 245; on World Series chances, 256; World Series Game One, 301–3, 304, 309; World Series Game Three, 330; World Series Game Four, 337, 338
Williams, Jimmy, 50
Wolter, Harry, 98
Wolverton, Harry, 188
World (New York), on sign-stealing rumors, 86
World Series (1903), 272
World Series (1912), 272
World Series (1914): gambling, 279–80, 279n, 280n; mascots, 257–63; Most Valuable Player ceremony, 291–92; rooftop seats for, 281–83; Royal Rooters (fans), 272–76; Smith's injury, 252–54; Stallings's strategy for, 250–51, 252, 255–56, 264–66, 267–71, 271n, 278–79, 287; team uniforms, 286–87
World Series (1914) Game One: arrival of fans, 284–86; lineup, 291–94; Most Valuable Player ceremony, 291–92; play, 295–300, 301–6, 307–10; press section, 289–90; team warmup, 286–88
World Series (1914) Game Two: double-play, 319–21; pitchers' duel, 312–18; Stallings on Boston Braves appearance, 311–12; Stallings's superstitions, 312
World Series (1914) Game Three: Boston Braves chances, 322; fans at, 323, 324; Most Valuable Player ceremony, 323; pitcher lineup, 323–24; regular innings, 324–27; tied and extra innings, 327, 328–35
World Series (1914) Game Four, 336–41
World War I news, 160–61, 176, 178, 198–200, 249
Wright, Harry, 9–10
Wyckoff, J. Weldon "Jack," 286, 288, 308, 309, 338

Young, "Cy," 16, 49, 71
Young, Nick, 34

Zimmerman, Heinie, 150, 214–17, 242–43
Zinn, Guy, 74–75, 121